THE WAR BEGINS

OUR TIMES

THE UNITED STATES
1900-1925

IV
THE WAR BEGINS
1909-1914

BY

MARK SULLIVAN

CHARLES SCRIBNER'S SONS
NEW YORK ، LONDON
1932

CONTENTS

CONTENTS

ILLUSTRATIONS

ILLUSTRATIONS xvii

ILLUSTRATIONS

THE WAR BEGINS

JUNE 28, 1914

The Day in America—as Pictured in Those Diaries of History, the Newspapers, and as Illustrated by Sundry Facets of the America that then Was. Together with Brief Allusion to an Event Which, Happening Far Distant from the United States, and Within a World with Which America Felt Sure It Had No Concern, Was Destined, nevertheless, to Make America a very Different Country. Some Interests, Preoccupations, Amusements, Points-of-View and Ways of Life of the People of the United States as It Was on a Day in Late June, in the Year Nineteen Hundred and Fourteen.

Two o'clock in the morning in that vast third of Continental United States stretching a thousand miles from the Rocky Mountains to the Pacific Coast. This immense region is deep in slumber, the peaceful stillness only broken by here and there the rumbling of a night train rolling down from Oregon, a lamp in a lonely ranch-house where a mother fosters a clamant new life, the droning hum of power plants along streams tumbling down the slopes of the Great Divide. In the cities, what movement goes on is subdued, furtive, "night-life" — in San Francisco's Chinatown the muffled crackle of dice on baize-covered gambling tables; along the Barbary Coast the tired tinkling of pianos behind closed and curtained windows; a sauntering policeman, twirling his club, yawns. In the far Western cities, morning newspapers have just been "put to bed"; their staffs are sleepily gossiping over rolls and coffee before they too "call it a day" and go home.

At the same moment it is four o'clock in the morning in the mid-third of the American Continent, the great food source of the nation, reaching from the Rockies eastward across endless fertile prairies to Illinois. Smoke is spiralling above the shingled roof-tops of a million farmhouses. In kerosene-lighted kitchens, wives and mothers are preparing breakfast on wood-burning stoves;

From the front page of the New York *Times* of June 29, 1914.

through the open doors and windows pours the fragrance of coffee, pancakes and syrup, frying ham. Men and boys carry milk-pails from house to barn; though the day is Sunday, and rural America will rest, morning chores must be done.

At the same moment it is five o'clock in the morning in

the Eastern third of the Continent, from Indiana to the Atlantic seaboard. In the great cities, belated roisterers are homeward bound. A doctor, kit in hand, rubs sleepy eyes as he hurries to answer a night-call. From dingy

The arrest of the assassin Gavro Princip.

car-barns motormen start out on their early runs. Milk-horses, trained to their slow-paced routine, clump over cobbled alleys, their clatter the city's chanticleer call to day.

America is abed, sleeping the sleep of the well-fed, the care-free, the confident.

At the same moment it is noon in the small foreign city of Sarajevo, capital of Austria-Hungary's newly acquired and sullen province, Slavic Bosnia. The heir to the Austrian throne, Archduke Francis Ferdinand, and his morganatic wife, the Duchess of Hohenberg, are driving to the palace from the City Hall, where the Archduke had been given a perfunctory welcome by the Burgomaster. As their automobile comes opposite the doorway of a barber-shop near the intersection of Rudolph Street, a young Servian student, Gavro Princip, fires two shots — "the first struck the Duchess low down

Archduke Francis Ferdinand of Austria and family.

on the right side, while the second hit the Archduke in the neck near the throat and pierced the jugular vein."[1] The chauffeur drives with panic haste to the garrison hospital. His royal charges, when taken from the car, are lifeless.

Only ten minutes have passed. In New York and Chicago late stragglers continue their way in the cool

[1] The New York *Times,* June 29, 1914.

of beginning dawn. In the mid-West, farmers' wives
go on with their lamp-lighted chores. In San Francisco,
Chinatown imperturbably gambles on.

From a drawing by Victor C. Anderson.

European news of June, 1914, had little effect at the "four corners."

America, still asleep on the Pacific Coast, or beginning
to arise in mid-West and East, is unaware of the tragic
act of a political maniac seven thousand miles away, has
no dream of the consequences to America that are to flow
from that mad deed.

II

At the time, the day was merely one in the flow of
eventless diurnities. Months later, some who cast their
memories back, could only recall it vaguely as a Sunday
in early mid-summer, associated with newly reaped
wheat stacked in fields, cattle knee-deep in shaded pools,

hay drying in the sun. Those who tried to remember
what they had been doing on the day that was a dividing-

From a drawing by L. Maynard Dixon.

Youthful hikers in the Rockies were happily unaware of a possible fate overseas.

point in history could identify only their accustomed
routine of pursuit and diversion; some could recall having gone to church and there to have been in a mood,
evoked by sermon, hymn, or ritual, of peace on earth,

good will towards men. It had been, in the American custom still strong at that time, a day of family dinners

From a drawing by Thornton Oakley.

Boston commuters reading of world events rushed for their evening trains as usual.

preceded by grace, of country drives—with horse and buggy in as many cases as automobile; of evening gatherings of young folks on wistaria-hung porches. The memories of many of the youths of the time associated the day with commencement week in high-school or college. It was these who had occasion, later, to realize,

From a drawing by N. C. Wyeth.

To the Pennsylvania farmer's son, life's routine was unruffled by events in Europe.

poignantly, that June 28, 1914, had contained the tragic omen of events destined to twist and make turbulent the stream of placid future they had supposed to lie ahead; before these awaited the scenes that, for many, ended

"Between the crosses, row on row."

In Flanders fields the poppies blow
Between the crosses, row on row,
That mark our place . . .[2]

[2] "In Flanders Fields" was written by Captain John D. McCrae, of Montreal,
Canada (killed on duty in Flanders, January 28, 1918). In full it reads:

> In Flanders fields the poppies blow
> Between the crosses, row on row,
> That mark our place; and in the sky
> The larks, still bravely singing, fly,
> Scarce heard amidst the guns below.
> We are the dead. Short days ago
> We lived, felt dawn, saw sunset glow.
> Loved and were loved, and now we lie
> In Flanders fields.
>
> Take up our quarrel with the foe!
> To you from falling hands, we throw
> The torch. Be yours to hold it high!
> If ye break faith with us who die
> We shall not sleep, though poppies grow
> In Flanders fields.

The second of the three best-known poems of the War was, "I Have A Rendezvous With Death," by Alan Seeger, an American aviator with the French Army:

> I have a rendezvous with Death
> At some disputed barricade,
> When Spring comes back with rustling shade
> And apple-blossoms fill the air —
> I have a rendezvous with Death
> When Spring brings back blue days and fair.

III

The youths, for whom that fate was destined, found no hint of it in the world about them. In the American newspapers of June 28 and the day following, there was no suggestion of the "thunder on the left" that was Rome's warning of impending storm, no hint that the day was to be one of the half dozen epochal dates in civilization, dividing modern history into pre-War and

---

It may be he shall take my hand
And lead me into his dark land
And close my eyes and quench my breath —
It may be I shall pass him still.
I have a rendezvous with Death
On some scarred slope of battered hill,
When Spring comes round again this year
And the first meadow-flowers appear.

God knows 'twere better to be deep
Pillowed in silk and scented down,
Where love throbs out in blissful sleep,
Pulse nigh to pulse, and breath to breath,
Where hushed awakenings are dear . . .
But I've a rendezvous with Death
At midnight in some flaming town,
When Spring trips north again this year,
And I to my pledged word am true,
I shall not fail that rendezvous.

    An English poem, elevated in spirit and form, was Rupert Brooke's "The Soldier":

If I should die, think only this of me;
  That there's some corner of a foreign field
That is forever England. There shall be
  In that rich earth a richer dust concealed;
A dust whom England bore, shaped, made aware,
  Gave, once, her flowers to love, her ways to roam,
A body of England's breathing English air,
  Washed by the rivers, blest by suns of home.

And think, this heart, all evil shed away,
  A pulse in the eternal mind, no less
    Gives somewhere back the thoughts by England given;
Her sights and sounds; dreams happy as her day;
  And laughter, learnt of friends; and gentleness,
    In hearts a peace, under an English heaven.

after. On the contrary, the press from its vantage-point of superior wisdom assured the country that the assassination at Sarajevo was merely "another mess in the Balkans." So far as any dealt with its international significance — and few did — they thought the death of the Archduke would, as a correspondent of the New York *Sun* put it, "make for peace in Europe," for the Arch-

From a drawing by William Oberhardt.

Where front-page headlines are made—the city editor.

duke had been a turbulent person and it had been apprehended that he would, on coming to the throne of Austria, be a trouble-maker.

Sarajevo was far out of the usual orbit of American editors, its name and the name of the assassin unfamiliarly foreign to American lips, the reason for the deed not understandable to American ways of thinking. So far as the newspapers treated the event editorially, they dwelt mainly upon the sorrows of the old Emperor, Franz

Joseph; his piteous lament, "Is nothing spared me!" catching the sympathy of the world, inspired editorials captioned "The Unhappy Hapsburgs." With that, the press dismissed Sarajevo, little thinking it would come back.[3] In the American newspapers of June 29, 1914, as surveyed in yellowed files some twenty years later, the assassination at Sarajevo appears as a temporary intrusion of violence from a distant world and an alien way of life, into an America intent upon the normal concerns of a peaceful country in a particularly peaceful time.

IV

The normal concerns of the America of June 28, 1914, are in most part to be found reflected in the newspapers of that and the following day. To identify and recall them, and to compose a picture of America as it was on that day, the author of this history eighteen years later asked editors[4] in all parts of the country to cull from

[3] It would be interesting to identify the American newspaper, or individual, to whom it first occurred that the assassination of the Archduke Francis Ferdinand might result in the United States' taking part in a war in Europe; and the date when that thought came first to any American. It is safe to say no one dreamed of the possibility until months after the assassination.

[4] All the headlines and other passages quoted in this chapter are from newspapers of two days, June 28 and June 29. The newspapers from which this picture of America on June 28, 1914, is made up are:

Atlanta (Ga.) *Constitution.*
Baltimore (Md.) *Sun.*
Battle Creek (Mich.) *Enquirer and News.*
Boise (Idaho) *Statesman.*
Cincinnati (O.) *Enquirer.*
Corning (N. Y.) *Leader.*
Dallas (Texas) *News.*
Decatur (Ill.) *Review.*
Des Moines (Ia.) *Register and Leader.*
Detroit (Mich.) *News.*
Detroit (Mich.) *Saturday Night.*
Elmira (N. Y.) *Star-Gazette.*
Fall River (Mass.) *Herald News.*
Fargo (N. D.) *Forum.*
Great Falls (Mont.) *Tribune.*

Harrisburg (Pa.) *Telegraph.*
Hartford (Conn.) *Courant.*
Jamestown (N. Y.) *Journal.*
Lewiston (Me.) *Daily Sun.*
Little Rock (Ark.) *Gazette.*
Louisville (Ky.) *Times.*
Lincoln (Neb.) *State Journal.*
Moline (Ill.) *Despatch.*
New York *Sun.*
New York *Times.*
New York *World.*
Oakland (Calif.) *Tribune.*
Oklahoma City (Okla.) *Oklahoman.*
Peoria (Ill.) *Journal Transcript.*
Pueblo (Col.) *Star Journal.*

their editions of June 28 and the day following items characteristic of that time.

The major interests thus revealed included a contest for the governorship of New York and the rôle played by a political party which the headlines called "Bull Moose" — a newcomer to the curious zoölogical nomenclature of American political parties, which had emerged

RELATIVE NEWS VALUES   —Enright in New York *Globe*

Figures in the headlines of 1914 and a few years previous.

full-grown into the arena two years before and for the time seemed equal to the elephant and the donkey in vociferous equipment for longevity. One headline reflected anxiety about the health of a national hero: "Ordered to Rest to Avoid Collapse, the Colonel Refuses" — the character then familiar to everybody as "The Colonel" being, it is necessary to explain to later generations, Theodore Roosevelt. Another headline dealt, somewhat excitedly, with an impending battle between two generals, Mexican, named Carranza and Villa — when newspapers of that time discussed "the war," as

Rochester (N. Y.) *Democrat &* *Chronicle*.
San Antonio (Texas) *Express*.
Spokane (Wash.) *Spokesman-Review*.
Springfield (Mo.) *Leader*.
Springfield (O.) *Daily News and Sun*.
Syracuse (N. Y.) *Herald*.

Topeka (Kans.) *State Journal*.
Troy (N. Y.) *Record*.
Utica (N. Y.) *Observer*.
Watertown (N. Y.) *Daily Times*.
Wichita (Kans.) *Eagle*.
Wilkesbarre (Pa.) *Sunday Independent*.

they frequently and portentously did, they meant the civil strife in Mexico, and, as to the great majority of newspapers, the danger and undesirability of our becoming embroiled. Another headline (larger in some news-

Copyright by National Photo.

Champ Clark, Democratic Speaker of the House, whose prophecy was three years short.

papers than the one about the assassination of the Archduke) recited that "Johnson Retains his Championship, Wins Decision Over Moran" — Jack Johnson being a colored prize-fighter whose winning the heavyweight championship from Jim Jeffries four years before[5] had added a new facet of the race-problem to the difficulties of making the American democracy workable.[6] Other

[5] July 4, 1910.

[6] In 1932 there was still upon the Federal statutes a law forbidding interstate transportation of prize-fight films, enacted by Congress soon after the Johnson-Jeffries fight, in simultaneous recognition of two objections: an avowed one that such films were evil, and a tacit one that they would show a black man victorious over a white and therefore might incite race riots.

headlines reflecting the major concerns of the America of June 28, 1914, included: "Suffragettes March on Capitol; Women Will Vote by 1917, Says Clark" — Champ Clark being the Democratic Speaker of the House of

From "Life," 1912.

"Women will vote by 1917," says Champ Clark. America was stirred, or amused, by news about suffragettes in England.

Representatives, and his prediction having to do with an amendment to the Constitution giving suffrage to women. (His prophecy was three years too short, since fulfilment did not come until 1920.) And "Underwood Stops Calamity Howlers by Plain Facts about Tariff" — Oscar Underwood being party leader of the House of Representatives in the Democratic administration of Woodrow Wilson, and therefore titular author of the tariff which the Democrats had written upon their entrance into power. How a low tariff would work was the principal political question of the day, Democrats claiming it would stimulate trade, Republicans that it would bring calamity. The argument, at the time seemingly important, was one of many controversies destined to be ren-

From an advertisement of the Goodwin corset about 1914.

From a *Vogue,* 1925, advertisement of the La Camille corset.

dered futile by the undreamed consequences of the shot at Sarajevo, which, within six weeks, were to launch upon the sea, and beneath it, and above it, influences upon trade that made tariffs impotent and every other preoccupation of America trivial.

The headlines quoted above, from newspapers of June 28,[7] 1914, reflect the chief interests, the public concerns,

A Redfern corset advertisement of about 1914.

of the America of that day. In the press of any one day, however, it is only the publicly important, or the unusual, or the showy, that the larger headlines portray. For a picture of the normal come and go of the day, the

[7] Some are from newspapers of the following day, June 29.

spirit and flavor of the time, one will search more fruitfully among the less obtrusive records on the inside pages,
including the advertisements, where, as in the living-
room and kitchen of a home, are to be found a more
intimate reflection of the life of the period than is provided by the front porch or the first page.

One intimate aspect of American life as mirrored by
those diaries of history, the newspapers, on June 28, was
discussed at Indianapolis, Indiana, at a meeting of a
women's national medical association, which waged
"Hot Debate Over Corset." Pro, Doctor Louise East-
man, putting personal candor into the service of a
cause, said, as reported in the Des Moines (Iowa) *Register*, that as she became "heavier" she "found the
'straight front' a friend that prevented her becoming
bunchy." Contra, Doctor Flora Smith of Newark, Ohio,
told her sister physicians she "could not see why women
thought it necessary to improve on nature; neither she
nor her mother had ever worn a corset." (If the lady
lived into the 1920's she enjoyed one of the rarest of
human satisfactions, the vindication of a pioneer, for by
1925 the corset had shrunk to an attenuated offspring,
and even that was not always considered essential.)

In Baltimore, a conflict between old ways and new
took the form of a debate over a proposal to permit baseball on Sunday, leading *The Sun* to discourse upon a
revolution that was under way. "Sunday," said the editor with gentle disapproval, "has become the gayest day
of the week." Sadly he recalled a different manner of
passing the day, called "observing the Sabbath," the aus-
terities of which were now softened by that potent
agency of human illusion, the tendency of time to
spread glamour over the past: "Twenty-five years ago
Sunday in the average househeld was set off from the
other days . . . There was silence and placidity.

Mother dressed for church early; father read his newspaper with the minimum of rustling; the children set off in starched white skirts for Sunday school with the feeling that an impalpable finger rested upon their lips imposing silence. The hoofs of the street-car horses seemed muffled. Certain things might not be done on a Sunday and respectability be maintained, even in a 'worldly' household. Novels might not be read, excepting perhaps those with a moral so obvious that it could not be overlooked; drives might not be taken; letters must not be written, nor visits made, except to maiden aunts or extremely poor relatives, when the excursions might be classed among the deeds of benevolence and charity."[8]

In 1914 that early Puritan spirit lingered in spots, and among some religious denominations. In Scranton, Pennsylvania, a gospel campaign had recently been conducted by the Reverend "Billy" [W.A.] Sunday, a former baseball player, now turned evangelist, whose exuberance of exhortation was sometimes called, by persons whose approval of Mr. Sunday was incomplete, "muscular Christianity" or "strong-arm religion"; one result was a revival locally of sentiment against Sunday baseball: "Bible-classmen have rented the grounds and details do guard duty each Sunday to see that the grounds are not used." In San Antonio, Texas, a sermon in the Prospect Hill Methodist Episcopal Church, reported by *The Express*, warned that "card-playing in the home has produced thousands of gamblers"; in Oakland, California, a sermon to the Pacific Union Conference of Seventh Day Adventists, reported by *The Tribune*, said that no Chris-

---

[8] The quotation is from a description, printed June 28, 1914, of the America of twenty-five years before, about 1889. Decorousness on the Sabbath had by no means disappeared in 1914. In many communities, and in families particularly religious or having a strong sense of tradition, the subdued manner of passing Sunday was still common, and in some cases continued as late as 1932.

tian can "attend a card game, billiard-room, theatre, or moving picture show."

These passages should be read with understanding that a picture of one day made up from newspaper records must be interpreted with discernment. In many respects, newspapers reflect the average of life, in others the ex-

From a photograph by J. R. Schmidt, Cincinnati, Ohio.

"Billy" (W. A.) Sunday in action. Former baseball player, turned evangelist.

ceptional. On that Sunday, June 28, 1914, in the 223,-000 churches that America then had, somewhat more than that number of sermons were delivered at morning and evening services, of which almost all consisted of conventional exposition of Scripture or unsensational discussions of public questions, and were therefore not reported in the newspapers.

Growing patronage of public amusements, Sunday and week-day, was the rule. The 176 plays (151 new, 19 adaptations, 6 dramatizations) which the New York *Times* enumerated on June 28 as having been presented in Manhattan during the season just closing, was high tide of the period when the spoken drama had

Scene from "The Perils of Pauline," a serial movie.

the theatre practically to itself. Rapid growth of a humble little Cinderella of the stage, not yet recognized as a competitor, was recorded in the *Register and Leader* of Des Moines, Iowa, where, out of a population of 100,000, fully 20,000 daily "stick nickels or dimes through the ticket-windows of 65 moving picture theatres"; the manager of one said that his "best business-getters are the serials, the stories which are continued week after week" — a very popular one was a lurid melodrama called "The Perils of Pauline." In the

Corning (N. Y.) *Leader*, a moving picture house advertised a "two-reel feature, two comedies, and an illustrated song—all for five cents." A despatch from Philadelphia recited that "Mrs. Cyrus Niver, member of the new state moving picture censorship board, after several weeks spent in passing upon thousands of yards of love

The famous four-sided Waldorf bar, New York City, in the days that were pre-War and also pre-Prohibition.

drama films, has decided that one yard is long enough for a kiss; young people should be torn from each other after 36 seconds."

A headline in the Cincinnati, Ohio, *Enquirer:*

COUNT OF TEN TO BE TAKEN TUESDAY NIGHT
BY BACCHUS IN PANHANDLE STATE

Long Dry Spell Coming

DROUGHT WILL BEGIN AS CLOCK STRIKES XII

Treasury Is Deprived of $600,000 Annually—Blue Says Man May
Drink at Friend's Home If He Doesn't Go There
for That Purpose

would need translation to an archæologist of the distant
future seeking data about the mores of the America of
1914. Interpreted at a time sufficiently near to understand the cryptic combination of the classics of Greece

From "Life."

Opponents of Prohibition predicted unhappy results. "Ha, Ha! Good! Now
there'll be lots of bad liquor drunk on the sly."

and the numerals of Rome with the slang of the United
States, it meant that West Virginia (by a majority of
92,000) had voted prohibition into its State constitution,
and that the gods, in a mood of punning, had arranged
that the name, as well apparently as the fame, of the
head enforcement officer should be Blue. Saloon-keep-
ers took the event gaily rather than funereally; plac-

ards on the walls and in the corners of the huge mirrors behind the bars warned patrons that "A camel can go nine days without a drink, but after July 1 you will have to beat the camel," and "Don't be alarmed if after July 1 you spit talcum powder." A Wheeling saloon-keeper, August Trabert, found solace for the death of his busi-

Brosnan's Ale House, Fulton Street, one of the oldest in New York. From a pre-Prohibition photograph.

ness in the pleasure he derived from contriving his first name into a play on words, at once pun and paradox, which he printed upon cards and presented to his patrons: "July first will be the last of August."

West Virginia was the ninth State that had gone dry on a state-wide basis; in some other States many counties had gone dry under "local-option" laws — the country was a mosaic of wet and dry; maps, whether by accident or intended symbolism, represented dry territory as white, wet as black. Difficulty encountered by dry communities

in keeping themselves hermetically sealed against leak-
age from wet was illustrated by an advertised "Mail
Order Price-List" in the Decatur (Ill.) *Review*, in
which a firm of liquor dealers in Springfield, Illinois,
solicited orders by mail from readers in dry territory.
This difficulty had given rise to a demand for nation-

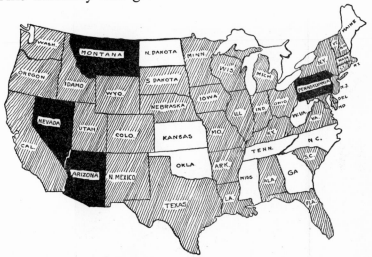

Map of Prohibition as it was in 1912. States shown in white had Prohibition
laws. Those in black had a license law, with practically no dry territory.
Those shaded had license or local option laws but contained much dry territory.

wide prohibition. The Utica (N. Y.) *Observer*, reported
that "a resolution asking Congress that the voters of
the country be allowed to ballot on a Constitutional
amendment to prohibit intoxicants was adopted at the
service at the Presbyterian Church yesterday."

Many advertisements of "male help wanted" included
a word which some years later came to be taken for
granted: the Fargo (N. D.) *Forum* advertised for "a
strictly sober all-round printer"; the Spokane (Wash.)
Spokesman-Review for "four sober, industrious men to
learn auto repairing." Among "Situations Wanted," the
New York *World* included proffer of services by a clerk

who recommended himself as one who did not consume the commodity he dispensed:

> BARKEEPER — Respectable young man, 33, thoroughly competent and reliable, neat and rapid mixer, total abstainer; excellent references.

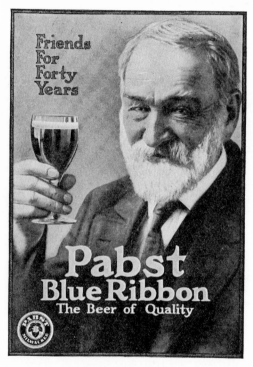

An ubiquitous beer poster.

The leading grocery firm in Oakland, California, Goldberg-Bowen, advertised in *The Tribune:* "Bourbon, $3.50 per gallon; Claret, 'the kind Omar liked,' $.40; white wine 'goes good with a fish dinner,' $.60." In the Cincinnati *Enquirer* those who were at once thirsty and thrifty were urged to "buy direct at distillery prices, Sandy River, the Best Whiskey made in Kentucky, 60 cents per full quart. 100 proof. Aged under government supervision. Not adulterated. Fully matured. Purity guaranteed. Unexcelled for medicinal purposes."

Progress of a disturbing invasion of women into a field

Map of woman suffrage as it was in 1912. Equal-suffrage States are shown in white, those with partial woman suffrage are shaded, and those with no woman suffrage are in black.

formerly left to males was reported by the Fargo (N. D.) *Forum:* "The first young people's suffrage[9] club in the state has been organized at Dickinson, composed of some of the most prominent young ladies of the city who are very enthusiastic"; the Springfield, Missouri, *Leader* described "the energetic work of women soliciting signatures to petitions for submitting the woman suffrage amendment at the November election."

In two far-Western newspapers of June 28 appeared items that were unconscious of the implications which

[9] The movement was for national woman suffrage, the 19th Amendment; women at this time had the right to vote locally in 10 states.

a subsequent historian could see in them: "An increase
in transfers of land," reported by the Fargo (N. D.)

In 1914 the horse was still going strong as the motive power for buggies, surreys,
spring wagons.

Forum, was attributed "to Eastern people who have come
here to live"; the Great Falls (Mont.) *Tribune* spoke,
in a "booster" spirit, of "homesteaders pouring into the
State by the thousands from every section of the Union."
That was the end of an epoch, the dribbling to a tiny
trickle of one of the most picturesque migrations of all
time, the "Go West!" impulse in America.

That the horse was still going strong was shown by the
pride with which the Wichita (Kan.) *Eagle* recorded

the purchase of a span for the local ambulance — "the horses are grey and are said to have cost $450"; and in the Corning (N. Y.) *Evening Leader* advertisement of the "finest livery service in the city — carriages and out-fits for weddings and socials."[10] Twilight for the horse, however (destined to become eclipse), was suggested in the San Antonio *Express* advertisement offering for sale "a lot of good, second-hand buggies, surreys, and spring wagons" — wagons equipped with springs were to some farm families, in that place and time, a comparatively recent advance in vehicular comfort. That 1914 was about the overlapping period, in which horse and auto-mobile competed, was implied in the phraseology of a Detroit *News* advertisement of a second-hand Cadillac which "will carry 1300 pounds and pull like a team of horses." Another advertisement, in the Fargo (N. D.) *Forum*, offered: "For sale: Velie 30 auto — drove it from Illinois; on account of roads I cannot drive it back." Dirt roads and the dust or mud that accompanied them were reflected in an advertisement of "automobile goggles," and in the Hartford (Conn.) *Courant* adver-tisement of "auto coats, in linen, natural and oyster shades, full length."

Among minor facets of the life of the time, the com-mencement exercises of the Watertown, N. Y., high school included, according to *The Daily Times*, the awarding of "a new Webster unabridged dictionary to a young man who wrote the best essay on the evils of ciga-rette smoking; a young woman, Miss Dorothy Hoyt, wrote the second-best essay on the same subject, and was awarded a volume of Longfellow's Poems." At Elmira, N. Y., *The Star-Gazette* reported beginning of the prac-tice of paying a salary to the mayor; it was to be $1500 a

---

[10] "Social" or "sociable" was the word for any gathering where men and women mingled for purpose of recreation or church fellowship.

year. (By 1932 it had risen to $7500.) At Atlanta, Georgia, *The Constitution* reported a sermon by Doctor A. B. Holderby about "the Great Conflict," by which

From a drawing by Rollin Kirby.

Dirt roads made "auto goggles," full length linen "auto coats," and veils necessary.

he meant the relations between capital and labor. Many papers reflected interest in, and some expressed indignation against, the new dances. In New York City *The Sun* asked: "Is the tango turning this country topsy-turvy?" and recorded a judgment, presumably facetious, expressed in the New York State legislature, that "the

Reo Touring Car $1000

For five passengers. Top extra.

The thing that counts most is get-there-and-back ability—every day in the year.

National

Beauty, Luxury and Utility

Write for illustrated catalogue. Depart-ment D. **SIX--$2375** FULLY EQUIPPED National Motor Vehicle Co. INDIANAPOLIS, INDIANA

Parts of two full-page magazine advertisements showing the progress made in five years in body design. The Reo was of 1909, while the National was of 1914.

tango, and the hesitation, and the one-step, and the grizzly bear, and the bunny hug, and similar dances, are not classical or truly terpsichorean."[11]

A Syracuse (N. Y.) *Herald* advertisement allured

From "Vogue," summer of 1914.

"Speeding the parting tunic and welcoming the coming long coat," *Vogue* suggested that Russian lines would prevail the following season.

women with a "Parasol sale, every new shade, women simply cannot pass them by." A Cincinnati department store offered "Ostrich feathers, guaranteed male plumes, one-piece, in black, white and colors, $1.98"; and an accessory of the women's skirts of that day, "placket fasteners, a dozen for one cent." A St. Louis department store advertised contemporary necessities for the adornment of women, known to the trade, it seems

[11] Ch. 10 has an account of the dances of the period.

necessary to explain to a "bobbed"[12] era, as "Hair Goods":

28 inch switches $2.98
Coronet braids $6.98
Transformations $1.29

A Hartford shop offered in *The Courant:* "Royal Worcester Corsets, a new medium-bust model, with long hips, made of good quality coutil, priced at 79

From an Yvette advertisement.

"These stylish coiffures can be arranged with the aid of a transformation, wavy switch, pair of pin curls and front fringe."

From "Vogue," summer of 1914.

"Every new shade, women simply cannot pass them by," said a parasol advertisement in a Syracuse, N. Y., newspaper in 1914.

cents." Yet further virtues were claimed for "Bon Ton corsets, non-rustable, make you look and feel younger."

12 One of the minor vexations of writing history has to do with point of view as respects time. This chapter is written in 1932, when women's hair is short. If read as many years from now as the author hopes, doubtless women's hair will again be long. This difficulty about perspective, here illustrated by a minor point, attends all historical writing, and is greater in proportion as the writing is close to the event recorded.

One of the Aeolian Company's advertisements of 1909. The reader will observe the abundance of hair worn at that time.

The Aeolian Company advertised "The Pianola — better than any other player-piano," of which the claimed virtue was, "You can play the piano as well as anyone." Book advertisements emphasized as "The best selling novel of the year," a romance by William J. Locke, "The Fortunate Youth" — title unconsciously ironic, considering that the fortunes of many of the youths who read it were destined to lead them to a different sort of adventure at Belleau Wood and St. Mihiel.

All over the country, communities were getting ready for the Fourth of July. The celebration at Decatur,

Illinois, announced a balloon ascension, a pie and bun-eating contest, and a "Jesse James Wild West Show"; one in North Dakota promised "Buffalo Bill in person." Baltimore scheduled "pageants, carnivals, parades, and a

Buffalo Bill as he was toward the end of his career.

sham battle" — but no firecrackers, for Baltimore had been one of the first to adopt the "safe and sane" Fourth.

The picnic season was on. At Wheatland, North Dakota, the Fargo *Forum* reported, a company of young ladies were entertained by a "ride in a hay-rack decorated for the occasion; everyone expressed themselves as having had a most enjoyable time."

Everywhere was whirring of reapers garnering the material basis for a felicitous content, which the Decatur (Ill.) *Review* put in words: "The wheat harvest is in full swing, the wheat is fine; several farmers have sold for 75 cents a bushel while some are holding for a higher price. The man who owns 160 acres of Illinois farm land is able to keep the wolf from the door, whatever happens to stocks and bonds or banking and finances."

The Peoria (Ill.) *Journal Transcript* stated that it was "a good year for bass." The Decatur (Ill.) *Review* reported the capture by John Chrisman of "a 6-pound cat-fish in Stevens Creek about half way between the wagon road and the river, the biggest catch of the season."

Mr. Chrisman, we feel sure, as he ate his catfish at breakfast, June 29, and read in his newspaper of the assassination at Sarajevo, was moved to more than the usual satisfaction which the average American felt with his lot, compared with that of the crowned heads of Europe. From them, and from assassinations and wars, Mr. Chrisman congratulated himself, America was far removed.

From a drawing by Edwin B. Child.

The glory of the Middle West wheat fields.

2

NEW ENERGY; NEW WEALTH

Difficulty Attending the Putting of Labels on this Era, or
on Any Era. Together with Some Observations about Minor
Fallibilities in the Writing of History. The Spirit of America During pre-War Years. A Dynamic Energy Accompanied by a Dynamic Humanitarianism. A New Social
Point of View That Accompanied the New Wealth. "Wealth
Is Motion." Woodrow Wilson Sadly Mis-reads the Times.

AMERICAN national life preceding the Great War was
too far-ranging in its vigorous adventuring, too varied in
the rich and ever shifting colors it presented to the world,
too many-sided in the strongly-marked expressions of its
robustious spirit, to be confined by any of those adjectival
designations, such as the "Gay Nineties," or the "Tragic
Era,"[1] with which historians describe, or put labels upon,
epochs and eras. Perhaps it would be more accurate to

---

[1] "Tragic Era" is the title of Mr. Claude Bowers' history of the reconstruction period, 1865–1870. The "Gay Nineties" was a common designation for the
1890's in the literature of about twenty years after they had passed. Likewise the
"Electric Nineties" and the "Yellow Nineties," and the "Golden," and the
"Mauve Decade." The "Splendid Idle Forties" (1840's) was the title of a book
by Meade Minnegerode.

Such designations achieve more convenience to historians than fidelity to the
spirit of the era which their happy phrases purport to sum up. The effect of
them has been to mislead the race about its past. I doubt, for example, if the
1890's in America were any more "gay"—or more yellow, or more golden, or
more mauve—than the 1880's that preceded, or the decade that followed. I doubt
if the 1840's were either more "splendid" or more "idle" than the 1850's or the
1830's. I doubt if the years subsequent to 1865 were any more the "Tragic Era"
than the years of civil war that preceded. I am skeptical about even such accepted terms as "Dark Ages" or the "Golden Age," and suspect that much which
went on in the one was not dark nor in the other golden. That time and use
have made these phrases classic does not alter the fact that originally they
were merely the happy inventions of historians, having for those who devised
them the usefulness of attracting attention by smartness of phrase and at the

limit this assertion to saying that the present historian is unable to think of any one word or compact phrase that could describe with sufficient inclusiveness or adequate exactness the American years preceding 1914. Of all designations of eras, those are most nearly possible of justification which rest upon association with some dominating personality. The American years preceding 1914 back to about 1900, in their spirit and flavor had a partial resemblance to the American who was dominant throughout them. If they must be called an epoch and if they must be given a name, the "Roosevelt

---

same time distracting attention from the lack of that labor which would have been necessary to create a correct and balanced picture of the era.

I distrust all epigrammatic summations, for I suspect that the devisers of them, at the moment of creation, are more intent upon the epigram than upon the truth; and I am confident that when attempt is made to press truth into the mold of an epigram, much of the truth falls outside the walls of the form, and much of that which is crowded in suffers sad distortion in the process.

I distrust, indeed, the whole dividing of history into "eras" and "epochs." The forces that make history do not observe the calendar nor conform to the clock; they do not stop work on Saturday night, nor begin on the first day of a century, nor stop on the first day of the succeeding one. Rarely do they adjust themselves to the convenience of historians by starting and stopping in just those years which facile authors name as the boundaries of an era or an epoch. Occasionally, but only rarely, a specific date can reasonably be picked out as a real landmark of history. Such a date, I think, is June 28, 1914, though even here, those tides of history, those sequences of events, which led up to the assassination of the Archduke Francis Ferdinand, and thence to the Great War, had beginnings which certainly were long anterior to the event, and were so complex, intertwined and obscure as to make it impossible to be sure whether the assassination of the Archduke, or something before or after, was the certain key-date that made the rest inevitable.

Of all definitions of eras, those are most nearly justifiable which name the age after the individual who happened to hold some place of power at the time, whether warrior or priest, king or queen. Even in these cases, I suspect the designation arises as much through allurement of accidental euphony as through identity of quality between the epoch and the individual after whom history names it. Had the name of the woman who ruled Great Britain from 1837 to 1901 been Bridget instead of Victoria, I cannot imagine how literary folk would designate those figures whom they now call the "Victorians" — Bridgetarians perhaps? There is in the case of Victoria a real identity of traits between the individual and the years in which she was dominant. Yet had the name of Victoria been Lucille or Susan, I suspect she would not have been the same temptation to the literary artisans of euphonic phrases; and the era of manners and standards that is now called Victorian might be called by some other name, with resultant emphasis upon different qualities of the period.

Era" has some aptness. Yet even here, the era had many
qualities differing greatly from those of the man; and

The Roosevelt Dam, Salt River, Arizona, completed in 1911 by the United States
Government at a cost of $3,890,000. Roosevelt had much to do with pro-
moting policies of conservation both as to water power and other natural
resources.

the extraordinary variety of the period far exceeded that
of even so wide-ranging a spirit as Roosevelt's. Some of
the forces which made the America of that day what it

was, had come with us from so early a period in our
national life, were so invincible in the vital strength of
their influence on our national character, that it would be
difficult to say, of the years from 1900 to 1914, whether
Roosevelt stamped himself upon this American period

A group of "dynamic humanitarians." *From left to right:* Robert C. Ogden,
President William H. Taft, Principal Booker T. Washington, and
Andrew Carnegie.

or whether America stamped itself upon Roosevelt.
Of the period as of the man the outstanding quality was
energy; energy physical, intellectual, spiritual — and,
throughout all, ferment. But not even Roosevelt is an
exception to the rule that in any history of a period,
heads of state become, to some degree, merely iridescent
bubbles on the surface, marking the course of deep
streams beneath.

It is futile — worse than futile, misleading — to suggest that the immensity of things happening in America

during those years of titanic vitality can be described in one word, or in a thousand. If there must be a condensed characterization, let us say that the time was marked by a prodigious energy, that much of the energy was ferment, and that the whole was infused by an altruism which, taking on the common characteristic, became a dynamic humanitarianism.

The dynamic humanitarianism was directly related to the dynamic materialism. It has been asserted by many poets, preachers, and politicians, that material enrichment results in spiritual starvation. Of that ancient cant, the America of 1900 to 1914 is sufficient refutation.

II

There had come into the world two new forms of physical energy. To speak of them merely as additions to man's stores of available power would be understate-

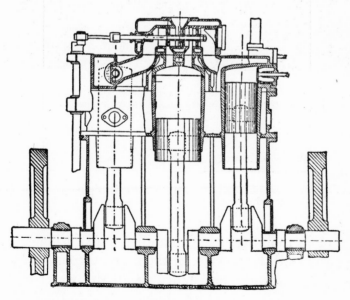

One of the two new forms of physical energy. A three-cylinder compound gas engine.

ment, for each of the new forms was greater than the
sum of all the energy that man had turned to his use in
all preceding time; each was far greater — taking into

The other new form of physical energy. Hydro-electric power station, Great
Western Power Company, Feather River, California.

account its mobility, its adaptability to diffusion — than
the sum of all the muscles of men, added to all the muscles of horses and oxen, added to all the water-wheels,
added to all the wind-mills, added, even, to the other of
man's comparatively recent acquisitions, steam.

The internal combustion engine in its most common form expressed itself in the hands of the average man as an Arabian Nights dream made real, a portable fountain of energy, the automobile, which, weighing only half as much as a horse, would do the work of sixty horses and keep it up without rest for practically an unlimited time.

Electricity was streaking up and down the country, literally like lightning — wires to provide it with a pathway were everywhere being extended, like long nerves of new growth, from central power houses, from the city to the suburb, longer and longer capacity for transmission carrying it to distant villages, from the villages to the farm — everywhere ending in a switch, by the turning of which man could tap for himself a practically limitless reservoir of physical power.

These new forms of energy were wealth; they constituted the greatest additions to man's material enrichment that had ever been created; added to the other forms of wealth which the new energies cumulatively produced, they enriched America to a degree never before paralleled. Compared to the wealth which America was transmuting out of the application of its new forms of energy to iron and forest and field, the gold and silver that Spain brought back from South America in the Sixteenth Century, the silks and jewels that Britain and Holland brought from the East Indies, were baubles and the trade built on them was the mere chaffering of bazaars. The very novelty of this new wealth and its abundance had an effect on men, made them open-handed, adventurous. They could not fear stratified poverty, and therefore did not practice tight-fisted holding on to what they had.

But the particular quality of this period in America was the diffusion of the wealth that was being created. Not only had that never been paralleled; it had never been to any effective degree attempted. Never before had the producers of wealth thought of wealth as a thing to be diffused. The old conception had been that wealth is static — things, and therefore to be amassed, stored away, withheld. Woodrow Wilson, thinking in these terms, and speaking at a time, 1906, when only the few had automobiles, said that "nothing has spread socialis-

Fashion at the wheel. From a Hupmobile advertisement in 1909.

tic feeling in this country more than the automobile; to the countryman they are a picture of arrogance of wealth, with all its independence and carelessness."

Woodrow Wilson did not see, in 1906, few saw at the time, a peculiar and unprecedented quality that had come into the world. The new wealth was not in the form of things, it was in the form of energy, of power of action; it was atoms in motion. Since the new kind of wealth was essentially motion, it did not lend itself to amassing or withholding; it could come into being only through use, and the use of it necessarily enriched the user. The entrepreneurs of the new forms of wealth, the industrial leaders identified with it, could make profit for themselves only insofar as they conferred upon the average man the power inherent in electricity and in the internal combustion engine; they could only enrich themselves by persuading the average man to use, and by enabling him to use, the new forms of energy.

Presently the desire to enable the largest possible num-

Reo Runabout $500

Folding seat, holding two extra passengers, $25 extra. Top extra.

A part of the Reo runabout advertisement of 1909 in magazines of the day.

ber of persons to possess and make use of the new form of wealth became a dominating motive. So far did this new conception go that Henry Ford — and later others adopting his point of view — came to think of his own laborers, of all workers, not according to the Adam Smith concept, as ones to be hired at the lowest wages they can be persuaded to accept, not as ones to leave with the employer the largest possible share of the fruits of industry, but as ones to be paid high wages in order that they might become maximum consumers of the goods Ford and others had to sell. Ford and others came to see labor not primarily as labor, but primarily in the rôle of consumer, and therefore to be enriched so that they might consume more. That was a revolution in economic thought and practice.

Politicians of the time, especially Bryan and LaFol-

lette,[2] thinking in terms of the classic definition of
wealth, dedicated themselves to putting limitations upon
the leaders of industry, to inciting labor against capital.
In general, they stirred the man who had no horse to suspicion against the man who had two. Some of the political thought of the period took the direction of Socialism, not calling itself by that name — the direction of
bringing it about that the man who had two horses should
give up one. Almost all the politics of protest, typified
by Bryan and LaFollette, took the direction of preventing the man with two horses from having more, certainly
from having many more.

At that very time, men in another world than politics,
men unnoticed by the politicians or the public (though
Edison was a familiar character, Henry Ford did not
emerge on the national consciousness until 1914) were
conferring upon both the man who previously had no
horse and him who formerly had two, not only the power
of one horse but of twenty or a hundred — as many as
either could possibly use or desire. Had all the proposals
of restraint ever devised by Bryan or LaFollette been
enacted into law, the sum of their effect — assuming the
effect would not have taken the form of disaster —
would not have procured for the average man even a
tiny fraction of the enrichment that Henry Ford conferred upon him.

As a result of Ford's contribution, Woodrow Wilson,

---

2 I have spoken here of the politics of Bryan and LaFollette and their disciples.
The other politics of the period, so far as it dealt with wealth, could be divided
into two main fields. The standpat conservative, Republican and Democratic, for
the most part just dug his heels into the ground, shut his eyes and resisted all
change — "stood pat." The other group, Roosevelt and his principal associates
in the Progressive movement, had a vision of the possibilities of the new forms
of wealth; they would have taken the legal brakes and impediments away from
the entrepreneur, and from the form of large organization that was indispensable
to him; they would not have penalized the entrepreneur as such, but only the
acts of those who committed crimes. This was one of the tenets of the Progressive party.

living until 1923, saw the time when every "country-man" had his "flivver," in which he could travel as far and as fast as any other, and therefore was moved to no socialistic jealousy of those whose Buicks and Packards differed but little except in trifling ornamentation from the farmers' Fords. The Woodrow Wilson of 1923 could have asserted the very opposite of what he had said in 1906. Hardly anything so disarmed the appeal of Socialism in America as the wide diffusion of the automobile, a diffusion so general as to be practically universal.

Yesterday.   To-day.

From *The Saturday Evening Post* of March 14, 1925.

3

HENRY FORD EMERGES, SUDDENLY

An American Melodrama, about a Poor Boy's Rise to Fame
and Riches, and Some of the Things He Did. He Raises
Wages—and the "Ford Idea" Becomes as Familiar as the
"Ford Car." Some Incidents Attending the Process by
Which a Man, Hitherto Obscure, Becomes a National Char-
acter; and Some Advantages, as Well as Embarrassments,
Which Attend that Role. The "Ford Jokes" Which, Accord-
ing to Variations of Individual Taste, Were as Locusts or as
Manna; the Natural History of the Type, and the Classifica-
tion into Species; Including the Tin-Can Joke and the Junk
Joke, and the Rattle-and-Shake Joke, and the "For-the-
Liver" Joke, Which Ultimately Led to the Word "Flivver."

FOR nearly ten years Henry Ford had been making the
largest quantity of the new vehicle that was revolution-
izing the country's life, and at a price that made it available to the largest number of people — by 1914 more
than half a million Model T's were on the nation's then
modest network of highways. Yet Ford as a man had
attracted no attention; there were no books about him,
no magazine articles. He had not been deemed eligible
for "Who's Who," national roster of the great and the
near-great and the would-be-great, which in its 1913
edition contained 18,794 names, including a Henry
Jones Ford, who was a university professor, and a Henry
P. Ford, who was an ex-Mayor of Pittsburgh — but not
the Henry Ford who was an automobile manufacturer.
In the newspapers[1] Ford's name appeared almost solely
as a signature to advertisements, chiefly in country week-
lies. A baseball player named Napoleon Lajoie was a
public character, but not Henry Ford. An actor named

---

[1] About 1901 and 1902, there had been some slight newspaper notice of Ford
as a driver of racing cars. (See Vol. I, "Our Times.")

Douglas Fairbanks was a public character, and a magician named Houdini; a moving picture actress named Mary Pickford and a reformed train robber named Al Jennings; a professional walker named George Weston and a speculator named Tom Lawson; a dancer named

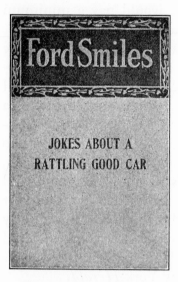

The cover of a "Ford Joke Book," which contained 151 pages of Ford jokes. (See page 62.)

Advertisement of Ford's Model "T" Coupé. In 1914 more than half a million were on the nation's highways.

"The Ford joke was told for the joke's sake only. It had no common pattern or point of view. It was as willing to compliment Ford and his car as to jeer."

Vernon Castle and an Indian athlete named Jim Thorpe; a blind girl named Helen Keller and a champion swimmer named Annette Kellerman — all these and a dozen others were public characters, their personalities familiar to the country, but Henry Ford was unknown. The name "Ford" was a brand, not a man — merely a proper noun linked with an article of commerce, like Fairbanks and scales, Ingersoll and watches, Colgate and soap, Lydia Pinkham and female restoratives, Singer and sewing machines. Like all these, "Ford" was to the public merely the first half of a trade-name. He was no more thought of as having a living personality than the dog in the Victor phonograph advertisement, or the Quaker of "Quaker Oats," or the twins of "Gold Dust," or the bull in "Bull Durham."

Then, in the afternoon newspapers of January 5, 1914, Ford announced that as a way of sharing his profits with his 13,000 employees, he would pay a minimum wage of five dollars per eight-hour day.

On the first pages and in the editorial columns of the next morning's papers, Ford's announcement overshadowed the war in Mexico and every other topic of national or local interest. Sensationally, a little appalled, with a manner of believe-it-or-not, the New York *Times* exclaimed: "The lowest paid employees, the sweepers, who in New York City may claim from $1.00 to $1.50 a day, are now to receive $5 in Ford's plant."[2] "It was," said the New York *Sun*, groping frantically for a sufficient superlative, "a bolt out of the blue sky, flashing its way across the continent and far beyond, something unheard of in the history of business."[3] "An epoch in the world's industrial history," said the New York *Herald*.

Headlines that proclaimed the sensation were followed by teeming columns of excited discussion. Ford became the man of the hour, his plan the topic of the day. Quickly the phrase "Ford idea" became as familiar as the Ford car. The discussion had two sides, and in-

[2] Some of the material dealing with the public reception of Ford's announcement is taken from Charles Merz's "And Then Came Ford."

[3] In the Detroit *Free Press* a versifier brought Whittier up — or should one say down? — to date:

Of all glad words
That now are roared,
The gladdest are these:
He works for Ford.

On the morning the new plan went into effect, 12,000 applicants for jobs swirled about the gates of Ford's factory, a modern variation of the old rushes to new-found gold-fields. Three days later, the influx continuing, Ford asked the newspapers of Indianapolis, Cincinnati, Milwaukee, and elsewhere to warn the workmen of their cities not to come to Detroit.

numerable angles. The plan was good, the plan was bad. It was a "magnificent act of generosity" (New York *Evening Post*); it was merely a cunning way of getting an advantage over competitors. It would make the workers self-respecting and independent; the workers would be robbed of their independence by Ford's paternalism. The workers would become home-owners and

Henry Ford, standing beside a racer, as he appeared in the days before he had built his first car.

build up savings; the workers would — time-honored concern of the "haves" for the best good of the "have-nots" — "spend their money foolishly." Ford was "an inspired millionaire" (New York *World*); Ford was a shrewdly self-interested business man.

To finding out just what sort of being this strange new Crœsus was, at once Midas and Messiah, to satisfying public curiosity about him, the country's mechanisms of publicity now dedicated themselves. In seven days the press of New York City alone printed fifty-two columns.

All over the country, managing editors wired "rush" telegrams to Detroit correspondents, who hastily sent out such casual information as was in their minds about their hitherto comparatively unnoticed fellow-citizen, in despatches to which they appended "more to follow." Writers and press photographers competed at Ford's door with the crowds of applicants for jobs; newspapers which formerly had sent only their advertising solicitors to the Ford plant now sent their star reporters, who found that, as the New York *Times* put it, "there was nothing about Ford's demeanor to indicate that he thought he had done anything remarkable." Over-night the press, from taking it for granted that Ford was of no more public interest than any other citizen, now combed his present and his past for anything that would help satisfy the public hunger for information about him. Not only was Ford himself "good copy," his wife, his son, all his relatives, his neighbors, his associates in business, his former teachers, all were tracked down by ubiquitous reporters with pencils poised lance-like. That curious and numerous army of baskers in vicarious publicity, the men who "knew him when," eagerly dropped their contributions into newspaper columns that gaped like hungry birdlings, and presses that panted for more.

The public learned that Ford liked skating and did not like Wall Street; that after he had become a millionaire he had continued to live in "a plain small house which would probably rent for $50 a month"; that in hiring men he set no extra value on a college education and was tolerant of former prisoners — one of his important executives was an ex-convict; that he liked outdoor recreation and had an adage (he later inscribed it over the open fireplace of his new house) "Chop Your Own Wood and It Will Warm You Twice"; that he liked birds — once to avoid disturbing a nest of phœbes

on his front porch he had used the back door of his house
for a week; that he raised pheasants on his farm and fed
them custard; that he did not approve of professional
charity — he had a principle, "the best use I can make of
my money is to make more work for more men"; that in
his business he was himself impatient of routine —
though devotion to rigid routine was the very heart of his
factory methods; that he was rarely to be found in that
part of his plant which was known as his office, and that
he often held conferences out of doors under trees.

Ford's hobby and his law of life, the press reported,
was to produce a good car at the lowest possible cost; to
save a few cents on each car he had dropped the "stripers"
who painted a slender ornamental line of yellow on the
bodies. When salesmen complained that customers demanded more ornament, in a time when other makes of
cars were sold largely on the basis of seductiveness of
appearance, Ford's answer had been, "They can have any
color they want so it's black." This, the press reported,
was a basic detail of the process by which Ford had made
his fortune. His formula of mass production had been:
make a thoroughly good car; make few models and stick
to them, thus avoiding the expense, immense in the automobile business, of equipping the factory for new models; make the car as inexpensive as possible by eliminat-
ing costly decorativeness, putting all the expenditure into
serviceableness only. Sell the car at the lowest price; by
that means achieve large sales; by large sales reduce the
manufacturing cost of each car; use this reduction of cost
to lower the price to the consumer; thereby get larger
sales — and so on, in an ascending spiral of expansion,
which in 1913 yielded Ford profits of about twenty million dollars. It was this twenty million dollars that Ford
now announced he would divide with his workers during
1914 by paying a minimum wage of $5 a day.

The question which everybody speculated about was, why had Ford decided to pay $5 a day to men he could have had for $2? Whatever may have been the motives in Ford's mind before he took the step, and whatever the relative weight of different reasons in the mixture of many motives that commonly lie behind any human ac-

The Ford Motor Company's factory as it appeared in 1903-1904.

tion, Ford was now to learn the truth of the worldly counsel, Never give your reasons at the time of an act, because thus you preserve for yourself a mobility which enables you later to adopt any of the motives that others attribute to you, or that which best fits the unanticipatable conditions that subsequently arise. Ford, within twenty-four hours after his announcement, could accept any one of almost as many reasons as there were sources of comment. The head of the rival Chalmers automobile factory attributed Socialistic leanings to him, and the New York *Times* sent a reporter to ask him, point-blank and accusingly, whether he was a Socialist, and if it was true that his purpose was to prevent his son from inheriting a cloying fortune. At the other end of the gamut of imputed motives, a mass-meeting of five hundred Socialists denounced Ford's act as a detestable trap: "Ford," they unanimously resolved, "had purchased the brains, life and soul of his men by a raise in pay of a few dollars a week;" the Socialist New York *Call*, seeing nothing to praise in

Outside the Ford factory in 1914, showing the tremendous output of chassis.

any "division of earnings between labor and capital," said it would be interested only "when the working class decides to cease dividing" with capital. Between these extremes of alleged motive ran an infinite range; Ford sought the favor of labor; Ford sought advantage over other manufacturers; Ford sought publicity for himself; Ford sought advertising for his car — and so on and so on and so on.

Ford's own statement of his motive, given to reporters — who called upon him in the spirit of demanding an explanation for having done an unheard-of thing — was that he had taken the step as "a plain act of social justice." This answer was too off-hand and simple to be acceptable as a carefully accurate statement of motives which actually must have been complex and must have sprung in part from little understood deeps of human psychology. "Social justice" was a rough-and-ready phrase, at that time much hackneyed by use as part of the creed of the Progressive party; it would come naturally to any one's lips, but it was rather too vague to explain so startling and original an act.

Ford's action could be regarded as a kind of unconscious expression of a deep and instinctive urge not understood by Ford himself. A more exact statement of his motive than he gave, and one not at all inconsistent with what he avowed, might say that the institution which Ford had built up had developed, like any living thing, a kind of cosmic urge of its own, an instinct to survive and grow and come to fruit; that the institution sensed that if it were to expand it must have a larger quantity of purchasers of the car it produced than was provided by the number of persons then able to pay for a car; that such new purchasers could only be created by bringing into the world the notion of paying larger wages to workers; and that this urge of the institution to function expressed itself in an inner compulsion upon Ford to do the thing he did. In short, that Ford the institution took possession of Ford the man, expressing its will to live in the form of cerebration on Ford's part that he called a hunch; that the step which the institution thus took was as much an instinctive act of nature as that of a tree reaching upward for sun; and that Ford, in throwing off into the world the idea of high wages for labor, was acting as instinctively, as blindly and as inevitably, on behalf of the institution of which he was a part, as the stamen of a flower when it sheds pollen upon the wind.

This hypothesis would comport with what later came to be realized as a fundamental law of such institutions as the Ford one, namely, that mass production can only exist by being fed with a constantly increasing purchas-

From a photograph by Brown Brothers.
Henry Ford.

ing power on the part of labor. And if we accept the theory that mass production was a normal and logical step in the development of civilization, then this hypothesis would explain the favor with which the world received Ford and his idea.

Ford became almost the one rich man whose wealth was not envied or contemned. For half a generation there was a curious contrast between Ford and that other rich man, John D. Rockefeller, whose leadership had provided the other half of the progress that made the automobile possible. Rockefeller's fortune, based on the fuel, was at all times under attack, Ford's practically never — although Rockefeller practiced lavishly the giving that is supposed to make the rich tolerable to the less-favored, while Ford did little or no giving and expressed disapproval for philanthropic institutions. When Ford, in the business depression of the early 1920's, was in difficulty, the country watched his efforts at self-rescue with as much sympathy as applauders of the home-team in a baseball game. Hardly could it have been possible that Ford as a matter of deliberate shrewdness devised the $5 day as an armor against envy and criticism; it is at least as credible to assume that Ford, acting upon one of the psychic impulses upon which he depended much, placed himself at the head of a tidal push of civilization.

At the least, any adequate account of the period this history covers must record, as an important innovation, that there came into the world, originating in the United States, widespread understanding of mass production, that to the public Henry Ford was the symbol of it; and that since the public thinks and feels mainly through symbols, its reaction to Ford was its reaction to the thing that Ford stood for.

Now, Ford was a public character, an exalted one, in a class by himself, an oracle, with opportunity to be a Titan — and willingness to undertake the role. Newspapers which formerly had referred to the Ford automobile as "a certain low-priced car" (in obedience to an office rule of some newspapers forbidding free publicity to institutions supposed to pay for their advertising) now sent reporters to pick up any chance pontifical remark he might have dropped to the barber in whose shop he had been seen; and begged from Ford himself the privilege of printing anything he might be graciously willing to say. He was solicited to speak, and with naïve sim-

Outside the Ford factory.

plicity — "he submitted to an interview as if it were a pleasure," said the New York *Sun* — gave such views as he had on corporation finance, which he disapproved; on railroads, which he thought were not well-managed; on tobacco, which he did not use; on labor unions, to which he was opposed; and on some other subjects more distant from his personal experience, including the gold standard, the civil war in Mexico, and the theory of evolution. If on some of these topics Ford's views lacked the benefit of complete information, the public nevertheless sensed his naïveté and unpretentiousness. Accepting simplicity as an adequate substitute for learning, and pre-eminence in one line as proof of capacity in all lines; assuming that the new god of a new order, mass production, must be godlike in all things, the public took Ford to its bosom. Within a month after Ford's announcement of his wage increase, a mass meeting of the Progressive Party in Calhoun County, Michigan, on February 8, 1914, endorsed him for Governor; movements to run him for President sprang up sporadically.

Ford, accepting perhaps too fully the judgment of the public about himself, took Olympian responsibility in some matters distant from the manufacture of automobiles. Passing easily from mass production of machines into the notion of mass-direction of men, Ford adventured into national and world affairs. Within a year he, in association with another wizard of the material world, Thomas A. Edison, embarked upon a crusade — "The Cigarette Must Go"; but the millions of copies of a pamphlet of denunciation, "The Case Against the Little White Slaver," were ineffective against the power of advertising that was at the cigarette's command. Within two years he embarked upon an enterprise of stopping the war in Europe, taking ship on December 4, 1915, with a go-getter purpose announced as "bringing the boys out of the trenches by Christmas," which would be about two weeks after his arrival in Europe. When he found the forces boiling along the Hindenburg Line not so amenable to the short cuts of standardization as the production of automobiles had been, Ford returned with a disillusionment which did not contribute as much restraint as it might have to his further adventuring in fields distant from his experience. Several other attempts to influence public affairs did not add to his stature; but neither did they diminish his permanent position in history, as the outstanding exponent of the most fundamental characteristic of the period, the diffusion of material goods, the enrichment of the average man.

II

In one quarter there was a qualification to the welcome given Ford's adoption of the five-dollar minimum wage, and the expansion of his business that followed. The doubling of Ford's plant, said the Detroit *News* on June 28, 1914, with the manner of a home-town's resentment against aspersion upon a local institution, "will make a certain type of vaudeville humor twice as insipid as it is now."

The Ford joke was, even more than the Ford car, a staple, like sugar or salt, as familiar a part of the conversation of the American people from about 1914 to about 1918, as their shop talk, or sports, or the weather. "Ford stories" were told by men in clubs and by women at tea parties, by boys in high school and elders in offices, by the fireman in the cab and the banker in the club car. To vaudeville monologists they were the staff of life, to toastmasters a rock of refuge in time of need. A clergyman would point his sermon with one, a doctor would carry them as part of his pharmacopeia of cheer. They were universal, and innumerable.

Where they started and how, who told the first one, and what there was about it that invited repetition, imitation and elaboration; why this brand of joke should have acquired a vogue and grown into a category, as standard and for the time greater in quantity than the "mother-in-law" joke, or the "two Jews" joke, or the "Pat and Mike" joke; what national characteristic of the American people caused them to like the Ford type of quip; why Henry Ford should have been the one human being in all time and his car the one commodity whose name became the brand-word of a form of wit; why the word "Ford" should have come to be followed

by the word "joke" as naturally and as frequently as
"Hamlet" is followed by "soliloquy" — all that composes a detail of this history that has eluded research and
left the author in the lame position of assuming that the
Ford joke must have come into the world by some kind
of spontaneous origination. One cannot even be certain
there ever was any one original Ford joke, Eve to the
race of them that was quickly begot with a fecundity
far excelling that of the guinea pig. Possibly they had no
one ancestor; maybe they came all at once, like manna
or locusts. It was like manna, if you liked them, or locusts if you did not, that they were upon us. They covered the country. They travelled East and West at the
same time. They sprang up anywhere, also everywhere,
and they travelled as the wind listeth, dropping frequent
progeny as they flew. A new one told at a Rotary Club
meeting in Kansas City would be carried by a drummer
on to a North-bound train; told in the smoking-com-
partment of the Pullman it found a new carrier in every
other drummer who heard it; introduced by these to the
dry-goods buyers in a dozen cities, repeated by each of
these at supper that night, told by the wives at sewing-
bees the next day and by the children at school, each
hearer a new focus of infection — within a week it covered the mid-West, within a month the nation. Presently diligent compilers with an instinct for commercial
opportunity collected them into paper-bound books
which found their way into the baskets of boys who in
the aisles of railroad trains cried "Peanuts, oranges,
candy, cigars and Ford Joke Books — two hundred good
jokes for only fifteen cents."[4]

[4] There must have been scores of different Ford Joke Books, and tens of
thousands of copies of each; but when in 1932, some seventeen years after their
burgeoning, I tried to find a copy, they were almost one with Nineveh and Tyre.
A search of the second-hand book-shops of Washington revealed not one; in the
Congressional Library, eight different ones were listed, but many were never
copyrighted and therefore never found their way to this or any other library.

The Ford joke was told for the joke's sake only. It had no common pattern or point of view. It was as willing to compliment Ford and his car as to jeer. It bore no malice, its exclusive purpose was to evoke a smile; a humble little roadside jester, it existed only to amuse. If more of them "kidded" the Ford than lauded it, that is only because humor tends more easily to take the direction of satire. If a whimsy could be anyhow made to fit a Ford, it mattered nothing what direction the implication took. Examining a collection of them now, one is able to sort them into categories, even though one feels a little the ghoulish guilt of an archæologist in fingering the dried mummies, and classifying into antediluvian genera and species things which so brief a time ago were so sprightly.

The most numerous species was the one whose point derived from the Ford's diminutiveness: A presumed economy of the Ford car, so the stories said, was that upon approaching a toll-gate you could get out, put the Ford in your pocket, and pass through at the price for pedestrians. The up-to-date cry of a junkman who kept abreast of the times was "Any old rags, old bottles, old Fords to-day?" "The life of a garbage man," said a philosophic member of the profession, "is gettin' harder every year; dead cats is bad enough, an' broken bottles is hell, but the worst on the temper and the fingers is sortin' out them damn little Fords." A clergyman who when pronouncing the benediction was annoyed by buzzing sounds among the congregation, protested, in clerically mild reproof, that while he had no objection to their bringing their Fords into the pews with them, he thought it would be more considerate toward him, and more reverent toward the Sabbath, if they would refrain from cranking the motors until after the services were completely over. Another whimsy in this category related the apprehension of a postman, about the increase in his burden, upon hearing that Ford was going to deliver all his cars by mail.

Something that Ford was about to do, some prediction of a startling innovation, furnished the formula for introducing many of the Ford jokes. His inauguration of a $5 minimum wage, and other departures from the conventional, conferred probability upon almost any intention that might· be ascribed to him, and gave similitude of seriousness to the facetious question with which many of the jokes began, "Do you know what Ford is going to do now?" Among answers as innumerable as Ford jokesters were fecund, the manufacturer was going to "paint his cars yellow so that dealers could hang them in bunches and retail them like bananas."

Next to tinyness came tinniness (both as respects the noises they made when running and the material out of which they were alleged to be constructed) as bases of the largest categories. Ford, always seeking innovations in the direction of resourceful utility, was going to make his bodies in future without doors, but would ship with each car a can opener with which the owner could cut his doors according to his taste. The Ford factory came to be considered a large consumer of tin, new or scrap, so that, not only in jokes but sometimes actually, the factory received shipments it had not ordered. In the stories, an Illinois farmer who had stripped the tin roof from his barn and sent it to Ford received a letter saying "While your car was an exceptionally bad wreck, we shall be able to complete repairs and return it by the first of the week." A thrifty New England housewife who had saved old tin cans shipped the collection to Detroit, and received a new car, accompanied with conscientious return of five cans that had not been needed.

The lightness of the Ford car, and the fact that its

body was deliberately high-slung to enable it to pass
through the mudholes and over the hummocks frequent
in the roads of that day, caused it to bounce, and thus
gave rise to a category of "rattle and shake" jokes: "Does
this car always make this racket? Oh, no, only when it's
running." A farmer in the chills and fever section of
Arkansas found the Ford car to be, among its miscellaneous utilities, a cure for ague: "When the chills seen
the brand o' shakes this car could put itself to, they just
naturally slunk away and hid." Henry Ford was a better evangelist than Billy Sunday, because "Ford has
shaken hell out of more people than Billy Sunday ever
saw."

The loose-jointed quality, less actual than presumed
for purposes of humor, led to a legend that the Ford
had a fault of shedding nuts and washers on the road;
hence Ford was about to provide, as an up-to-date acces-
sory with each car, a trained squirrel of exceptional agil-
ity, which could leap from the car, retrieve a dropped
nut and return without the car slowing down. The same
pun provided the point for Irvin Cobb's story about the
crazy man who stole a Ford, found it enjoyable, and with
a philanthropy associated with incompleteness of intellect determined to share his pleasure with two Chinese
laundrymen. The outing of the three came to an unhappy end through the crazy driver's failure to estimate
correctly the speed and momentum of a railroad locomotive at a crossing. When the train crew returned to the
scene, "all they could find was a nut and two washers."

Many of the quips, reflecting the keeping-up-with-
the-Joneses trait in the American spirit, imputed social
inferiority to the Ford: "Why is a Ford like a bath-tub?
Because you hate to be seen in one." The demeaning of
the Ford was subtly suggested in a garage-owner's

choice of words for his sign: "Automobiles Repaired; Fords Mended."

One species took its point from the Ford's sturdy dependability: "Why is a Ford car like a motion to adjourn? Because it's always in order." A man about to die had one death-bed request, that his Ford should be buried with him, because he had "never been in a hole yet where his Ford didn't get him out." The Ford's strength, coupled with its smallness, inspired the story of the owner of the Cadillac (or the Pierce-Arrow or the Peerless or the Packard) who always carried a Ford in his tool-box "to pull him out when he got stuck in the mud." Another virtue accompanying the Ford's smallness was its economy of operation: A colored man asked at the filling station for "a pint of gasoline"; the dealer, salesman-minded, suggested the buyer had better get more. "No," said the Ford owner, "I don't want to give it any more; I'm weanin' it."

An American trait of seeing a commercial motive for every phenomenon, which had assumed that Ford's announcement of the $5 day must have been designed to get free advertising, now gave rise to a legend that the Ford jokes were manufactured in the Ford factory, or at the least that Ford welcomed the jokes:

> Ford has made a million cars
> Out of paint and iron bars. . . .

> Each single car has had one joke
> Cracked by an envy-ridden bloke
> Flung at its fancied size and jars —
> So Ford has sold a million cars.

> If we could think of something, too,
> To sell to you, or you, or you,
> We'd like it made the butt of joke,
> By ev'ry green-eyed guy that's broke.

A nearer approximation to Ford's actual state of mind was the story of a smoking-car volunteer of wit who asked a stranger: "Have you heard the last Ford story?" The reply, "I hope so," was, to the average American mind, so extraordinary as to call for investigation, which revealed that the stranger was Henry Ford.

A story, often asserted to be veracious, recited the experience of a farmer whose Ford broke down on a remote country road. A man drove up in another Ford, courteously inquired about the trouble, left his own car, and with a manner of expert familiarity, made the needed repairs. The farmer tendered a dollar. The stranger declined it, saying that he was the manufacturer of the car and that it was not only courtesy but duty to help out any Ford owner who had trouble. The farmer, unable wholly to let polite gratitude overcome his resentment at being thought gullible, and reflecting a common American point of view to the effect that Mr. Ford's distinction lay not in his expertness as a manufacturer but rather in his wealth, stepped sullenly into his car, remarking, "If you had that much money, you wouldn't be driving a Ford."

One quip made a joke of the Ford joke itself: a man who remained in his theatre seat after the rest of the audience had gone and was told by an usher that the show was over, retorted: "That can't be — I haven't heard a Ford joke yet."

If one were to attempt, through these and other reclaimed fossils of the Ford jokes, to separate them into, so to speak, geologic strata, one might venture the hypothesis, erected chiefly upon surmise, that the "Ford story" began with a more inclusive genus, the automobile joke; and that the automobile joke emerged as a kind of spontaneous folk-lore, arising naturally out of the appearance among men of so startling an innovation. One might surmise further that the earliest stratum, the so-to-speak archæozoic age of the new means of loco- motion, was represented by the joke about the automo-

From a photograph by Keystone View Company.

Mr. Ford when over sixty was still a good skater. He is shown here on the ice while on a vacation at Wayside Inn, Sudbury, Massachusetts.

bile and the roadside skunk, which seems to reflect the earliest impact of the automobile upon a generation to whom it and its attributes, including the scent that ac- companied it, was new. By the time of the proterozoic and subsequent ages of the automobile, the smell of gaso- line was familiar, taken for granted; babies inhaled it with their first intaking of breath, and the mature, especially those living in the lower stories of city apartment houses, would have been startled by absence of it. To the earlier generation, however, who knew the automobile as an innovation, the scent of gasoline, and of the exhaust of it, had a vividness which would account for the mephitic series of the jokes, and would seem to fix the time of them as the earliest era of the automobile joke.

The skunk, for uncounted generations, had been conscious of possessing a weapon of defense that made him safely arrogant toward all other animals, including, and especially, man. Any skunk whose nocturnal adventures called on him to travel across the road knew he had nothing to fear; an approaching pedestrian, or a horse and buggy, would stop and courteously wait until the skunk had completed his occupation of the right of way. Now, however, came a vehicle which did not stop or slow down or detour, which daringly drove past or over the skunk — and that astonished animal, as the odor of the exhaust struck his startled nostrils, knew the reason for man's newly acquired daring; knew also that the daring was soundly based — knew, in short, that he had encountered a competitor in aromatic warfare to which he would always be inferior. That situation, giving rise to the group of stories which pictured the roadside skunk as throwing up his hands in complete and permanent surrender and taking to the deep woods, must have been, one surmises, the earliest stratum of Ford jokes.

To support that theory, however, there is only the tenuous type of evidence known as inherent probability. Perhaps this subject had best be left with some other and minor aspects of Ford history that seem to defy research. Why was a Ford car called a "tin Lizzie"? A suggestion is that it was after "Lizzie" as the name of a mare; but in the American nomenclature of horses, "Lizzie" was not common. And why, when, and by whom was the term "flivver" first applied to a Ford car, and the term "jitney" to a Ford that carried passengers? Both words were unknown to the compilers of the edition of Web-

Henry Ford in his first car.

ster's Dictionary that appeared in 1909, or else were deemed as not yet having the degree of permanence that would entitle them to lexicographic approval. A supplement added in 1927 to record words that had come into the language since the preceding edition included:

Flivver — A small and inexpensive automobile; hence anything that is small of its kind and cheap or insignificant.

If one should accept the Ford jokes as valid clues to the folk-lore that germinated at the time, we should be informed that "flivver" arose out of a presumed phar-

maceutical attribute of the Ford car. That the car had
a vibrator effect was the theme of many of the jibes. Because it shook, it stirred up the liver, hence: "for the

The twenty-millionth Ford car, completed in 1931. Mr. Ford and his son Edsel
watch the car leave the production line at the Rouge River plant.

liver," abbreviated to f'liver, condensed to flivver. The
theory is borne out by a limerick of *circa* 1914:

> There was a fat man of Fall River,
> Who said as he drove his Ford "flivver,"
>   "This bumping and jolting,
>   To me is revolting!
> It's hell! but it's good for the liver."

Many of the Ford jokes were just puns or conun-
drums, and were told as such, baldly. Others lent themselves to elaboration. An artist could surround them with
atmosphere and build them up with engaging detail,
thereby providing, on very slight foundation, delicious

laughter. One such story, very American in its emphasis on mechanical ingenuity and commercial resourcefulness, took as its principal not the driver of the Ford car, but the keeper of a junk-shop. The junk-dealer on a slumberous afternoon leaned against the front of his store, reflecting somberly upon the dearth of customers. An automobile drew up, towing a dead Ford. The man in the Ford, entering the junk-shop, began pawing purposefully over the stock strewn on the floor, with a manner of knowing just what he wanted. One by one he gathered up odds and ends which the watchful junkman listed as: four feet of bed spring, a broken fly-swatter, the handle of a decrepit baby carriage, a yard of the intact portion of an old garden hose, and the faceless works of an alarm clock. With these materials assembled under his arm, the visitor paid the thirty cents asked by the junk-dealer, left the shop, lifted the hood of his Ford, worked a few minutes, closed the hood confidently, entered the Ford and drove off. The junk-dealer, after a few moments of concentrated cerebration, looked up at his sign, went to the back of his store, returned with some paint and a brush, painted out "Junk of All Kinds" and replaced it with "Ford Parts and Accessories."

4

NEW WAYS IN INDUSTRY

Which Resulted in Larger Production of Goods at Lower Expense of Human Effort. "Scientific Management," Which Was Different from, but an Aid to, "Mass Production." A Voltaire of Industry. "Taylorism" and "the Taylor System." "Time-Studies." Some Remarks Concerning a Relation between Organized Industry and Plain Human Nature.

THE heart of the system practiced in Ford's factory was an "assembly line," a conveyor belt running the length of a long well-lighted factory nave. Standing along each side are hundreds of workmen, each with his appointed task to perform while the slowly moving conveyor passes by him. Coming in from the sides are "feeder" belts, bearing parts: carburetors, complete and ready for installation; motor blocks still hot from the foundry — forty-eight hours before they were inert ore; screws and bolts, windshields, wheels, batteries, gasoline tanks. At the head of the conveyor belt, deft-handed, quick-moving workers place chassis frames on the assembly conveyor, each at a fixed interval from the next, two or three or more a minute. As the conveyor-belt carries the chassis along, workers trained to perfection in their minutely specialized duties attach parts to them, the whole process following a programme thought out in meticulous detail in advance, a process in which the human factor is reduced to a minimum.

The process, the speed and precision of it, was symbolized in a popular, and of course apocryphal, legend that a worker who dropped his wrench found, by the time he had picked it up, that fourteen cars had gone past him. The system, as practiced by Ford, and with appropriate variations by manufacturers in many lines, was known as "mass production."

II

Mass production was dependent partly upon, though very different from, another industrial development of the period, a carefully thought out, severely tested philosophy of producing goods called "scientific management." The phrase came to public attention in 1910, when Louis D. Brandeis of Boston, later a Justice of the United States Supreme Court, stated, with much attendant publicity, before a Congressional committee, that the railroads of the country could save one million dollars a day in operating costs if they would adopt scientific management.

An aspect of the new idea that caught the interest of the country, giving rise to much discussion in 1911, was "time-studies," conducted with a stop-watch.

To the public, time studies, as pictured (with some sacrifice of facts to picturesqueness) in magazine articles embellished with charts, graphs, and photographs, had the mystic fascination of a witch's incantation. The making of them consisted of observations by a trained engineer — the photographs showed him usually as a well-dressed, alert-faced man in the early thirties, rimless eye-glasses perched on a thin inquisitive nose, stop-watch and other gadgets of his profession in his hands — standing behind a bricklayer or a shoveller in a pit or a machine operator in a factory and making notes on how the workman moved his arms, hands, and fingers. Next the engineer was pictured as taking his data and retiring for a period of concentrated thinking. After that, he would emerge with a brand new set of motions which would lessen the number of movements of a bricklayer's

Brandeis Attacks Price-cutting

Favors Price-maintenance Under Competitive Conditions

Louis D. Brandeis

"Price-cutting of the one-priced, trade-marked article eliminates the small dealer, and ultimately ruins the market for the article."

"Encourage price-maintenance under proper conditions of competition, and you will aid in preserving the small dealer against capitalistic combinations."

"The most intolerable of monopolies are those where the price is not a matter of common knowledge, and where the discrimination in prices is used oppressively to annul competition."

It takes courage of the highest order to stand firm against uneducated public opinion —for the public's good.

Louis D. Brandeis, the eminent lawyer, has never taken a step in the interest of all the people that will arouse greater comment than the following article.

Many people who have not studied the subject are against price-maintenance. The consumer thinks it a device to make him pay more; the merchant feels that when he buys the goods of the manufacturer they are his, and that it is an infringement of his rights to establish his selling price.

Careful study of the subject, however, shows that the same price everywhere is for the best interests of the buying public, the independent dealer and the independent manufacturer.

Price-cutting on articles of individuality, Mr. Brandeis maintains, would enable men controlling vast combinations of capital to win local markets one by one, and create monopolies on the things we eat and wear, then raise the prices higher than before.

This article is published by a number of the leading magazines in the belief that by giving wide publicity to the views of Mr. Brandeis, the real interests of the enterprising individual manufacturer, the small dealer, and the public will be served.

Half of a two-page advertisement published in a number of leading magazines of 1913, giving publicity to Mr. Louis D. Brandeis' (later Justice Brandeis) views about price-cutting.

right hand from ten to nine, or shorten by so many inches the distance a laborer's hand needed to move drilling a given number of holes in a given time. The objective was economy, labor-saving; the method was specialization, a specialization in which it appeared that the efficiency expert was sometimes willing to require the man to adapt himself to the machine.

That was "time-studies" as the average man understood it, after being filtered to his mind through articles in the popular magazines. The average man took "time-studies" seriously, as he did all of scientific management, but not so seriously that he would refrain from "kidding" it, or smiling when some one else "kidded" it. He took delight in such extravaganzas as the story of that zealot for scientific management who, having put his mind upon the economical collection of garbage, observed that time could be saved, and rhythm of effective motion attained, if the men on the left side of the cart were chosen from among the left-handed; and that in order to have a supply of "southpaw" scavengers equal to the demand the public schools should train every other child to be left-handed.

Scientific management (of which time studies were but a detail) evolved from many separate origins and was developed by many men. The name most identified with it, and the man most justly to be credited with pioneering it, was a Philadelphia engineer, Frederick W. Taylor.[1] Taylor, son of a Quaker father, born at Germantown in 1856, unable to finish at Exeter Academy because of weak eyes, went to work for the Midvale Steel Company as laborer, became a mechanic, rose to be fore-

[1] Friends of Taylor, and of scientific management, who have been kind enough to read drafts of this chapter, insist that several distinctions be made clear: "Scientific management" differed sharply from "mass production," which Taylor did not greatly approve. Scientific management was not, decidedly not, the same thing as "efficiency engineering," which apostles of Taylor regard as a "bastard perversion" of the master's creed. Mr. H. S. Person, Managing Director of the Taylor Society, wrote to the author: "Taylor retired before the period of real mass production; he was never sympathetic with its unregulated development. Taylor's era was the era of the small and medium-sized plant

man and then general technical adviser, meanwhile qual-
ifying as a mechanical engineer at Stevens Institute of
Technology.

It was a driving urge of Taylor's nature to be skep-

Frederick W. Taylor, father of scientific management.

tical, iconoclastic, toward the conventional; to resist and
combat man's inclination to accept what is. In a period
when "I'm from Missouri" and "You've got to show
me," thrown off in a million conversations every day,
were the road-signs of a growing propensity to question

making various products on multiple-purpose machines; not the era of large
plants making homogeneous products on single-purpose machines." Mr. King
Hathaway, long an associate of Taylor and now (1932) a director of the Taylor
Society, wrote to the author: "The term 'scientific management' for the type of
organization and management evolved by Taylor and his associates was adopted
about 1910, previous to which Taylor had for want of a better term called it
'task management.' Popularly it was known as the 'Taylor System,' to which
Taylor objected on the grounds of personalizing, and that 'system' was not
sufficiently comprehensive."

the familiar, Taylor went far beyond, into a stark Voltairean world of agnosticism where nothing, absolutely nothing, was to be accepted on faith, and where force of tradition was to be not respected but indicted. His "whale of a New England conscience" expressed itself in an abhorrence of waste and a compulsion to subject to inquisition every accepted method of industry. Whatever was time-honored was Taylor-suspected.

Such a spirit of crusading agnosticism, had it been all there was to Taylor, might have made of him merely a fault-finder. But Taylor had an additional equipment which, complementing his genius for recognizing and diagnosing the spots of decay or error in a manufacturing plant, made him, on the whole, the greatest surgeon of industry of his time. Taylor had ingenuity, inventiveness, common sense; above all, patience.

Some of Taylor's feats of resourcefulness in solving problems became legends of the engineer's craft, told and retold wherever engineers foregathered. He was given at Midvale a job of reconstructing a chimney that had got out of plumb. He had to work while the chimney was in use, which meant that he and his helpers had to contend with extreme heat and noxious gases. Taylor finished the task, without injury to man or property, and without causing a moment's stoppage of the plant. The stack's similarity to a giant corkscrew drew jeers from every one, caused shivers to run down the spines of orthodox engineers — but the pull it gave to flue gasses was such as no other chimney had ever achieved. Called in as a consultant by the manufacturers of wood-pulp, Taylor revolutionized the industry and reduced the cost of production from twenty dollars a ton to "eight dollars and fifty-eight cents." In the Paris exhibition of 1900 Taylor startled even the visiting Germans, who rightly prided themselves on the progress they had made in the

mechanical arts, with his high-speed lathes which cut
through hard metals with the ease and speed of a wood-
drill in soft white pine. It would be difficult to exag-
gerate the importance to industry of Taylor's work with

From a photograph by Ewing Galloway.

In the Ford plant. What resemble two long stretches of notched floor in this
picture are really cooling racks covered with Ford car body parts.

cutting steels; it was revolutionary. He spent fourteen
years in making thousands of tests and the wealth his
work created would ransom a thousand kings. What he
learned he epitomized in a rule: "The best measure of
the value of a tool lies in the exact cutting speed at which
it is completely ruined at the end of twenty minutes."

It was not in Taylor's nature, when faced by resistance of conservatism, to make concession of diplomacy. He disdained tact, regarded it as a weakness, a

waste of time, and therefore a sin against the code that was his only religion. When he encountered an opinion opposed to his own, he crashed into it, head on like a bull. He browbeat his clients[2] and flaunted his contempt for their opinions. His temperament led him almost to court conflict; his crusading zeal, leaving, as often, little room in his cosmos for humor, led him to carry his attempts at innovation into areas where he could not give them the recommendations of increased profits. As a tennis player, he "improved" the game with a spoon-handled racket which, whatever might be said in derogation of it by the orthodox, was the implement in his hand when he won a national championship. Golf, with its disdain for innovation, its Scotch inertia against the spur of progress, aroused in Taylor an almost frantic evangelism. He experimented with synthetic "greens." In his tool-shop he made, and after assiduous practice gained skill in the use of, a long-shafted driver, a filed mashie, and a fork-handled putter, only to be unfeelingly rebuffed by the golf authorities who outlawed them all for tournament play.

With organized labor, which regarded him with sullen suspicion, Taylor was ever at furious war. He would grow indignant at the charge by labor that his ideas would make men subordinate to the machine and that his system would eventually destroy the livelihood of multitudes of workers; steadfastly he maintained that scientific management was the solution of the problem of producing goods and that it would in the end lead the worker out of bondage, reduce the hours of man's labor, increase the period of his leisure.

In time a new generation of workers grew up, for

2 When he left the employ of the Midvale Steel Co. in 1890 he "retired" in the sense that he never afterwards charged a fee for services to any of the scores of manufacturers who asked him to introduce scientific management in their plants. He had means sufficient to permit him to live comfortably and had no wish to pile up a fortune as he undoubtedly could have done.

whom Taylor's methods involved no change, but were themselves the accepted and familiar. Before Taylor

From a drawing by Thornton Oakley of October, 1912.

An example of industrial efficiency. The building of the Grand Central Station, New York City, where excavating, rock-drilling, erecting steel and stone are all going on at once, while train service remains uninterrupted.

died, in 1915, he had the satisfaction of seeing part of organized labor, in the textile and clothing-making trades, swing wholeheartedly to his point of view and voluntarily adopt scientific management on a basis of sharing the increased profits with capital.

A generalized definition of scientific management by Taylor himself said: "The basic principles include: first, the development of a science for each element of a man's work, to replace the old rule-of-thumb method; second, the selection and training of workmen to follow the science laid down; third, the payment of extraordinarily high wages to workmen who approach the standard performance set up, and of ordinary wages to those who take more than the standard time allowance; and, fourth, the dividing of responsibility between men and management on a basis of scientifically determined function."

As science, as efficiency, this was unassailable. In practice, however, Taylorism, or, rather, the corruption of it by efficiency engineers, meant requiring men, often middle-aged, to change life-time ways, to drop motions that had become so instinctive as to be parts of their nature. A hod-carrier was outraged to the depths of his soul when told that he could save six seconds of time and eliminate one motion out of ten by picking up a brick with thumb and fingers disposed in a manner minutely specified by an engineer. On many a scaffolding occurred combats between orthodoxy and reformation not inferior in dignity and certainly not less white-hot in emotion than Martin Luther before the diet of Worms.

It is conceivable that some of the acolytes and camp followers of scientific management may have become enamored of system for system's sake; that there were occasions when the workman's instinct was right, the engineer's science wrong — the workman's instinct in accord with nature, the engineer's science a perversion of nature. Popular prejudice thought so. A story of the day, invented without doubt to deride the profession, took pleasure in the case of an efficiency engineer who was summoned from his New York office to a distant factory. The engineer, stepping off the train on a winter day, was bundled into a horse-drawn hack by a driver who thoughtfully tucked a buffalo robe about his passenger's knees. During the process, the expert showed uneasiness and finally said, "Now see here, my man, there's a right way and a wrong way to do everything; this is a small matter but it should be done right; this robe should be wrapped with the leather side out, and the fur inside, where it will fit more snugly around the legs and be warmer." The driver, obeying an efficiency of his own which said it is always wise to let the man who pays the bill think he knows best, chuckled. When the engineer's passion for pursuing phenomena to their ultimate causes led him to ask what the hackman was laughing about, the latter replied, "Oh, I was just thinkin' what a joke it was on them buffalos that they didn't know **that.**"[3]

The village hackman was one of the last survivors of individually owned and operated industry — his brother in the cities became about this time the hireling of a corporation, required to conform to a time-clock in the office and a meter on his cab. To the old-time workman who owned his business and operated his own tools, efficiency engineering was the ultimate modern antithesis. The two were at opposite poles of the spiritual world. The war between them went steadily against the individual. By 1914, it was rare to find anywhere any old-time artisan, any shoemaker[4] who walked down the street to the

[3] Proofs of this chapter which the author submitted to an engineer for criticism were returned with this comment pencilled in the margin: "It's a bully good story — but all the same, fur side in *is* the most efficient way to get the most warmth out of a robe."

[4] In the Pennsylvania village in which the writer of this history was a child, there was still, during the 1880's and early 1890's, an old-time shoemaker, who

tanner's, bought a roll of leather, carried it back to his
shop, pausing genially to pass the time of day with such

From a painting by Stanhope Forbes

"The village industry" in contrast to present-day methods as pictured on the
opposite page.

neighbors as he met; sat down on his solitary bench,
throne in the shop that was his personal kingdom; and

took orders for shoes; and the old-time type of tailor, dress-maker, seamstress,
and wagon-maker; and a miller who ground wheat for a percentage of the grist.
All were survivors from a past order of industry; separation of production into
mass manufacture in factories and distribution through retail stores was already
well under way; but these were living relics of an age in which the maker and
the seller of goods were one, and the customer dealt directly with the provider.

addressed himself to the making of a shoe, waxing his
thread and sharpening his awl in a spirit of leisurely an-

The Chevrolet assembly line.

ticipation; taking pleasure in the variety of the task, in-
dulging his mood by turning from sewing the upper to
hammering the pegs in the sole; doing it all in a tempo
that permitted thought and reflection about his own small
affairs and those of the universe; finally getting a glow
of satisfaction from the sense of completeness — "This
have I done, and it is good"; the whole in a spirit that
was kin in its humble way to Raphael painting one of his

Madonnas. A long way that was from the efficiency engineering method, its leisurely conformance to the worker's spirit far distant from the grim concentration upon a routine task that thrust itself upon the factory worker at a fixed and imperative pace determined by the manager and having no relation to whatever might be the tempo of the worker's mood.

To the new vogue, choice by the worker of his own task, and the turning from one to another as his mood suggested, or his tired muscles urged, the determination by the worker of his own pace — to the new all that was wrong. Heresy also was that little excess of motion, the flourish that was the exuberance of spirit in an artisan finding joy in creative work. A worker who would have sung at his task, and made the swing of his tools conform to the rhythm of his song, would have been a startling phenomenon along the Ford assembly-line, and would have been regarded by the efficiency engineer as having no place in industry.[5] A village blacksmith forging a shoe for his neighbor's horse inspired a Longfellow to verse, and other poets and singers have been similarly stimulated by the farmer in the dell and the miller by the stream. The poet has not yet emerged who will

[5] An engineer who read the proofs of this chapter in July, 1932, criticizes: "There is no reason why the worker on an assembly-line should not sing or whistle if he chooses, and provided he does not annoy the men about him. I should imagine the men in Ford's plant joke and banter each other just as people everywhere else do. I think you should say, in justice to large-scale production, that it has many advantages over the older, less specialized method. While the old-time cobbler eked out a straitened livelihood by sticking to his last from dawn to darkness, the modern worker in a progressive, scientifically managed factory needs to labor only seven or eight hours, at a pace carefully planned not to unduly fatigue him, and earns enough to enable him and his family to enjoy comforts and advantages such as the old-time workman did not dream of. It was not in the experience of the worker of an earlier day, as it is a commonplace to-day, to get in eighteen holes of golf between knocking off work and dinner-time, and in the evening take his wife to the movies or go for a ride in his car. Once this depression is over I believe you will see scientific management continue its destined course of making life more worth living for the working man."

write a lyric about workman Number 8602 punching hole 69 with drill B-61 in automobile Number 6,-841,682.

The recommendation of scientific management and mass production was that they would permit the workman to reduce the procuring of food and other necessities to a chore of two or three days, leaving the rest of the week free for art or other use of leisure as his soul might summon him to. It is true that hours of labor per day, and days per week, were materially reduced during a period simultaneous with mass production. Believers in it held that the one was the effect of the other, and that the liberation of labor would go farther. The ideal, life divided between work and leisure, with generous emphasis on the latter, work and satisfaction to the soul kept in separate compartments, held out as the ultimate social goal of scientific management, had not, at the time this history was written, fully arrived.

From "Life," 1913.

Efficiency Crank: Young man, are you aware that you employed fifteen unnecessary motions in delivering that kiss?

5

ART FINDS A PATRON

The Function of Diffusing Goods Creates a New Market for the Talent of Persuasiveness. A Changed Objective for the Quality of Allurement in Words. A Change That Took Place in the Economic Bases of Newspapers and Periodicals. "Grub Street" Disappears. Increased Access to Art by the Average Man. Increased Production of Art and Increased Diffusion of it, but Without Conspicuously High Achievement, or the Emergence of Unusual Intellects. Some Poets of the Day. One Art, Architecture, Which, Because of an Unusual Condition, Made Indisputable Progress, Attaining Much Greater Distinction than Ever Before.

HAND in hand with mass production went mass distribution. The result enriched the average man, enormously. The processes by which diffusion was accomplished wrought deep-reaching changes in American institutions, points of view, ways of life.

"Scientific management" in production became "scientific salesmanship"[1] in distribution. "Overcoming sales resistance" was professional patter for the process, "sign on the dotted line" the objective of it. This, too, became a school and a cult, its practice a highly developed art, its experts and acolytes a lavishly paid profession. Any one who possessed in his personality the gift of persuasiveness found the richest market for his talent

[1] Defined by the Detroit *Free Press* as "selling a dress suit to a man who went into the store to buy a celluloid collar." That quip adequately implies the spirit of "scientific salesmanship," but to describe the art in terms of a single transaction is to under-suggest its scope. "Scientific salesmanship" was a thing of organization, with armies of salesmen drilled as carefully as soldiers, campaigns based on elaborate surveys, built up along lines of sales psychology, synchronized with advertising.

in the business of influencing men to buy goods. Elo-
quence, imagination, power of exhortation, magnetism
of personality, all those endowments which give to the
possessor of them ability to move other men, the talents
which in previous ages would have been exercised primarily in the world of ideas and of the spirit, convert-
ing masses of men to accept new creeds or abandon old

A double-page advertisement in a magazine in 1909.

ones, persuading them to support one political party or
oppose another — these talents were now dedicated to
enticing men to buy more automobiles, more bath-tubs,
more phonographs, more hats, more shoes, more soap.
Talent for exhortation which in former eras taught man
to prepare for the next world now taught him to use
more goods in this.

Salesmanship evolved a technique more refined than
pulpit or platform oratory; advertising became more subtle in method, more concrete in results than any form of

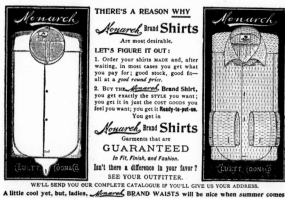

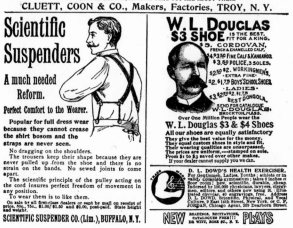

A page of magazine advertisements of the early 90's. A later development of the Cluett advertisement is shown on the opposite page.

proselyting argument. The art which Milton[2] put into selecting words which should make man think about God was excelled by the care with which American writers of advertisements assembled words designed to persuade man to consume more chewing-gum. The man, or ad-

[2] "Few sonnets ever written — and we assume that the sonnet is one of the most finished forms of literary art — have been prepared with the thought and anxiety (we grant the poet divine afflatus!) that go into the creation of an effective and compelling advertisement. . . . We do mean to say, therefore, that the written word in the form of advertising such as made possible swift universal acceptance of the automobile exercised an influence upon society far beyond that of anything but the masterpieces of the greatest masters of thought. There

vertising agency, who wrote an effective selling slogan, such at "It Floats," received far greater compensation than Milton for "Paradise Lost." And just as the poets and prophets of earlier ages considered that the main concern of man was to think about eternity, so did the

The BELMONT & the CHESTER are the new **ARROW COLLARS** with the notch that makes them sit perfectly. 15¢ 2 for 25¢

The CHESTERFIELD is the new **Cluett SHIRT** with the bosom that cannot bulge. $2.00

A double-page magazine advertisement of the Cluett, Peabody Company, 1910.

Miltons of mass production and advertising come to look upon man as existing for the primary purpose of consuming more goods.

II

Advertising which preceding the 1890's had consisted of little more than formal announcements, designed mainly to supply the seeker for goods with the name and address of the merchant who had them to sell, was now

is not a writer of fiction or prose in the world to-day who can command even the passing attention of three million readers; but there are many writers of advertisements whose work must not only compel the attention of millions of readers every week, but must in addition *impel these readers to open their pocketbooks and spend, in the aggregate, billions of dollars!*" From a pamphlet, "The Written Word," in which a large advertising agency, N. W. Ayer & Son of Philadelphia, devoted itself to advertising the art of advertising.

directed toward inspiring in readers the wish to buy. Advertising became mass stimulation to buy. To provide forums in which it could function, newspapers ex-

A page of advertisements from the 1890's.

panded; periodicals increased in size, multiplied in circulation.

In bringing about this change, the principal agency was the automobile.[3] Here was a new commodity, with an

[3] The automobile, with its accessories, was the principal agency in the increase in size and circulation of periodicals. The department store, coming into existence a little earlier, shared with the automobile responsibility for increase in the size of newspapers.

enormous potential market, sold at a price much greater than any other commodity that ever before had had a popular sale. The larger price of the automobile permitted a

An advertisement of 1909.

larger appropriation for advertising than any other advertised goods had ever afforded; an automobile selling for a thousand dollars could readily allocate as much as a hundred dollars for advertising. And here was an immense void, a market wholly unoccupied, which in the quarter century to come would absorb thirty-five million cars. Manufacturers, sensing the opportunity, could realize that the prizes of the new industry would go, other things being equal, mainly to those who through advertising first impressed their brands upon the public

The tingle in the air tells of Fall overcoat-time.

If you are guided by the Kuppenheimer name, you'll get all that an overcoat should be—with style dated far enough ahead to make sure that you will lead.

You'll find our garments at the better clothiers

The House of Kuppenheimer
CHICAGO   NEW YORK   BOSTON

A magazine advertisement in 1909: note the lady's peach-basket hat and the upholstered shoulders of the men.

consciousness. This suddenly expanded demand for advertising space created an immensely broadened opportunity for periodicals and newspapers, and for the authors and artists who supplied reading matter or adornment to them.

A consequence was an arrangement in which, directly

or indirectly and in one degree or another, materialism became the patron, art and ideas the protégés, in a function
of which the objective was the sale of goods. Newspa-

Copyright 1909 by Hart Schaffner & Marx

BETTER be sure your thin summer clothes are of all-wool
fabrics if you want them to hold shape and style.

Our mark is the sign; a small thing to look for, a big
thing to find. Send for Spring Style Book; six cents.

Hart Schaffner & Marx Good Clothes Makers
Chicago   Boston   New York

Another men's clothing ad of 1909. Though the names of the artists are not
given, these advertisements were usually done by capable illustrators
of the day.

pers and periodicals became, as to the principal economic
base of them, agencies for stimulating the consumption of commodities. Newspapers and periodicals which
up to about 1890 had depended for most of their income
on money paid by the reader for the ideas, information,

or entertainment they contained, now received the major
portion of their revenue from advertisers. The advertising, which in newspapers of the 1890's was a rather

From the "Saturday Evening Post." Nate Collier's cartoon.

A joke which pictured the indispensability of advertising to mass distribution
during 1900. The man who made the best mousetrap, but didn't advertise, waits for the world to make a beaten path to his door.

grudgingly tolerated[4] fringe of simple announcements
along the edges of reading matter, or in periodicals was

4 A time when the greatest of metropolitan newspapers could prosper on
revenue received from readers alone, was described by Edward P. Mitchell (of
the New York *Sun*) in "Memoirs of an Editor":
  "During the period [1872–1881] the dividends of *The Sun* ranged almost continually upward from twenty-eight per cent to fifty, with an annual average of
thirty-six per cent. The returns for advertising were almost a negligible item
then in the earnings of the concern; so much so, indeed, that for years Dana
cherished the idea of rejecting advertisements altogether and depending upon income from circulation alone. To newspaper publishers of to-day [1924] this early
dream of his must seem fantastic, but it was nevertheless seriously entertained
and frequently discussed. The vision dissolved only when the . . . sudden development of department-store advertising conspired to shape the Brobdingna-
gian format. But the fact remains that with a comparatively slim advertising
patronage *The Sun* in a dozen years yielded dividends amounting to fourfold
its entire invested capital."

confined to a very few pages in the back, was now expanded and elaborated until it occupied the major portion of the space; while reading matter receded relative-

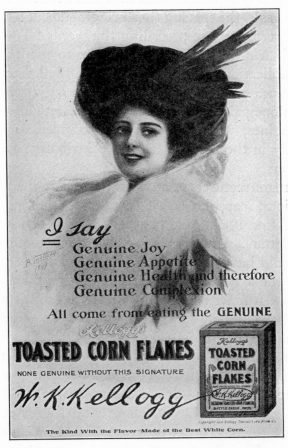

Pictures of pretty girls were in great demand by advertisers throughout this period.

ly to the position, and the economic status, of in part a frame for the advertising, in part an allurement drawing the reader's eyes to it. Many writers of fiction accommodated themselves to the new basis; the writing of "serials," designed primarily for publication in magazines rather than as books, became a recognized technique, in which an observable detail was that the affairs of heroes and heroines came to successive climaxes at points which happily coincided with the end of the installments in periodicals, the spacing thus bringing about a moment of high suspense just preceding the words "To be continued." A novel which omitted thus to adapt itself to serial publication suffered detriment in the literary market, because publication in book form only, where the reader alone paid the bill, was rarely as remunerative as in magazines, where much of the compensation came indirectly in the form of a joint contribution from the advertisers.

The manufacturers of automobiles, ready-made clothing, lotions, soaps, breakfast-foods, and other advertised commodities, became, so to speak, associated patrons of art and letters. A writer who in eighteenth century England would have dedicated his book to a noble lord for bearing the expense of publication — and who thereby put himself under obligation to conform to his patron's political and other views — could, in the America of 1914, have appropriately dedicated his book to a joint association composed of General Motors, Hart, Schaffner & Marx, the American Tobacco Company, and the manufacturers of Listerine, Ivory Soap, and Heinz's Baked Beans. The relation did not entail the servility that went with the old form of patronage, and was in respects felicitous. The new type of patron asked nothing of the author except that he please the reader — attention from the reader's eyes was all that the advertiser desired. The over-suspicious sometimes found in the arrangement an implied limitation on the writer's freedom of expression. A Socialist and life-long protestant against what is, Upton Sinclair, wrote a book, "The Brass Check," in which he pictured literature and art as the "prostitutes" of business. This view surprised and amused or angered both parties to the relation. True, a writer who was a cog in a mechanism for the dif-

Old and new (1899 and 1925) in tooth-paste advertisements.

fusion of goods could not readily say that diffusion of goods was evil; but few authors ever wanted to say it, and little of the public desired it to be said. And even an advocate of Socialism, or an ascetic Ghandi preaching a philosophy of doing without goods, would have encountered no curtailment of his liberty of expression, provided only that he wrote entertainingly.

What business in general sought[5] was merely that the reader should be led to read, and thereby notice, the advertising on the adjoining column or page.

The arrangement was fruitful of advantage in many directions. An author who in a dollar-and-a-half book might have reached twenty thousand readers found in the *Saturday Evening Post* or *Collier's* several millions. A reader who would not have bought one book in a year, received, for an annual subscription to the *Saturday Evening Post*, half a dozen novels and as many as two hundred short stories and a similar number of articles. Periodical literature flourished as print had never flourished before. Those that had the largest circulation included in their contents and carried to millions of readers the best writing of the time.

To author and artist the arrangement was extremely remunerative. Writers and painters prospered almost like stock-brokers. "Grub Street" as an indigent accompaniment of literary life became a quaint antiquarian phrase. A writer of short stories or serials, who in the early 1890's would have received $100 from a magazine as his share of what readers paid for the total contents, received in 1914 ten times that sum as, in the main, his

---

[5] There were exceptions. The author of this history, writing in *Collier's Weekly* in 1913 arguments against the tariff on woollen manufactures, "Schedule K," encountered the disapproving attention of a corporation engaged in the woollen textile industry, which, in a polite letter, pointed out that they could not advertise in a periodical which in its reading columns contained arguments against their interest. *Collier's* published the letter.

Another type of conflict between the interest of advertiser and public was illustrated by an experience of the Boise (Idaho) *Statesman*. The publisher, Calvin Cobb, a man of exceptional public spirit, exceptional force of personality, wrote me, January 26, 1925:

"We had a smallpox epidemic here and I insisted on publishing the fact and demanding action to control it. The local merchants said I was hurting the town and business and made a movement toward organized boycott of *The Statesman* by refusing to advertise in it. I sent them word to go ahead, that I could get along without their business better than they could get along without *Statesman* space and hoped they would try it out. There was no more talk of boycott."

share of what advertisers[6] were happy to pay for having a distinguished and competent author write excellent reading-matter alongside which they could print their announcements. Many artists received exalted compensation direct from manufacturers for painting handsome young Adonises who in the advertisements wore Cluett collars, or B.V.D. underwear; or alluring young ladies whose beauty, poise, and charm, so the advertisements said, arose from divers cosmetics, corsets, dentifrices, and medicaments. Other artists, including many of the best — Frederick Remington, Maxfield Parrish, Jessie Willcox Smith, Charles Dana Gibson — found a generously remunerative market for their work, not available to artists of previous generations, in the magazine covers or frontispieces of the better class of popular periodicals, and in illustrating magazine fiction. Pictorial and literary art, including the best that was produced, experienced a wide diffusion, riding the same waves of distribution with mass diffusion of goods — hitch-hikers, so to speak, upon the progress of the automobile, joy-riders upon the one institution that dominated the period, mass production of goods.

III

Reason for the Extraordinary Development of the Short Story in America

The mutually serviceable arrangement between materialism and art led to an expansion of the latter, certainly an expansion in quantity. In one field of letters there was an elevation of quality.

Diffusion of goods demanded advertising, advertising

---

[6] With the coming of the radio and the development of it as a vehicle for advertising, the subsidizing of writers (as well as singers and actors) went farther. The performer was paid directly, or often through an advertising agency.

called for periodicals as media, periodicals found the
short story to be the form of writing best adapted to their
use, authors found in periodicals such a market for short
stories as had never existed before. The short story, when
confined for its market to book publication, had rarely
been widely distributed or remunerative. Now editors
combed the country for talent that could tell a tale within the length adapted to periodical publication, from
four thousand to twelve thousand words. If in America
any professional author had a good short story in his
brain, there was urgent incentive for him to produce it.
Amateurs who had never written before were stimulated
to creation by the demand for the short story. Such an
infinite variety of topics and situations were treated in
the almost universally circulated periodicals that any
reader having the faintest urge to create was sure to find,
one time or another, a suggestion stimulating him to construct a story out of something in his own experience.
Any fairly good short story from a new author would be
followed by a visit from a scouting editor bent on de-
veloping the possible mine. Every experienced author
had competing editors on his door-step pleading for
more.

The result was a cultivation of American short story
talent such as had not existed before and would hardly
have taken place without the subsidy of materialism.
America in more than a hundred years had developed but
one outstanding writer of short stories, Poe. The early
1900's produced more than a score whose output was distinguished. The most popular at the time, O. Henry,
who developed a new technique, the surprise ending, became the model most widely followed by young writers.
His work was less worthy, however, than that of some
others. One, Irvin Cobb, produced, within a mass of
output, a few stories not inferior to Poe's.

Cover of *Judge's "Advertising Number"* (November 17, 1923), suggesting to some extent the use of the pretty girl in advertising. Among those present: The Misses Heinz, Holeproof, Venida, Mavis, Hinds, Gainsborough, Life Saver, Zip, Mulsified, Mum, Coca Cola, Dorin, and the Palm Olive and Luxite sisters.

The short story was the only form of letters that profited through the subsidy by materialism, in the sense of attaining a higher standard. The other forms profited in the sense that the public was made widely familiar with them. It was recognized by European critics that the short story had a greater development in America

O. Henry.

than in Europe. The short story developed in America more greatly than any other form of literary art. For both these results, a main cause was the subsidy given by materialism.

IV

The flourishing of arts and letters expressed itself, not as conspicuously in the emergence of unusual intellects, nor in outstanding individual achievement, as in the spread of a great quantity of art and letters of average quality, and in increased acquaintance of the masses of people with it. So far as the intellectual energy, the creativeness, of the time expressed itself in distinguished achievements by unusual minds, in really epochal new standards, the advances took place almost wholly within the world of science[7] or, if among the arts at all, among the utilitarian ones. Hardly any book written by an

Joyce Kilmer, a "century-plant" among poets.

American author during the period was rated, twenty years later, a permanent or indispensable[8] addition to literature.

V

No poem produced in America during the period was rated as high as Emerson, Whitman, or Poe; none was as widely quoted as those of Whittier, Longfellow, Low-

---

[7] This judgment is queried by the very discerning editor of *Poetry*, Miss Harriet Monroe. Advances in science, she says, "give immediate proofs of their rank; the rank of new expressions of art is proved more slowly." This is true; and the condition constitutes one of the handicaps of writing history from a short perspective.

[8] Miss Harriet Monroe, having read a proof of this chapter, remarks, with some spirit, that 1932 is too early for so confident a judgment.

ell, and Bryant had been when they were creating. The nearest approach to such popularity was attained by a practically solitary poem of Joyce Kilmer,[9] "Trees," of which the opening and closing couplets are:

> I think that I shall never see
> A poem lovely as a tree. . . .
> Poems are made by fools like me,
> But only God can make a tree.

"Trees" was the most widely quoted poem produced in America during the period. The quality which causes a poem to be widely quoted may or may not be identical with elevation according to critical standards. Much of America's inclination to memorize verse during this period was absorbed by an English poem, Rudyard Kipling's hymn to steadiness in time of stress, "If," which came to America in 1910. As late as 1932 it stood first on lists of favorite poems of college graduating classes:

> If you can keep your head when all about you
> Are losing theirs and blaming it on you . . .[10]

Theodore Roosevelt, in the extraordinary range of his interests, noticed[11] a poem by Edwin Arlington Robinson,

[9] Joyce Kilmer was one of those century-plants of art who produce one outstanding flower and never another of any consequence.

[10] The speed with which "If" attained popularity was facilitated by an accident of quick appreciation on the part of a magazine editor of elevated taste, John S. Philips. Mr. Philips wrote me in 1932: "I found 'If' when looking over the advance copy of Kipling's 'Rewards and Fairies,' shown me by Frank Doubleday at Garden City. We arranged by cable for its use in the October 1910 issue of *The American Magazine* which I was then editing. 'If' was in all probability suggested by the wise, firm conduct of George Washington in the Genêt episode of 1793. The story 'Broad-Toes' in 'Rewards and Fairies' is concerned with that episode and 'If' appears at the end of the tale. Lord Charnwood, in the historical prelude to his 'Lincoln,' refers to 'If' in connection with Washington and the Genêt affair. Most if not all of the interleaved poems in this and other books of Kipling are related to the matter of the stories they accompany."

Another poem of Kipling appeared during the period and was widely quoted, "The Female of the Species." See page 194.

[11] The poem was called to President Roosevelt's attention by his son, Kermit, who brought home with him from Groton School the volume of Robinson's called "Children of the Night." Roosevelt sought out Robinson, found him in a

was moved to write an article about it for *The Outlook* in which he described the lines as having "in them just a little of the light that never was, on sea or land," and by his commendation made much of America, for a little while, familiar with "The House on the Hill"[12]:

> They are all gone away;
>   The House is shut and still.
> There is nothing more to say.
>
> Why is it then we stray
>   Around that sunken sill?
> They are all gone away.
>
> There is ruin and decay
>   In the House on the Hill.
> They are all gone away —
> There is nothing more to say

— in the circle of Roosevelt intimates the lines were quoted with a personal meaning when Roosevelt left the White House in 1909.

1913 and 1914 were years of the first or early appearances of new poets in sufficient numbers to make these years a kind of Renaissance in American verse. Edgar Lee Masters published, beginning in *Reedy's Mirror* (St. Louis, Mo.), May 29, 1914, and later in a volume, a series of autobiographical epitaphs ascribed to persons beneath the tombstone in the cemetery of an Illinois village. Amy Lowell, leading critic of the day, thought the " 'Spoon River Anthology' . . . may very

---

situation in which his affairs were going no better than is the usual lot of an unknown young poet, and offered him a post in the New York Customs House, which Robinson held for four years. Even more than by the job, Robinson's fortunes were suddenly bettered by the effect of a President's published appreciation of his verse. "This wholly unanticipated assistance," wrote Robinson to the author in 1926, "came at a time when things were rather dark. . . . I shall always have a deep and very special feeling of gratitude for a most unusual act of appreciation and kindness on the part of a most unusual man. I don't like to think how my affairs might have gone on as they were going then if their course had not been rather suddenly changed."

[12] Though "The House on the Hill" became, through President Roosevelt's attention, the most widely known of Robinson's poems, it was not his best.

well come to be considered among the great books of American literature; no book, in the memory of the present generation, has had such a general effect upon the reading community; its admirers are not confined to those who like poetry, people who have never cared for a poem before are enthusiastic over 'Spoon River.'" Masters' epitaphs had a grim and acid cynicism, a despairing disillusionment, that was a shock[13] to the spirit of the America of 1914 but was prophetic of the post-war America of about 1924. One epitaph, written about a Civil War soldier, lent itself to the mood of a later generation who wished to express skepticism about the imputation of glory to the Great War, or any war:

KNOWLTE HOHEIMER

I was the first fruits of the battle of Missionary Ridge.
When I felt the bullet enter my heart
I wished I had staid at home and gone to jail
For stealing the hogs of Curl Trenary,
Instead of running away and joining the army.
Rather a thousand times the county jail
Than to lie under this marble figure with wings,
And this granite pedestal
Bearing the words, "Pro Patria."
What do they mean, anyway?

Other poets of the 1914 Renaissance included Robert Frost — the very titles of his poems possessed, to any one who had ever known and loved New England, the power of a magic carpet, able to carry an exile across seas and continents back to the land of "North of Boston," "The Birches," "The Pasture," "Mowing," "Mending Wall," "Stopping by Woods on a Snowy Evening," "The Thawing Wind," "After Apple-picking," "The Woodpile,"

---

[13] Publication of the "Spoon River Anthology" was followed by an outburst of reproach and commendation extending beyond the circles in which poetry is ordinarily a matter of disputatious concern. Mr. Masters, writing to the author of this history in 1932, asked, as if with rue mingled wih pleasure: "Maybe you remember the literary storm; maybe you remember a bigger one; I don't."

"The Mountain," "The Hill Wife," "The Gum Gatherer," "An Old Man's Winter Night."

What Robert Frost did for New England was done for Chicago and the mid-West by Carl Sandburg, Sandburg's rugged force, however, differing from Frost's gentle serenity about as the Chicago stockyards differed from a New England orchard. Sandburg, in his "Chicago," seemed almost to use words as boulders:

Hog-butcher for the world,
Tool-maker, Stacker of Wheat,
Player with Railroads and the Nation's Freight-handler;
Stormy, husky, brawling,
City of the Big Shoulders . . .

Fierce as a dog with tongue lapping for action, cunning as a
    savage pitted against the wilderness,
    Bareheaded,
    Shovelling,
    Wrecking,
    Planning,
    Building, breaking, rebuilding.

Nicholas Vachel Lindsay,[14] Illinois-born, as American as the Mississippi River, tramped the West reciting a drumming, thumping, rolling type of verse, of which the earliest and perhaps the best were "General William Booth Enters Heaven" and "The Congo." His style is illustrated by "Simon Legree," which, he directed, is "to be read in your own variety of negro dialect":

Legree's big house was white and green,
His cotton-fields were the best to be seen.
He had strong horses and opulent cattle,
And bloodhounds bold, with chains that would rattle. . . .
Legree he sported a brass-buttoned coat,
A snake-skin necktie, a blood-red shirt.
Legree he had a beard like a goat,
And a thick hairy neck, and eyes like dirt.

[14] Several critics who have read this chapter in proof are earnest in asking that Vachel Lindsay be given broader credit than the one extract which is all that limitation of space will here permit. Edgar Lee Masters thinks that Lindsay's songs "will feed the classic allusions and national traditions of America."

Bliss Carman was best-known for his joint authorship with Richard Hovey of "Songs from Vagabondia." Amy Lowell was at once competent as poet, inspiring as friend of poets. It was a sign of the state of poetry during this period that Miss Lowell was less commonly identified as

" 'September Morn'
Clothed as she was born,"

was more interesting as nudity than important as art. Exhibited in 1912 it gave rise to much discussion and some attempts at repression.

a poet than as the sister of the president of Harvard University, and through a legend that she smoked big black cigars. A school of verse that flourished during the period was the "Imagist." An eccentric departure vivaciously discussed within the craft, but little known outside, was "free verse," better known, where it was known at all, by the exotic name which marked its alien origin, "vers libre."[15]

[15] Edmund Lester Pearson, having read this passage, writes the author:
"I think, that *vers libre* was really Walt Whitman's kind of poetry, taken to France, written, rather feebly, by French poets, given a French name, and then

VI

A departure in pictorial art, similarly alien, similarly bizarre, similarly ephemeral, was called "Cubism,"

From an abstract painting by Picasso.

Figure.

sometimes described as "insurgency in art," and designated "bedlam in art" by conservative critics who likened it to the cave ornamentation of prehistoric man. Critic Royal Cortissoz said it was the trick of "post-

discovered and brought back to America by Americans! As we send Mississippi white-fish eggs to Russia to come back as caviar, and Louisiana cottonseed oil to Italy or France to be labelled "Huile d'olive." Not perfect comparisons — as Whitman's was the real stuff, not the imitation."

impressionism" carried one step farther. A poet of the day, Harry Kemp, as eccentric in letters as "Cubism" was in art, after visiting an exhibition of the new genre in New York in the spring of 1913, wrote with an air of being torn between not really liking it and wishing to approve anything that was outré:

> I cannot shake their wild control;
> Their colors still go roaring through my soul, . . .
> Strange cubes evolving into half-guessed forms,
> Cyclones of green, and purple rainbow-storms.
> Thus artists on huge Jupiter might paint
> (Or some mad star beyond the earth's constraint) . . .
> You go out with a whirlwind in your head.
> The thing, at least, is not inert and dead;
> There's life and motion there, and rending force,
> Color-Niagaras thundering on their course,
> Power that breaks like a great wave in spray —
> And what it means we'll let To-morrow say!

By 1932, "To-morrow" had arrived — and did not think it worth while to say anything.

VII

The one art that made notable progress was architecture — and architecture is that one of the arts having the largest utilitarian value, most directly integrated into the material world. In this field the one greatest achievement was a building called the Woolworth Tower, erected with profits from the sale of five- and ten-cent articles, and devoted to the housing of lawyers and business offices — a cathedral of trade.[16] Architecture sub-

---

[16] The architect who planned the Woolworth Building, Cass Gilbert, thinks that "cathedral of trade," as well as the other phrase frequently applied to the Woolworth Building, "cathedral of commerce," is particularly inept because, as he writes the author: "It has none of the aspects of a cathedral and was not intended to have. If the Woolworth Building bears a resemblance to any previous structure, or any of its details are derived therefrom, it is to the Town Halls in Flanders, the Netherlands, and France, such, for example, as the Town Hall at Middleburg and the Cloth Hall at Ypres, the Town Hall at

mitted to the limitation put upon it by the spirit of the age, that it must conform to the broad movement of material advance. That limitation, it was thought in the beginning, made beauty impossible; buildings erected to conform to commercial uses, the "International Encyclopedia" had said in 1904, could not have grace: "Hitherto in the history of the world no architecture of any value has been developed out of any such conditions." But American architecture, accepting the limitation, accepted also the advantages with which American engineering endowed it, structural steel, concrete, hollow tile, wire-cable, and the passenger elevator. Out of these, architecture, with characteristic American adaptability, contrived for itself a revolutionary addition to its scope and variety, actually a new dimension, practically unlimited verticality. With this addition to its resources, American architecture, incarnating the spirit of the time, created the most distinctively and characteristically American thing in the world, the skyscraper, having the beauty of line as well as the beauty of massiveness and power.

Architecture's release from the limitation of proportions in line and perspective that had been dictated by the need of keeping buildings close to the ground, within heights attainable by climbing stairs, amounted to almost a new art.

Brussels, the Hôtel de Ville at Rouen, and the house of Jacques Cœur at Bourges. In other words, its architecture is *civic* and *not ecclesiastical.* As a matter of fact, the Woolworth Building has no prototype."

Mr. Gilbert, as a pioneer in whom imagination was combined with fine restraint, had more to do than any other person with overcoming the fixed conviction of architects and critics that buildings devoted to business, especially skyscrapers, could not be made beautiful. He is, therefore, more responsible than any other person for the outstanding development in architecture during this period in all the world.

6

NEW WORDS

Which Coming into the Language Were an Index of the Spirit of the Age. The Speed with Which New Words Came, which was an Index to the Tempo of the Age. Difficulties Encountered by Dictionary-makers in adapting themselves to the Etymological Fecundity of the Time. Evolution of the Word "Sell."

A REFLECTION of the spirit of any age is the new words that come into the language; an index to the era's tempo and energy is the number of the words, and the speed with which they come. An epitome of the history of any period could be achieved by an operation in arithmetic: take a dictionary of, say, 1914; subtract from it a dictionary of 1900; the result, the new words that came into being, would be a summary of what happened.

About the year 1888 a company of scholars undertook to assemble all the words in the English language in a dictionary, an opus of the sort ambitiously designed to be definitive, complete. It was to consist of ten volumes and to consume forty years in the making. But as the venerable scholars toiled, the world raced past them. While they were upon the letter "A," about 1893, a new medical term for a disease came into common use, "appendicitis," too late to get a place in the dictionary. An important new element in chemistry, "argon," suffered similar exclusion through neglecting to be discovered until after the dictionary compilers had closed the door on the A's. While they were at work upon "C" there emerged a new thing called the "cinema" (in America the motion-picture). The lexicographers, too late to include the word among the C's, inserted it, with some exertion of main strength, one assumes, in the K's, "kinema." Four hundred and one other words beginning with "C" were too late.

By the time the dictionary-makers had completed the ten volumes, in April, 1928, they found that while they had worked there had come into the language about one new word for every ten old ones. Instead of resting from their labors they were obliged to set about compiling a supplementary volume. And since in the progress of science there is a cumulative quality which breeds new words with almost the fecundity of guinea pigs, one guesses that by the time the scholars, if they live long enough, have completed their supplementary volume, material for yet another will be clamoring at the doors of their cloister.

II

Classification of the new words yields light upon the era in which they emerged. The "Oxford English Dictionary" compilers, to cover adequately an expansion and refinement of material luxury, found themselves asked to find space in their supplementary volume for forty-three new words of color, to express newly devised shades of silk stockings. When the dictionary-makers began in 1888, stockings had been of two colors, both adequately described by ancient words, black, and white. This new nomenclature for the shades of stockings, the compilers black-balled. The imperative and important words that could not be denied were in another category, science.

In the supplement to the 1929 edition of "Webster's International Dictionary," comprising accretions to the language that came into common use between 1909 and 1927, are about three thousand[1] new words. By classifying a characteristic group of them we can find a clue

[1] This number is misleading. It is the number in the "New Words" supplement of Webster's 1929 edition; but it is only a fraction of the new words, many technical, that came into use during twenty years preceding.

to the changes taking place during the period, a pattern of the very spirit of the age. Of the 299 words beginning with "A," more than two-thirds, or 221, were in science, physics, chemistry, invention, medicine; and seven more were in the allied world of machinery. Just one word of the 229 was in the world of art, an abstruse new term for an attenuated refinement in music, "atonality."

Examination of the 229 words in "A" finds:

Eighty-two arising out of aviation, including airplane, airman, aircraft, airdrome, airport, air-mail, aeroboat, areomechanic, aviator. (Compilers of "Webster's," designed for popular use, were unduly exclusive: aviation, first practised on December 17, 1903, had acquired twenty-three years later, according to a "Nomenclature for Aeronautics," published by the National Advisory Board for Aeronautics in 1926, a vocabulary of more than 2,000 words.)

Twenty-seven for chemistry, including activator, alcosol, aldazine, aldebarnium.

Twenty-two for medicine, including antiserum, aspirin, atophan, ambrine.

Seven for machinery, including autogenous welding, autotruck.

Seven for electricity, including anode rays, aperiodic circuit.

Aside from the 228 for science and invention, there were but 71 in all the other fields of human activity. The complete classification[2] was:

SCIENCE

Aviation	82
Meteorology	13
Electricity	6
Radio	32
Psychology	11
Psychoanalysis	13
Physics	7
Chemistry	27
Engineering	2

[2] A grouping necessarily arbitrary, for some words might as properly be classified under one heading as another.

Medicine...................... 22
Zoology...................... 3
Biology...................... 2
General...................... 1
    Total.................... 221

MISCELLANEOUS

Machines..................... 6
Finance...................... 1
Legislation.................. 1
Geography.................... 1
Military..................... 16
Abbreviations................ 7
Arts (Music)................. 1
Unclassified................. 45   78
    Total.................... 299

These words, and the preponderance among them of science, terms having to do with the material world, airplane and automobile, gasoline and argon, helium and insulin, are an infallible index of the spirit of the time, a true gauge of the history of the period, an accurate reflection of the major preoccupation of men's minds — just as, in another time and a different country, the emergence of such words as iambic and dactyl, comedy and tragedy, ionic and doric, were the reflection of preoccupation with a different area of man's spirit; just as in yet another country and time such words as colonel and lieutenant, vedette and redoubt, brigadier and grenadier, were an index of war as the principal interest of man; just as in other times and places reformation and predestination, crusader and pilgrim, baptism and penance, reflected concern of man's mind with his future life.

III

If we must have a word that will sum up the years this history treats, which shall serve as a title[3] for the period,

3 For a discussion of nomenclature in the writing of history, as applied to eras and epochs, see pages 37 et seq.

at once attention-compelling and reasonably truth-tell-
ing, we may find it here.   But we shall need to construct
it, by synthesis, or by a process of extraction.   Distill
the new words coming into the dictionary, boil them in a
pot like a dish of alphabet soup, and take the essence.
Or take a syllable each from physics, chemistry, and
medicine, another syllable from machinery, a diphthong
from psychology, and from art an iota.   The combination, in about these proportions, would express the spirit
of the years 1900–1914.

IV

The emphasis on material things in the new words
that came into the language has unmistakable meaning.
Equally significant is a new meaning that was acquired
by an old word.

The verb "sell" in "Webster's Dictionary" for 1929
was still defined as to transfer goods for a price.   But in
universal practice, to an extent that the dictionary must
soon record, "sell" and the process it connotes, had enlarged its domain.   To the material world that had been
the word's habitat since Christ said, "Go and sell that thou
hast and give to the poor,"[4] and in a direction different from Christ's admonition, "sell" had invaded the spiritual and intellectual world.   To convert a man to a new
conviction or point of view was to "sell him the idea."
To impress yourself favorably upon another's attention
was to "sell yourself to him."   The missionary who a
generation before would have described his function as
to convert unbelievers, might now have described it, or
certainly it would have been so described in the common
idiom, as to "sell religion to the heathen."   A political
leader who in the time of Abraham Lincoln would "go
to the people" on the question of abolition, or in 1896

4 Matthew 19:21.

would "educate the people" on the gold standard, would at a later date "sell the League of Nations to the country" or the World Court, or the high tariff or the low tariff. And he would have expressed success in the transaction by saying, in terms of conclusion of a deal, that he had "put it over."

If a commercial interest wished professional aid in "putting over" a new idea, it could find paid practitioners of the art, who called themselves "public relations counsel." That euphemism was successor to "publicity agent" — the substitution being achieved as a commercial adaptation of Talleyrand's epigram, "The chief business of statesmen is to find new terms for institutions which, under their old names, have become odious to the public."

The word "publicity" had passed through a transition similar to that of "sell," but in the reverse direction. As late as the time of Theodore Roosevelt, "publicity" meant letting in the light. Usually it was used in a sense of disinfection, of destroying something undesirable by making the people see and understand it — Woodrow Wilson thought that "pitiless publicity" would cure many of the ills of government. Almost at once "publicity" was annexed by the material world as part of its jargon for acquiring advantage in the world of the mind. "Publicity" was now mainly an art for causing the world to take notice of, and think well of, goods; or of policies which the makers of goods wished to make popular. The word was coming to be synonymous with advertising.

A word that suffered even greater demeaning was "propaganda." In the 1890's it meant, generically, any institution or function of propagating a doctrine; specifically it was most familiar as the name for an institution in the Catholic Church, the College of Propaganda, founded at Rome in 1622 for the oversight of foreign missions and the education of missionary priests. During almost three hundred years the word retained that sacred connotation without taint from the secular world. During the Great War it came to be used for indoctrinating enemy troops or civilians behind the enemy line with ideas designed to undermine their morale — in plain English, to disseminate deceit artfully. Then it came to be used, with "reverse English," so to speak, as a word for disseminating a different sort of falsehood among the home peoples, with the design of stiffening their morale, or stirring them to greater exertions, or to more bitter hatred of the enemy. From its military use, the word during the 1920's passed into political use. Propaganda became, to each side of a controversy, a word to describe ideas expressing the other's point of view. Soon the business world annexed it as in part a new synonym for "publicity."

7

THE GENIUS OF THE AGE

A Nation in a Hurry to Become Better, Determined to
Bring about a Better Here and Now. A Time of "Causes."
"Social Justice." "Child Labor." "Woman Suffrage."
"Feminism." "Direct Elections." "Abolition of War."
"Initiative and Referendum." An Earnestness for Reform
Which Led "Mr. Dooley" to Exclaim, "Oh f'r a Moses!"

THINGS were in the saddle. But this must not be understood to mean that the condition was to the disadvantage of the average man. It meant that America was
mainly preoccupied with things; but it meant also that
the average man had greater access to things than ever
before. With profusion of things, went willingness —
more than willingness, eagerness, of those who had
much, to share with those who had less. Also accompanying the profusion of things was an earnest concern
to make the world a better place; with dynamic materialism went dynamic humanitarianism.

As conspicuous as new words like "gasoline" and "airplane" in the material world were some phrases in the
area of philanthropy, either new, or now greatly enlarged in use, "social justice," "child labor,"[1] conservation, arbitration, juvenile courts, workmen's compensation; and some words of politics, connoting greater power

[1] By 1932, "child labor" had become familiar, for the cause had largely tri-
umphed and become a thing accepted. In 1912, child labor in this sense was new,
and abolition of it a crusade. In August, 1912, Senator Albert Beveridge of
Indiana, leader of the movement to prevent employment of young children in
factories, addressed a banquet of Progressives in a Chicago hotel, on the eve
of the national convention in which the Progressive party was born. I sat with
my wife at a table, across from Douglas Robinson and Mrs. Robinson, who was
the sister of Theodore Roosevelt. As Beveridge rang the changes in his theme,
Robinson leaned across the table and in a hoarse whisper loud enough for half
the room to hear, asked: "Child labor, child labor, what does it mean? It
sounds as if we were in a lying-in hospital."

for the average man, such as "direct primary," "initiative and referendum," "recall of judicial decisions."

Whether because of some attribute of humanity inherently associated with the new kind of wealth and the new conception of it, and the new abundance of it;

From a photograph by Ewing Galloway.

School improvements spread throughout the country. The school pictured here was at Beverly Hills, California.

whether because it is in times of well-being that men become kindly and open-handed and only in times of economic depression and spiritual fear that they become wolfish towards each other — for whatever cause the period was characterized by concern with the fortunes of fellowmen, a desire to make the world better, an awakening to the possibility of a finer way of life, a fervor of many souls to bring in a juster, more lovely era, a supersensitive over-eager determination like the conscience of a fifteen-year-old boy — the whole resulting in a budding and flowering of an extraordinary number, and to an exceptional degree, of those impulses and movements, individual and mass, that are grouped within the words, philanthropy, reform. This was the outstanding spiritual characteristic of the period.

We saw it ourselves and were proud of it. "Fifty years from now," said the editor of *Collier's Weekly*,[2] appealing to a presumed-to-be omniscient arbiter, the "future historian will say that the ten years ending about January 1, 1914, was the period of the greatest ethical advance made by this nation in any decade." The editor of *The World's Work*, Walter Hines Page,[3] writing in January, 1912, an epitome of the year just closed, said with as much matter-of-factness as if he had been reciting statistics of the wheat crop, "Our great activities go on well, such as road-building, school improvement, sanitation, helpful concern for the unfortunate, and the growth of our interest in one another." A summary of topics discussed in magazine articles about 1911 included: better tenements; improved conditions in mines; fresh air campagns; education about tuberculosis and other diseases; war on flies and other insect pests; pure food; abolition of white slavery; workmen's compensation; city government; rescue of poor children; juvenile courts; agricultural improvements; police problems.

We were in a hurry about it. We wanted not merely that "promise of a better future" with which in ordinary times politicians could satisfy the people about this world and clergymen about the next one. We wanted a better here and now. Rather more than each of us wanted it for himself, he demanded it for his fellows. We were proud of our intentness upon it, irritable toward any who questioned the inherent value of it or the ultimate success of our efforts, resentful against interruption of it. The complaint of *Collier's Weekly* against President Wilson's policy about Mexico was that "here in the United States we are in the middle of an intelligent at-

[2] January 24, 1914.
[3] Later Ambassador to Great Britain under Woodrow Wilson.

tempt to carry out experiments in idealism" and **Mr.** Wilson's action about Mexico "would postpone indefinitely our own domestic programme."

So breathless were we that a humorist of the day, George Fitch, found it a little hard to keep up (though he was a fine personality and wished not to miss any of it). "Progress," he said, "is so rampant that we wake up each morning with a half century of advancing to do and go to bed exhausted at night having covered the half century, and in the meantime having uncovered enough new and vociferous necessities to leave us a whole century behind."

With it went a spirit of self-blame, a passion for putting on a hair-shirt as a spiritual luxury, a mood of accusing ourselves for having postponed so long the things we were now determined to accomplish in a hurry. "Never," said an English visitor to America, "has there been such an example of a nation sitting in judgment on itself as America of this year 1911." The self-accusation, the passion for a better order, the hurry to bring it about, were satirized by "Mr. Dooley":[4]

Oh, f'r a Moses to lead us out of th' wilderness an' clane th' Augeeyan stables an' steer us between Silly an' What's-it's-name an' hoist th' snow-white banner iv civic purity an' break th' feathers that bind a free people an' seize th' hellum iv state fr'm th' pi-ratical crew an' restore th' heritage iv our fathers an' cleanse th' stain fr'm th' fair name iv our gr-reat city an' cure th' evils iv th' body pollytick an' cry havic an' let loose th' dogs iv war an' captain th' uprisin' iv honest manhood agin th' cohorts iv corruption an' shake off th' collar riveted on our necks by tyrannical bosses. Where is Moses?

Whether all the experiments in reform would be as happy in execution as in intention was, to some, a matter of imperfect certainty. The periodical *Life* thought some of the tendency reflected "an immense propensity nowa-

4 "Dissertations by Mr. Dooley," Peter Finley Dunne.

days to get in between fools and their folly." Be that as it might, the wish, the impulse, the determination was the dominant note of the time to an extent and with a width of diffusion among average men never before equalled.

II

In our determination to bring a better day, we set about our first deliberate alteration of our fundamental plan of political organization, which for more than a hundred years had been regarded as perfected, and had only been amended before as an incident arising out of civil war. With one amendment, adopted May 31, 1913, we changed election of senators by State Legislatures to direct election by the people — and felt sure we had taken a considerable step toward political millennium. With another, made effective February 3, 1913, we provided for a tax on incomes, and for the graduation of it on an ascending scale, so that the rich should pay not only more, but at progressively higher rates, than the well to do; while those of moderate income could be exempted entirely. By yet another amendment, just beginning to be pressed and destined to be adopted in 1920, it was hoped that liquor would be taken out of politics — put out of existence utterly. By yet another, eagerly pressed at this time and adopted in 1921, we proposed to put females upon the same footing as males as respects participation in government.

III

"The circumstances may be easily imagined, in which women may speak, vote, argue causes, legislate, and drive a coach, and all the most naturally in the world, if only it come by degrees."—EMERSON, "Essays."

The movement for woman suffrage had begun as early as the movement to abolish slavery, and in somewhat the

same spirit.   It was no more a mass movement of women
demanding their "rights" than the anti-slavery movement was an uprising of blacks. What happened in both
cases was that certain individuals, such as William Lloyd

A pioneer for woman's suffrage, Susan B. Anthony (1820–1906).

Garrison and John Brown, in the case of slavery, and
Susan B. Anthony, in the case of suffrage, moved
by some mysterious idiosyncrasy of personality, or by
some uniqueness of bitterness-provoking experience in
their own lives, set out to demand rights for masses who
had not theretofore felt they were being deprived of
anything they particularly desired. It was only after
more than three generations that any considerable number of American women came to feel any acute interest
in the steps which self-appointed individuals were taking in their behalf. Women, indeed, were as a rule more
scornful than men about the movement, being content

with their status, including the privileges and the deference which tradition accorded them.

The movement in America was stimulated between 1909 and 1914 by sensational despatches from England,

English suffragists, Mrs. Pankhurst and Miss Christabel Pankhurst, in prison dress, 1912.

describing the extraordinary actions of leaders of the suffrage crusade there, notably a Mrs. Emmeline Pankhurst and her daughter Christabel, who called themselves "militants," and in the spirit of that designation threw stones through shop windows, set fire to churches and country mansions, destroyed letter-boxes, ballot-boxes, and paintings in museums, and, when sent to jail, went on "hunger strikes." In America the "suffragette" movement indulged in no violence, except, in the very early days, a few attempts to vote which were punished by fines, and, in the later period, demonstrations which aimed at catching public attention, such as a parade from New York to Albany by some women whom a Bishop of the Protestant Episcopal Church, William C. Doane,

From "New Cartoons," by Charles Dana Gibson, copyright by Charles Scribner's Sons.

When Women Vote. Mrs. Jones officially notified of her election as sheriff.

considered to be "a band of silly, excited and exaggerated women."

The woman's suffrage movement in America was part of a broader trend, which in the whole of its manifestations was called "feminism," an emancipation of women from ancient taboos of all kinds. Women suffered disadvantage as litigants in courts, as owners of property and heirs to it. A woman author, Mary Roberts Rinehart, when she wrote a play, felt obliged to give herself a masculine pseudonym, "Roberts Rinehart," partly in deference to a doubt in some circles whether it was quite delicate for a gentlewoman to write for the stage, partly to forestall a sentiment that a play written by a woman could not be so good as one composed by a male. Women suffered many such imputations of inferiority. Prominent in feminism was a feeling of rebellion by women — and of sympathy for their point of view by men — against continuance in marriage after the relation had become coercive, merely. The law gave to husbands many rights which made their wives much less than equal, accepted custom gave the husbands yet other privileges. Against all this, feminism arose. The movement, in America, achieved rapid momentum through methods which at no time invited the forceful attention of the police. So far as there was controversy between old ideas and new, it took place in the field of forensic debate, and in exchange of barbed quips. A suffragette lecturer appealed to reason with an argument saying: "I have no vote, but my groom has; I have great respect for that man in the stables, but I am sure that if I were to go to him and say, 'John, will you exercise the franchise?' he would reply, 'Please, mum, which horse is that?'"

The opposition to suffrage, like the advocacy of it, took to a great degree the form of good-natured jibing. "Imagine," said *Puck*, "a long line of skimpy skirts tackling an election-booth — each one having to stop and powder her nose, and fix her hair, and adjust her belt, and look through her handbag, and wonder who the occupant of the next booth is voting for; the elections would have to be held 'the first two weeks in November,' or perhaps longer." Even those more aggressive assertions of feminism which demanded complete participation in all rôles hitherto assigned to men, excited no opposition more determined than could be expressed in humor. "Is Man coming to this?" asked *Judge*, as it pictured the male of the species saying to his wife, "Mary, I am positive there is a woman under the bed." Triumph of the cause and accepted superiority of the female were portrayed in:

> Peter, Peter, pumpkin eater,
> Had a wife and tried to beat her;
> But his wife was a suffragette,
> And Peter's in the hospital yet.[5]

The aim of feminism was equality. In its final phase it seemed to go a little beyond, or for other reasons to shock us. One of the earliest and most loyal devotees of the movement was William Allen White. By 1914, he observed, a little ruefully, and with the deliberate exaggeration of humor, that he had "supposed 'feminism' meant giving a latch-key to mother," but had found it meant "taking the latch-key away from father."

Woman suffrage, many felt confident, would introduce into politics the presumed-to-be superior ethics of women; and into the business of government their housewifely traits and other desirable qualities. A few skeptically doubted whether mere doubling of the electorate would necessarily increase its capacity to function.

IV

Diminution of sale of intoxicating liquors was making progress along lines of statutory enactment. Diminution of consumption of them — a somewhat different concept — was making progress along lines of voluntary temperance in use, or, in many cases, total abstinence. An accurate index was embodied in an observation in which Elbert Hubbard[6] recorded his experiences during the winter 1913–1914: "During the last six months I have attended forty-seven banquets. Sixteen were dry. Eighteen were semi-arid; these have started with a cock-

[5] *Judge,* February 10, 1912.   [6] *The Philistine,* July, 1914.

tail and stopped there. The rest, thirteen, were the old-fashioned kind beginning with cocktails, running into wine, and often there were beer and whiskey." This percentage of liquidity of public banquets was probably higher than that of individuals, because in most cases banquets could get liquor without cost — it was thrust

Elbert Hubbard.

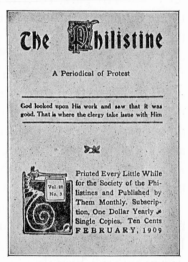

The cover of Elbert Hubbard's little publication *The Philistine*.

upon them for advertising purposes by "wine-agents," who asked only that the names of the brands be printed on the menu. That sixteen out of forty-seven banquets in the winter of 1913–14 should be without liquor was a marked access of temperance. Mr. Hubbard, and every other American of his age, could "well remember a time when a banquet without booze was considered a barren ideality, worse than Hamlet with the melancholy Dane omitted."

Gradual progress in self-imposed moderation or voluntary abstinence was too slow for the breathless reform that was in the air. That spirit included a disposition to do good to one's fellow-man without always consulting the latter about what he regarded as his best good, a trait reflected in a quip which interpreted "W. C. T. U." (Women's Christian Temperance Union) as "We see to you."

This aggressive benevolence accounted in part, though only in small part, for the organized effort to settle the liquor problem by complete, nation-wide prohibition of its manufacture or sale. Much more, however, that movement, and the Anti-Saloon League that crusaded for it, arose as reaction against the political power exercised, arrogantly and ruthlessly, by the organized liquor interests. They exercised their power not only to end or neutralize temperance movements, not only to resist and defy attempts at regulation; they went into politics in a broad way, setting up in states and cities political machines which dominated public business.

That extermination of the commercialized liquor business would result in depriving the individual of the right legally to buy liquor and drink it was a condition which did not weigh heavily. The conviction among the majority who at that time came to accept the idea of total prohibition was that even if the individual must sacrifice his right legally to drink, nevertheless the commercial liquor business must be extirpated. The commercial exploitation of liquor was too flagrant an agency against good, too stubborn a combatant against betterment, to escape the spirit of reform that was in the air.

v

Energetically and confidently, and with the accompaniment of considerable melodrama, we attacked some aspects of evil associated with "the most ancient profession in the world." Some amelioration was achieved —

how much by statute and how much by other influences would be difficult to apportion. The current excitement expressed itself in an inflammatory phrase "white slavery." The thing that "white slavery" originally and literally meant had an actual though extremely limited existence, a commercialized business, very loosely organized, of procuring young women chiefly in Europe and shipping them to houses of prostitution in seaport cities of North and South America, mainly the latter.[7]

The phrase, when it appeared in newspaper headlines, had great potency to excite crusading minds, and also minds with an appetite for pornography. Congress appointed a committee, and issued a document "The White Slavery Traffic." The Wisconsin legislature created a commission "to investigate the White Slave Traffic and Kindred Subjects." The Massachusetts legislature, exact in thought and characteristically cautious, added a word implying questioning at the end of the title of the commission it set up to investigate the "white slave traffic *so-called*," the duty of which, so the Massachusetts legislators somewhat skeptically phrased it, was "to determine so far as possible by what means and to what extent women and girls are induced or compelled by others to lead an immoral life or are brought into this commonwealth for that purpose." Investigations by grand juries and other official or altruistic organizations sprang up everywhere. A former head of the New York police, General Theodore A. Bingham, wrote a book, "The Girl That Disappears." Magazine articles were numerous. Minneapolis set up a Vice Commission; Syracuse, New York, a "Moral Survey Committee," and Chicago a commission whose report, "The Social Evil,"

---

[7] The phrase arose in France. A conference on the subject held in Paris had called the traffic "Traite des Blanches," largely because a conference held a century before, to deal with African slavery, had been called "Traite des Noires."

was exceptionally thorough and exceptionally useful.

Agitation about the evil led to exploitation, by some parts of the stage, press, and films, of the sensational possibilities associated with the idea, an exploitation as commercial in motive as the traffic itself. There were "white slave" plays, "white slave" motion pictures. This in turn led to a popular hysteria which believed that "white slavers" procured victims by carrying a "poisoned needle" with which they stupefied young women beside whom they, in the artful pursuit of their business, seated themselves in street-cars. "How far," asked the New York *World*, "is this ridiculous delusion to go? If the popular imagination is to become heated to a point where it discerns an attempt at abduction in every dizzy feeling of momentary illness suffered by a young woman in a public place, it will be unsafe for a man to offer the slightest civility to a person of the opposite sex whom he does not happen to know." So prevalent became the vague but sensational accounts of mysterious disappearances, that it became prudent for the press, some of which had incited the hysteria, to quiet it by procuring from physicians authoritative testimony to the practical impossibility of drugging an unwilling person by injection from a hypodermic needle in a crowded street-car.

To a more elevated level of readers and for a more sincere motive, a novelist of high quality, Miss Elizabeth Robins, wrote "My Little Sister,"[8] fine as a novel and almost great as a horror story, a tale of two young English girls who travel by train to London, are met by a supposed relative, and are lured into a house of prostitu-

---

[8] Of "My Little Sister," a critic wrote in *Life*, April 10, 1913:

"A generation ago no one but a few particularly daring parents would have read such a book if it had existed, and they would either have burned it afterwards or have hidden it behind Fox's 'Book of Martyrs' on the top shelf of the book case; whereas, to-day the chances are that most of the parents who read it will do so because (with some preliminary cautionings) it has been recommended to them by their daughters."

tion, whence one of the girls escapes and tells the story, the other being lost forever in the underworld. The book went rapidly through four editions, was made into a play, became the talk of the day, and amounted to a kind of "Uncle Tom's Cabin" of white slavery. To assertions that Miss Robins was hysterical and had exaggerated, she replied that between fifty and sixty such cases had been known to the London police within a year.

The curative statute passed[9] by Congress, called the "White slave traffic act," included in its prohibitions an embracing phrase "or for any other immoral purpose"; with the result that enforcement descended not only upon the professional procurers and shippers of white slaves in the true sense, but also upon many philanderers who incautiously paid the railroad or taxicab fare of a lady across a state line, and thereby made themselves liable to prosecution later by a woman scorned, or by one who had planned blackmail from the beginning.

Other legislation by Congress, promoted by Senator William S. Kenyon of Iowa in 1913, successfully wiped out a "red light" district in Washington, on a site which had been the camp of General Hooker's division in the Civil War, and which under the colloquial term "the division," had been a place of disorderly houses during the nearly fifty years since Hooker's soldiers had left. In states and cities, segregated districts were broken up. There was, beginning about 1910, a diminution, almost a disappearance, of the form of vice which, once common in every city under the name "houses of prostitution" had included a kind of semi-bondage on the part of inmates. It would not be safe to say that the quantity of unsanctified or non-legalized relations between unmarried persons became less; but those odious aspects of it which included commercialization by entrepreneurs, and

---

[9] June 25, 1910. It was called the Mann Act, after its author and advocate, Congressman James R. Mann of Chicago.

a degree of forced detention of prostitutes in houses, disappeared in many cities. The reasons were not wholly confined to statutes enacted by legislatures, or raids by police, or crusades by vice societies. They included a rise in the economic status of women, an extension of the occupations opened to them, an elevation of their pay.

VI

Roosevelt while in the White House preached that peace could be attained and preserved only through carrying "a big stick"; after he left office, many of us thought that peace could be achieved by processes which would permit us to split the big stick into kindling for the hearth fire, or cut it into gavels for purposes no more belligerent than registering decisions at meetings in Andrew Carnegie's Peace Temple.

"The war" during the early years of Woodrow Wilson's presidency meant a civil war current in Mexico. A few Americans, but very few, were trying to make it a war *with* Mexico, having in mind material advantages and national grandiosity presumed to inhere in territorial expansion. "I think," said Wingo of Arkansas in Congress, "those hearing me will live to see the Mexican border pushed to the Panama Canal." Upon which a versifier in the Chicago *Tribune*, Bert Leston Taylor, expressed at once the larger and more elevated section of American opinion:

> Wingo
> Jingo

The policy of President Wilson about our neighbor's internal strife was described by him in a phrase that became famous, "watchful waiting" — waiting, that is, not for selfish opportunity for us, but for the triumph of that one of the Mexican factions which Mr. Wilson deemed most virtuous. Fear lest even this pacific parti-

sanship might involve us in some kind of military benevolence led, on the part of some of the press, to watch-
fulness over President Wilson. What the President desired for Mexico, he had said, was "a settlement of the
agrarian land question, such as that followed by New
Zealand;" to which *Collier's Weekly* observed, "Isn't
there some irony in this? Can any one imagine Mr. Wilson, or any other American politician, proposing the single tax as a plank in a political platform for domestic
use? To enforce in Mexico with the Army and Navy a
system that the administration would not dream of proposing at home for legislative debate would add a good
deal to the gaiety of nations." Wilson's difficult problem,
to practice as much firmness toward Mexico as was necessary to guard our rights, yet to avoid going to war
against a weak and unhappy and comparatively helpless
neighbor, brought upon him criticism at once from those
who thought he went too far and others who felt he did
not go far enough. The criticism expressed itself in a
witty analogy to a dance popular at the time, which said
our policy about Mexico was "the Wilson tango: one step
forward, two steps backward, side-step, hesitate."

That we should refrain from making war on Mexico,
or even intervening between the factions, was the over-
whelming American determination, a self-denial imposed on ourselves as our small contribution to an ideal
which said that all war is wrong, and a confidence which
said that no more war would be. That we would never
have a war ourselves, we were quite sure; with a kind of
aggressive humanitarianism, characteristic of our attitude toward all proposals of benevolence, we were trying, by our initiation of arbitration treaties, and our participation in international peace movements, to confer
peace on others. *The World's Work*[10] published an In-

[10] December, 1911.

ternational Peace Number — the editor, Walter H. Page, lived to take an important part in the Great War, as American Ambassador to Great Britain during the years from 1913 to 1918. William H. Taft, then President, was sure the cause of "permanent international peace is growing; this sentiment, comparatively new in the world, has made enormous strides during the past few years." Woodrow Wilson, about to be President, felt that "many powerful influences are at work which make for peace" but prudently deemed it "important that we should not be impatient, that we should not be too easily disappointed." William Jennings Bryan, newly installed as Secretary of State in the Wilson Cabinet, ambitiously laid before thirty-six nations a proposal for an agreement that no nation should begin hostilities until after investigation of the cause of dispute, that the investigation should be made by a permanent commission set up by the nations entering into the proposed agreement, and that the commission should have power to undertake investigation of its own motion, without waiting for a request from either party to a controversy.

A sale just made by our government of two second-hand battleships, the *Idaho* and *Mississippi*, to Greece, was widely disapproved, on the ground that the ships might be used for war. The money received by us, we felt, was over-balanced by the ethical objection to our making a potential contribution to a possible future conflict. Opposition to war, certainty that war would never be, was a characteristic of the time. The periodical *Life* thought that a "naval holiday," then contemplated, should be called by a term denoting greater permanence, "naval holiyear"; and printed a symposium about "Universal Peace Among the Leading Powers of the World,"[11] in which David Starr Jordan said that "great

[11] October, 1912.

international wars are already practically at an end"; and Norman Angell that "cessation of military conflict between powers like France and Germany, or Germany and England, or Russia and Germany . . . has come already. The nation which we have all been taught to regard as the most military in the world, Germany, has not gone to war for over forty years, and it has been visible to all who have eyes to see during the last six months that far from these great nations being ready to fly at one another's throats, nothing will induce them to take the immense risks of using their preposterous military instruments if they can possibly avoid it."

The period was, literally, "a time of peace, wherein we trusted"; a time, said Elmer Davis, looking at it retrospectively twenty years later, "of incredible innocence and security." We had used up the word "Armageddon" to describe a war of words made in 1912 by the Progressive Party in behalf of social ideals. We had come to think of war as a primitive rudeness like a backwoods feud, or an outmoded standard of honor, like duelling, as something outlandish, unlikely to occur again, except in small and unstable countries such as Latin America and the Balkans. This confidence, on June 28, 1914!

VII

What might have been the next stage of the America that was on June 28, 1914; what direction might have been taken by the evolution of that combination of materialism, diffusion of the fruits of materialism, and crusading altruism — all that became, by the shot at Sarajevo, one of the "ifs" of history. It is fair to surmise that this interruption of the course upon which America was intent constitutes the greatest of all indictments against war.

8

CARNEGIE, TYPE OF HIS TIME

A SYMBOL of the time, of a Peter Pan quality it had, of its sentimental faith in progress, of its odd union of furious energy in pursuit of materialism with aggressive evangelism to bring about a better world, of fervent getting accompanied by fervent giving[1] was Andrew Carnegie. Carnegie, in his ambition to be rich coupled with his impulse toward benevolence, his earnestness of reform, and his reverence toward education, was the average American of the time, apotheosized by success. Carnegie it was, rather than Roosevelt, who typified the period, for Roosevelt did not function in the world of materialism and therefore could hardly be fully representative of an age in which materialism played so large a part.

Carnegie was an ironmaster, the greatest of his era or of any era — for three decades preceding 1900 the word "Carnegie" was practically synonymous with "steel." He amassed the largest[1a] fortune ever made by one man, amassed[2] it largely by pursuing more ruthlessly than any other the cut-throat business practices of the time. In

---

[1] Carnegie's getting was pretty ruthless. For an account of it, his business career, the crushing competition he practised, his hard bargaining, see "Our Times," Vol. II, Ch. 18.

[1a] Up to that time. The fortune of John D. Rockefeller subsequently became larger.

[2] For an account of Carnegie's rise and of the business practices of his time, see "Our Times," Vol. II, Ch. 18.

1889, he announced[3] and carried out a personal policy of magnificent giving:

"This, then, is held to be the duty of the man of

From a photograph by Alman and Company.   *From a photograph by Pach Brothers.*

Carnegie at the time he was engaged   When he was engaged in "fervent
in "fervent getting."   giving."

wealth: 'To set an example of modest, unostentatious living, shunning display or extravagance; to provide moderately for the legitimate wants of those dependent

[3] In a magazine article in the *North American Review* for June, 1889. Gladstone called it to the attention of his friend, W. T. Stead, who reprinted it in the *Pall Mall Gazette* under the title "Gospel of Wealth." In 1900, Carnegie republished it, with other essays, in a book also called "Gospel of Wealth."

upon him; and after doing so, to consider all surplus rev-
enues that come to him simply as trust funds, which he
is called upon to administer . . . in the manner which,
in his judgment, is best calculated to provide the most
beneficial results for the community — the man of
wealth thus becoming the mere trustee and agent for his
poorer brethren."

That sounds a little pompous, like unction taken on for
print and meant to evoke approval. Actually it was the
public avowal of a private conviction that had germinated in Carnegie as a young man. Twenty-one years
earlier, in December, 1868, he had scribbled a memoran-
dum — it was found among his papers following his
death — describing the sort of life he wanted and soon
expected to live:

"Thirty-three and . . . $50,000 per annum! Be-
yond that never earn — make no effort to increase fortune, but spend the surplus each year for benevolent purposes. Cast aside business forever, except for others.
Man must have an idol — the amassing of wealth is one
of the worst species of idolatry, no idol more debasing.
To continue much longer overwhelmed by business cares
and with most of my thoughts wholly upon the way to
make more money in the shortest time, must degrade me
beyond hope of permanent recovery."

That was in 1868. For thirty-three years the "debasing idol" continued to hold Carnegie to its service.
Bound to the machine — like many a one among the
humblest of his employees who drearily drew his pud-
dling-tool back and forth through molten metal the
while he thought of whatever little Cathay was his private dream — Carnegie accepted the dictation of circumstance, the tyranny of to-day's duty over the vision
of to-morrow's pleasure. By 1901, he was the richest
person in the world, and an old man, sixty-five. Taking

the $250,000,000 in securities that J. Pierpont Morgan paid him for his steel properties, he sailed for Europe, feeling that the "solemn change" had come. For several years he could not force himself to visit the old plant — "This would recall so many who had gone before; scarcely one of the old men would remain to call me 'Andy.' "

To the employees of the Carnegie Steel Company he

The Homestead Steel Works, one of the Carnegie plants.

made a gift of $4,000,000, and beamed under "their sincere thanks and earnest wish and prayer that his life would be long spared." To hundreds of former comrades, now indigent, including men who had served under him when he was a railroad superintendent forty years before, he gave pensions, graduated in size to needs which Carnegie himself passed upon, the whole amounting to a yearly outlay of $250,000. "I was only a boy when I first went among the trainmen," he wrote, "and got to know them by name; they were very kind to me. . . . I had sweet satisfaction from this source."

With that intimate claim upon him satisfied, Carnegie

turned to what was, up to that time, the greatest[4] career of systematic giving in all history. In a letter to universities and technical schools in the United States and Canada in 1905, he announced creation of the Carnegie Foundation for the Advancement of Teaching, with an endowment of $10,000,000 (later increased to $29,250,000). "The least rewarded of all the professions," he declared, "is that of the teacher in our higher educational institutions. The consequences are grievous. . . . Able men hesitate to adopt teaching as a career, and many old professors whose places should be occupied by younger men cannot be retired."[5] From beneficiaries of this thoughtfulness, mainly retired teachers, Carnegie received "most affecting letters — these I can never destroy; for if I ever have a fit of melancholy I know the cure lies in re-reading them."

Carnegie gave money to Lehigh University for a building to be called "Taylor Hall" in honor of one of his old employees, Charlie Taylor; when Taylor protested against the distinction to his modest name, Carnegie replied: "No Taylor, no Hall." He gave to Dickinson College a building to be called "Conway Hall," after his old friend, Moncure D. Conway; established at

[4] John D. Rockefeller's philanthropies reached a greater aggregate; Carnegie gave a larger proportion of his fortune, was prior in beginning, and was the pioneer in laying down the "gospel of wealth."

[5] To the members of the teaching staffs of those institutions which came up to the Foundation's standards, retiring allowances were made, at first as a matter of right and under fixed rules as to age and length of service. Later a change was made whereby younger men were required to pay nominal insurance premiums.

Among the scholars and teachers who have received retiring allowances have been: Professors William James, Palmer, Peabody, and Toy, of Harvard; Beers, Sumner, Ladd, and Woolsey, of Yale; Corson and De Garmo, of Cornell; Burgess and Chandler, of Columbia; Stoddard, of New York University; and Edgar Gardner Murphy, Secretary of the Southern Education Board; Presidents Eliot, of Harvard; Patton, of Princeton; Remsen, of Johns Hopkins; Seelye, of Smith; Taylor, of Vassar; Gordon, of Queen's University; Northrup, of Minnesota; Jesse of Missouri; Jordan, of Leland Stanford; William Pilot, President of the Council of Education of Newfoundland; and William T. Harris, United States Commissioner of Education.

Kenyon College (Ohio) the "Stanton Chair of Economics," in honor of Edwin M. Stanton, "who greeted me
kindly as a boy in Pittsburgh when I delivered telegrams to him"; gave the "John Hay Library" to Brown
University, and the "Mrs. Grover Cleveland Library"

An early picture of Andrew Carnegie. From a carte de visite by
J. E. McClees, Philadelphia.

to Wells College; gave two Elihu Root funds to Hamilton College and the "Mark Hanna Chair" to Western
Reserve University.

He gave $10,540,000 ($5,000,000 in the United
States) to found the "Carnegie Hero Funds" to reward
valor wherever found and support the dependents of heroes "who perished in an effort to serve or save their fellows." For the "Hero Fund" in England and Germany,
Carnegie received a letter signed "Edward R and I";
"As a mark of recognition I hope you will accept the

portrait of myself which I am sending you"; from the German Kaiser — "How pleased His Majesty is with the German Hero Fund!" For various benefactions he was given many honors: Knight Commander of the Legion of Honor by the French Government; the Order of the Grand Cross of Orange-Nassau from Holland,

Carnegie coaching with friends in Britain.

the Grand Cross Order of Danebrog from Denmark, a gold medal from twenty-one American republics.[6] Carnegie commented: "Such honors humble, they do not exalt, so let them come. They serve also to remind me that I must strive harder than ever and watch every act and word more closely that I may reach just a little nearer the standard the givers — deluded souls — mistakenly assume that I have already attained."

[6] In recognition of Carnegie's gift of a building, one of the most beautiful in Washington, to the Pan American Union. Carnegie's and the Union's purpose was to foster harmonious relations between the republics of Latin America and the United States.

He was elected twice Lord Rector of St. Andrews; was made a member of learned societies, institutes, and

Two of Andrew Carnegie's residences. *Above:* Skibo Castle, Scotland. *Below:* Fifth Avenue and 92d Street, New York.

clubs to the number of over 100; was given the "freedom of the city" by towns and cities in such numbers that he wrote, naïvely: "Once started upon a freedom-getting career, there seemed no end to these honors. With headquarters in London, I received six Freedoms in six consecutive days, and two the week following, going out by morning train and returning in the evening. . . . Nothing could excel the reception accorded me in Cork, Waterford, and Limerick." In all, Carnegie received fifty-four "Freedoms" of cities in Great Britain and Ireland — a record, Gladstone coming second with seventeen.

He started a tradition of "principals' week," during which each year the heads of the four Scottish universities and their wives or daughters visited him and Mrs. Carnegie. He gave annually a dinner to writers and editors, and another to his former partners; was called "Saint Andrew" by Mark Twain; caused Richard Watson Gilder to remark that among all his acquaintances Carnegie could recite the greatest number of poetical quotations.

Part of his leisure Carnegie used to write an autobiography in which he laid no more emphasis, indeed rather less, on his business career than on his contacts with men of science and of letters or otherwise distinguished. He recited how Mrs. Gladstone, one morning at Hawarden, had said to him: "William tells me he has such extraordinary conversations with you" — one wonders if "extraordinary" may have had one meaning to the naïve Carnegie and another to the sophisticated Mrs. Gladstone. Elsewhere Carnegie described Gladstone, at the end of some remarks by Carnegie about the philosophy of civilization, exclaiming: "I like that; I like that." He wrote down that he was present when Herbert Spencer "peevishly pushed away Cheshire cheese when presented by the steward, exclaiming: 'Cheddar, Cheddar, not Cheshire; I said Cheddar.'" One whole chapter Carnegie devoted to "Meeting the German Emperor," who said to him, "I have read your books." He recited with pride his contacts with Presidents McKinley, Harrison, Roosevelt; Joel Chandler Harris ("Uncle Remus"), Joseph Jefferson, Richard Watson Gilder, Earl Grey, Matthew Arnold, Lord Morley.

II

In this use of an old man's money and leisure, there is confession of the long-repressed dreams of one whose inner soul had preferred, or thought it preferred, literature and public life, rather than money; a case of desires postponed as ordinary as that of the humblest bookkeeper who has had to stick to his desk while he dreamed of Kashmir and Xanadu. The comment during Carnegie's lifetime that called him vain was a little undiscriminating and more than a little cruel. The emperors under whose patronage Carnegie beamed, the statesmen whose hands he shook, the literary men he brought to dinner, were Carnegie's private whim, and the whim died with him. What was immortal, the public importance of him, lay in the career he had as the world's most magnificent giver.[7]

[7] A friend who had the opportunity of observing at close hand the unfolding of Carnegie's programme of giving writes me:

"The ways in which Carnegie spent his money indicate the long thought out nature of his plan. In everything he did, he was intensely personal; there is no doubt that his ego was highly developed. Practically all his gifts are a reflection of his own personality — of the needs and ambitions he had felt as boy and man. The evils he set out to cure were mainly the things he had felt. The whole explanation of Carnegie as well as his benefactions, can be found in his boyhood in Dunfermline. Dunfermline, during Carnegie's earliest years, was a headquarters of the peace movement, and public meetings denouncing war were continually taking place. Carnegie came of a reading family; the difficulty of obtaining reading matter was always before his eyes. Carnegie's distribution of pipe-organs is also explained by his love for music — a fondness which was evinced in other ways. This love of music he acquired early, in the little Scottish town where he was born."

III

Carnegie had begun his giving while still in business. In 1881, forty-five and not yet greatly rich, he had given a library to Allegheny City, partly in the spirit of a memorial to his father and the other weavers of Dunfermline who had maintained the tiny little free library from which he had got his first sip of books:

My own personal experience may have led me to value a free library beyond all other forms of beneficence. When I was a working boy in Pittsburgh, Colonel Anderson of Allegheny — a name that I can never speak without feelings of devotional gratitude — opened his little library of four hundred books to boys. Every Saturday afternoon he was in attendance at his house to exchange books. No one but him who has felt it can ever know the intense longing with which the arrival of Saturday was awaited, that a new book might be had. It was when reveling in the treasures which he opened to us that I resolved, if ever wealth came to me, that it should be used to establish free libraries, that other poor boys might receive opportunities similar to those for which we were indebted to that noble man.

Five years after his gift to Allegheny City, Carnegie presented to Pittsburgh the first sums of a total that aggregated $28,000,000, for school buildings, reference and circulating libraries, art galleries, and museums and assembly rooms for learned societies, known collectively as the "Carnegie Institute of Pittsburgh." Part of it, the "Carnegie Institute of Technology," is a co-educational college designed to give opportunities for self-betterment to youths situated as Carnegie had been, the sons and daughters of working people.

Following the giving of his first library, Carnegie was flooded with requests from all parts of the world. He granted them, to communities in English-speaking countries, subject to conditions, and in accord with a technique developed through experience. Carnegie would give the building and fixtures, but the community must provide the site and pay the cost of operation. In the beginning, local architects in small cities, with too little experience and too much ambition, reveled in ponderous or ornate exteriors, with an uneconomical allotment of interior space. This Carnegie corrected by having his own designer prepare standardized specifications. By 1926, funds had been supplied by Carnegie for 2,811 library buildings, of which 1,946 were located within the United States, costing thirty-eight millions of dollars.[8]

To foster good music Carnegie presented 7,689 organs to churches, 4,092 in the United States. "A rigid system was developed," he wrote. "A printed schedule requiring answers to many questions has to be filed be-

[8] The record of libraries completed (up to 1926), the sums expended on them, and their location according to States, is:

State	No. of Libraries	Amount	State	No. of Libraries	Amount
Alabama	14	$195,800.00	Nebraska	61	$634,288.00
Arizona	3	54,000.00	Nevada	1	15,000.00
Arkansas	4	138,600.00	New Hampshire	9	139,000.00
California	128	2,415,397.79			
Colorado	20	649,943.00	New Jersey	32	1,015,934.00
Connecticut	6	82,640.00	New Mexico	3	32,000.00
District of Columbia	2	415,000.00	New York	99	6,074,614.36
			North Carolina	6	102,945.00
Florida	9	188,000.00	North Dakota	7	107,700.00
Georgia	22	471,756.00	Ohio	99	2,866,464.00
Hawaii	1	100,000.00	Oklahoma	24	409,500.00
Idaho	10	138,000.00	Oregon	27	428,000.00
Illinois	106	1,662,000.00	Pennsylvania	49	4,299,512.84
Indiana	139	2,200,442.38	Porto Rico	1	100,000.00
Iowa	97	1,461,706,00	South Carolina	13	204,700.00
Kansas	56	846,496.00			
Kentucky	23	795,300.00	South Dakota	24	246,500.00
Louisiana	9	380,000.00	Tennessee	12	310,500.00
Maine	18	235,450.00	Texas	32	649,500.00
Maryland	8	202,000.00	Utah	19	213,470.00
Massachusetts	38	1,050,500.00	Vermont	4	80,000.00
Michigan	55	1,549,700.00	Virginia	3	88,000.00
Minnesota	64	950,900.00	Washington	41	998,500.00
Mississippi	11	145,500.00	West Virginia	3	81,500.00
Missouri	29	1,401,643.84	Wisconsin	62	1,027,761.50
Montana	13	166,700.00	Wyoming	14	234,000.00

1,539 $38,256,864.71

fore action is taken. The department is now perfectly systematized and works admirably because we graduate the gift according to the size of the church." A later de-

The Carnegie Library, Washington, D. C. There were in all 1,539 Carnegie libraries in the United States in 1926.

velopment was to "ask each congregation to pay one-tenth the cost of the new organ."

With $22,000,000 in five per cent bonds of the United States Steel Corporation, Carnegie founded, on January 29, 1902, the "Carnegie Institution of Washington," "to secure if possible for the United States leadership in discovery and utilization of new forces for the benefit of man." The Carnegie Institution conducts research in botany, experimental evolution, geophysics, marine biology, meridian astronomy, history, solar observation, nutrition, and terrestrial magnetism. Its contributions to advance in scientific knowledge, if listed in detail, would include a plurality of the fields ranging alphabetically from archæology and astronomy, through law, linguistics, and literature up to thermodynamics

Andrew Carnegie in his later years, in his library in Scotland.

and zoology. Researches of one kind or another have been carried on in nearly every country. Two by no means the most important, but familiar because spectacular, are the non-magnetic yacht of wood and bronze, the *Carnegie*, which for an aggregate of distances more than eight times the circumference of the earth, voyaged up and down the seven seas, correcting the errors of earlier ocean surveys, and making new advances in terrestrial magnetism; and the Mount Wilson Solar Laboratory in California, for the study of solar phenomena and the measurement of star distances and dimensions, equipped with a 60-inch refracting telescope — through it more than 200 new worlds have been brought into the ken of man, some so distant as to require years for light from them to reach us.

Largest of Carnegie's agencies for good is the "Carnegie Corporation of New York," created in 1911 with an endowment of $125,000,000, "for the purpose of receiving and maintaining a fund or funds and applying the income thereof to promote the advancement and diffusion of knowledge and understanding among the people of the United States, by aiding technical schools, institutions of higher learning, libraries, scientific research, hero funds, useful publications, and by such other means as shall from time to time be found appropriate." This institution, the last of Carnegie's great foundations, is the logical working out of his "gospel of wealth," that a rich man should during his life expend his wealth for the benefit of humanity; that, as Carnegie phrased it, a man who dies rich "dies disgraced."

The Corporation had a wider purpose than any of Carnegie's other benefactions. While it may aid the other Carnegie institutions in the development of their work, these latter can claim only a minor part of the income of the great trust. That income must remain unencumbered, capable of being turned to whatever cause or agency the trustees of succeeding generations may judge most worthy. In short, the Carnegie Corporation is a permanent reservoir of social energy. If the trustees in any one year or generation fail to guess correctly what is the highest purpose, they will have used the income only; the principal will remain, to endow the trustees who follow them the same potential ability for human development.

Carnegie planned this Corporation so that for all time its income shall be in mobile form, capable of being turned to the solution of those problems and to the aid of those causes that the trustees of each generation may find most fruitful in promoting the increase and diffusion of knowledge and understanding. The "Carnegie Corporation," grim business-sounding name, suggesting the steel mills out of which it grew, might to-day fairly be described as "Human Good, Incorporated." Its sole limitation lies in the intelligence of its trustees, their varying capacity from age to age to know just what "good" is.[9]

Carnegie in his will gave the bulk of what he had left to the Carnegie Corporation of New York. To his widow and daughter he left about twenty million dollars — the

---

[9] Most of the institutions Carnegie founded were intended by him to exist in perpetuity, and to this end he in many cases made it an iron-bound condition that the principal of the endowment must always be conserved in toto and that never in any one year could more than the income be spent. A later point-of-view, having as its chief exponent in America Julius Rosenwald — a thoughtful and high-minded business man of Chicago who for a generation until his death in 1931 had been one of America's greatest and most intelligent givers — was that donors should direct that the funds given by them must be spent at such a rate that they would be completely exhausted at the end of a generation or so. Mr. Rosenwald believed that no one is capable of envisaging the changing future and planning intelligently for it, and that consequently an institution which renders a needed service to-day may to-morrow become ineffectual. Mr. Rosenwald cited, in *The Atlantic Monthly* for May, 1929, a number of endowments that have long since outlived their usefulness, among them a Bryan Mullanphy fund, established in 1851, at the time when the covered wagon hegira to the West was at its height, for the relief of "worthy and distressed travellers and emigrants passing through St. Louis." The fund, a godsend for a brief day, later became a burden to its trustees who had difficulty in finding any beneficiary eligible under the terms of the trust. "Benjamin Franklin," wrote Rosenwald, "in drawing his will assumed that there would always be apprentices and that they would always have difficulty when starting in business for themselves in borrowing money. In addition, he assumed that a loan of three hundred dollars was enough to enable a young mechanic to establish himself. With these assumptions, Franklin set up two loan funds of a thousand pounds each. One was for the benefit of 'young married artificers not over the age of twenty-five' who had served their apprenticeships in Boston, and the other for young men of similar situation in Philadelphia. The accumulated interest as well as the principal was to be lent out for a hundred years. . . . Great as Franklin's intellectual powers were, he had miscalculated at every point.

sum, though large, was less than the Biblical tithe. In all, by outright gift during his lifetime, or by his will on his death, Carnegie disposed of approximately three hundred and fifty million dollars.[10]

IV

Of all the things Carnegie bought, of all the things he gave, of all the satisfactions his money brought him, the greatest was a purchase, made for him by a friend after difficult negotiations, which enabled his agent to wire him on Christmas Eve, 1902: "Hail! Laird of Pittencrieff." Pittencrieff was some seventy acres of park owned by a local laird near Dunfermline in which Carnegie had been born. As a poverty-stricken lad of the people Carnegie had been barred from it. "The lairds of

[10] Summary of gifts and grants by Andrew Carnegie and Carnegie Corporation of New York:

Free Public Library Buildings (2811)	$ 60,364,808.75
Carnegie Institute and Carnegie Inst. of Tech...	26,719,380.67
Other Colleges	20,363,010.11
Church Organs (7689)	6,248,309.00
Carnegie Corporation of New York	125,000,000.00
Foundation for Advancement of Teaching	29,250,000.00
Carnegie Institution of Washington	22,300,000.00
Carnegie Hero Funds	10,540,000.00
Carnegie Endowment for International Peace..	10,000,000.00
Simplified Spelling Board	280,000.00
Central American Peace Palace	200,000.00
New York Association for the Blind	114,000.00
War Grants	2,792,500.00
Miscellaneous	36,523,644.87
	$350,695,653.40

Of this amount $49,817,450.54 was appropriated from the revenues of Carnegie Corporation of New York. Figures are taken from *A Manual of the Public Benefactions of Andrew Carnegie,* compiled and published by The Carnegie Endowment for International Peace, 1919. Other publications consulted by the author in preparing this chapter on Carnegie's benefactions include:

A Manual of the Public Benefactions of Andrew Carnegie, compiled and published by The Carnegie Endowment for International Peace, 1919;

A Carnegie Anthology, arranged by Margaret Barclay Wilson, 1915;

Autobiography of Andrew Carnegie, Houghton Mifflin Co., 1920;

Philanthropy in the History of American Higher Education, Jesse Brundage Sears, Bulletin, 1922, No. 26, Department of the Interior.

Pittencrieff for generations had been at variance with the inhabitants." To Carnegie the spot was "saturated with childish sentiment. It always meant paradise to the child of Dunfermline. It certainly did to me. Happy were we if through an open lodge gate, or over the wall, or under the iron grill over the burn now and then we caught a glimpse inside of the abbey and palace grounds. Its high hills grandly wooded . . . the busy crows fluttering around in the big trees. In all my childhood's air-castle building, nothing comparable in grandeur approached Pittencrieff. Its Laird was to us children the embodiment of rank and wealth. My Uncle Lauder predicted many things for me when I became a man, but had he foretold that some day I should be rich enough and so supremely fortunate as to become Laird of Pittencrieff, he might have turned my head. And then to be able to hand it over to Dunfermline as a public park — my paradise of childhood! Not for a crown would I barter that privilege."

V

The attitude in which the public received Carnegie's gifts does not constitute the most agreeable manifestation of the American spirit. There was gratitude enough of the formal sort that expresses itself in stiffly starched resolutions, and testimonials of esteem in the form of honorary degrees from colleges, or set speeches on public occasions. Much genuine gratitude there was, too, from the direct beneficiaries of specific gifts. But Carnegie must have seen, one time or another, the less lovely side of human nature, sometimes in the form of cringing cupidity, sometimes carping criticism. He must have had many occasions to realize, as personal truth brought home to himself, the adage that gratitude is the expectation of favors to come; and many other occasions to learn that the true rule of human conduct is not the one which says one good turn deserves another, but rather the reverse, that one good turn leads to a request for another.

Fortunately, Carnegie was a little blind to lack of appreciation. He was likely to see it less as a reason to be emotionally depressed, than as opposition, to be combated, sharply. By the rules of his giving he excluded the undeserving, those already provided for, those institutions which were receiving help from the government, and those receiving aid from religious bodies. This irritated some groups of clergymen and sectarians. On the other hand, some colleges abjured their religious ties in order to qualify for the pensions, and this angered other portions of the clergy. One such instance was described by Bishop Warren A. Candler, in a jeremiad pamphlet, "Dangerous Donations and Degrading Doles."

As for the general public, which Carnegie enriched as no man or prince had ever enriched it before, its response was usually tinged with a slightly jeering note which assumed that part of Carnegie's motive was self-exaltation.[11] If he was not guilty of selfish exaltation, then he was of some other kind. So suspicious were we of caste that we did not like even a superior order of givers. As Stuart Sherman put it: "Large-scale beneficence — doing good to towns and entire classes of society and nations — establishes one as a member of a privi-

[11] One person who could never work up much enthusiasm over Carnegie or his benefactions was his fellow-Pennsylvanian, Philander Chase Knox, Attorney-General under Roosevelt, Senator from Pennsylvania, Secretary of State under President Taft. In a conversation with Taft at a time when the munificence of the endowment of the Carnegie Corporation was still a matter of wondering interest, Knox, in a mood half facetious, half serious, said: "Now, Mr. Taft, all that old Scotchman is investing this money for is to have a funeral oration preached over him once a year at the anniversary of everything he has put a nickel into. He has bought up most of the orators of the world to-day, but what is worse, he is bribing everybody who will be able to talk from now until eternity." — "Taft and Roosevelt," Archie Butt, p. 612.

leged order, which the average man regards with a certain unease." Such must be, in the characteristic American phrase, "taken down a peg." An expression of this attitude was a skit published in the Portland (Ore.) *Oregonian*, and reprinted in the New York *Sun*, May 5, 1904: "An Epitaph Fifty Years Hence":

HERE LIES
JOHN PITTSBURG SKIBO SMITH
WHO WAS BORN IN A
CARNEGIE TOWN
EDUCATED IN A
CARNEGIE LIBRARY
AT THE AGE OF 30 BECAME A
CARNEGIE HERO
AND HAS GONE TO BE WITH
CARNEGIE

1932 is too early to estimate the results of Carnegie's munificence, to appraise the influence of his philanthropies upon history. Only after many years will it be possible to judge whether the thousands of libraries and organs Carnegie scattered over the earth really gave a perceptible lift to human culture and appreciation of music; whether the millions he gave to science and education increased man's knowledge by a margin; whether, in a word, he gave a push to human progress, accelerated the slow unfolding of evolution. In the main, Carnegie's benefactions have had the effect of democratizing culture, making available to millions possibilities for self-improvement and for enjoyment of things of the mind that would otherwise have been withheld.[12] Whether

---

[12] Stuart Sherman wrote:
"If Carnegie had not taken from us that $350,000,000 we might all and each have had the credit of contributing to the purchase of those organs, the foundation of those libraries, the establishment of those hero funds, the building of that Palace of Peace, the pensioning of those employees, the endowment of those universities, that great fund for the advancement of knowledge. True, we might have contributed. We might have taxed ourselves at that rate. We might have made similar investments in human progress. But we know pretty well that we wouldn't have done so."

man's destiny in the long run can be bettered or even altered by such influences is a matter within the realm of speculation.

VI

One of Carnegie's most grandiose plans, the one which synthesized his finest and loftiest aspirations, went disas-

Carnegie and Dunfermline Trustees on board the yacht *Seabreeze,* Scotland.

trously awry during his lifetime — the result broke his heart. In all else he had been successful, according to his lights. His colossal fortune had been a modern Aladdin's Lamp enabling him to endow millions of his fellow-men with pleasures of the mind and spirit, to liberate necessitous old people from the terrors of want, to build magnificent temples of education, galleries of the finest art. It would not be strange if, seeing the magic his philanthropy had wrought, he had come to feel that money was omnipotent.

Long before his retirement from business he had written of war as "our deepest disgrace," had prayed that "it surely must soon be abolished." With this problem his mind was incessantly busy. For years he served as president of the Peace Society of New York. When Andrew D. White suggested that Carnegie endow at the Hague a Temple of Peace where nations could go with their disputes, he was delighted, and accepted subject to the condition that the overtures must be made not by him but by the Dutch Government. The King of the Netherlands, complaisant, asked Carnegie for the money. Carnegie, boyishly pleased, wrote: "The government drew upon me for it, and the draft for a million and a half is kept as a memento."

In 1910, Carnegie launched the long-pondered project which he believed would have the effect of mobilizing world sentiment for peace and make war impossible. To a board of carefully selected trustees, including President Taft as Honorary President and Elihu Root as President, he turned over $10,000,000 to be used "for the abolition of international war, the foulest blot upon our civilization." To the institution he gave the name "Carnegie Endowment for International Peace." So compelling was his wish that the foundation should accomplish its ends that, hard-headed though he was, he let the wish become father to the thought and deluded himself into believing that, as a consequence of the endowment's creation, never again would civilized peoples settle their differences on the battle-field. In that spirit he advised the trustees as to their course in the Utopia that was to come. With war ended, he wrote, the trustees should consider "what is the next most degrading evil whose banishment, or what new elevating element, if fostered, would most advance the progress and happiness of man; and so on from century to century without end my Trustees of each age shall determine how they

Photograph © Underwood and Underwood.

Andrew Carnegie in his old age.

can best aid man in his upward march to higher stages of development unceasingly."

Carnegie wrote that in 1910. Four years later came Sarajevo.

Carnegie concluded, or rather broke off, the writing of his autobiography in the summer of 1914. The last paragraph he wrote begins: "As I read this to-day what a change! The world convulsed by war as never before. Men slaying each other like wild beasts."

The editor who prepared the autobiography for publication wrote: "Here the manuscript ends abruptly."

Carnegie lived on until August, 1919, less and less seen or heard by the public, beginning to be forgotten by a world intent upon the sound of guns along the Hindenburg line. He died eighteen years after retiring from business, eighty-four after his birth in a tiny Scottish cottage, seventy-two years after as a child he had exulted over his first job. He is buried in Sleepy Hollow Cemetery, in a grave a little shorter than average. By 1932, to a generation that enjoyed the fruits of his benefactions, he was little more than a name carved in stone over a library door.

© *Detroit Publishing Company*

The Crowning of Pittsburgh. The main panel of John W. Alexander's "Apotheosis" of Pittsburgh, in the Carnegie Institute, Pittsburgh.

9

NEW INFLUENCES ON THE AMERICAN MIND

Disappearance, Partial in Most Cases, Entire in a Few, of Old American Points-of-view, Old Ways, Old Customs, Old Traditions. New Ideas, the Sources of Some, and the Paths by Which They Came. The Whole Resulting in a Material Change in the Entire Range of American Culture.

THE average man found himself thinking differently, or in a greater number of cases, found his children thinking differently from himself. The man who was adult between 1900 and 1925 had acquired his stock of ideas[1] some decades before, through association as a child with his family and through school life during the 1890's, 1880's or 1870's. Many of these ideas had become, by the 1900's, so antiquated as to seem, to the newer generation, humorous or quaint, or in some cases odious — ancient fogyisms, to be laughed at, or amiably tolerated, or savagely attacked, according to the attitude of any individual youth towards his elders.

The sources of the new ideas, and the channels through which they found their way into the American mind, were as various and intricate as the fabric of civili-

---

[1] For a summary of what is meant by culture, see "Our Times," Vol. II, p. 1: What is commonly called, loosely, a nation's culture includes the points of view every one has about individual conduct and social relations; his attitude towards government and towards other peoples; his habit of mind about the family, the duty of parents to children and children to parents; his standards of taste and of morals; his store of accepted wisdom which he expresses in proverbs and aphorisms; his venerations and loyalties, his prejudices and biases, his canons of conventionality; the whole group of ideas held in common by most of the people. This body of culture comes to every individual mainly through well-recognized channels, through parents and elders who hand it down by oral traditions, through religion, through schools, and through reading, of books and of newspapers and periodicals.

zation. Neither source nor channel was commonly known by the average man. Indeed, he did not ordinarily recognize that his point of view had undergone change. As for the young, the new ways came to them not as new but as part of the world about them, as taken-for-granted as the air they breathed. Any reflective person, however, upon reviewing even a brief span of years,

From a drawing by A. B. Walker in "Life."

In 1909 the chaperone was still in vogue.

could observe that what had once been shocking, such as talk about sex, was now accepted; what had been taboo, such as smoking by women, was now general; what had been authoritative, such as permanence of marriage, was now ignored or questioned; what had been an imperative requirement, such as chaperons for young women, was now passé; what had been universal custom, such as grace at meals and family prayers, was now rare; what had been concealed, such as women's legs, was now visible.

Conventions which had been respected, traditions that had been revered, codes that had been obeyed almost as precepts of religion, had been undermined or had disappeared. In their place had come new ways, new attitudes of mind, new manners. The sum of the changes had a deep-reaching effect on the generation that was young as the Great War began; coupled with the war, it made a different America.

The sources of the new, the causes of the change, the routes by which the new came, were in most cases vague, indirect and not readily recognizable. To find the springs and trace the paths of all the new ideas would be impossible.[2] A few, including some of the more important, are susceptible to the processes of historical investigation; they came from such concrete sources and by such direct routes as to lend themselves to exact identification.

II

Ideas That Came from an Austrian Physician

The largest single group of new ideas, and the ones that were most fundamental in the changes they wrought, appeared in America between 1909 and 1914. They had originated in Europe, some thirty years before.

About 1881, in Vienna, a physician named Sigmund Freud (his practice was mainly with the mentally ill) evolved some startling new theories about personality and conduct, which denied every existing hypothesis about human behavior.

Freud claimed that the personality is divided into two parts, the conscious and the sub-conscious[3] or unconscious, the latter in turn divided into the true sub-con-

---

[2] Certainly it would take a lifetime of research; and the results would fill many volumes. The best that can be done here is to devise what seems a sound method of historical writing and to apply the method to a few concrete cases.

[3] As between the terms "sub-conscious" and "unconscious," Freud personally habitually used the latter. Freud's early classification was "unconscious" and "fore-conscious." "Sub-conscious," however, became the term familiarly used by Freudians and the public. I have therefore used it in the present discussion.

scious and the censor. Between the conscious and the
sub-conscious, Freud asserted, there is constant war, with
the censor acting as a busy little mediator.

Freud's theory held that the conscious is that respectable and superficial part of the personality which presents
itself to the world as a civilized and self-disciplined human being, but that the sub-conscious is the fundamental
part, the irrepressible part, the primitive personality;
that the conscious is the well-ordered parlor of the personality, while the sub-conscious is the cellar of cave-
man passions; that between conscious and sub-conscious
there is constant struggle, the sub-conscious striving to
carry out its animal impulses and instincts, the conscious
engaged in a continuous process of repressing, or else
camouflaging with a veneer of civilization, the tenden-
cies of the powerful sub-conscious — a never-ending
strife between sub-conscious as the caged beast and conscious in the rôle of keeper and only partially successful
tamer.

Freud held that in the sub-conscious, and therefore in
the personality as a whole, the fundamental and universal basis of all human action is the sex-urge; that
within every individual, the biologic urge to reproduce
and perpetuate is the sole[4] driving force that inspires all
emotions, impulses and actions; that our strivings, and
our exultations in achievement — which the world
theretofore had called ambition and let it go at that —
were really expressions of sex impulse, of the cosmic urge

---

[4] In Freud's early announcements, he treated sex as the sole basis of conduct;
in later presentations he and his disciples modified this to the extent of admitting
the individual wish to achieve, to conquer and to grow, as a minor partner of the
sex-urge.

In 1909, a distinguished New York psychiatrist, Frederick Peterson, wrote:
"He [Freud] is perhaps extreme in this opinion [that sex is the basis of all
conduct]. But we might grant him half, since, roughly speaking, fifty per cent
of the trends, wishes, desires that inspire our activities are for the perpetuation
of the species, and fifty per cent for self-preservation." [Quoted in "History of
Psychoanalysis in America," by Doctor Clarence Oberndorf.]

to perpetuate the race; that where actions seem spiritual, it is merely a case of the personality "sublimating," putting a better color on, a process which in the sub-conscious remains always savage and always sex; that the sex-urge exists, functions and is in evidence from the moment of birth — indeed some of the Freudian school asserted its beginning to be prenatal, "intra-uterine."

A corollary of the Freudian theory was that religion is merely "an unconscious transference of love energy from human to divine objects . . . a symbolic satisfaction for hidden impulses and primitive emotions, a forcing of unconscious desires into forms acceptable to the moral consciousness."[5] Another corollary was that dreams are the vicarious gratification, sometimes symbolic or indirect, of suppressed wishes — the sub-conscious escaping from the tyranny of the conscious, going on the loose and taking its fling in time of sleep, while conscious the keeper is off guard.

The Freud theory came to the United States first through medical journals, the earliest mention in an article entitled "The Psychopathology of Everyday Life," by Boris Sidis, in the *Journal of Abnormal Psychology* in 1906.[5a] By 1909, medical periodicals had much of it. In September of that year, Freud came in person to deliver a series of lectures "Concerning Psychoanalysis," at Clark University, Worcester, Mass. By 1910, allusions to the new concept of psychology began to appear in the lay press, usually with angry disapproval. "So far," said the *American Magazine*, in November, 1910, fingering the subject rather gingerly, "no other leading psychopathist has accepted this sweeping and audacious theory." Two years later the *Scientific*

[5] "Freudian Essays on Religion and Science," Cavendish Moxon.
[5a] The earliest champion of the Freudian theory in the United States was Doctor Abraham A. Brill.

American Supplement[6] spoke, with repugnance, of Freud's "disgusting and wild interpretations."

That was the average normal layman's reaction to initial acquaintance with a theory which was utterly con-

Sigmund Freud.

trary to religion and subversive of every existing conception of romantic love. To the average American of about 1910,[6a] it would be difficult to imagine anything more

[6] November 9, 1912.

[6a] As late as 1932 some three hundred outraged citizens of North Carolina united in a petition to Governor O. Max Gardner against inclusion in the library of the University of North Carolina of Freud's "General Introduction to Psychoanalysis."

repellant. A not too imaginative reader would have interpreted Freud's theory to mean that a devotee kneeling before the Cross is unconsciously satisfying a sublimated form of desire of the flesh, and does not differ from a pagan bowing before a phallic symbol; that every baby in his cradle is a leering philanderer; that a boy-child throwing his arms about his mother is an incestuous libertine; that every girl-child has an incestuous love for her father accompanied by a murderously jealous hate of her mother; that protective tenderness shown by an adult toward a child of the opposite sex is a scandal; that a Romeo sighing beneath his Juliet's balcony is merely the two-legged and more musically voiced equivalent of any male cat yowling to his tabby on a back-yard fence — some of the early and zealous converts to Freudianism would have implied that the tom-cat was on the whole the more laudable, since he practiced no debasing dissimulations or indirections.

The new theory did not come to the average man directly nor in its stark form; the average man, indeed, rarely heard the name Freud, and never grasped the meaning of "Freudian" even after the word got into the 1927 edition of Webster's Dictionary. Nevertheless the world about the average man, the books, magazines and newspapers he read, the plays and motion pictures he saw, the manners and point-of-view of the people about him, including ultimately his own, were profoundly modified by the ideas of the Viennese physician of whom he knew nothing, coming to him through processes of which he was never aware.

The medium through which Freud's ideas were impressed upon the country and altered its standards, consisted mainly of the novelists, dramatists, poets, critics, college teachers, and a type of intellectual called, somewhat condescendingly, "high-brows." These, seizing upon the new "ism" avidly, were soon talking animatedly in its outré terminology: "Psychoanalysis," meaning the study of man's sub-conscious motives and desires, or the act of a practitioner in analyzing the sub-conscious mentality of an individual; "sublimation," meaning the diverting of sexual energy into intellectual channels or creative work; "fixation," meaning the unconscious arrest and crystallization at an early age of a sub-conscious tendency, for example, the affection, alleged by Freud to be wholly or mainly sexual, of a child for a parent; "repression," meaning the keeping from consciousness of primitive desires or mental processes that would be painful for the conscious to admit; "complexes," meaning obscure mechanisms arising in the sub-conscious as a result of the tyranny of the conscious or of the outside world — a series of associated ideas, the touching of any one of which stirs the whole series into action; "libido," meaning originally sexual hunger but broadened to include what the philosopher Bergson termed the "vital impetus" and becoming almost synonymous with all forms of instinctive energy.

Chatter of all that stirred the air wherever intellectuals met; by the 1920's there were more than two hundred books dealing with Freudianism. Among intellectuals as well as high-brows and those who were impressed by them, it became a fad to be psychoanalyzed, abbreviated to "psyked." To meet the demand practitioners arose. Lucrativeness attracted charlatans; at the height of the vogue, advertisements offered to psychoanalyze by mail.

The dramatists, novelists, and poets, by accepting the new theory, caused practically the whole of previously written English literature, so far as it dealt with love or religion, to become, as they said, old-fashioned. A novel such as Hawthorne's "Scarlet Letter," dealing with the struggle between conscience and conduct, became, to these intelligentsia, valueless unless interpreted in terms of the Freudian formula. Romantic love, as it had been described by novelists like Thackeray, or poets like Tennyson, was considered a sentimental glossing over of animal instincts. "He for God alone, for God in him," would have been analyzed by an American intellectual of about 1914 as a "father fixation" suffered by each lover. The romantic tradition in literature came to be regarded as passé, and was jeered at. The Puritan tradition both in literature and morals began to be derided. Hardly any intellectual revolution in history was more complete than the transition from reverence for Emersonian Puritanism up to about 1910, to fierce jibing at it subsequently. It was a denial, by American authors, of the most American standard, almost the only American standard, we had — a rejection of the austere morality of a New England philosopher to make way for the biological theory of an Austrian physician to diseased minds. The new novels and plays written from about 1914 until about the middle of the 1920's took the Freudian thesis, in one degree or another, and by that name or under the designation "realism," as the basis of the love-episodes they contained. Eugene O'Neill, considered during the 1920's to be the ablest American dramatist, followed the Freudian concept starkly, almost slavishly.

Through all this, romantic love, not only in literature but in life, had a rough time. A generation of youth, made familiar by novels and the stage with the exclusively biological explanation of love, came to be a little ashamed of romantic love, or became heretics denying its existence. By 1932, Sophie Kerr alluded with sentimental regret to the passing of the age of innocence, literary and human, about 1910: "The simple merry days before Freud and his three slaves, Inhibition, Complex and Libido, had got to working on sex and marriage and love life generally, and 'made them what they are

Freudian influence in the theatre. A scene from Eugene O'Neill's play, "Desire Under the Elms."

to-day' — yes, long before the very kindergarten children knew ALL."[7]

Interest in Freud and his theory removed the taboo upon sex as a topic susceptible of discussion in what used to be called "mixed company"; once sex as a subject of conversation became permissible, it became, naturally, general, to the considerable embarrassment of persons aged thirty or more, who could recall when the word

[7] *Saturday Evening Post,* April 9, 1932.

"leg" was questionable, and the word "sex," for example, not questionable at all, but strictly forbidden. By 1915, William Marion Reedy was moved to remark, "It's sex o'clock." The phenomenon, until we got used to it, was acutely disturbing; the New York *World* spoke of 'our present popular hysteria, sex-madness"; a Philadelphia author distinguished, if somewhat cloistral, in her personality and in her art, Miss Agnes Repplier, spoke of it as the "repeal of reticence."

Much of the new thought about love was sincere, some was a mere rushing to adopt the novel, not a little was meretricious. Just as in the field of mental pathology there had sprung up many self-styled psychoanalysts who had the same relation to psychiatry that Lydia E. Pinkham or old Doctor Munyon had to the science of medicine, so in literature and the drama, and especially in moving-pictures, there were some who used the new theories as an excuse for money-making pornography. A joke of the period represented a motion-picture magnate as saying "two and two make four, four and four make eight, sex and sex make millions."

Meanwhile, by the time the Freudian theory had seeped down through the intellectuals to affect the masses, the novelists and dramatists who had sponsored the movement began to jeer at it. Dream interpretation was ridiculed in a farce called "Suppressed Desires." Later came a satirical book, "Is Sex Necessary?" and then "Whither, Whither, or After Sex What?" — parodies of some of the pretentious titles used by solemn investigators of the sub-conscious. By 1927 Freudianism had reached the stage at which limericks laughed at it:

> A progressive young lady of Rheims
> Had confessed some astonishing dreams,
> And was justly annoyed when the great Dr. Freud
> Said, "a surfeit of chocolate-creams."

In 1932, *Vanity Fair*, village newspaper of the sophis-
ticates who as evidence of up-to-date-ness had eagerly
adopted psychoanalysis, now, in a new up-to-date-ness,
recommended Freud as a candidate for oblivion, decried
his theory as mainly error.

The movement left some enduring effects. Such valid
residuum of it as was able to withstand criticism, modified greatly the science of psychology, both the medical
aspect of it and the teaching of it in colleges. It revolutionized the treatment of the mentally ill. Freedom
from self-consciousness about talking of sex between the
sexes led to evaporation of some false sentimentality
about women. The mere experience of acquaintance
with a new point of view, of seeing an ancient and accepted convention brought under attack, had an intellectual effect of "shaking up" even where the new view was
rejected. Some of the new frankness and the new understanding had partial value. There was much validity
in the supporter of Freud who said of the older order
that "sending the young out into life with such a false
psychological orientation was as if one were to equip
people going on a polar exploration with summer clothing and maps of the Italian lakes."

Between those entranced by Freud and those outraged
by him, battle raged for more than twenty years. "The
ideas of no other living man are so directly responsible
for so many printed pages."[8] The controversy could have
no conclusion. The basis of the Freudian theory was not
within the world of proof or disproof; it was not the end
of a syllogism, but the beginning; it was a premise, upon
which many conclusions, sound or fantastic, were built,
by which many practices, good or bad, were justified.

[8] Joseph Jastrow: "The House that Freud Built," 1932.

To the writer of this history, it seems that — so far as we accept the biological theory at all — weight should be given to another animal instinct, which we may call the urge to function. Any one who has ever had intimate acquaintance with a bird-dog, or seen a rat-terrier in action, or observed the zest, the almost hysterical anticipation, of a hunting-dog of any type when he sees his master pick up a gun, knows that the animal is impelled more continuously and with more acute concentration, by desire to do the thing that nature created him to do, than by either the sex-urge or the instinct of self-preservation. It seems tenable to suggest, since this whole field is pretty vague anyhow, that every human being has some one function which the law of his nature drives him to do; and that the urge of an artist to paint, of a poet to rhyme, of a horseman to ride, of a farmer to plow and plant, is as powerfully animating a motive of behavior as those suggested by Doctor Freud. In organized society as it is, not everybody finds the opportunity to do the thing for which nature gave him the desire. A man born with a passion for the sea may through circumstances be carried into the career of bank-clerk, or spend his days in an elevator-cage. Such a man becomes as much a case of "repressed desire" as any case that Freud catalogues.

Finally, may one add, physicians, psychiatrists, like Doctor Freud and his disciples, have their own urge to function; and their zest in it may carry them, and the theories they evolve, to extremes — at which they encounter the historian's urge to doubt.[9]

9 Freudianism is one of the most controversial subjects in the modern world. In the effort to state the theory fairly I have submitted this chapter to some of the ablest exponents of it in America, to one of Freud's relatives, and to several neurologists who either disapprove Freudianism or are judicial about it. The final form of the chapter here presented will not satisfy all the advocates of Freud. Fundamental difficulties in achieving either fairness or clearness are several: the subject is extremely technical, Freud has modified his views from time to time, the position of Freud is not always identical with that of many of

III

Ideas That Came from a Persian Skeptic

The ideas of Freud came to America between 1910 and 1914. Another influence had begun to come in the 1890's, had spread greatly, and infected each succeeding generation of youth.

During the years from about 1050 to 1123 A.D., there lived at Nīshāpūr, in Persia, a man named Ghiyā-thuddĭn 'Abulfath 'Omar Bin Inrāhīm, to which was added a descriptive designation taken from his father's occupation, which was tent-maker, Al-Khayyāmī. By occupation he was a mathematician; for diversion he composed epigrams in rhyme, called rubā'īs. Some eight centuries later a manuscript of these, in the Bodleian library, came to the attention of an English orientalist, Edward Fitzgerald, who translated them into English verse at various times between 1859 and 1880. During the latter part of the nineteenth century this English translation appeared sporadically in the United States, by 1895 in considerable numbers.

---

his apostles, and the popular understanding of Freudianism sometimes differs from the medical.

As to judgments about Freudianism in 1932, Doctor William A. White, head of Saint Elizabeth's Hospital, Washington, D. C., writes the author:

"To my mind, Freud's greatness lies in his having evolved an entirely new point of view and a new method which will ultimately discover the facts which it is capable of discovering and discard the errors which are incident to its employment, just like any other scientific method or point of view. . . . The whole situation in my mind is quite similar in its history to the development of anatomy and utilization of dissection. There was just the same feeling of outrage against the early anatomists who insisted upon dissecting the human body, and these same early anatomists discovered all sorts of things that were not so, and subsequently had to be corrected by future observations more accurately checked up. It is quite the same with the analysis of the human mind. It is equally resented, and I have no doubt mistakes are made in the same way."

Another eminent neurologist, Doctor Frederick Peterson of New York, in a letter to the author in 1932, declared, with italicized emphasis, that *"Freudianism is a voodoo religion characterized by obscene rites and human sacrifices."* He adds that psychoanalysis has in innumerable cases caused mental aberration, insanity or suicide, and that much of the work of present day neurologists has come to be the "reconstruction of unfortunate victims of Freudianism."

By 1900, the book had begun to be extremely popular throughout America. By 1905, a volume of "Omar Khayyám," glamorously illustrated, was a favored birthday remembrance, especially among young folks; many

Copyright Houghton Mifflin Co.

From an edition of Fitzgerald's translation of the "Rubaiyat of Omar Khayyám," illustrated by Elihu Vedder and published by Houghton Mifflin Co., 1884.

a youth and maiden saved for months to give one to a sweetheart. By 1910, millions lay on parlor tables upon which, incongruously, the only other book was in many cases the Bible. Tens of millions of individual quatrains were printed on desk-cards, "pyrographed" in leather on sofa-cushions, hand-painted as ornaments for walls — upon which their companions were quotations from Emerson and "God Bless Our Home."

By that diffusion, a generation of American youth

made acquaintance with an oriental philosophy. Trained during their Sunday-school years in the austere tenets of the Christian religion, they became acquainted in their impressionable adolescent teens with the epicurean fatalism of a Persian atheist, the latter expressed with a charm of poetic words much more alluring to youth than the cold commandments of the Christian Scriptures.

Warned by the Bible that "God now commandeth all men everywhere to repent,"[10] the youth was now told by Omar to scorn penance and follow a gayer life:

> Come, fill the cup, and in the fire of Spring
> Your Winter garment of repentance fling;
> The Bird of Time has but a little way
> To flutter—and the bird is on the wing.[11]

Promised by Old Testament prophets that there is a future life, that the "dead . . . shall rise,"[12] and shall "possess life everlasting";[13] and that "in my flesh shall I see God"[14] — he was advised by Omar to enjoy the here and now:

> Ah, make the most of what we yet may spend,
> Before we too into the dust descend;
> Dust into Dust, and under Dust to lie
> Sans Wine, sans Song, sans Singer, and sans End.[15]

Told by the Bible that he will be judged, and his fate throughout eternity determined, by a God "who will render to every man according to his deeds,"[16] who will give "eternal life to them who by . . . well-doing seek for glory and honor and immortality"[17] — he was now assured by Omar that there is neither reward, nor punishment, nor eternal life:

> Oh threats of Hell and Hopes of Paradise
> One thing at least is certain — this life flies;
> One thing is certain and the rest is lies;
> The flower that once has blown for ever dies.[18]

[10] Acts 17:30–31. [11] Quatrain VII. [12] Isaiah 26:19.
[13] Nathan 19, 28, 29. [14] Job 19:26. [15] Quatrain XXIV.
[16] Romans 2:6. [17] Romans 2:7. [18] Quatrain LXIII.

Admonished by the Bible to pray — "I will therefore that men pray everywhere, lifting up holy hands without . . . doubting";[19] and promised that "whatsoever ye shall ask in prayer, believing, ye shall receive"[20] — he was now counselled by Omar:

> And that inverted bowl they call the Sky,
> Whereunder crawling, cooped, we live and die,
> Lift not your hands to it for help — for it
> As impotently moves as you or I.[21]

Assured by the Bible that God concerns Himself with the salvation of man: "God . . . tempteth not any man" — he was told the opposite by the Persian Voltaire; Omar, in a mood of especial bitterness, accepting for once the existence of God in order to deride Him, railed:

> Oh Thou, who Man of baser earth didst make,
> And even with Paradise devise the Snake;
> For all the sin wherewith the face of man
> Is blackened, Man's forgiveness give — and take.[22]

Assured by the Bible that God is a God of mercy, compassionate, kind, and a father to all: "We are the children of God, heirs of God and joint heirs with Christ . . . that we may be glorified together"[23] — he was warned by Omar that God is indifferent, cruel:

> But helpless pieces of the game He plays
> Upon this checquer board of Nights and Days;
> Hither and thither moves, and checks, and slays,
> And one by one back in the closet lays.[24]

Told by all the accepted sources of American standards of conduct that life should be lived according to the Puritan philosophy of the hair-shirt; told to accept this life with resignation because endurance of poverty and other denials here was the key to the kingdom of

19 Tim. 2 :8. 20 Matthew 21 :22. 21 Quatrain LXXII.
22 XCI. 23 Romans 8 :16, 17. 24 Quatrain LXIX.

Heaven; told by the Bible to "mortify the flesh"[25] because "man doth not live by bread alone";[26] told by familiar maxims from McGuffey's "Fifth Reader" that

Copyright L. C. Page & Co.

From an edition of Fitzgerald's translation of the "Rubaiyat of Omar Khayyám,"
illustrated by Gilbert James and published by L. C. Page & Company, 1898.

the present should be subordinated to the future; told by
Bryant to "so live that when thy summons comes . . .";
told by Longfellow that "Life is earnest" — young
America was now sedulously advised by the Persian poet
to live for the day, was allured to a course of life in
which languorous ease, sensuous self-enjoyment was the
only objective worth while:

> A book of verses underneath the bough,
> A jug of wine, a loaf of bread — and thou
> Beside me singing in the wilderness —
> Oh, wilderness were Paradise enow.[27]

[25] St. Paul to the Romans 8:13.   [26] Deuteronomy 8:3.   [27] Quatrain XII.

Some for the Glories of this World; and some
Sigh for the Prophet's Paradise to come;
Ah, take the Cash, and let the credit go,
Nor heed the music of a distant drum![28]

It was not that many American youths really believed
Omar, or embraced him as a practicable philosophy of
life; few did that, any more than they took the Sermon
on the Mount as a practicable rule of business. But the
young American was made aware, in this generation for
the first time in a wholesale way, that there is more than
one philosophy of life; he was started to comparing and
reflecting — was started, in short, upon an intellectual
path that put every sort of dogma under inquiry, that
took away authority from all dogma. Many an American, adult in the 1920's, remembered as a landmark the
day he read Omar's line, "I myself am Heav'n and
Hell." The spirit of Omar Khayyám, not recognized as
a philosophy or a body of doctrine, but more persuasive
than anything so unappetizingly labelled, the mood of
him, and the mood he induced in readers, seeping into
the minds of successive generations of American youth
from about 1895 on, had an effect of sapping and undermining, relaxing and making pliant, the very foundations and granite pillars of what had formerly been the
characteristic American structure of standards of conduct.

IV

Ideas That Came from a British Artisan of Plays

About 1879 there had come to London from Dublin,
where he had been born (though he was as distant as
possible from being what the world knows as an Irish-
man), a young man named George Bernard Shaw. Be-

[28] Quatrain XIII.

MR. BERNARD SHAW

Mild surprise of one who, revisiting England after a long absence, finds that the dear fellow has not moved. Max Beerbohm's caricature of Bernard Shaw, published by E. P. Dutton & Co.

cause of conflict within his own nature and an additional war between his nature and his circumstances, he had lived a bitter boyhood. Within himself, shyness and sensitiveness were at war with a passion for assertiveness. These traits, all his personality, had been racked and rasped by his family's poverty, by their inability to live up to the social station to which they had some title and which they regarded as important; by an unhappy and tension-provoking relation between his father and mother; by continuous irritation of the boy's soul because the intellectual ability which he really had did not count for him with other boys but rather against him, while his physical timidity, his shrinking from boisterousness, marked him as inferior in the only quality which his young associates esteemed. The whole of his unhappy cosmos led him to take on insolence, an incredible impudence, as an armor of defense against a world which, whatever way he turned, wounded his ego.

His outstanding trait was assertiveness, the wish to be seen and heard and noticed, a wish so passionate as to amount almost to abnormality; he was of a type recognized by modern psychologists, and familiar to every one who has seen in schools, or in other groups of young people, a boy who will do any desperate thing to attract attention to himself — a type which, under sympathetic conditions, becomes a "show-off," and under indifference or repressive conditions turns to an almost hysterical anxiety for conspicuousness — and young Shaw's conditions had not been sympathetic. In London Shaw's bitterness, his spirit of rebellion against frustration, his desperate sense of failure to get the world to accept him at his own valuation (which was high, and really deserved to be), was increased by an experience of writing five novels without finding a publisher for one, earning during four years exactly 5 pounds, 15 shillings, 6 pence.

By this time Shaw was mature enough to reflect that, other means failing, a man can surely cause the crowd to look at him by standing on his head on the pavement.

Applying this device to the world that he knew best, and in which he lusted to function, the world of ideas, Shaw reasoned that, by standing any familiar idea or accepted convention on its head, the world can be shocked into paying attention. Upon this formula, Shaw began to write plays, plays in which the fundamental device lay in a trick of taking any universally held view or universally

From "Vanity Fair," 1914.

Mrs. Partick Campbell in "Pygmalion."

cherished tradition, turning it inside out, and holding the reverse before the audience or the readers. His first, when produced, was "not . . . a success, but I had provoked an uproar, and the sensation was so agreeable that I resolved to try again."[29]

In "Mrs. Warren's Profession," a prostitute and keeper of a house of prostitution is to be not looked down upon but respected as much as any other compe-

[29] Preface to "Plays Pleasant and Unpleasant," G. B. Shaw, Vol. I.

tent head of a business; in "Man and Superman," the man does not pursue the woman, the woman pursues the man; in "Arms and the Man," soldiers are *not* brave and war is *not* glorious; in "Cæsar and Cleopatra," the world has made no progress since the time of the Roman Empire; in "Pygmalion," there is no reason why the word "bloody"[30] should be taboo — and so Shaw had Mrs. Patrick Campbell say it, upon which a visible and audible shudder from the audience became as definite a part of the performance as anything done on the stage.

In addition to his plays, Shaw practiced his trick of paradox in hundreds of mechanically devised epigrams: "Better never than late," "too true to be good," "my reputation grows with every failure," "lack of money is the root of all evil"; and a thousand assertions that reversed accepted views, negatived established traditions: people should be painted and photographed naked, marriage is the quintessence of license, a woman seeking a husband is the most unscrupulous beast of prey, no one should eat meat. As a detail and refinement Shaw denounced the country in which he lived, reviled Englishmen.[31] He prospered by, and brought about in his disciples, a deification of the perverse.

Other than this trick of paradox, Shaw had scant equipment for play-writing.[32] Of plot he attempted lit-

---

[30] The author of this history was behind the scenes at the first performance of "Pygmalion" by Beerbohm Tree and Mrs. Campbell in London in April, 1912. The newspapers, in advance information about the play, had hinted — Shaw was adept in getting this sort of provocative publicity — that a familiar forbidden word, inferred by everybody to be "bloody," would be spoken. On the stage, the tension of the players as the time for the word approached, and the gasp of the audience when Mrs. Campbell spoke it, overshadowed everything else in the play. "Bloody" had in England the status which, in America, goes with a phrase imputing canine maternity to a human being, a phrase curiously and illogically singled out as not to be uttered in polite society, nor used in print ever — though its equivalent, such as "yellow dog," can be spoken or written with impunity.

[31] As in Napoleon's long speech in "The Man of Destiny," and the comic character of Britannus in "Cæsar."

[32] Some critics who have read this manuscript question the assertion that Shaw lacked the equipment of a dramatist. What they mean, I think, is that

tle; of men, he knew nothing; of women, less — his female characters, Frank Harris said, "lack mystery, grace,

G. Bernard Shaw, from the photograph by Frederick H. Evans, London.

divinity, allure or charm, they are like synthetic women
made up in a laboratory." Of characterization, Shaw
had no faintest art — such characterization as he lugged
in to put semblance of flesh upon his stark ideas, was
taken largely from Dickens, Ibsen, Molière or others.

Shaw had an instinct for the dramatic (which is quite a different thing) and
knew superbly the art of being dramatic. To be dramatic was the very corner-
stone of Shaw's ability, a fundamental part of the one indisputable genius he had,
the genius of assertiveness, of calling attention to himself and to his ideas.

Ideas were Shaw's one asset. He held them sincerely, as any egotist does. Most of them were new or revolutionary, lending themselves to the method of presentation by paradox. In putting his ideas forward, he had daring inventiveness, persistency and consistency, an instinct for the startling phrase, some wit — much of it having the rather mechanical quality that expresses itself in paradox or other deliberately striking form of words. Shaw introduced, or carried further than any one before had, the idea of using the stage as a vehicle for discussion, argument. As Walter Prichard Eaton put it, Shaw "intellectualized the stage and made thinking, not feeling, prevail."

Paradox served Shaw well. With success in it, he carried it to a supreme extreme. For a man in Shaw's position, the conventional thing would be to conceal his sham; Shaw in an apotheosis of his trick, proclaimed his sham, described himself, in scores of witty epigrams, as the arrant showman that he was. "Force of assertion," he said in self-revealing candor, "is the Alpha and Omega of style . . .; he who has something to assert will go as far in power of style as its momentousness and his conviction will carry him." In an extreme of self-exhibitionism, he said, "I can't guarantee myself as the greatest living hokum merchant, but I am certainly one of the first ten."[33]

So limp a bag of tricks[34] would hardly have carried

---

[33] Quoted in Frank Harris' "Bernard Shaw."

[34] Walter Prichard Eaton, ardent Shavian, one of our most discriminating and respected American dramatic critics, having been kind enough to read a draft of this chapter, disagrees — I go so far as to say violently — with much that is here said about Shaw.

"Shaw has vast inventiveness, sparkling humor of the kind which best enlivens stage repartee, an eye for ironic contrast of character types, an ear gifted to make speech ring right when spoken. In many ways he has the best equipment for writing comedy possessed by any dramatist on the English stage since Sheridan. The reason Shaw often seems formless and undramatic is because he has deliberately chosen to throw overboard the tricks of the older drama in order to intellectualize his stage and make thinking, not feeling, prevail. He

Shaw as far as it did, but for one greatly favoring condition. In every age and place, there are scores of conventions, accepted ways of doing things, which have no other justification except that they started that way, which are no more logical, and in no respect better, than the opposite way would have been had accident in the beginning adopted it — a typical example is the wearing of trousers by men, skirts by women — in some Eastern countries the reverse works equally well; or turning to

---

has, no doubt, created the driest laughter since Congreve, but he has done it no less deliberately, and the result, on the whole, has been to compel most dramatists after him to abandon to the movies a vast deal of the ancient trickery of situation found in former playwrights. Shaw, even to-day, still has more performances than any other living writer; 'Arms and the Man' is still acted somewhere nearly every week.

"Shaw himself, as well as his plays, has stood the light of merciless publicity (Shaw has seen to that!) for almost half a century now, and he still is acted, he still is respected, he still stands for the things he began standing for. He deliberately sought publicity, I admit, and was the best press agent of his age. He wanted attention for his plays. But even that was in part a sign of the sincerity of his convictions. He stood on his head *for* his convictions — which isn't quite what you have implied.

"What I think you fail to say, as any treatment of Shaw should say, is that he is a master of English prose, particularly argumentative prose, and will probably be classed among the literary great on this score alone. He is certainly the best pamphleteer since Swift. Nobody in English has ever written more consistently interesting, arresting, witty and well mustered sentences than he in his prefaces. Shaw was, and is, a fine literary artist, a natural dramatist of great endowments, endowments employed to put over intellectual ideas, and finally a man whose ideas, hammered home for 40 years, have altered (whether for better or worse is beside the point) both our ways of thinking and our ways of writing plays. Only pretty great men, and certainly only sincere men, alter the world to anything like this extent."

I think that some of the admiration for Shaw remaining in the affections of those who, like Mr. Eaton, were young when Shaw's plays were new, is part of the familiar illusion that throws glamour over the past. The young American intellectuals of the early 1900's were thrilled by Shaw in part because he gave expression to, "put over," new ideas that were dear to the rebellious young eagles of that day. Their sustained devotion to Shaw is part of a fine loyalty for the man who gave potent voice to their discontent at a time when that required the courage of a pioneer. I doubt if Shaw, viewed by the newer generation of intellectuals, seems so great.

It seems to me significant that Walter Eaton, who was my classmate at Harvard College in 1900, thinks Shaw great; while my daughter, who graduated in 1931 at Bryn Mawr College, thinks Shaw a prosy old poseur. The generation that is over fifty recalls Shaw as having the courage and glamour of an innovator; to the generation under thirty Shaw's innovations are outmoded, tepid.

the right to pass on the road — England gets along just as well by turning to the left. Many rules of conduct, even ethical standards, so-called, are equally arbitrary, equally capable of working as well if reversed. At any time the world can be entertained, amused or shocked by the device of merely standing these established ways on their heads.

In the England in which Bernard Shaw began to write plays (during the early 1890's), there was an exceptional accumulation of conventions that had lived beyond their time and were peculiarly subject to satirical assault because of changes that were coming into the world. England for more than fifty years had been under the political and social tutelage of one leader, a woman, Queen Victoria, whose every trait of temperament and character inclined her to prize conventions and conserve them, to esteem conformance, to reverence tradition. England was living under a code of manners, political ideas and social points of view almost as out of date as feudalism. On every Sunday, in every Sabbath school and at many other services of the Church of England, and in America at services of the Protestant Episcopal Church, millions of people from earls to menials, from millionaires to servants — and servants and menials rather more earnestly than millionaires or earls — prayed God to give them grace "To submit myself to all my governors, teachers, spiritual pastors and masters . . . to order myself lowly and reverently to all my betters, and to do my duty in that state of life into which it shall please God to call me."[35]

That prayer was the supreme expression of a ritualized point of view, of crystallized conventions in every area of life, surviving from an older type of social and political organization, into a world in which the spirit of democ-

[35] The Episcopal Catechism.

racy had routed every vestige of aristocracy except its antiquated forms; a world in which the officially sancti-fied virtue of contentment with lowly station had become

Queen Victoria, from a photograph taken in 1887 by Hughes & Mullins, Ryde, I. W.

not a virtue at all but, especially in America, almost a sin, and certainly a lack of proper spirit in the individual who supinely practiced it; a world in which such words as "masters" and "betters" had become so obsolete as no longer even to inspire jeering but only an amiable smile; an age in which worldly commendation, if not religious, was only for those who denied "submission," defied

"masters" and "betters," scorned "lowliness" and "reverence"; an age which felt that the state of life in which
a man found himself was not the decree of God, but the
fault of the individual, and that the only quality deserv-
ing divine approval was ambitious striving to raise one's
self, or certainly one's children, to a higher state.

That contrast between the fossilized form and the living spirit was meat for totem-wreckers of every degree.
Beneath the ancient stratification of established order in
the England of about 1890, lay the explosive materials
of revolution, inherent in changes that had come into
every area of life. To touch the match of satire or invec-
tive to the powder came Bernard Shaw in the world of
letters, Lloyd-George in the political world. To each,
the body of outworn Victorian conventions was a gold-
mine, and each knew how to exploit it. Both had much
the same technique, a deliberate iconoclasm, concocted to
shock; possibly of all the provocative sentences ever
uttered in politics, none, not even the incitements to blood
in the French Revolution, ever had so great an effect
of concussion as the sentence with which Lloyd-George
attacked England's system of primogeniture in the descent of land holdings, "the eldest son of a duke is only
the oldest whelp of the litter."

The furore that Lloyd-George and Shaw created in
England affected American thought, already in high
ferment of its own. Shaw's plays, acted in America long
before they were accepted in England, put into words
subversive new ideas that were already common among
intellectuals, and carried those ideas into widening
circles of the population. The intellectuals, in naïve delight at finding the notions that were already inchoate
in their own minds, now put into pungent words by the
English dramatist, hailed Shaw as seer, sage and philosopher; thought of him as in the same class as others

who really were authentic philosophers or artists, such as
Nietzsche and Ibsen (from whom Shaw borrowed);
failed to see that Shaw's distinction, and success, arose
chiefly from his superiority in showmanship. Shaw's

Photograph © Harris & Ewing.

Rudyard Kipling.   H. G. Wells.

vogue was great, and lasted for nearly thirty years. If
some historian of sardonic temperament were to seek the
most damning possible epitaph for the American intellectuals of the first quarter of the twentieth century in
America, he could find none better than to say, "They
took Bernard Shaw seriously." This judgment about
Shaw's quality does not modify the fact that his plays
greatly expedited the substitution in America of new
conventions for old.

v

There were many other sources and vehicles, literary
or otherwise, of new ideas. H. G. Wells had a point-of-
view parallel with Shaw's, and Wells' influence in Amer-

ica — because among his other qualities he was a teller of charming tales, an authentic literary artist — went deeper among the masses than Shaw's. The plays of a Norwegian dramatist, Henrik Ibsen, as literature more indisputably hall-marked than Shaw's, contributed to a less sentimental view about women and family life. Rudyard Kipling, though as distant as possible from being an iconoclast — reverence for the established order was Kipling's primary passion — had acquired through youthful contact with Orientals a point-of-view about women which, expressed in pungent verse, was widely quoted in America and measurably contributed to modifying the national inclination towards chivalry. Kipling's early "The Colonel's lady and Judy O'Grady are sisters under the skin," had an effect even in the not formally stratified social structure of America, of partially de-sentimentalizing the attitude of men toward women. His later "Rag and a bone and a hank of hair," and "The female of the species is more deadly than the male," when first published in America, led almost to censorship.

Most of the new ideas came from across the sea, from Shaw in England, Freud in Austria, Nietzsche and Schopenhauer in Germany, Tolstoy and Gorki in Russia, from Omar Khayyám in Persia and nine centuries ago. Such idol-wreckers as arose in America as a rule owed what conspicuousness they achieved to their adeptness and quickness as adopters and adapters of new thought that came from abroad; America had no really important image-smasher of its own. During the 1870's, '80's, and '90's, Walt Whitman had originated new ideas and new forms of poetry; Henry George had made familiar a new theory of organized society; Robert ("Bob") Ingersoll had made agnosticism familiar though decidedly not popular. Minor iconoclasts of religion were Elbert Hubbard with his bizarre little magazine, *The Philistine*, and a fiercely belligerent atheist who reached the average man with a fiery, cheaply printed, paper

Count Tolstoy.

(often consumed in bonfires by angry believers), called *Brann's Iconoclast.* At all times, especially in church and university circles, there was querying of some portions of orthodox religion. "Higher Criticism" was a euphemism — devised as armor against accusation of heresy — for attempts made by churchmen and collegians to construct an intellectual bridge between religion and Darwinism. Darwin's "Descent of Man," published in England in 1871, was, of course, the source of practically all modern questioning of the Bible. It never reached the average man directly, though the effects of it seeped down to him from the colleges.

The seeping was slow; as late as 1925, the outstanding sensation of the country for a month was the trial of a Tennessee school teacher, John Thomas Scopes, for giving instruction in biology which included Darwin's theory — contrary to a statute of Tennessee which read:

Be it enacted — that it shall be unlawful for any teacher in any of the universities, normals, and all other public schools . . . which are supported . . . by the public school funds of the State, to teach any theory that denies the story of the Divine Creation of man as taught in the Bible, and to teach instead that man has descended from a lower order of animals.

VI

For the exceptional responsiveness of America to new ideas, and exotic ones, for the fact that foreigners like Shaw became popular in America long before they were accepted in their own countries, there were reasons easily identifiable. America, as a people, did not have deep roots in the soil upon which it lived; the oldest community in the United States was, in 1914, but little over three centuries old, the average less than a hundred — merely a morning-hour of sunrise compared to the length of continuous life and unbroken tradition among European peoples. America had no separate body of culture that had germinated[36] here; such traditions as we possessed had come to us with early settlers or with waves of immigration, and had experienced arrest of growth by transplanting, had suffered attenuation in the new soil, and attrition by rubbing against differing traditions from

[36] A critic who has read this chapter in manuscript makes the point that there were some areas of indigenous culture in America, the local customs associated with plantation life in the South, ranch-life in the West, life in the Southern Appalachians; and the parochial social codes of some cities, Charleston, S. C., New Orleans, Baltimore. This, however, is using the word "culture" in a narrower sense, and a much less fundamental sense, than is intended in this chapter. Such variations from the national culture were no more important than the variations of pronunciation of the English language that prevailed in the same communities.

other sources. America presented to the assaults of change no such crystallized front of long accepted, indigenous culture as did older peoples. American culture was still in the melting-pot, still in a flux into which new ideas could be thrown and become part of the whole.

Immigrants at Ellis Island, New York, waiting to be passed for entry into the United States.

This fluidity of the American body of ideas, this receptivity to the new, was kept alive by constant waves of new immigration. The immigrant, because of the quality of mind that led him to migrate, was susceptible to change; one who of his own impulse had sought the new, was pliant to the new when it came to him from any source.

VII

Influence of New York on America

A fundamental fact about America, constituting a special cause for its quick receptivity to new ideas, and necessary to be taken into account in any thoughtful attempt to understand the country's culture and its social history, is a unique relation that existed between America's metropolis and America itself.

In every country, changes in culture originate in the

Ellis Island Immigration Station, New York Harbor, seen from an airplane.

metropolis and from there spread out. One reason is the tendency of the provinces to regard whatever is done in the great city as "the thing," and to imitate it. Another reason is that, in any country the largest city, because of its aggregation of wealth and other conditions, is, so to speak, the culture capital. A more direct reason is similar to one of the laws of mass production in the material world: the metropolis of a nation is the densest and most easily accessible market for all those forms of art and culture which are the vehicles of new ideas for new plays, new books, new music, including new popular songs. The purveyors of these aim at the population of the metropolis for their primary market. Innovations of every kind, including new styles in clothes and new vogues in manners, commonly sink their first roots in the metropolis. What the metropolis adopts is certain to spread out through the country; the influence of a metropolis on a nation's culture is irresistible.

Photographs © Ewing Galloway.

Above: Interior of a dairy barn of an electrically equipped farm. *Below:* Government scientist testing milk.

This law of culture operates as to all countries and all metropolises. In almost all cases, it conforms to natural law, is a part of normal evolution. The people of the metropolis are of the same racial stock as those of the country, have the same traditions, the same habits of thought, the same affections and loyalties, the same prejudices and biases, the same folk-spirit. The normal metropolis is a cross-section of the nation, merely a dense aggregation of characteristic individuals. The changes that originate in the great city are likely to be natural modifications of the main body of culture, the new closely integrated to the old, the process and the result constituting a slow, normal tangent of cultural change, without violent interruption or reversal.

But about the metropolis of the United States there was a unique condition making it, and the country trib-

From "The Theatre Magazine," September, 1908.

"Why stir up the Dust Demon to a frenzy like this?"

Through the introduction of vacuum cleaners, choking clouds of dust have become relics of barbarism.

utary to it, peculiarly susceptible to innovations. The metropolis of the United States was made up mainly of peoples different from the country whose culture it modified. Nowhere,[37] either in the present world or in history, was another case of a city exercising the influence of a metropolis on a country without being made up of people of that country.

[37] Vienna was the case of a metropolis containing comparatively few representatives of some of the races that made up minor divisions of the country. To that fact is attributable some of the instability of the Austro-Hungarian Empire. But Vienna, in a cultural and racial sense, was more truly the metropolis of Austria than New York of the United States.

New York had been, up to about the 1880's, a sufficiently American city, its population composed of the
same elements as the rest of the country, its recent immigrants the Irish, English, and Germans, homogeneous
with those out of which the nation had been composed.
But New York during the period this history covers had

"Some Day." Cartoon by Arthur Young in *Life*.

come to be made up to an increasing extent of immigrants — almost exclusively of immigrants if we include
the first generation born in America. Of greater consequence in its bearing on cultural change,[37a] a rapidly
growing preponderance of the new immigrants came
from countries which had not before contributed to the
make-up of the American people. The new immigrants,
racially alien to the old stock, and in many respects cul-

[37a] The effect of the composition of New York's population upon American
culture was illustrated by a change that took place in the public schools. Because a large proportion of the pupils were Jews, city and school authorities,
to avoid offense to them, minimized school ceremonies associated with the Christian faith or with Christian holidays. Considering how much of American culture, in the broadest sense, especially its folk-ways, are related to the Christian
religion, the effect is obvious. For the same reason and to the same effect, in
the teaching of Shakespeare, "The Merchant of Venice," because of the character
Shylock, was sometimes omitted.

turally different, came from Italy, Russia, Poland, Austria-Hungary, and the rest of Southeastern Europe.

In the population of New York City in 1910 the relative proportions of alien stock and native American stock were:[38]

Stock	Persons	Percentage
Alien	3,748,000	78.6
American	1,020,000	21.4

The essential condition went farther than the figures show. The classification "alien" includes only persons actually born abroad and their children. In many cases grandchildren of aliens (who in the classification are grouped with American stock), having been born and spent their lives in New York, took on the color of New York's alien influences. To this, add that a considerable number of those listed as of American stock were negroes. One feels justified in doubting whether as much as ten per cent of New York's population was American in the sense of possessing, in the form of heritage, old American ideals, customs, characteristics, traditions. Fully 90 per cent of New York's population was not identified with that background and base of American social structure which has American ideals as an inheritance from white American ancestry and intertwined with the appealing sentiment of blood and family. New York City was the metropolis of America only in the sense that it had the largest population. It was not the largest American city. It was the largest Italian city in the world, and the largest Jewish city; but as a city of native Americans it was exceeded in numbers by Los Angeles, and several others.

Had the immigrants brought their native cultures with them, and held to them, New York might have

38 Census figures.

Fifth Avenue and 33d Street, New York, looking north. The upper picture was taken in 1900 showing the old Waldorf-Astoria on the left. *Below:* The same corner in 1932 shows on the left the lower floors of the Empire State Building. The buildings show that the neighborhood has changed from a residential to a business section.

been, as respects culture, a polyglot city. To a slight degree this took place. There were Yiddish theatres and an Italian press, as well as a German theatre and newspapers in some twenty-three tongues. These, however,

During the period of this book, work on the Panama Canal was being pushed. This drawing by William H. Foster, 1910, shows the dredges at work in the channel by moonlight.

catered only to successive groups of newly arrived immigrants. They did not tend to perpetuate in New York the cultures of the peoples who made up the city. The trend was against New York becoming a polygot city in the sense of being made up of separate peoples and separate cultures existing side by side. The trend, very strong, was toward New York becoming a "melting-pot" city.

Above: The Princeton Stadium in the process of construction. *Below:* Excavating for the Yale Bowl in 1913.

Lawrence Perry in 1914 in an article on "The Stadium in College Athletics" stated: "Stadia now exist at Harvard, Syracuse, Yale, Princeton, the College of the City of New York, and at Tacoma; are in course of construction or are projected at University of Michigan, Columbia, Cornell, and the University of Washington, Seattle."

What happened was that the immigrant, as he arrived at Ellis Island, was moved, in a rather fine spirit, to drop his native culture, to cease to be an Italian, Russian, or Pole, to become an American. But if he stayed in New York he had little opportunity to become American in the sense of taking on American culture, American ways; he found about him only uprooted Europeans like himself. As for the children of immigrants, their wish to drop the ways of their parents was self-conscious and aggressive — they tended to be a little ashamed of their parents' ways, often in rebellion against their parents' codes. They were determined to be American, or what they understood to be "American"; but they, like their parents, found about them not Americans but only uprooted orphans of culture like themselves. It was the common observation that what the younger generation in New York picked up as "American ways" was tragically inferior to what their alien parents had possessed as inherited and cherished traditions.

The consequence was, New York, while exercising the influence that a metropolis inevitably has upon a country's culture, did not itself have an American culture, nor a polyglot culture, nor any standard of culture at all. New York was a culture-void. To the new it presented no resistance of indigenous custom or native tradition. To any chance seed brought by the wind, it opposed no granite of crystallized tradition, but rather gave the febrile welcome of a hot-house. Such a soil is one in which new ideas, new points of view, new ways of life, can easily take root. The city, naked of tradition or ancient standard, was subject to infection by any ephemeral vogue that might arise from any source, whether generating spontaneously, or coming from abroad, or thrust upon it by commercial entrepreneurs. If from time to time it should generate momentary standards, they would

A well-known Washington landmark, thirty years ago. The New Jersey Avenue Station of the Baltimore and Ohio Railroad, as it appeared after successive remodellings.

A modern terminal, from the air. This photograph of the Union Station at Washington shows the arrangement of tracks.

From 1909–1914 many railroad terminals were rebuilt, including the Grand Central and Pennsylvania in New York. These pictures show the contrast between the old Baltimore and Ohio Station at Washington, D. C., and the new one which houses all the lines entering Washington.

be something new and hybrid, not felt to be kin to any nation that is homogeneous or has traditions.

New York, without culture standards of its own, wrought upon America the inevitable influence of a metropolis. It was America's culture capital. New York was, as it was expressed by one of the most genuinely American writers of his generation, Hamlin Garland, "the jury of final appeal," not only for Mr. Garland's art, but for all art, as well as manners, ideas — all that composes culture in the sense in which the word is used in this chapter. It dominated the theatre. Plays either were written for New York or were dependent for their survival on suiting the taste of New York. If New York liked them, they were successful and were sent with road companies to impress themselves on the taste of the rest of the country. The motion-picture business (though operated in California because of conditions of sunlight) was dominated from New York, and productions were aimed at New York audiences as their primary market. New York was the largest market for books. Of the sales of an average book, more than half would be made in the metropolitan area. Most of the critics whose applause or disapproval had influence on the success of books either lived in New York or reflected the New York spirit. The newspapers of New York, written necessarily to meet the taste of that city, became the models for the press of the rest of the country. Practically all the country's forms of art, almost all its vehicles for the introduction of new ideas, took their color from New York.[38a]

New York's lack of any relation to American stand-

[38a] Many persons, sensing strongly but vaguely the effect of New York on the country's culture, have undertaken to explain it on the ground that the authors and producers of many plays originating in New York are aliens, or New Yorkers affected by the alien influences of that city. Authorship has little to do with it. It is in New York as a market for culture — New York as audience — that the true explanation lies.

Theatre time in New York—ONCE.

Theatre time in New York—NOW.

From the New York *Herald Tribune,* December 23, 1928.

ards, its lack of any traditional standards whatever, made
it a hot-house for the new. Much of the new that took
root there was fine and wholesome. To no new play was
New York ever more spontaneously sympathetic than to
so gentle a phantasy as "Peter Pan" or so spiritual a revival as "Everyman." New York gave as hearty a welcome, as prolonged a patronage, to a simple American
play, "Lightnin'," and to the play of New England life,
"The Old Homestead," as to any importation from
abroad or any innovation generated in New York itself.
That many of the experiments in art which took hold in
America were good, that many of the new ways of
thought were an improvement, goes without saying.
Since practically all got their impetus from New York,
and since many were accepted by the country and were
generally approved, we must conclude that there was advantage for the nation in the quick receptiveness such a
soil as New York had for the new.

It was, however, a soil in which weeds could spring
up. The part of America lying outside New York City
felt itself frequently infested by noxious seeds carried
by the winds from the metropolis. Much of the social
history of the United States, and not a little of its political history, consisted of resistance by the country, especially the rural portions of it, to influences emanating
from New York. "Seen from the West and South,"
Hamlin Garland said, "Manhattan is a city of aliens
. . . who know little and care less for American traditions. After a lecture trip in the interior I return each
time to New York as to a foreign port. It is in the small
towns of Ohio, Indiana, Illinois, that I overtake the van-
ishing America of my youth."

On the one hand was the country clinging with instinctive affection to its old standards, on the other a
metropolis which generated fitful gusts of change, hectic

successions of vogues. With one instinct, that of imitation, entertained chiefly by the young, the country tended
to accept the innovation from the metropolis just because it was new, "the latest thing." With a deeper instinct, the country resented and resisted. Frequently the
opposition was organized, formal, statutory, expressing
itself in such devices as censorship of motion pictures by
towns or states. Practically always, however, for good or
ill, the new prevailed, until supplanted by another new
from the same spring.

VIII

Ideas — that is, products of the intellect — were no
more important than moods, that is, states of emotion.
Moods were invoked in part by art. Among the arts,
music, in its range from good to commonplace, had more
power to bring about moods than any other form. The
potency of music to incite national moods is illustrated by
the martial music of many peoples, the use of the "Marseillaise" by the French, of the "Wacht am Rhein" by
the Germans. It would not occur to the French military
authorities to sound their troops off to war with "Au
Claire de la Lune," or to the German high command
to have the military bands play "Stille Nacht, Heilige
Nacht."

The permanent effect of music on national moods and
states of mind was understood by Plato,[38b] who said that
"styles of music are never disturbed without affecting
the most important . . . institutions, manners, and customs"; by Mussolini, who, as a defense against American
jazz, decreed that at least half the programme at public
musical performances must be Italian; and by the philosopher who said "Let me write the ballads of a nation

[38b] The passage, from Plato's Republic, is printed more fully on page 245.

and I care not who makes its laws." (In this saying, it is the tune, not the words, that is important — the "Marseillaise" or the "Wacht am Rhein" sung with different words would have the same inspiration to a warring mood.)

In popular music as in other forms of art, New York was the source of the new themes and motifs which inundated America with increasing rapidity. Song-writing ceased to be the chance inspiration of a tuneful soul here and there. In the "noisiest, maddest quarter of the metropolis," called "Tin Pan Alley," the improvising of new tunes became an energetically pursued vocation, a highly commercialized trade. From this source came most of the music the people sang, hummed or whistled, or heard. In this quarter were born the songs that "fill the nation's fifteen hundred motion picture theatres, its eight hundred vaudeville houses, its six thousand dance halls, its eleven hundred cabarets. Most of the music in the air for which the three million radio sets reach out nightly is of Alley origin. It is the composing commissary for America's [popular music]."[38c]

In the process, the technique of salesmanship and promotion counted rather more than the technique of composition. "Songs are sold to you as deliberately and as grimly as beans. If you are under the innocent impression that the tune you whistled in your bath this morning got into your head by chance, it is only because the advertising of a song is more subtle than the advertising of beans, and the means by which you become familiar with it, less visible to the naked eye. If you are a vaudeville patron, you have often heard some one rise in the balcony and with apparently impromptu impetuosity, sing the refrain of a song that had just been sung on the stage. You think that such volunteered singing is just the

[38c] New York *Times,* February 8, 1925.

impulse of some lark who cannot resist bursting into the chorus of so infectious a melody. Actually the lark was engaged at a salary of $5 a week to encourage in this manner a song that was being introduced. . . . In Chicago, in Detroit, in San Francisco, like greyhounds straining at the leash, the pluggers[38d] of the branch offices are waiting for the word to carry the song to every cabaret and movie orchestra. The new tune drenches the country with the suddenness of a cloudburst. The very selling method[38e] is as much a part of the pace and rhythm of [rag-time and jazz] as that music, itself, is part of the pace and rhythm of America in the third decade of the twentieth century. Something of the nervousness, the jumpiness, and excitement of jazz itself, is in the very air of a music publishing house.[38f] . . . Faster, faster, faster — it is the tempo of a time which seizes upon a song, worries it to death, and throws it away — all in six months. On to the next and the next."[38g]

IX

Those whose profession is words, historians as well as critics, essayists, and other literary artists, frequently assume, perhaps through pride of calling, that new ideas, changed habits of thought, come into the world only or mainly through words. They assume that of all the

38d The commercial device of plugging was described by Charles K. Harris, who claimed to be its inventor: "I conceived the idea that I would have some one in the gallery to start the applause. The rest of the audience would surely follow. That was the real beginning of song plugging, a word suggesting the exploitation or advertising of a song by calling the public's attention to it either by singing it or applauding."

38e A New York song publisher says: "When we decide to get behind a song, every member of our organization works twenty-four hours a day trying to get it to the ear of the public. We don't overlook a chance, even to getting newsboys on the streets to whistle it."

38f This passage is made up of quotations adapted from a New York dramatic critic, Alexander Woolcott.

38g For a further discussion of the effect of popular music on "Institutions, Manners and Customs," see page 249 et seq.

sights that pass into man's mind through his eyes, the ones that work changes in his thinking are black marks upon white paper. It is tenable to suggest that the intellectual innovations which came to America during the period this history covers were due more to changes in the material world about him than to anything that came

Louis Bleriot leaving France. He was the first to cross the English channel in a monoplane, July 25, 1909.

to him through the pens of intelligentsia; that the average man's mind was modified more by the automobile than by any so-called leader of thought; more by Wilbur and Orville Wright than by the author of "The Origin of Species" or of "Mrs. Warren's Profession."

The changes wrought by books and plays were as a rule superficial, mere substitutions of new conventions for old. The changes that came from natural causes went deeper, were, one might almost say, changes in the very fibre of man's mind, at least in his mental processes.

Of all the agencies that influenced men's minds, that made the average man of 1925 intellectually different from him of 1900, by far the greatest was the sight of a human being in an airplane. Man had been taught and had believed since the beginning of time — indeed, he had not been taught, he believed through instinct — that he could not fly. The common form of words with which to express absolute utterness of impossibility was

· L I F E ·

From a drawing by E. B. Kemble in "Life," 1912.

THE FLIGHT OF TIME.

1901—Speed 10 miles an hour.	1912—Speed 50 miles an hour.
"Now do be careful, Fred.	"What's the matter, John?
You're scorching."	Can't you go a little faster?"

"he can no more do that than he can fly." Impossibility of human flight was one of the immutable certainties, one of the unalterable facts of nature, like death, the law of gravity, and the succession of the seasons. Negation of flight was in the same category as affirmation of God.

And now man saw human flight. That uprooting of one of man's oldest and most deeply imbedded immutabilities may reasonably be described as the most potent one intellectual influence of the time. If this immutability was mutable, what other dogma or authority might not be questioned; what other tradition or convention was sacrosanct? Of all the influences that worked for the liberation of men's minds, for emancipation from servitude to the accepted, the airplane was the greatest.

This was the symbol and the apotheosis of all the intellectual changes, superficial or fundamental, that came

THE STAGE COACH.
In '76 the "Flying Machine," a springless wagon, took two days to go from New York to Philadelphia.

THE MOTOR BUS
The modern Pullman motor-bus makes the trip from New York to Philadelphia in 4½ hours.

From *Vanity Fair*, July, 1926.

to man out of the material world, from new applications of natural law, new understandings of it.

The automobile acquainted the average man's mind with rudiments of physical law, to an extent that formal education as practiced at that time never would; working with gasoline, oil, and electricity gave to his thinking the greater exactness, the better understanding of cause and effect, which accompanies even elementary acquaintance with chemistry and physics.

Use of the new vehicle brought man freedom from

world-old limitations, from ancient subjections to circumstance. It modified time and distance. What had
been an hour became five minutes, what had been ten
miles became one. Before the motor-car came, the market in which man could sell his labor was limited to the
area he could reach on foot or by horse, or to the lines
of railroad or street-car along which he lived. With the
motor car, man could choose the buyer of his labor anywhere within a radius of thirty to fifty miles. By its
gift of quickly achievable distance, the automobile released man from subjection to small and stratified circles of public opinion. If the radius of a normal unit
of community hegemony and interdependence had been
five miles, it became, with the motor-car, thirty to sixty.
The automobile actually broke up the old cell of organized society, substituting an enlarged one. The process, going on for more than thirty years, gave rise to ferment and flux in every area of life.[39]

The average man, by the new scenes to which the automobile carried him, by the new sights brought before
his eyes through the motion-picture, by the immensely
increased quantity of reading matter brought to him
through growth of newspapers and periodicals and increase of books and spread of libraries — the average
man cerebrated, within his limitations, as he had not before. By these causes and by the diffusion of pictorial
and literary art, as well as information, the intellectual
energy of the period, looked upon as a quantity or in
terms of intensity, was measurably increased and speeded
up. But — excepting in science, invention,[40] and related

[39] So brief an exposition of the changes brought by the automobile as is possible here is sadly inadequate to the scope of the theme. Willa Cather, distinguished novelist, clear-sighted and sympathetic observer of her times, said in 1932
that the automobile brought greater change into the world than the Great War.
[40] See Chapter 2.

fields — it expressed itself not conspicuously in the emergence of unusual intellects, nor outstanding heights of individual achievement, but rather in an enlargement of the intellectual functioning of the average man in the aggregate; a quickening of the speed with which he thought, within his limitations, and an enlargement of the field in which he thought, again within his limitations. By the necessity put upon him of dealing with a more complex and faster-moving world, and of handling familiarly some intricate embodiments of physics and science, his mind was quickened. The older American who could nod upon the back of his horse, or let the lines lie slack upon the dashboard of his buggy while his mind occupied itself with reflection or revery, was succeeded now by one whose brain must be every minute upon the steering-wheel and pedals, his senses alert for signals and for danger. Man's mind was sharpened, though not necessarily deepened.

The new was accompanied by some illusion. The quantity of new facts brought before man by increase of printed words, the sights brought by the motion-picture, the words brought by the later-invented radio, did not necessarily bring him more wisdom. The ability to distil wisdom from experience remained what it had always been, a quality varying with the individual's ability to assimilate and reflect. And reflection, under the new order, became less possible. The speed of the new ways, the quantity of voices and sights rushing in upon man from the world, the enforced obedience to signals on the road, the summoning of bells in office and the home, reduced the time for reflection, made the mood for it difficult. The value of a message coming over the radio was not increased by the distance over which it came; that remained dependent upon the mind at the microphone.

It still remained true as it was when Carlyle said it, "Produce great men, the rest follows," and there was no proof that the new ways brought a larger number of great minds. The effect of many of the inventions and new ways was to make man less an individual, more a unit in the herd. The act of picking up a newspaper, and even more, of turning on the radio was in effect the slipping of a clutch which geared the individual into the common emotions, the mass thinking of the crowd, making him more subject to slogans, more responsive to stimulus, by those who wished to move the mass for their own ends. Man, surveying some of the results of the new, might reasonably have asked the inventors and innovators to reverse, for a while, their talents and direct themselves to a new need, insulation and isolation.

x

To catalogue the changes that came to men's minds would be to survey the whole of civilization. Much of the changed direction took the form of releases, chiefly releases from fears.

Man was freed from fear of hell — the notion of a literal hell of fire and brimstone receded to the backwaters of primitive sects in isolated communities. Man was freed from fear of divine wrath — God as a god of vengeance largely disappeared from men's minds. To some extent man was freed from fear of sin and sense of guilt — states of mind previously regarded as sin, such as doubt about literal interpretation of Scripture or some other religious dogmas, now became a virtue, at least in the world of intellect. Man was released from many arbitrary imperatives, from authoritative "thou shalts" and also "thou shalt nots." A command, whether its source was religion, government, or public opinion, unless it appealed to the reason of the individual, or to the accepted standards of those whose opinion he happened to respect, was often ignored and could always be questioned without sacrifice of society's esteem. With the command not to doubt passed the command to have faith — men had faith, perhaps as much as ever, but it

From a photograph © Underwood and Underwood.
Michael Pupin.

was a faith that germinated within himself and was maintained by inner conviction rather than outer rule.

Intellectually, and to a large extent in religion, it was the "Why?" era. Many of man's ancient speculations had been answered by science, many of his apprehensions dissipated. With the answers came freedom from many forms of dread, from dread of what, because it had not been understood, was supposed to be supernatural. By increased acquaintance with cause and effect, by new understanding of natural phenomena, the world, or certainly America, was almost wholly released, in many cases within a lifetime, from superstition.[41] A physicist of the period, Michael Pupin, who in his maturity became America's outstanding authority on the laws of sound, had been taught in his boyhood that thunder was the noise of Jehovah's car as he careened about the heavens.

XI

Whether the new was in every case better than the old is merely matter for philosophical dissertation; whether the convention of women smoking was better than the convention of women not smoking; whether any of the new ways was better or worse than that which it displaced, is neither here nor there. The fact of history is that the new conventions came in great numbers, and in every area of life.

Whether the average man, the world, was happier for the changes, is a question only to be answered adequately by answering inconclusively; by remembering that the "average man," while a useful abstraction for historians and statisticians, does not exist in fact. There is no such thing as a "world" that feels happiness or lacks it; the world is made up of flesh-and-blood human beings of every variety of temperament and predilection. Probably the number who entertain the delusion that all the old was golden, is roughly equal to the number who believe the fallacy that all the new is good. Some like change; others feel always the need of stability and security, of

---

[41] Not wholly. In 1922, the wife of the then President of the United States, Mrs. Warren G. Harding, frequently consulted an astrologer. The advertising columns of newspapers revealed that reading the future, by the palms of the hands or other empiric device, was a remunerative, if small, occupation. It is probable, however, that the patrons of such seers were, by the 1920's, mainly young folks out for fun, or acutely interested in their own egos; or, if older, were persons whose minds had not grown with their years.

fixed anchorages of faith, authority, rule, command, familiar paths, fixed ways, appointed hours, the protecting walls of rutted courses. These had a rather unhappy time. "Mr. Dooley," speaking for some of them, recalled the time when "half th' congregation heard mass with their prayer-books turrned upside down, an' they were as pious as anny." For himself "Th' Apostles' Creed niver was as con-vincin' to me afther I larned to r-read it as it was whin I cudden't read it, but believed it."

The Woolworth Building which held the record for height in the early years of the century.

DANCES OF THE DAY

The "Rag-Time Revolution" and the Dances It Introduced;
Including the Fox Trot, and the Turkey Trot (Which "De-
served All the Abuse It Got"); and the Bunny Hug, Which
Made the Transition from Rag-time to Rag-time's Dynastic
Descendant, Jazz. Together with Some Account of the High
Vogue of the Two-Step, and of the Temporary Eclipse of the
Waltz; and Brief Allusion to Some Older Dances of Candle-
lit Romance, the Schottische, the Polka, the Quadrille and
the Reels, Which Were Danced to the Music of "Pop Goes
the Weasel," "White Cockade," "Fisher's Hornpipe," "Old
Dan Tucker," "Virginia Reel," and Other Alluring Music.

"The winter of 1913–14," remarked a humorist of the
day, George Fitch, "will live in history because of the
dances, which have spared neither young nor old."

An account of the evolution of popular dances in
America during our times can appropriately begin with
a list of the earlier ones, set out metrically in the chorus
of a popular song written in 1890, "The Party at Odd
Fellows Hall":

Waltzes, polkas, lancers, gallops, glides;
Portland fancy, quadrilles and reels and slides![1]
High-lows, di-dos, how we danced them all!

[1] This enumeration of the dances familiar in 1890 and in the late 1880's and
before, omitted, for reasons of metre perhaps, the Mazourka, the Gavotte, the
Schottische, the Newport, the Redowa, the Varsovienne, the Knickerbocker,
the German, the Cotillion.

Also, this metrical list, since it had to do with "society dances," omitted a
group of solo dances, the clog, the jig, the buck-dance or buck-and-wing, the
highland fling, the hoe-down, which, to the tune of the fiddle, the mouth organ,

From a drawing by Gordon Grant.

An invitation to dance.

Old style.　　　　　　　New style.

"May I have the pleasure of the next　　"Say, kiddo, I've got you cinched for
waltz?"　　　　　　　　　　　　　the Bunny."
"I shall be very happy, I am sure."　　"Right, old sport.　Guess I'll keep
　　　　　　　　　　　　　　　　you a-hopping."

That compilation of the popular dances of the early
1890's had intimate association with the highest aca-

---

the accordion, or the jewsharp, had at all times been danced in quarters not designated as "society."

The jig was, from the earliest days, the most familiar solo dance in America
(and was still, in 1932, familiar in the Southern Appalachians, in the hills of
Arkansas, in the West, and in other parts of the country where old ways survived).

The airs to which the jig was danced — many of them served also for reels
— had names suggesting liveliness, almost of themselves enough to stir one's
toes to gaiety. Many of them came from England, or, in a larger number of
cases, from Ireland. "Haste to the Wedding," "May Morning," "Fox-hunter's
Jig," "Mug of Brown Ale," "Connaught Man's Rambles," "Bunch of Currants,"
"Smash the Windows," "Top of Cork Road," "Over the Stone," "Wink and
She Will Follow You," "Toss the Feathers," "Up the Road to Lancaster,"
"Rocky Road to Dublin," "Pretty Girl Milking the Cow," "Kerry Girls," "Irish
Lassies," "Little House Under the Hill," "The Maid on the Green," "Money
in Both Pockets," "Drop of Brandy," "Barn Door," "Paddy Whack," "Young
May Moon, "Garryowen."

President Theodore Roosevelt said that for him all music was divided into
two classes, "Garryowen" — and the rest.

Garry Owen (JIG.)

demic circles. Fate seems to have had a determined intention that the Harvard College Class of 1891 should be known by the Episcopal bishops it produced: Bishop Rhinelander of Pennsylvania, Bishop Slattery of Massachusetts, Bishop Root of Hankow, China; together with such secular dignitaries as Nicholas Longworth, Speaker of the House of Representatives, 1925–1931; and Frank Hitchcock, Postmaster-General in the administration of President Taft. Some impish little brother of fate, however, brought it about that for several college generations the Class of 1891 was most familiarly remembered for the light-hearted singer who wrote "The Party at Odd Fellows Hall."

Jacob Wendell, Jr. — abbreviated to "Jac" and called as if spelled "Jack" — was the son of a New York merchant of the old-time type, the youngest of four brothers, all Harvard students and three of them graduates, a diversely talented four. One, Evert Jansen Wendell, was among the fastest college sprinters of his day; another, Barret Wendell,[2] was long Professor of English at Harvard, where he wrote books about literature, caused generations of students to remember him for his stern insistence on accurate use of "shall" and "will," and led the country to think of him as an ultra-purist in

[2] Barrett Wendell's books included "The Temper of the Seventeenth Century in English Literature," "Cotton Mather," "A Literary History of America."

taste with an attitude of permanent deploring toward many things that pleased the multitude.

The youngest brother wore feathers of a brighter color. "Jac" Wendell had tastes and capacities which made him the most gay-natured, and perhaps the most

Courtesy of the Players Club.
Jacob (Jac) Wendell, Jr.

beloved, Harvard man of his day. He could play the cornet — to hear him "double-tongue" a polka or draw out the long tones in the "Lost Chord" was marvellous; he could likewise whistle double, could actually whistle duets all by himself — whistle successions of thirds and keep one note going on while he whistled the tune with, so to speak, another voice; through a similarly extraordinary power of super-ventriloquism he could imitate, not merely a dog-fight but a dog riot — big dog, little dog, bull-dog, setter-dog, and sundry more species, all in a violent medley of barks, growls, yaps, yips, yowls, and every other vocal expression of canine emotion. Finally, "Jac" Wendell could write songs.

One morning in the autumn of 1890, during a "Fine Arts" lecture by the revered Charles Eliot Norton, which Wendell was "attending without attention," his mind wandered into the world of the more vivacious arts, and he wrote the words of "The Party at Odd Fellows Hall." Immediately after the lecture he whirled his classmate and friend, Robert W. Atkinson,[3] to a piano in the "Hasty Pudding Club," where Atkinson composed music appropriate to the lively spirit of the words. The song was sung at a Hasty Pudding show just before the Christmas holidays, came to the attention of Oliver Ditson Company, was published, and ranked almost with "Daisy Bell" and "Down Went McGinty" as a popular song of the nineties.[4] To-day, "The Party at Odd Fellows Hall" has historical value, as a list of popular dances that came spontaneously to the mind of a young man of 1890 when in a mood of recalling his own dancing pleasures.

II

The Coming of the Two-Step

Jacob Wendell, writing his metrical list of the dances of 1890, did not mention the two-step, because it did not exist. Within that year, John Philip Sousa came to the front of the American stage with his incomparably stirring march, "The Washington Post" — and when America's ears heard the "Washington Post March," America's feet were moved to a new beat and a special

[3] Son of Edward Atkinson, an economist famous in the 1890's and himself distinguished as a musician and composer.

[4] Wendell, after some years of amateur association with the Comedy Club of New York, went on the professional stage, and was making headway when in 1911 he died of pneumonia contracted while rehearsing a part in "Bluebird."

quality of liveliness. Therein was born the "two-step."[5]
It was a simple dance, not much more than a double-
quick march, with a skip in each step, done as rapidly as

From a photograph by Marceau.
John Philip Sousa.

a couple could conveniently go forward, backward, and
turn. Its vogue — and no dance of American origin ever
had a greater or a longer — was sustained partly by its
own merit, partly by the succession of march tunes with
which Sousa supplied music for it — march tunes "with
swank and valorous rhythm fitting the gay spirit of
youth, tripping, laughing" — "Stars and Stripes Forever," "Liberty Bell," "El Capitan," "High School Cadets," and some ninety more. For fully a quarter-century the name "Sousa" had a definite connotation, be-

[5] Sousa, then leader of the United States Marine Band, wrote this march as
the result of a chance street meeting with one of the proprietors of the Washington *Post* newspaper, which was sponsoring a gathering of school children for
June 15, 1889.

came almost a common noun; as generally as Sherlock Holmes meant detective stories, or Edison electricity, so did Sousa mean marches, two-steps.

Sheet Music Edition
P. 951   *To Gen. Frank Hatton and Mr Beriah Wilkins.*

THE WASHINGTON POST.
MARCH.

Printed through the courtesy of Carl Fischer, Inc.

III

Some Dances That Passed

The two-step wrought a revolution, elbowing into retirement the older dances that had served to express lively spirits. Into oblivion went the schottische, the gallop, the polka (with its variation, "heel and toe," — one, two, three, hop; one, two, three, hop), with all of which one could caper and kick up one's heels. Went also about this time, for whatever reason, a charming group called square-dances.[6] The lancers (with its variation, the Saratoga) disappeared entirely, taking a seat alongside the minuet[7] in some gallery where former belles of the

[6] So called because danced by four couples standing so as to compose a square.

[7] The minuet had practically disappeared at least a decade before 1890, though one man not yet elderly, with whom I talked during the preparation of this chapter, Mark Requa of San Francisco, recalled learning the minuet at

dance looked on at a new generation in occupation of the
floor. Into semi-oblivion went the quadrille,[8] with its
glamorous figures, often called out by the orchestra
leader, or by some one on the floor who became master of
ceremonies by personal initiative and common consent,
and was known as the "figure caller," a position of some
elevation in the circles that danced the quadrille: Choose
Partners![9] Address your Partners! All Promenade!
Gentlemen Forward! Ladies Forward! Form Circle!
Centre and Back! Ladies Chain! Balance All! Cross
Over! Swing Partners! All Hands Round! Right and
Left! Change Partners! Forward and Back! Form

dancing school. It is doubtful if the minuet was ever danced as a number on an
ordinary programme after 1860. Older persons, however, still had affectionate
memories of the formality of its opening: Salute Partner Right! Salute Partner Left! Salute Corners! All join hands — and its grave crescendo of stately
steps; slew step, balance step, minuet; and its formal bows by the men and
sweeping curtseys by the ladies (accompanied by a gesture of opening the fan),
and the small presents, called "favors," that were a feature of it. The minuet
was a dance of dignity and grace of carriage, a dance of the day when the test
of a good dancer was sometimes expressed by saying: "He could dance with a
glass of water on his head."

Mrs. Frederic McLaughlin (Irene Castle), who knows much about dancing,
having read the proof of this chapter, doubts whether "favors" were an incident
of the minuet, though they were of the cotillion. She writes also that she doubts
whether "the minuet could be danced with a glass of water on one's head; the
gentlemen's bows were exceedingly low, and the head was supposed to drop
forward while bowing; the ladies' curtsey was a little more upright, the head
tilted on one side."

8 Some who have read the proofs of this chapter assert strongly that it was
not the quadrille, but the reel, in which there were "figures" and a "figure-
caller." Others remember the custom to have been as here described. The fact
appears to be that in most parts of America the terms "quadrille" and "reel"
were interchangeable.

The quadrille was danced commonly to the music called "plain quadrille."
It could be danced, and often was, to some other familiar music. In the South
and Southwest, the quadrille was sometimes danced to music locally favored,
"Natchez Under the Hill," "The Arkansas Traveller," and — intriguing name —
"Cotton-Eyed Joe."

9 The figures are given here, not in the order in which they took place, but
merely as they come back to the memory of one who has not heard their joyous
imperativeness for more than thirty years. For that matter, the order of the
figures was not fixed, but varied with the whim of the caller.

Another series of calls, quoted from a memory of the 1890's, included:

Honor your partner!　　　　　　　Promenade across!
Corners the same.　　　　　　　　Promenade back!
Head couples right and left through!　Change your ladies!

Arch and Balance Through! All Join Hands! All Chassez![10] and, at the end, Thank Your Partner Kindly!

With the square dances went their close relatives, the reels and hornpipes, called, when they first came out of

From a drawing by J. Paul Burnham in "Judge," February, 1912.

Where are the good old decent dances of yesterday?

France, "Contre danses." The French phrase was pronounced, imperfectly, "contra dances" by teachers who called themselves "professors of the terpsichorean art"; and was still more imperfectly translated, in the average American vernacular, to "country dances." From "country dances" the descriptive classification was sometimes

[10] Often pronounced, and sometimes spelled, when spelling was called for, "sashay."

changed to "barn dances"; for this name there was no
justification except that one of the most familiar of the
tunes was called "Dancing in the Barn." Some of the
best-known were "Miss McLeod's Reel" (known wherever there was dancing); "The Fisher's Hornpipe"
(equally familiar); "Money Musk," "Pop Goes the

Miss Mc Leod's Reel.

Weasel" — the very name was wine to the heels — "Old
Dan Tucker," "Portland Fancy," "Harvest Home,"
"Speed the Plow," "The Irish Merry-Making," "Sail-
or's Hornpipe," "Devil's Dream," "Pigeon's Wing,"
"Holes in the Carpet," "Peas Upon a Trencher," "White
Cockade," "Green Fields of Erin," "Rakes of Mal-
low," "Irish Washerwoman," "Bricklayer's Hornpipe,"
"Blackberry Blossoms," "The Wind That Shakes the
Barley," and the "Sir Roger de Coverly," known in
America as the "Virginia Reel."[10a]

Those were all dances of candle-lit romance;[10b] the
only one that survived[11] into electric light was the "Virginia Reel," which as late as the early 1900's was frequently danced as a kind of jolly finale to the evening,
just before the dancers sang "Auld Lang Syne" as they

[10a] Many of the tunes for reels served also for jigs, and the names of some
reel-tunes will be found in the list of jig-tunes on page 224 (footnote).

[10b] Mrs. Barrett Wendell, Jr., who has read the proofs of this chapter, recalls
the lancers was danced in Boston as late as 1903.

[11] During the 1920's Henry Ford attempted to revive these old-time dances.
Visitors to Dearborn on business or other affairs of serious import had the experience of being led to a room in which fiddlers played "Old Dan Tucker" or
"Pop Goes the Weasel," and of being swept by Mr. Ford and members of his
family and his staff into the figures of the reel and lancers. Mr. Ford dedicated part of a weekly periodical he published, and made other efforts to cause
the rest of America to appreciate the old dances as much as he did; but found
it more difficult to popularize the lancers than the automobile he made. The
very fibre of America seemed to have been attuned to a new tempo, to which
Model T was more adapted than the graceful sweep of the quadrille.

sought their way to the sleighs or buggies that would take them home.

IV

Hey-Day of the Waltz

During the late 1890's and the earliest of the 1900's the two-step and the waltz were substantially the whole of American dancing, dividing every program about equally between them.

The "programme" in those days was a literal thing, a little card-board folder, decorated in the spirit of its purpose, containing a formal list of the dances to be played, and opposite each dance-title a blank space in which the dancers wrote — with a tiny pencil attached to the programme by a silk cord — the names of the partners to whom they had engaged themselves. Days before the ball, in some sections the "hop," youths called girls upon the telephone, or, in homes where the telephone had not yet arrived, sent messages or called in person to ask the pleasure of the first waltz, or the first two-step, or in the failure of priority, for the first dance the girl had free. Those old programmes containing the names of Laura and Lydia and Edith and Rebie and Bess, Tom and Will and Jim and Jack, became treasured mementoes of persons who, when they became the parents of debutantes in the 1920's, saw with some regret the pell-mell modern dance in which there was no programme, the music never paused, and the whole effect seemed, to the older generation, a little hoydenish, certainly less sentimental and stately than the way such things had been conducted about the turn of the century.

Persons who were at the dancing age[12] during the late

_____

[12] At that time the dancing age commonly ended with the late twenties for women and the early thirties for men. Hardly any woman danced after thirty. The man who kept it up after thirty-five was called an "old beau," he had to

1890's and early 1900's, up to about 1910, carried for the rest of their lives affectionate memories of some very popular waltz-songs which, looked back upon in the light of a quarter-century later, can be recognized as marking the end of an era, their passing the sign of a deep-reaching change in manners, popular mood, and the tempo of the national pulse.

"The Band Played On"[13] (1895), "Waltz Me Around Again, Willie" (1906), and "Yip-I-Addy-I-Ay"[13a] (1908) were far from being at the head of popular waltz-music; that distinction was kept by "The Beautiful Blue Danube" throughout the entire period of the waltz's leadership among dances. Nor were these American pieces, as music, as good as Franz Lehar's "The Merry Widow Waltz,"[14] the other Viennese creation which, during the early 1900's, divided waltz leadership with the "Blue Danube."

---

have bachelorhood as an excuse, and even then suffered some dis-esteem; was looked upon as one who made dancing and its associated diversions his career, and therefore not to be taken seriously in his ordinary vocation.

[13] As well or better known by another name, the words of a line in the chorus: "Casey Would Waltz With the Strawberry Blonde."

[13a] Some persons who have read the proofs of this chapter and who have affectionate recollections of the dance-tunes of the early part of the century, insist that "Over the Waves" should be included in any list of the best waltzes, or the most popular.

[14] Formally called "I Love You so" (1907). The words accompanying really achieved the spirit of the waltz. Some lines that became familiar were:

> Golden glowing lamps are throwing light above,
> While the swaying tune is saying love, love, love!
> And the feet of dancers sound it as they go . . .
> Though our lips may say no word,
> Yet in the heart a voice is heard . . .
> Love that hovers over lovers, speaks in song,
> In the fingers' clasp that lingers close and long.
> And the music answers swaying to and fro,
> Telling you "It's true, it's true, I love you so."

These words from "The Merry Widow" are printed here through the courtesy of Chappell-Harms, Inc.

Other words sung to the "Merry Widow Waltz," as they lingered in the memory of Carolyn Wells (Houghton) in 1932 were:

> If I say not what I may not let you hear;
> Still the swaying waltz is saying love me, dear.

"The Band Played On," "Waltz Me Around Again, Willie," and "Yip-I-Addy-I-Ay" were not only good dance music, they lent themselves to song. Whenever at dances the orchestras swept into either of them, young voices all over the floor broke joyously into the words, the chorus floating through open windows to stir the summer trees in a charming burst that was "youth and love and that sweet time." By whatever quality it was in these two songs that inspired the dancers to sing as they waltzed, they had the effect of reviving, for the few years of a passing vogue, one of the oldest and most spontaneous traits of the human race, the association of dancing and singing.[15] "The Band Played On" and "Waltz Me Around Again, Willie," followed the older tradition that a popular song must be a ballad, tell a story. The stories in these were about characters that dancers would naturally be fond of, waltz "fans."

In "The Band Played On" the hero was one Matt Casey, who "hired a hall" and "formed a social club that beat the town for style."[15a]

Casey's club was typical of that time:

> When pay-day came around each week,
> They greased the floor with wax . . .
> Each Saturday you'd see them,
> Dressed up in Sunday clothes.
> Each lad would have his sweetheart by his side.
> Such kissing in the corner,
> Such whispering in the hall,
> And telling tales of love behind the stairs.

[15] In the period of man's earliest expression of emotion, singing and dancing were one action. Which was the earlier impulse, whether dancing suggested singing or *vice versa,* is a point about which the erudite differ. The painstaking "Encyclopedia Britannica" leans to the view that "the dance had its origin in the mimetic actions which are the natural accompaniment of rudimentary song."

[15a] The words of "The Band Played On" are printed here through the courtesy of Shapiro, Bernstein & Co.

In every line of the song Casey was emphasized as "the favorite," "the man that ran the ball." No mere "dancing fool" was Casey; he had initiative, energy, organizing ability, and the other attributes of leadership, including strong personal magnetism.[16] As is becoming to worthy leadership, Casey accepted responsibility for his full share of the kissing and love-making. So also of the dancing:

> When Casey led the first grand march,
> They all would fall in line
> Behind the man who was their joy and pride.

At one point Casey was torn between two summonses to his function of leadership:

> At twelve o'clock exactly, they all would fall in line,
> Then march down to the dining hall and eat.
> But Casey would not join them . . .
> He stayed upstairs to exercise his feet.

> While the others went off for the lesser delight,
> Casey would waltz with a strawberry blonde,[17]

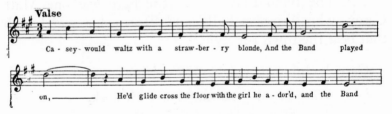

Ca - sey would waltz with a straw-ber - ry blonde, And the Band played
on, _____ He'd glide cross the floor with the girl he a - dor'd, and the Band

> And the band played on.
> He'd glide 'cross the floor with the girl he adored . . .
> He'd ne'er leave the girl with the strawberry curls,
> While the band played on.

Casey was always last to leave the floor:

When the ball was over and the band played "Home, Sweet Home" . . .

16 The terminology of the 1920's would say Casey had "IT," or "sex appeal" abbreviated, in the motion-picture world, to "S.A."

17 To the average American, the subjunctive "Casey would waltz" seemed too weak for the spirit of this song. Many sang it in the affirmative, "Casey, he'd waltz." A strawberry blonde was merely a red haired girl.

[Casey] thanked them very kindly for the favors they had shown,
Then he'd waltz once more with the girl that he loved best.[18]

Finally, conforming to the current taste which in several forms of art insisted upon explicit assurance that the hero and heroine married and lived happy ever after:

Most all the friends are married now that Casey used to know,
And Casey too has taken him a wife,
The girl he used to waltz with upon the ball-room floor,
Is happy Mrs. Casey now for life.

"Waltz me a - round a-gain Wil - lie, a - round, a - round, a - round;___ The

"Waltz Me Around Again, Willie" was also about a waltz enthusiast, in this case a lady:

Willie Fitzgibbons who used to sell ribbons,
And stood up all day on his feet,
Grew very spooney on Madeline Mooney,
Who'd rather be dancing than eat.
Each evening she'd tag him, to some dance hall drag him,
And when the band started to play,
She'd up like a silly and grab tired Willie,
Steer him on the floor and she'd say:

Waltz me around again Willie, a-round, a-round, a-round,
The music is dreamy, it's peaches and creamy,
Oh! don't let my feet touch the ground.
I feel like a ship on an ocean of joy,
I just want to holler out loud, "Ship ahoy!"
Oh! waltz me around again Willie, a-round, a-round, a-round.[18a]

Willie De Vere was a dry goods cashier,
At his desk he would sit all the day,
Till his doctor advised him to start exercising,
Or else he would soon fade away.

18 In the reprinting of some of the popular songs in this chapter, the author has taken the liberty of assuming that the writers of the songs would not object to immaterial changes of grammar and spelling.

18a "Waltz Me Around Again, Willie," is printed here through the courtesy of the Paull-Pioneer Music Co.

One night this poor looney met Madeline Mooney,
Fitzgibbons then shouted with joy,
"She's a good health regainer, you've got a great trainer,
Just wait till she hollers, my boy,

"Waltz me around again, Willie."[19]

E—Yip - I - Ad-dy -I - Ay, - I - Ay!   E—Yip - I - Ad-dy -I -

"Yip-I-Addy-I-Ay" (1908), beginning the departure from the ballad tradition, was merely an episode:

Young Herman Von Bellow, musical fellow,
Played on a big cello each night
Sweet melodies rare in a dance garden where
Dancers danced round and round with delight.
One night he saw dancing a maid so entrancing,
His heart caught on fire inside;
And music so mellow he sawed on his cello,
She waltzed up to him and she cried:
Yip-I-Addy-I-Ay-I-Ay!   Yip-I-Addy-I-Ay!
I don't care what becomes of me
When you play me that sweet melody
Yip-I-Addy-I-Ay-I-Ay! My heart wants to holler: Hurray!
Sing of joy, sing of bliss, home was never like this,
Yip-I-Addy-I-Ay![19a]

A bit of verse that originated in 1890 and lasted as
long as the waltz's high popularity was "Learning Mc-
Fadden to Waltz," reciting the endeavors of one Clarence McFadden, who, craving to be able to dance, sought
a teacher, and was told:

One, two, three, balance like me.
You're quite a daisy, but you have your faults;
Your left foot is lazy, your right foot is crazy,
But don't be unaisy, I'll learn you to waltz.

19 "Waltz Me Around Again, Willie," was adapted to a political use by cartoonists to picture the position of William R. Hearst when, in the exigencies
of his candidacies for Governor and Mayor of New York, he embraced political
leaders from Tammany and elsewhere, whom formerly he had denounced.

19a Reproduced here through the courtesy of Shapiro, Bernstein & Co.

These waltz airs, and the youths who sang them as they danced, may be said to have been present at the beginning of a temporary eclipse of the waltz. It was about

From a Victrola advertisement of 1914.

Dancing the hesitation waltz in 1914.   Note the hobble-skirt in the foreground.

1910[20] that this, following the other older and slower dances, gave way (with a stately bow, we may be sure) to

[20] While the waltz was temporarily eclipsed, it did not cease to be danced, and as late as 1914 continued to compete with rag-time and jazz. In that year, Mrs. Carolyn Wells [Houghton] writes the author, "I translated the words of an opera by Franz Lehar which contained the most beautiful waltz song he ever composed. The opera opened at Washington, where Secretary of War Lindley M. Garrison gave me a box party. The chorus ran:

"Waltz, you siren of melody, soft and sweet,
Waltz, I follow you ever with tireless feet;
Waltz, you lure me away to a dream of bliss,
Waltz, you're like the soft glory of love's first kiss."

a vogue of dances with a more strident tempo, a jerkier motion.

The waltz was a dance for gentle folk; it must have developed in the upper stratum of the formal society of continental Europe, since, for its best rendition, it called for the ample floor-space of stately halls to accommodate its graceful sweep. Physically, the waltz must have felt a little cramped in the comparatively small parlors of American homes during the 1890's, but essentially that leisurely dance was in tune with the spirit of the American generation whose favorite it was. With the growth of cities, and with the preponderance of the city in determining American usages in every field, came flats, later called apartment houses, and also public halls, where any one was admitted that had the fee, the crowded floors of which were better adapted to the up-and-down jerkings of newly devised dances, than to the spacious sweep of the waltz. The change was symbolical of what was going on in several other aspects of American life. "The Band Played On," but for a different kind of dance, in a changed world.

The jilting of the waltz was expressed with rather heartless frankness in a song of 1907,[21] "I'd Rather Two-Step Than Waltz, Bill":[21a]

> Waltzing is fine, Bill, but not for mine, Bill;
> It isn't in it with the two-step a minute.

And later, even more roughly:

> But waltzing, dearie, makes me so weary[22] . .
> That slow dance is no dance, dearie . . .

It was not the two-step that elbowed the waltz into desuetude; the two-step generously shared the floor about equally with the waltz for some twenty years.

[21] The two-step was popular before this, as early as the 1890's.
[21a] Printed through courtesy of Remick Music Corp.
[22] Not in the physical sense, for the waltz was less fatiguing than its hoydenish successors. "Makes me weary" or "makes me tired" was slang of that time for "bores me," or "irritates me."

Then, about 1912, two-step and waltz alike became victims of a new style of dancing called, generically, rag-

A section of the drawing by F. Matania in the London "Spur," 1913.

Rag-time dancing in the new ballroom of the Ritz-Carlton Hotel, New York. The society craze for dancing new and strange steps spread over the country, affecting young and old alike.

time, after the music that went by the same name, the fantastic variations of which were described, with singular aptness, by the names of various animals.[23] Before these pushing newcomers, one can see the waltz retiring, its disdain concealed by the self-controlled manners of its day, as it went to join the minuet and the lancers, all, for the time, wall-flowers to the temporary taste. "The slow tempo, the softness, the gentle sentimentality of the waltz lent itself peculiarly to song, and to memory"[24] — and in memory it was destined chiefly to abide for a generation or so. The waltz never left the floor completely, however, nor the affections of those who had danced it; it was "like a strain of poetry that we cannot forget, a bit of our best selves that does not desert us." The waltz could never die; rather, one might say, it preferred to "sit out" a few numbers, so long as the rowdy gate-crashers monopolized the floor.

v

The Rag-Time Revolution

A little before 1900 there appeared, on an occasional dance floor, in a pause on the programme between a waltz and a two-step, the cake-walk. The cake-walk was not really a dance, but a solo performance of a high-spirited youth, at first young men only, who imitated a colored man strutting in a prize contest, the distinguishing characteristics being the head held high, chin up, elbows out, shoulders thrown back, and, especially prominent, an exaggerated frontal protuberance. Occasionally it was walked, or pranced, by a couple in a side-by-side position, arms locked. The cake-walk was the first appearance of a negro movement in ball-room dancing, harbinger of more to follow, much more.

About 1895 a touring player, visiting New Orleans,

---

[23] For an account of the rag-time dances, see page 244.
[24] The quotation is adapted from Mr. Gilbert Seldes.

observed something which, years later, he described: "It was in a café, and there was a little negro at the piano. He would play one of the standard songs of the day, and then announce, 'Here's the new music, the way us plays it.' . . . I'll never forget the way that negro chased himself up and down the piano."[25]

The "new music, the way us plays it," was what later came to be called rag-time.[26] The word, primarily the name for a new type of musical syncopation, was later applied to both the music and the dance that came to accompany it. Strictly, rag-time was not, in the beginning, a "new music," nor any kind of music, but rather

[25] Fred Stone.

[26] And still later, after some evolution, jazz. The precise connection between rag-time and its successor jazz is a point about which the present historian is insufficiently musical to be technical. Authorities prevailingly agree that rag-time led to jazz, that rag-time was wholly negroid in origin, and that jazz added to rag-time some traits from other primitive sources.

About the origin of jazz as well as rag-time there are innumerable theories and versions. A distinguished musician, Mr. Robert W. Atkinson, who has read the proof of this chapter, writes me: "It seems probable that rag-time and jazz are both the same. But rag-time began at the piano as narrated above in the text, whereas the most plausible explanation that I have heard of the term jazz is: there was once a negro drummer in a band whose nickname was Charles, colloquially abbreviated to 'Chaz.' It was his custom, when the trio of a march was repeated by the band, to embellish it with remarkable rhythmic variations on the drum; and the leader would call upon the drummer on these occasions by saying, 'Now, Chaz' or 'Now, Chaz it.' Thus jazzing a tune on the drum was rhythmically little different from 'ragging' a tune on the piano."

Mr. William O. Inglis, a journalist and author of books, with an accurate mind and vise-like memory, who had a wide-ranging experience in the America of about the turn of the century, agrees with others that New Orleans either was the starting place of rag-time or was a scene of its early development. He writes: "I saw negroes dancing rag-time in negro dives 'back of town' in New Orleans in 1892."

Mr. James W. Fitzpatrick, long a performer on the vaudeville stage during the early part of the century, admonishes the author that "you, like Woolcott and Seldes and the rest, are all wrong in the explanation of rag-time and jazz when you say it was a *conscious* jeer at the older music. You all make the mistake of reading something into the thing its authors and promoters never dreamed of. It was simply a new form of musical composition which caught the public fancy because it was *new*, because it had an unconscious but direct sex reaction, and because people who were ordinarily tone deaf and tune dumb were able to sing it. But to imagine that Berlin and his imitators had a definite message to convey or were trying to interpret a national mood is, to me, silly. Besides I have come to the conclusion that explanations of anything are usually wrong."

a comic perversion of music, a whimsical caricature, like a fringe of gargoyles on a cathedral. It was not negro music; it was negroes "kidding"[27] white man's music. After the negro had been freed from slavery, his dawning sense of release, together with his natural exuberance of spirits, led him to entertain, when among his own kind, an attitude of inward chuckling toward many of the white man's ways and highly formalized institutions — his own comic relief for the unctuous deference he felt obliged to pay to white usage when the white man was looking. Negro "ear-singers" in barber-shop quartettes, performing to audiences chiefly of their own race, took comic liberties with the white folks' music. Singing "Home, Sweet Home," they took advantage of the pauses in this slow music to repeat the regular melody — but with the accents quickened and shifted, making an effect of comical pertness. The humor of it lay in the surprise; hearers recognized the authentic music of an old familiar favorite, but done in a quickened[28] tempo, as far as possible from the original mood. White folks, hearing the new syncopation, were amused, regarding it as a ludicrous travesty. With encouragement, negro singers, and white fabricators of negro music, expanded what at first had been a whimsical curlicue on the notes of old music, to a point where the original notes were almost displaced by the injected syncopation. Musically, the effect was one of melody with a fringe of tatters — "ragged time" music. With the vocal variations on the notes went a shuffling of the feet, and this was the genesis of rag-time as a dance.

At first, both the music and the dance that accompa-

[27] Rag-time, after it developed, was called "kidding the classics." An epithet hurled at it was "musical profanity." Irving Berlin called jazz "musical pandemonium."

[28] The process, years later, supplied a new verb, to "rag," subsequently to "jazz," or "jazz up," or "pep up," and was used in areas far afield from music, in all sorts of situations where speed and action were called for.

nied it were performed by negroes for their own amusement; frequently, negro song and dance men, professionally engaged in catering to honky-tonks and cabarets, would give a rag-time performance for white men, who applauded it in somewhat the spirit of going slumming. Rag-time was, as Booth Tarkington put it, indigenous "to the underworld or circles where nature is extremely frank and rank." Occasionally a white youth, on a dance-room floor, would introduce, as an amusing and slightly shocking stunt, an imitation of a darky dancing rag-time.

After about ten years of this dubious existence, as an habitué of cabarets, and an occasional intruder on dance-floors, tolerated as amusing, but decidedly not approved, rag-time came, about 1910, into conjunction with a young musical genius. The result of that juxtaposition was a revolution in American popular music, which marked or accompanied, or was the cause or the expression, or all four, of a change in national manners, such as Plato must have had in mind when he said:

The introduction of a new kind of music must be shunned ... since styles of music are never disturbed without affecting institutions. The new style, gradually gaining a lodgment, quietly insinuates itself into manners and customs; and from these it issues a greater force, displaying the utmost impudence, until it ends by overturning everything, both in public and in private.

VI

Irving Berlin (born Israel Baline) was destined later to have a wide and elevated fame, to excel every other American composer of popular music during his generation, in the sense of writing the largest number of good songs on the widest variety of themes, having his songs sung by a larger number of Americans, and — particular cause of his importance — exerting a greater influence[29] upon American popular music. As a part of his versatile talent, Berlin was to show a capacity for writing exquisite songs of sentiment, beautiful waltz rhythms — of being, indeed, extremely sentimental.

Irving Berlin.

That Berlin had within him the capacity to achieve such variety was due to his possession of that attribute of genius which is able to take on the atmosphere of its surroundings, to "sense" the spirit of its locale, and having sensed it, to express it in art. "Berlin," wrote Gilbert Seldes, "succumbs to influence, from his own life and from [his] surroundings." And Berlin's surroundings when he came into conjunction with rag-time had been the surroundings in which rag-time at that stage was

29 "I can hardly remember the time when I was not singing something by Berlin; a whole generation of adults in America has grown up on his songs." — Gilbert Seldes.

likely to be; his background and experience up to that time illustrating the sad limitation which too often constitutes America's careless welcome to its immigrants.

Berlin,[30] brought from Russia when he was four years old, deprived of his father at eight, was thrown into the

A colored jazz orchestra in action.

welter that was New York. He sold papers, carried telegrams, sang songs in saloons for such pennies as the sentimental would chuck on the sawdust at his feet. He slept where he could get a bed for ten cents a night; changed his name for a time to an Irish one, Cooney; became a "busker"[31] on the Bowery; "plugged" songs from the balcony of Tony Pastor's Music Hall for five dollars a week; became a singing waiter in a Chinatown restaurant, "Nigger Mike's Place," where he swabbed the floor foul with butts of Sweet Caporals, and took ad-

[30] Berlin was the youngest of eight children of a refugee rabbi who, harried from village to village in Russia, fled with his family to America in 1892.

[31] A singer who seeks his audiences on the streets, or where he can.

vantage of occasional moments of leisure to pick out, imitatingly, on the black keys of the piano, the tunes he had heard the day before on the barrel-organs of China- town. Then, at twenty-three, he wrote the song from which rag-time really dates, "Alexander's Ragtime Band."[32]

With "Alexander's Ragtime Band," Berlin lifted rag-

Come on and hear,........ Come on and hear............ Al - ex - an - der's rag-time band,........ Come on and hear.....Come on and hear,........... It's the best band in the land,...........

(Reproduced with permission of copyright owner, Irving Berlin, Inc.)

time from the depths of sordid dives to the apotheosis of fashionable vogue. The suddenness of the transforma- tion was sensational. "From Chinatown," said his biog- rapher, "Berlin dropped into Broadway as abruptly as if he had come by parachute. He set the shoulders of America swinging with the syncopated jubilance of 'Al- exander's Ragtime Band' . . . wrought with a tune which no one had ever consciously heard before.[33] This was the first full free use of the new rhythm which had begun to take form in the honky-tonks where pianists were dislocating old melodies to make them keep step with the swaying hips and shoulders of the spontaneous dark dancers. New York was soon noisy with the boom

[32] The story of Berlin's life given here is paraphrased and condensed from the movingly sympathetic biography that Alexander Woollcott wrote.

[33] Mr. Woollcott does not mean that "no one before had ever consciously heard" rag-time. All the emphasis on Irving Berlin as the "king of rag-time," as the one who impressed rag-time on America, is quite accurate. But the faint beginnings of rag-time had come at least fifteen years before, as early as 1895. See page 243 (footnote 26).

and blare of the song which was promptly caught up by bands and orchestras and cabaret singers in endless succession. It infected other song writers. It smote its day and generation as few songs have."

"What was needed," said a New York critic, "was a crystallization, was one song which should take the whole dash and energy of rag-time and carry it to its apotheosis. With a characteristic turn of mind Berlin accomplished this in a song which had no other topic than rag-time itself. 'Alexander's Ragtime Band' was . . . utterly unsentimental and the whole country responded to its masterful cry, 'Come on and hear!' "[34]

"Alexander's Ragtime Band," said Berlin's biographer, "stamped a new character on American music." The definition of the new character after it had established itself, was given, somewhat harshly, by Clive Bell:[34a] "Impudence is its essence — impudence in . . . revolt against nobility and beauty; impudence which finds its technical equivalent in syncopation; impudence which rags."[35]

The triumph of rag-time was not merely a case of one type of music succeeding another. It was a case of conquest, achieved, as if by assault, accompanied by a kind of truculence toward older types, an example of what Gilbert Seldes calls "frank destruction of sentimentality." Rag-time drove to the front in the spirit of overthrow, of revolution. It consciously jeered at the older

---

[34] Gilbert Seldes, "The Seven Lively Arts."

[34a] In the essay "Plus de Jazz" in the volume called "Since Cezanne."

[35] Mr. Bell's indignant jeremiad was directed not only against rag-time music, but against the rag-time spirit in some other forms of art. While I do not, at this place, imply, on my own account, any relation beyond co-existence in time, I call attention to the fact that the period in which rag-time blared forth coincided, roughly, with the beginning of free verse in poetry; cubism, vorticism and what-not in art; and, in literature impressionism, together with a particular variety of realism having to do with sex. Obviously, there is occasion here for a more extended examination than the present writer is able to make.

music, always in spirit, often in words, as in Alexander's Ragtime Band" itself:

Come on and hear, come on and hear Alexander's ragtime band,
Come on and hear, come on and hear, it's the best band in the
land. . . .
And if you care to hear the Swanee (*sic*) River played in rag-
time,
Come on and hear, come on and hear Alexander's ragtime band.

"Swanee River" was only one that rag-time lampooned. "Everything that could be syncopated, and some that could not, paid their quota to rag-time."[36] The "ragging" (*i.e.*, transposing into rag-time) of other songs had been, from the beginning, the essential technique of the new syncopation. The resulting travesty, with its effect of jeering, was part of rag-time's method of conquest. It became a direct and conscious barbarity upon older types of song. As it was put in a 1900 song,[37] indicating a rag-time addict:

You've massacred Beethoven, and you've upper-cut de Koven,
And you've slaughtered Tosti till he looks a sight.

In this technique, the solemn "Rosary" was made the subject of "When Rag-time Rosie Ragged the Rosary." John McCormick's lovely "Mother Machree" became "Mother Machree looked like a chicken to me"[38] — the outstanding example, the pinnacle (if that is the right word) of the rag-time spirit. Even psalms did not escape the cacophonic Herod. When a rag-time tune parodied the hymn held in highest affection by most Americans, a New York teacher of music, Madame Anne Kaufman, stirred the newspapers with her indignation, charging that artisans of the new music "stopped only a few inches short of setting the Bible to rag-time. . . . The most absolutely irreverent burlesque I have

36 The quotation is from Gilbert Seldes.
37 "We'll Have No More Coon Rag-time Songs Tonight."
38 This was a line in "At the Fountain of Youth."

ever heard lies in the tune[38a] built upon 'Nearer My God to Thee.' The young folks think it is funny. A halt should be called before this system of ridicule shatters our every tradition and ideal."

VIII

To such conservatives as had a feeling for the more

The Turkey Trot and the Grizzly Bear.
Modern dances barred from dance halls but popular in society, drawn by A. B. Walker in *Life*.

formal type of music the rag-time syncopation was unpleasing enough, but the words thrown together to fit the syncopation were even more distasteful. The idea that a popular song should tell a story was dismissed. In a febrile section of New York City called "Tin Pan Alley" — where nine-tenths of the country's popular music came to be produced — hectic artisans, hurrying frantically to take advantage of the new vogue, threw together words having no pretense of narrative, or logic, and only as much poetry as the assonance of love with

[38a] This burlesque began, "Nero, my dog, has fleas."

dove, moon with June, or, attained by main force, tune
with soon, or maid with said. In the rag-time songs, the
words were merely a series of ejaculations, the music a
sequence of panting gasps.

If the words were banal, the utterly revolutionary rag-
time dances that came with the new music were no less
than shocking. Some achieved the effect of double-en-
tendre by motion. If, as *Figaro* remarked, what cannot
be said can be sung, rag-time discovered that what cannot be sung can be danced. An early one of the impish
series was celebrated in a song that Berlin wrote, a song
which partly described the not very intricate motions[39]
— motions rather than steps — of the parvenu dances,
and partly placated scruples against it, the placation consisting of what was coming to be sufficient justification
for a good many things, "Everybody's Doin' It Now"
(1911):

Honey, honey, can't you hear funny, funny, music, dear? . . .
Can't you see them all, swaying up the hall?
Ev'rybody's doin' it, doin' it, doin' it.
See that ragtime couple over there,
Watch them throw their shoulders in the air,
Snap their fingers, honey, I declare,
It's a bear, it's a bear, it's a bear! There!
Everybody's doin' it now![39a]

The spawn of new dances that rag-time begot, called,
generically, "animal dances," included the fox trot and
the horse trot, the crab step and the kangaroo dip, the
camel walk and the fish walk, the chicken scratch and
the lame duck; the snake, and the grizzly bear; and —
especially common, in both senses of the word — the
turkey trot,[40] which Elizabeth Marbury said "deserved
much of the abuse it got." And the bunny hug, which

39 "The word 'step,' " said Booth Tarkington, "is somewhat misleading, nothing done with the feet being vital to the evolutions."

39a Printed here through the courtesy of Irving Berlin, Inc.

40 Louis H. Chalif, founder of the Chalif School of Russian dancing in New
York, thought that the women's dress which was the vogue of the day, the hob-

made the transition from rag-time dancing to rag-time's dynastic descendant, jazz — and which was sufficiently described in a witticism in the Harvard *Lampoon* during 1912:

He: Shall we bunny?
She: No: let us just sit down and hug.

From a drawing by Gordon Ross.
The Grizzly Bear.
But, in heaven's name, what kind of conversation goes with this?

The "grizzly bear" inspired two popular songs: "I Would Like to Try It" (1912) in which a young girl repined:

But mother said I shouldn't dare,
To try and do the grizzly bear.

———

ble skirt, had a relation to the turkey trot. "If a lady's feet are tied so that she cannot dance, other parts of her will dance, and they did — the shoulders and hips. The original turkey trot consisted of very short steps and very ample body movements. The steps but not the spirit came from the hobble skirt. For a while we had the curious phenomenon of women dressed like moderns and dancing like Hottentots. The spirit of this dance came from the music, which came from the Africans, who got it from nature. . . . The spirit of the dance could not be resisted."

And an Irving Berlin song:

> Listen my honey, do, and I will show to you
> The dance of the Grizzly Bear.
> All your other lovin' dances don't compare.
> Hug[41] up close to your baby.
>
> Throw your shoulders toward the ceilin'
> Lawdy, Lawdy, what a feelin'.
> Snug up close to your lady.
> Close your eyes and do some nappin'
> Something nice is gwine to happen.
> Hug up close to your baby, sway me everywhere.
> Hug up close to your baby,
> Hypnotize me like a wizard,
> Shape yo'self just like a lizard,
> Snug up close to your lady.
> If they do that dance in Heaven,
> Shoot me, "hon," tonight at seven.[42] . . .

IX

The rag-time dances, at first, made even New York a little squeamish. Battle raged. William R. Hearst's New York *American*,[43] taking a shot at a double target, the new dances and "society," recorded that "New York and Newport society are just at present manifesting a craze for the disgusting and indecent dance known as 'Turkey Trot.' " A distinguished critic of music, H. E. Krehbiel, wrote that "in this year of pretended refinement, which is the year of our Lord 1913, the [rag-time dances] are threatening to force grace, decorum, and decency out of the ball-rooms of America." The New York *Sun*[44] asked: "Are we going to the dogs by the rag-time route?" and

---

[41] The transition from the older dances to the rag-time ones was marked by many features denounced as objectionable, among them the extinction of space between dancing partners. Another was "backing the lady." A professional teacher of dancing, Albert W. Newman, wrote in 1914: "Backing the lady was considered exceedingly bad form only a few years ago, but now, with the new dances, everything has changed, and it is quite the thing."

[42] In the "Grizzly Bear" (1910) as here printed, some lines are transposed. The song is reproduced here through the courtesy of Irving Berlin, Inc.

[43] February 8, 1912.   [44] June 23, 1912.

hurled harsh phrases, "decadent drivel," "rhythmically attractive degenerator which . . . hypnotizes us into vulgar foot-tapping acquiescence."

In the end, the new dances won. Not only did they win in the ordinary dancing circles of the city; they carried their conquest into areas of life where dancing had been dropped with the passing of youth. The "dancing age" leaped as high as the sixties; the "frontiers of senescence," as Elmer Davis put it, were "pushed back forty years." For the old of both sexes, and those of generous girth, the new dances became, as Betty Lee daintily said, "a substitute for the Turkish bath and the masseuse." One popular dance-tune of the period, "Everybody's Doin' It," was parodied to "Everybody's Over-doin' It."

With universality came condonation. *Collier's*[45] urbanely thought that "more collars than high resolutions will be melted, and more shirt-bosoms than moral principles." *Life*,[46] with a tolerance that condoned the dances, and a complacence which felt sure that whatever New York approved, the country would accept, frowned upon "the disturbance which is proceeding about the prevalence in this city of modes of dancing which do not commend themselves to the guardians of our manners and moralities. The 'turkey trot,' the 'bunny hug,' and the 'grizzly bear' spread up and down and far and wide through our metropolitan society. Little Italians dance them in Harlem, polite cotillions at Sherry's have been diversified by them, and they flourish above, below, and between. Dancing masters are besought to teach them; the cabaret performer of a Broadway restaurant who is thought to be most proficient in them is said to be overrun with demands for instruction from learners out of fashionable families. The dancing set in our town must

[45] February 14, 1914.   [46] February 1, 1912.

be at least half a million strong, and it makes a difference how it dances."

X

With approval by the metropolis began inundation of the country. Rural communities, and cities other than New York offered resistance. All over the country, newspapers charged that rag-time was vulgarizing the young, undermining respect for sacred things, and was "responsible for deterioration of manners, taste, and right thinking. . . . The real danger to the community is the songs that give young folks a false and perverted impression of love and romance, and which hold a pure and romantic sentiment up to slangy ridicule." The Comfortville (N. Y.) Beethoven Society, rather pathetically, according to a newspaper[47] headline, "Relegated Rag-time to its Proper Place." In Philadelphia, uncompromising disapproval by a conscientious guardian of young women was reflected in an episode reported in a newspaper dispatch which described the turkey trot as "taboo at the office of the Curtis Publishing Company; fifteen young women were dismissed to-day after they had been detected enjoying the suggestive dance at lunch time by Edward W. Bok, editor of *The Ladies' Home Journal*."[48] A Paterson (N. J.) court imposed a fifty days' prison sentence (as the alternative of a $25 fine) on a young woman for dancing the turkey trot. At Millwood, N. Y., Miss Grace Williams, eighteen years old,

[47] New York *Evening Post*, November 2, 1911.
[48] New York *Sun*, May 29, 1912. The dispatch is here condensed. A careful historian does not vouch for the accuracy of every newspaper dispatch printed during these years about Mr. Bok and *The Ladies' Home Journal*. Mr. Bok and his institution were made the target of stories and witticisms almost as frequently as Henry Ford was made the butt of jests about his automobile. Such stories are, so to speak, artists' illustrations of the life of a period, rather than camera photographs. As artistic exemplifications of the spirit of an era they have their own kind of value, differing from, but sometimes not less useful than, photographs of detail, or literal transcriptions.

was arraigned on complaint of former Justice of the
Peace Ogden S. Bradley, who charged that she was
guilty of disorderly conduct in frequently singing
"Everybody's Doin' It Now," as she passed his house,
and dancing the turkey trot. "Squire" Bradley said that

Edward W. Bok.

he and his wife thought that both the song and dance
were highly improper and that they had been greatly annoyed. Lawyer Stuart Baker demanded a jury trial.
Miss Williams said she sang the song because she liked
it, and danced because she could not help it when she
heard the catchy tune. Lawyer Baker volunteered to
sing the song in court. The prosecuting attorney objected,
stating this would make a farce of the trial. Judge Cha-
deayne overruled him and told Baker to go ahead. The
lawyer, who had a good baritone voice, sang the ditty.
When he reached the chorus, "Everybody's doin' it, doin' it, doin' it," spectators joined in. The jurors called

for an encore. Again taking out his tuning fork to pitch
the key, the lawyer sang the second stanza with more
feeling and expression, and as he sang he gave a mild
imitation of the turkey trot. The jurymen clapped their
hands in vigorous appreciation, and after five minutes'
deliberation found Miss Williams not guilty.[49]

Churches, regarding the new songs and dances as in
the category which St. Augustine had described as "can-
tica nefaria" (that had caused concern to the church as
early as the sixth century and led the Council of Agde
[506] to forbid Christians to frequent assemblies where
they were sung), took notice in a manner that was
summed up later for the purpose of serious history in
"Nelson's Encyclopedia": "During 1912–14 these steps
. . . were so universally danced, notwithstanding their
doubtful character, that they incurred the serious dis-
pleasure and the condemnation of many churches and
respectable people. In January, 1914, an official disapproval was issued by the paper of the Vatican in
Rome."

The outstanding teachers of dancing at this time, Vernon and Irene Castle,[50] a couple who shared distinguished
manners, grace in their art, and elevated taste, to an extent that made them national characters, started "Castle
House," sponsored by several persons important in the
life of New York, in which the announced purpose was
to turn the tide against "the orgy that the world indulged
in during the vogue of the turkey trot." Their effort

[49] Condensed from the New York *Sun*. September 11, 1912.
[50] Vernon Castle subsequently met death while training as an aviator during
the Great War.
   Mrs. Castle (now Mrs. Frederic McLaughlin) wrote me in 1932, too mod-
estly giving most of the credit of the vogue of the Castles and Castle House
to her husband: "I think you have credited Vernon Castle with too little influence. . . . I was really of no importance to him in this work, and I did not
teach, but he did, a great deal."

was less to overcome the new steps than to have them
danced unobjectionably.[51]

An energetic and earnest, if humble, contribution to
the battle against rag-time had been made some years
earlier by Mike Clancy, as described in a 1900 song:

Vernon and Irene Castle.

Mike Clancy's almost crazy, and his wife's near had a fit,
  On account of his young, lively daughter, Annie;
For when Mike comes home at night she's bangin' out with all
    her might,
  Those nigger ragtime songs on the pianny.

"Now I'll have no more coon ragtime songs tonight,
If there is there's surely goin' to be a fight . . .
I have listened to you strangle Promise Me,
And throw knockout drops in Far Across the Sea;
Sure I think I've said enough, and what I tell you is no bluff,
That I'll have no more coon ragtime songs tonight."

[51] Mrs. Castle disapproved particularly the "strangle-hold," and hoped to
introduce a style of dancing in which "the man should touch only his partner's
finger-tips."

A quip of the day described the feminine partner in the close-clutching dances
as "more danced against than dancing."

Whether honest Mike Clancy's protest stemmed the tide of rag-time in his own family, history does not relate. In the state to which the juvenile attitude toward parental authority had come, it probably did not. Anyhow, the winning of one family skirmish was immaterial. Rag-time by its persistence achieved the favoring fortunes that attend vice when vice can manage to be seen often enough.[52] Neither the orders of parents nor the ban of the church, neither the disapproval of dancing masters nor the outcry of newspapers, neither country squires nor the editor of *The Ladies' Home Journal*, neither Philadelphia nor Comfortville was able to stop a vogue that had the momentum of New York behind it. In 1913, Booth Tarkington, writing "Penrod," described the conquest of America by the type of dance popular in that year: "At last it reached the dives of New York, when it immediately broke out in what is called civilized society. Thereafter it spread, in variously modified forms — some of them disinfected — to watering-places, and thence, carried . . . over the country, being eagerly adopted everywhere and made wholly pure and respectable by the supreme moral axiom that anything is all right if enough people do it. Everybody was doing it." By 1913 rag-time was more than a music and a dance; it was a new national tempo and attitude of mind, affecting everything:

> Oh, the ragtime of the present
> Is in many ways unpleasant. . . .
> It is not in music solely
> That its influence unholy
> Is exerted the proprieties to balk,
> But it permeates existence
> With insidious persistence,
> And it gets into our thinking and our talk.[53]

---

[52] The allusion is, of course, to "Vice is a monster of so frightful mien. . . ."
[53] *Life,* June 26, 1913.

Final universality was recorded in the near fulfilment of a song, written as a whimsical extravaganza:[54]

> I got a ragtime dog and a ragtime cat,
> A ragtime piano in my ragtime flat;
> Wear ragtime clothes from hat to shoes,
> I read a paper called the *Ragtime News*.
> Got ragtime habits and I talk that way.
> I sleep in ragtime and I rag all day;
> Got ragtime troubles with my ragtime wife,
> I'm certainly living a ragtime life.

And by 1913, Irving Berlin wrote jubilantly:

Lon-don dropped its dig-ni-ty____   So has France and Ger-man-y____

What did you do, America? They're after you, America!
You got excited and you started something,
   Nations jumping all around;
You've got a lot to answer for, they lay the blame right at your
  door,
The world is ragtime crazy from shore to shore.

London dropped its dignity, so has France and Germany,
All hands are dancing to a raggedy melody full of originality;
Dukes and Lords and Russian Czars, men who own their mo-
  tor cars,
Throw up their shoulders to that raggedy melody full of orig-
  inality;
Italian opera singers have learned to snap their fingers,
The world goes round to the sound of the International Rag.[54a]

XI

It was said, after rag-time (and its descendant, jazz) had proved that nothing succeeds like success, that this was a "peculiarly American product";[55] that it was the spirit of America";[56] that it was "the national idiom";[57] that it is "our one original and important contribution to

[54] Supplied, from memory, by Carolyn Wells (Houghton). The title was "I'm Certainly Living a Ragtime Life" (1900). [54a] Printed here through the courtesy of Irving Berlin, Inc. [55] *Life*, April 2, 1912. [56] Otto Kahn. [57] *Time*, 1928.

music" and that it contains "the true American spirit";[58] that it "seems to fit the nervousness of our climate and our people";[59] that "the dash and vim of it is in the American blood";[60] that it is "the rhythmical and melodic expression of life in the modern United States."[61]

Maybe. The writer of this history does not know, but doubts. Perhaps some one with sympathetic understanding of the deeper subtleties of our national psychology, and of the conflict[61a] between New York City standards and older American ones, might say that the triumph of rag-time and jazz was merely another case of a new vogue taking root like a weed in the heterogeneous welter that the American metropolis was, and from there inundating the country; and that the genuinely American thing was not rag-time, but the instinctively defensive — and pathetically futile — effort of the older generation in the rural parts of the country to ward off this assault on the older American melodies at which rag-time jeered. Can one imagine "rag-time" springing up spontaneously and indigenously on the prairies of the Midwest or on the farms of New England, as the old out-door dances sprang up on the village greens of England, "Annie Laurie" in the glens of Scotland, "Garryowen" at the country fairs of Ireland, the "Volga Boat Song" on the steppes of Russia, or "El Manicero" ("Peanut Vender") in the purlieus of Havana, or "O Sole Mio" on the canals of Venice?

The new music was hailed as "peculiarly American," and the man who gave it impetus, Irving Berlin, as the authentic inventor of American popular music. "Irving Berlin," said Jerome Kern, "has entrenched himself in a shell-proof, impregnable position, as commander-in-

[58] "How Music Grew": Bauer and Peyser.
[59] *Life,* June 3, 1909.   [60] Vilmos Westony, Hungarian pianist.
[61] W. Frank Harling.   [61a] See page 197 *et seq.*

chief of all the purveyors of American light music. . . . .
He *is* American music." The assertion was confirmed by

A page from "Life."

On with the dance.
Why stop to eat?
Interpretation of the dance craze in America.

some competent authorities even in the field of classical
music, which but rarely lifts its high hat to popular
songs. An American composer of admitted distinction,

John Alden Carpenter, named Berlin's rag-time composition, the "Everybody Two-Step," as the sole American contribution worthy to be included in a symposium of the world's greatest masterpieces of musical art. "I . . . believe," he said, "that the musical historian of the year 2000 will find the birthday of American music and that of Irving Berlin to have been the same."

Again, maybe. Berlin, at the time he wrote "Alexander's Ragtime Band," had been out of New York City just once; a brief trip to Binghamton, New York, had been his sole opportunity to know the part of America that lies west of the Hudson River. "What music Berlin knows," said his biographer, "he learned on the sidewalks of New York. . . . He transmuted into music the jumbled sounds of his life—the wash of the river against the blackened piers, the alarums of the street cars, the roar of the elevated, the frightening scream of the fire engines, the polyglot hubbub of the curbs and doorsteps of his own East Side, the brassy jangle of the hurdy-gurdies, the cries of the fruit venders and push-cart peddlers, the chants in the synagogues, the whines and squeals of Chinatown, the clink of glass and the crack of revolvers in saloons along the Bowery." To Berlin, "above all others of his day, a youngster carried out of Russia in the hold of a ship and pitched into the swarm of life in the lower East Side, it was given to catch the rhythm of his land and time."

One wonders. Berlin's background was ideal for catching the spirit of New York, but did it equip him to catch the spirit of America, the true "rhythm of his land"? Can one be certain Berlin would have arrived at rag-time as the national music if his formative years had been passed, not on the East Side of New York, but in California, or Kentucky, or Oregon?

Possibly it was one of America's major misfortunes

Miss Maude Allan as "Salome."   La Sylph.

Miss Gertrude Hoffman in "The   Mlle. Adeline Genee, in "The
Blue Danube."   Silver Star."

Four leading interpretive dancers of 1909–1911.

that this musical genius and fine spirit did not happen to spend his youth where he could have heard, and absorbed, and transmuted into a different synthesis of national music, the sigh of the pines on Mount Katahdin, the roar of the surf and storm against Cape Cod, the low of cattle in Pennsylvania meadows, the old-time melodies of dwellers in Appalachian valleys, the call of roustabouts on the Mississippi, the song of cowboys on the Texas plains, the twanging of banjos in Alabama, the summons of church bells in rural Ohio, the cries of children playing "One, Two, Three, O'Leary" in Virginia school yards, the honking of geese south-bound in autumn, the drum of rain against the windows of Nebraska farm houses, the notes of bob-white in Indiana wheat fields, the thunder of Niagara, the howling of a Dakota blizzard, the whisper of rustling corn on July nights in Illinois, the whine of dynamos at Conowingo dam, the homely whirr of the mowing-machine in June hay-fields, the bay of coon-dogs in North Carolina woods, the scream of an eagle in the Sierras, the crow of chanticleer in Maryland barnyards, including, as any complete synthesis of characteristic American sounds should — the cry of the hog-caller across rolling Kansas plains.

11

CHANGE; FERMENT, IN GREAT MATTERS AND LITTLE

From the Horse-drawn Victoria of President Taft in 1909 to
the Automobile of President Wilson in 1913, Which in Time
Was Four Years, but in Fundamental Change Was Nearer
Twenty Centuries. Some Minor Facets of a People in Ferment. More Divorce, Fewer Children. From Outdoor
Work to Indoor Exercise. From Farmhouse to City Apartment. From Sheerness to Dearness in Women's Raiment.

IT was a time of endings and beginnings, of the commotion that goes with clash of old against new, the momentum of the innovation against the inertia of the established. The most cultivated American scholar of that
day, Henry Adams, writing his autobiography in 1906,
felt, he said with gentle resignation, like a man who
had come down from centuries before. His education
(which he had received in the 1850's and 1860's at the
best American and European sources), had fitted him
well to live in the time of Julius Cæsar — but not at all
to live in the time of Theodore Roosevelt. The figure
of speech was not too far-fetched; the changes that took
place within a single lifetime spanned centuries in terms
of culture; the number and importance of the changes
in the material world that took place during the life of
Theodore Roosevelt were greater than the sum of those
that had taken place during two thousand years preceding.

When in 1909, at the end of Roosevelt's administration, his successor, William H. Taft, went to the Capitol to be inaugurated, the horse-drawn vehicle he rode
in did not differ essentially, except that it had four wheels

instead of two, from the carriage (*carruca*) in which the Cæsars rode out to the Roman baths during the first century of the Christian era. In principle the American Presidential victoria of 1909 and the Roman chariot of

A *carruca,* or Roman chariot; (*below*) the carriage used by Roosevelt and Taft at Taft's inauguration in 1909; both horse-drawn, and although a difference of twenty centuries in time exists they show but little change; while the automobile in which President Wilson rode a few years later marks a radical change—the gas-engine having practically superseded the horse.

the year 1 were identical. Both depended for motion on horses, on horsepower in the ancient and literal sense; both were creations largely of wood and leather and a few pounds of metal. About the greatest difference, the one detail that marked the Taft vehicle as the more modern, was that the wheels of Taft's carriage were tired with bands of solid rubber.

Four years after Taft's inauguration, his successor in the Presidency, Woodrow Wilson,[1] rode to the Capitol in a complicated product of physics and chemistry, compounded of gears, levers, pedals, rubber, cloth, glass, wire; and powered by an engine which generated motion as a result of electrically induced explosions of gasoline in expansion cylinders. The Wilson equipage had no flesh-and-blood horses; but had what engineers described as thirty to sixty horsepower of effective energy, compactly housed under a steel hood, not a quarter as large or heavy as a real horse. It consumed, not hay, nor oats, nor corn, but gasoline and mineral lubricating oil; and was started not by a coachman's "gid-ap," and not by crack of a whip, but by pressure of the driver's foot on an electric self-starter.

The distance between the Wilson automobile and the Taft carriage was, in time, four years; in material change, it was fully twenty centuries. The distance between the Taft carriage and the Roman chariot had been, in time, twenty centuries; in material change, practically nothing.

Such contrasts were all about — in grave matters and small, overlapping of new upon old, accompanied by clashings of standards of conduct and manners. On January 12, 1910, at a dinner in the White House, the wife of the Russian Ambassador, Baroness Rosen, desiring to smoke, asked President Taft for a cigarette. Taft relayed the request to his military aide, Archie Butt, who in some agitation procured one from the leader of the musicians. When Taft, cosmopolitan in experience and

[1] Wilson was the first President to take his inaugural ride in an automobile.

gracious even when graciousness involved risk of criticism, lit and held a match for the lady, the military aide[2] "hope[d] the press would not hear of it," and was virtuously "glad to say that the American women present did not indulge."[2] The wife of a subsequent Russian ambassador, Madame Bakmetieff, as late as April 6, 1912, encountered greater rigidity of American resistance to the European indulgence. Dining with another Russian lady in the Hotel Belvidere, Baltimore, "the two women lighted cigarettes; other diners gasped and the manager courteously requested the visitors not to smoke, explaining that it was not the custom at the hotel; the women accepted the situation gracefully and did not appear offended."[3]

The new practice, nevertheless, was making headway in America. A few young women smoked as a self-conscious defiance of convention, characteristic of youth at all times. President Roosevelt's oldest daughter, Alice, reproved for smoking in the White House, said, very well, she would smoke outside, and took her few puffs on the roof. Other girls and young matrons smoked with the feeling that it was the "latest thing," a spirit reflected in a quip in the Newark, N. J., *News:*

> You folks are being taken up by society, aren't you?
> Well, we don't believe in bragging, but we know three ladies who smoke cigarettes.

Smoking by women had not always been completely taboo in America; a generation or two before, a few immigrant women had smoked clay pipes, and a few native frontierswomen had smoked corncobs, sitting on cabin steps in the ease of the evening. Their daughters, a step up in the world, concealed the maternal indulgence as a skeleton in the closet; the daughters of these in turn,

2 Archibald Butt, who told the story, naïvely, in "Taft and Roosevelt."
3 Baltimore *Sun,* April 7, 1912.

about 1914, took up smoking cigarettes as a smart imitation of European high-life, transplanted to New York
and then to the country.

About a subject which Wallace Irwin called the "in-

From a drawing by Charles Dana Gibson in "New Cartoons" © Charles
Scribner's Sons.
Grandfather contemplates granddaughter smoking.

creasing decrease" of woman's raiment there was much
print: humorous on the part of *Life*,[4] which said that
"persons who claim to be informed assert that of all
the details of under-raiment that belonged in a woman's
wardrobe ten years ago, the only one that survives is the

[4] November 26, 1914.

"Butterick Fashions."   *"The Ladies' Home Journal," March, 1911.*

The spring sport suit of 1932.   The new spring tailor-made suit of
                                   1911.

From an advertisement in "The Theatre Magazine," 1913.

In 1913 silk stockings were, thriftily, mostly lisle. The silk and lisle met just
above the hem of the skirt. As skirts grew shorter the lisle receded
until, in the 1920's, it vanished.

stocking"; more serious on the part of the president of
the New York Cotton Exchange, George W. Neville,

who deplored that scantiness of woman's under-dress "has reduced consumption of cotton fabrics by at least

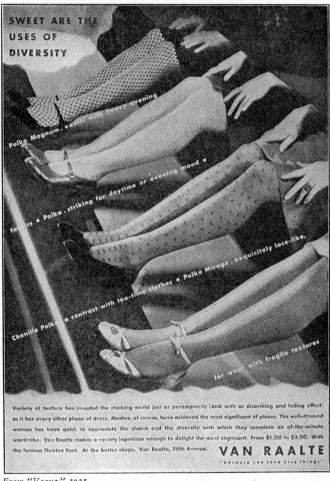

From "Vogue," 1931.

An advertisement by a stocking manufacturer, showing that by 1931 lisle tops had completely disappeared and stockings of transparent mesh were most popular.

twelve yards of finished goods for each adult female inhabitant."[5]

Decrease of quantity was not accompanied by decrease of cost. Defying economic law and following

[5] New York *Tribune*, April 4, 1912.

that of style, sheerness was accompanied by dearness. In 1900, an average woman paid less than five dollars for a year's supply of stockings; they were of cotton or of

From "The Theatre Magazine."

A golfing costume selected by a fashion expert after a tour of the New York shops in the summer of 1913, in the days when "suntan" was just plain "sunburn." Every precaution was taken to prevent exposure to the direct rays of the sun.

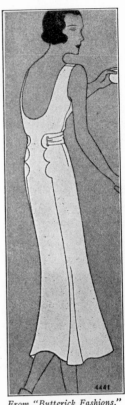

From "Butterick Fashions," Summer of 1932

A tennis frock—"nudity has an important place in sports fashions; this backless dress gives you that chance for uniform suntan," said the fashion expert of 1932.

wool, and they were black or they were white. Not one woman in ten thousand wore silk; the only place she or any one else ever saw silk stockings was on the stage or in shop windows. As skirts began to recede from the

ground, stockings began to be chosen for purposes additional to warmth and utility; they had to be silk, or near-
silk, and of colors so various that some forty new words
were invented for the spectrum of shadings that could

Photograph courtesy of Universal.
A long bob with ringlet ends, permanently
waved, is the smart coiffure of 1932.

"The Ladies Home Journal,"
1911.
Hairdress of 1911.

be seen on women's calves. By 1912, *Judge*[6] estimated
twenty-five dollars as the annual cost of the average
woman's stockings. Silk stockings called for more ex-
pensive shoes; the honor of both demanded costlier
dresses and hats. "The silk stocking is the foundation of
needless extravagance," said *Judge*, pleading, unsuccess-
fully, that it would be "hygienic, moral, and financial
wisdom to return to the saner practice of the preceding

6 February 10.

Modesty in 1893.

"Her first appearance in this costume. She thinks, on the whole,
she feels more at home in a ball dress."

Modesty in 1914.

generation about foot and limb covering" — *Judge,* as late as 1912, though it had the license of a semi-humorous periodical, was careful to say "limb," not "leg."

A rhymer of the day, Strickland Gillilan, counting

From a drawing by Wallace Morgan in the "New Yorker," August, 1932.

Modesty in 1932.

Mystery, as a feminine charm, had almost disappeared.

too confidently on the permanence of social taboos — in the dawning of an era in which the only permanence was the certainty of change — penned a dirgeful ditty about the disappearance of a little girl's legs into the cloisterhood of reticence, "Good-bye, Legs":

Tomorrow I'll be sweet sixteen; no more I'll be a "girl."
From that time on, around you, legs, some lengthened skirts
    must swirl.
I shall be legless till my death, for 'mid Dame Grundy's whims
Is one that says small girls have legs, but big ones just have
    "limbs."
. . . You've done no harm, old friends, that I can see,

From an advertisement © "Ladies Home Journal," 1911.

A theatre toque.

From an advertisement © "Ladies Home Journal," 1911.

An American evening hat.

THE HATS OF 1911

Oh, those hats! awful hats
   Garnished with the fur of
     cats;
The feathers of a hen,
   And defying tongue or pen;
Tilted up and tilted down;
   With a washtub for a crown;
And a pompom, pert or prim,
And with width enough of brim
   Oh, those hats!
     —New York *Press*, 1909.

From an advertisement in the N. Y. "Herald Tribune," July 31, 1932.

"A softly draped toque, tilted becomingly over the right eye."

But ne'er again must you be seen by any one but me!
You're in disgrace, I know not why, and no one else can tell me;
You must be hid, or social ranks would certainly expel me;
I must not even mention you.
How you must envy those two things above that are my arms!

From the "Ladies' Home Journal," 1912.

The little boy and girl of 1912 wore long stockings.

From "McCall's Fashions," 1932.

By the 1920's socks were worn the year round.

They get to keep the name they've had — are counted 'mid my charms;
But you must drop from sight and thought by stern convention's whims —
You are a guilty secret now, since you've become my "limbs."

That was printed in *Puck* on February 14, 1912. If the heroine of the ditty lived ten years, her legs became as visible a charm — assuming that in this individual case they had the good fortune to be a charm — as her arms.

New understanding of the cause and nature of disease, accompanied by changes in living which took men away from nature's ways, led to self-consciousness about health. Millions of Americans whose ancestors since the beginning of time had spent ten or twelve hours each day in the sun and outdoor air, in contact with the soil, now passed in a single generation to spending their days

So this is progress

Drawing by C. D. Batchelor, in the "Public Ledger," Philadelphia.

From outdoor work to indoor exercise.

moving pens over paper, or tapping typewriter keys, or in other forms of indoor life. Less perspiration dripped from the average man than ever before; to earn one's bread by the sweat of one's brow became merely a figure of speech, as unreal to modern life as some other passages in the Bible. For adaptation to the new way, came ingeniously equipped gymnasiums; elaborate country clubs where men whose fathers had swung a hoe for a living now swung a golf-club for recreation. A prejudice against "night-air," logical before men learned that malaria is transmitted not by miasmic vapors but by a mosquito, which had expressed itself in tightly closed windows, was succeeded by a vogue of out-door sleeping:

> We are s-s-sleeping on the roof,
>> We are b-b-bathing on the stoop,
> We are d-d-dining on the lid
>> Of a b-b-backyard chicken coop.
>
> In the snow upon the l-l-lawn
>> Sits the bubbubbaby fat and cool,
> And the older chuchuchildren go
>> To the Fresh Air Public School.[7]

Understanding of the way tuberculosis is transmitted led in practically every city to ordinances against spitting; when it became apparent that American regard for the rights of the individual — and the ease of getting a political friend to speak a word to the magistrate — would not often countenance punishment for so slight an offense, policemen were reduced to handing printed warnings to offenders. In bar-rooms and other places of public congregation, signs appeared: "Gentlemen *will* not, others *must* not spit on the floor." A more cutting admonition said, "If you spit on the floor at home, you can do it here." Concern about sanitation led to the passing of the old-fashioned roller-towel, recorded in a quip in the San Francisco *Argonaut:* "Say," asked the hotel guest of a man in the washroom, "don't the owner of this hotel know it's against the law of the State of Illinois to use roller-towels now?" "He knows it all right enough," was the reply, "but that law wasn't passed when this towel was put up."

Concern about physique led to much talk — but very little practice — of a modification of the romantic basis

[7] Newark *Evening News,* April, 1911.

of marriage; it is doubtful if there was as much as one[10]
authentic case of a "eugenic marriage":

> He chose her, not because her eyes
> Were like the stars that glow at night

but because

> Her biceps were of goodly size
> And she was of superior height.[11]

A magazine article captioned "Twilight Sleep," conveying an implication of childbirth made easy, arrested
to a sensational degree the attention of millions who had
never heard of the long-used drug mandragora, or its
modern derivative, scopolamine, or the modern barbit-
uric acid compounds. Childbirth was not made any
easier by the phrase than it had for some time been made
by the drugs; and neither by phrase nor drug was the
willingness of women to endure childbirth increased.
American obstetricians deplored the excessive hopes held
out for combinations of drugs they had been using for
some years before.

Divorce was becoming more usual, stern disapproval
of it from pulpits being displaced by quips in comic
papers about "the go-getting male who turned in his old
wife for a snappy new model." "Are you unmarried?"
asked the lawyer of the woman on the witness-stand.
"Sir," she replied, "I have been unmarried four times."

There was much argument about the word "obey" in
the marriage ceremony. A conference of bishops of the
Church of England suggested a cautious "schedule of
permissible variations" of the Book of Common Prayer,
which omitted "obey" from the wedding ceremony, and
from the rite of baptism omitted the dogma that babies
are conceived in sin. A pioneer in new conceptions of
education and new liberalness in thought, Doctor Charles

---

[10] If there was, it would be interesting to survey the result, in the light of
twenty years or so after.
[11] *Life*, February 24, 1914.

W. Eliot, about the time he retired from the presidency of Harvard University in 1911, said that public schools ought to teach physiology more frankly: "We have got

Drawing by C. D. Batchelor, in the "Public Ledger," Philadelphia.

The old American home—and a new one.

to get rid of the idea which has been taught us for thousands of years, that man is born in sin. The transmission of life is the sacredest and holiest thing in life. We must get rid of those monstrous things brought down to us from Leviticus."

Migration from country to city, from farm-house to flat or skyscraper apartment, led to many changes in human relations. A father who, to visit a friend would

have saddled his horse and ridden three miles along country roads, could have a son whose trip for a similar purpose would have been down an elevator, through a sub-
way and up another elevator. Apartment dwelling did
not make for neighborliness. *Life*[12] epitomized the new
condition in:

> "The woman across the hall from us is dead."
> "How did you find that out?"
> "I happened to see it in the paper."

For children reared in city apartments, immune from
farm chores and the exercise that went with them, summer camps arose — the hills of Vermont and New
Hampshire came to be dotted with them. Apartment
life was unfriendly to children, even to their existence:

> "So you won your divorce suit?"
> "Yes! I got an absolute separation with alimony, and the
> court awarded me the custody of the dog, too."[13]

Migration from small town to larger led to a nostalgia
for neighborliness. In 1905, in Chicago, was started a
Rotary Club, of which one of the rules was that at the
once-a-week luncheons members must call each other by
their first names. By 1932, there were, in addition to
Rotary, three major organizations similar in type, Ki-
wanis, Lions, Civitan, and many smaller ones, with thousands of local clubs all over the country containing hundreds of thousands of members.

Largeness of the unit of industry, coupled with standardization, led to impersonality. The submergence of
the individual came to be recognized as a little repellent
to human feeling. About 1914, appeared evidences of a
desire upon the part of heads of industry to recognize
what they called "the human factor." At the point
where immense corporate organizations came in contact
with the public, pains were taken to assure the customer

12 March 2, 1911.   13 *Life*, August 24, 1911.

that the corporate employee whom he faced was something more personal than a biped tentacle of the corporate soul. Upon the teller's cage in banks, and at the desks of hotels, were hung brass plates which gave the customer the opportunity, if he chose, to address his fellow-man by a name. Travellers in Pullman cars had long felt that relations so intimate and friendly as those with the colored servitors should be evoked by something more personal than the call of "Porter!" and had conferred on all that friendly tribe the generic "George." About 1920, railroads began to supply passengers with the name of the Pullman conductor; by about 1925, the porter and the dining-car waiter were recognized as having had human ancestors and having been baptized.

II

Some Facets of American Life, 1909–1914

The log-cabin passing off the scene as the favored birthplace of candidates for office — by 1928 came the first candidate for the Presidency whose asset was that he had been born in a city tenement, "Al" [Alfred E.] Smith. . . . Wrist watches, beginning to be worn by men — and giving rise to a completely serious belief that the wearers were effeminate, in a pathological sense: "Personally," said the Dallas (Texas) *News*, "we think it is all right for a man to wear a wrist watch in warm weather, but in winter we think he looks better carrying a muff." . . . "High-brow" and "low-brow" were new in current slang, the former described carefully by the *Ohio State Journal* as a person who reads Browning, talks about anthropology, attends grand opera, and says "eyether"; the latter as one who goes to see moving pictures, plays euchre, and says "eether." . . . The first income tax — very mild compared with what came later

— collected in the early part of 1914. A humorist of the day, George Fitch, observed that "it will be an exclusive circle, this income-tax class — one which the ordinary wage-earning man cannot hope to enter," and suggested that these élite should "organize the Sons of Simoleons with a golden ribbon on the coat lapel for a badge." . . . An experiment in the education of tiny children, the Montessori System, named after an Italian woman, Dotoressa Maria Montessori, who in 1913 delivered lectures in America in which she expounded, with widespread approval, a theory that we should permit children to develop through self-education, "self-activity"; enough of the new theory survived to materially modify American education of the young, in the direction of less emphasis on arbitrary discipline, less on teaching the child, more on permitting him to learn. . . . An "ethical culture" movement designed as a substitute for or addition to formal religion. . . . Rapid triumph of the safety razor over the old-fashioned "hone-your-own" . . . A vogue of ping-pong led to a joke about a presumed difference between New York and Boston:

New York.   "Do you know ping-pong?"
Boston.   "No, who wrote it?"

The commission form of city government coming in rapidly with the pleased approval of many who thought it would get rid of the evils of municipal politics; in 1912, one hundred and eighty-two cities and towns had it. . . . A phrase of revival, "The New South," coming into print to describe full recovery from the Civil War, and what, for the South, had been worse than war, reconstruction. . . . High-tide of "correspondence schools"; Irvin Cobb had a joke about a youth who was careful to fix the stamp on an envelope in a particular position, because "that's our college yell." . . . "Bottle-babies," meaning ones not suckled — the wet-nurse succumbing to the progress of science. . . . "End-seat hog," a person who in summer trolley-cars caused incoming passengers to edge past him. . . . "Billikens," mock-gods made of clay which, seated on one's desk, were supposed to avert bad luck; a presumed resemblance to William H. Taft provided some of the political wit of the day. . . . It was hey-dey of the gramophone, the Victrola, and other forms of mechanically reproduced music, a pleasure to most, but, like the radio that displaced it, causing fretfulness to some who asked, with George Fitch, "How can a man who doesn't like gramophone music visit his friends in comfort?" . . . The trade-call of the street-car conductor, "Step lively!" sometimes accompanied by "please," more often not; by the 1920's, on the New York subways, vocal urgency having turned out to be insufficient, was succeeded by men employed to shove. . . . A former train-robber, Al Jennings, who, after serving his penitentiary sentence, wrote a book, became a popular lecturer, was taken up by some sentimental folks, and ran for Governor of Oklahoma.

The "Black Hand," to which were ascribed, by the more lurid part of the press, most crimes of violence or vengeance, especially those in which an Italian was either the victim or the suspected criminal. Some such crimes actually had their origin in Sicilian or Corsican vendettas, or in traditions brought from there which decreed that satisfaction for injury is a matter to be handled by the injured party, or his family, rather than by organized society. Exploitation by press and film of this habit of mind, and of the mystic symbol of it, was carried to a point where a bill collector, or other small fiduciary, could explain discrepancy of a few dollars between what he collected and what he delivered to his employer, by reporting a hold-up by the "black hand" or mafia. A boy, given reason to wish for revenge on a teacher or a larger youth, could acquire a simulation of satisfaction for his wound by drawing upon the door of his oppressor or enemy the semblance of a hand in black.

Slang that was new, "flossy," in 1912, as assembled by *Life*[14]: Beat it! Peeved. Sure! Classy. It's a cinch. What do you know about that? Fussed. Speedy. Peachy. Nutty. Getting your goat.

The profusion and diffusion of wealth caused "Mr. Dooley" to remark, with an Irish wink: "Th' day whin we millyonaires bought yachts an' brown stone houses with mansard roofs onto thim an' were proud iv havin' thim has gone by, Hinnissy. 'Twill not be long befure none will be so poor as not to own a private yacht, an' th' nex' time a Coxey army starts f'r Wash'nton, it'll ride in a specyal vestibule thrain. What was luxuries a few years ago is mere necessities now." . . . It was, said *Judge*,[15] in an adventure into epigram, "The Living Age." *Life*,[16] less venturesome in condensation, epitomized it more lengthily: "This is a get-things-done-quick age. It is a ready-to-put-on-and-wear-home age, a just-add-hot-water-and-serve age, a new-speed-record-every-day age, a take-it-or-leave-it-I'm-very-busy age."

But perhaps as accurate an epitome as any was that of Mr. Patrick J. Murphy of New York City, who day-times managed a leather-goods shop and nights was the wittiest after-dinner speaker of the time: "To stay where you are in this country you must keep moving."

[14] August 1, 1912.   [15] In 1912.   [16] July 6, 1911.

12

ROOSEVELT NOMINATES TAFT

A Process of Which the Principal Part Consisted of Preventing the Nomination of Himself, and Another Part Consisted in Persuading the Public That Taft Was the Equivalent of Himself. The Story of a Friendship, Political and
Personal. Together with Allusion to the Wives of the
Two Friends and Their Families, and the Parts They Played.

RARELY in public life, or private, rarely in any area of
human relations has there been so appealing a picture
as the years of the friendship of Theodore Roosevelt and
William H. Taft. It began when both occupied subordinate government posts in Washington, from 1890
to 1892, Roosevelt as Civil Service Commissioner, Taft
as Solicitor-General. They lived near each other, met
frequently at the homes of each other and of mutual
friends, often lunched together. Mornings they walked
to their offices together—Roosevelt quick-stepping,
short-paced, eager; Taft slow-paced, rolling-gaited,
placid—passing the White House, then occupied by Benjamin Harrison, and turning unconsciously to glimpse its
unfailing glamour (though it was Roosevelt alone of the
two whose thrill was associated with a personal dream).
After advancement in their careers separated them from
Washington and from each other, they kept their friendship alive through letters. When Roosevelt became President, the friendship took on to some extent the relation
of giver and receiver, benefactor and beneficiary.

Roosevelt, entering the White House in 1901, found
Taft among the subordinates in his administration, as
Governor-General of the Philippines. Roosevelt ten-

dered his friend elevation, in the form of a place on the Supreme Court — Roosevelt's face beaming with pleasure at the happy combination, the opportunity of making so exalted a gift to so loved a friend, his sense of Taft's fitness for the post, his knowledge that it was what Taft in his soul most desired.[1]

Taft's wife intervened. She had begun to believe it was possible her husband might some time be President and felt that immurement on the Supreme Court would side-track him at a dead end, away from the course leading towards the higher goal. The Supreme Court, she said, was "settlement in a 'fixed groove' I had talked against so long."[2] Taft's declination puzzled Roosevelt, but did not abate his ardor for the rôle of giver. A year later he made Taft another offer, the post of Secretary of War. This, in Mrs. Taft's judgment, "was much more pleasing than the offer of the Supreme Court appointment, because it was in line with . . . the kind of career I wanted my husband to have."[2]

II

The years when Roosevelt had Taft beside him as Secretary of War were the golden time of the friendship. When the two were in a White House room together their laughs, Roosevelt's high-pitched, Taft's rumbling, would reverberate through the corridors; "It's always that way when they're together," Mrs. Roosevelt said.[3]

[1] The proffer was made late in 1902. For an account of the early friendship between Taft and Roosevelt, see "Our Times," Vol. III.

[2] "Recollections," Mrs. Wm. H. Taft. Taft in part had, and gave to Roosevelt, a reason for his declination not associated with his wife's reluctance; namely, his feeling he could be more useful in his Philippine post.

[3] To Archie Butt. Butt was a curious figure, utterly unimportant in the making of history, but — because of the diary he kept — very important to the writers of it. His formal name, Archibald Willingham Butt, comported with the ornateness of the uniform he wore, his rather strutting air, his erect largeness of figure, the gallant look of him upon a horse, his naïvely snobbish adula-

"Three Musketeers."

The two, with Elihu Root, jocularly thought of themselves, in intimate conversations, as the "Three Musketeers." In Cabinet meetings, or at gatherings of friends, Roosevelt's "Isn't that so, Will?" was his way of getting what he regarded as the most convincing buttressing of his own opinions — a confidence of expectation never abated by the fact that at evening gatherings in the White House study the question would sometimes wake Taft from a nap. Whenever Roosevelt spoke to Taft, or spoke of him to others, pleasure shone from his own countenance. He loved Taft and admired him, extravagantly. "You know," Roosevelt once said,[3] "I think Taft has the most lovable personality I have ever come in contact with. I almost envy a man possessing a personality like Taft's. One loves him at first sight." In scores of such private conversations and in public statements Roosevelt expressed his pleasure about Taft. Not only his affection, but the regard he had for Taft's ability, his gratitude for Taft's services. "If only there were three of you," Roosevelt wrote to Taft, "then I would have one of you on the Supreme Court, one of you as Secretary of War, and one of you permanently Governor of the Philippines." Once, in a letter to Henry Cabot Lodge, Roosevelt recited his current troubles — the Russo-Japanese war, a dispute with England over New-

---

tion toward persons deemed to be of social importance, and the Southern ancestry of which he was rather grandiosely conscious; but "Archie" was more appropriate to his real kindliness, his gayety at informal parties, and above all the golden loyalty he gave to the two Presidents whom he served as military aide. That loyalty, in an indirect way, killed him, literally. He first served Roosevelt and was utterly devoted to him; then, when Taft became President, Butt remained as White House aide. As Taft and Roosevelt drew apart, poor Butt's turmoil of tension between his earlier loyalty and his new one, brought on physical sickness. Taft told him to take a vacation at a European cure; he did, and on his way home on April 14, 1912, went down on the *Titanic*.

It was Butt's practice, each night, to address a letter to his sister-in-law, or otherwise set down a gossipy account of what he had seen and heard during the day. This record, in effect a diary, preserved by Butt's family until most of the persons mentioned in it had died, was published in 1924 and 1930, "Taft and Roosevelt," two volumes, and "The Letters of Archie Butt."

Though the keeping of this record of intimate conversations overheard was an outrage in the social sense and dubious from the point of view of propriety as practiced in the army; and though Butt sometimes failed to grasp the full significance of what he overheard in the circles about the Presidents he served, his letters are of extreme value to a historian who tries to trace the evolution, the precise shading from day to day, of the relations of Roosevelt and Taft from friendship to something different.

foundland fisheries, the Railroad Rate bill — but concluded, as if with a sigh that implied confidence to face
all troubles, "Taft has been the greatest comfort to me."
In another letter to Lodge, he told of picking a successor
to John Hay as Secretary of State, and of hesitating between Elihu Root and Taft — "for Taft, as you know,
is very close to me." Deciding upon Root (because thus
he would have both Root and Taft about him) he said,
"Taft is a big fellow; he urged me to bring Root into the
Cabinet." In public and formal testimonials and allusions to Taft, Roosevelt searched his vocabulary for
superlatives: in "courage," "capacity," "inflexible up-
rightness," "disinterestedness," "wide acquaintance with
governmental problems, Taft stands pre-eminent."

These gifts of praise that Roosevelt heaped on Taft,
coupled with the offices and honors, constituted much of
the place Taft came to have in the public eye. So far as
it was a little more than Taft could live up to (and also
different from what he was adapted to), it became a
part of his subsequent tragedy. "Taft," said his secretary years later,[4] attempting an explanation of Taft's
fall in public esteem after he became President, "had
the finest press agent ever a man had, in Teddy;
Teddy was talking Taft, and the people took Taft at
Teddy's estimate."

If Roosevelt was a generous giver, so was Taft an ap-
preciative receiver, a loyal payer of the obligations that
generosity gives rise to. When at a banquet in Boston,
while Taft was Secretary of War, a speaker[5] poked fun
at Roosevelt, alluding to him as "Theodore the First,"
and saying that he was "a blue pill which the nation had
to take," Taft rose ponderously: "When I love a chief,"
he said, "and when I admire him from top to toe, I can-

---

[4] Charles D. Hilles, as quoted by Archie Butt.
[5] Simeon Ford, in private life keeper of the Grand Union Hotel, New York;
publicly, prominent as a caterer of wit to banquets.

not be silent and permit such insinuations, although they may be hidden in a jest."[6]

The relations between the two — Roosevelt as giver, Taft as recipient, Roosevelt as chief, Taft as subordinate, Roosevelt as initiator, Taft as aide — were comfortable to Taft. From his youth, he had been one whom fortune liked to favor. Though not born with a silver spoon in the money sense, he was the son of a father, Alphonso Taft, who had been a Cabinet member and whose position in Cincinnati made the son's way easy. Young Taft's hugeness of physique attracted attention to him; his ruddy amiability transmuted attention into affection, caused people to like him and made the early offices he received comparatively easy to get. After an elder half-brother, Charles P. Taft, had become wealthy, he gave William H. an amount of securities the return from which was a sufficient private income to enable Taft to remain in the various public offices Taft received — holding public office was, for Taft, "just lighting one fresh cigar from the butt of the last one." Taft gave fine service in the offices to which he was appointed, complete loyalty to those who befriended him.[7] Taft, in his relations to Roosevelt, was completely loyal, highly efficient, and perfectly happy. No ambition for a higher position clouded his contentment, though, knowing the relation must come to an end with the close of Roosevelt's administration, he would have been glad of elevation to the life-office that was ever his heart's desire, a place on the Supreme Court.

When Taft had served two years as Roosevelt's Secretary of War, Roosevelt for the second time gave him

[6] "From Harrison to Harding," Arthur Wallace Dunn.

[7] His death, in 1930, had as its immediate cause a trip he had taken, against the advice of his physicians, to the funeral of the dead half-brother whose generosity had helped make his public career possible.

the opportunity of going on the Supreme Bench. Taft longed to accept, spent four months of hesitancy between his own inclination and the pull of what proved to be a stronger force. Mrs. Taft, seeing her husband now well

Birthplace of President Taft, Cincinnati, Ohio.

advanced on the path that led toward the Presidency, was annoyed at an offer that pointed toward another career — "The subject of my husband's appointment to the Supreme Court," she wrote, with a rather acid side-glance at Roosevelt, "cropped up with what seemed to me annoying frequency."[8] Still later, Roosevelt, anticipating yet another vacancy on the Supreme Court, (which did not materialize) spoke a third time to Taft about his adaptability to the Bench. This time, Mrs. Taft was more than annoyed. The Presidential year

8 "Recollections," Mrs. William H. Taft.

1908 was ahead, and the way open, to say the least, for Taft to get the Republican nomination. With the outlook what it was, Mrs. Taft felt that Roosevelt's urging of her husband toward the Court reflected a reluctance on Roosevelt's part to see Taft make progress toward the Presidency; reflected, perhaps, even a Machiavellian intention on Roosevelt's part to take the succession for himself.[9] Mrs. Taft was vehement, excited — there was innuendo about Roosevelt's using Taft as a stalking-horse around whom to assemble delegates who on a last minute coup would be drafted to Roosevelt himself.

III

The same instinct that led Roosevelt four times to urge Taft to take a place on the Supreme Court must have inspired him unconsciously to a reluctance, never clearly recognized by himself, to put Taft in the Presidency. The reluctance may have been increased by the doubt of Mrs. Roosevelt whether it was wise to push Taft into the Presidency, doubt whether the country would be well served, or Taft himself happy. Mrs. Roosevelt[10] did not press her view on her husband; had she done so much of subsequent history might have been different.

[9] The authority for this statement is a member of Roosevelt's Cabinet, who told it orally to the author of this history, basing it on an entry made in his diary at the time.

[10] Roosevelt's wife had greater insight into men than her husband, and sounder judgment in many respects. Some intimates of the White House during the Roosevelt régime felt that, however great Roosevelt was among men, Mrs. Roosevelt was even greater among women. That her code kept her in the background deprived the public of knowing not merely one of the great women, but one of the great persons of her time. For much that Roosevelt got approval for, Mrs. Roosevelt was not only inspiration and partner, but actually principal. Her education was broader than Roosevelt's, her reflection deeper. In manners, in everything she had a literally perfect sense of taste. All this Roosevelt knew well, and admired her extravagantly. Part of her greatness lay in the quiet rein of graciousness and humor she kept upon her husband's sometimes reckless

It was not until January, 1908, five months before the convention, that Roosevelt decided fully, and then only because his secretary, William Loeb, told him he must act. Loeb's pressure, and Roosevelt's primary decision, was not that he should back Taft but that he should back somebody — because otherwise the convention might re-nominate Roosevelt himself. "You should have a candidate," Loeb told him one morning. "You are under pledge not to run again. I propose that you make people understand you intend to keep it. Some people believe that a deadlocked convention might force you to disregard it. Others believe you . . . are manipulating things so as to force a deadlock. The air is full of such talk. The way to settle it is to have a candidate."

Roosevelt agreed — "We must have a candidate." After surveying in his mind the possibility of backing Root, and re-surveying Charles E. Hughes, he turned to Taft — with a reluctance only to be explained as the caution of his instinctive question about Taft's adaptability, acting as a brake on the natural impulse of his friendship. Once Roosevelt determined to turn the nomination toward Taft, he went about the elevation of his friend with as much gusto as he would have taken in promoting his own fortunes. To getting the nomination for Taft he devoted all his political resourcefulness,

---

exuberance. Some persons still living in 1932 could remember the smile, the twinkle in her eye and the affection in her voice on occasions at the White House table when her "Theodore!" would put a gentle brake upon her husband's headlongness. The President's response on those occasions was always to become meek, always took the same form of words: "Why, Ee-die, I was only" — The way in which she helped him most, however, lay in her infinitely superior insight into men, their motives and characters. It is safe to say that never, when Roosevelt had his wife's judgment, did he go wrong or suffer disappointment. The White House circle between 1901 and 1909 knew the power and the immense obligations of the country to this woman, who was never in the public eye, and never in politics. One of the White House intimates of that day, Owen Wister, distinguished author, putting his memories into words, wrote: "She was the perfection of 'invisible government.' Was Roosevelt ever wholly aware of what she did for him? Is any husband wholly aware of a devoted and tactful wife until he has lost her?"

taking in it somewhat the pleasure of a father in promoting the fortunes of a particularly beloved son, somewhat the pleasure that an adept in an art takes in showing off his skill in the presence of and for the benefit of a
loved and loyal admirer.

The job really was not difficult in proportion to the

Drawing by Lamdin for the Syracuse "Herald," 1909.
"Passing on the Torch."

éclat that Roosevelt put into it. The act of bestowing the
Presidency on Taft consisted chiefly of declining to take
it himself; more accurately, in preventing its being thrust
on him. The only other candidate constituting any im-
pediment to Roosevelt's nominating Taft was Charles
E. Hughes, then Governor of New York.

IV

Roosevelt Disposes of Hughes

Hughes, Governor of New York, was at high tide of
the prestige that had come to him as a result of his investigation of insurance[11] abuses two years before. His
availability, his obviousness for the Republican Presi-

11 See "Our Times," Vol. III.

dential nomination was really greater than Taft's —
Roosevelt himself had thought he might "feel it my
duty to be for Hughes."

Hughes, following a characteristically austere conception of propriety, refraining from announcing himself a candidate, hesitant even to allow the use of his
name, came finally to a point where he "felt that those
who were earnest in the movement were entitled to support me if they saw fit."[12] In that spirit, and in response
to urgent solicitation, Hughes, on January 21, 1908,
wrote to the Republican Club of New York City, saying that if the Club would hold a meeting on January
31 he would appear "to make such further statement as
may be appropriate." The announcement was universally interpreted as meaning that Hughes was a candidate, and that his coming speech would "lay down the
platform on which he would be willing to run."[13]

Anticipation flamed. The New York Republican
County Committee, January 29, 1908, endorsed Hughes
as their candidate. Similar resolutions or informal steps
were taken in New England and elsewhere.

Newspapers, fanning anticipation, said that Hughes
would "make plain his views on all important national
issues"; and mobilized their facilities to carry to the public the speech which Hughes was to deliver about eight
o'clock on the night of January 31. The public, its interest excited, waited in suspense — it was thirteen years
before radio broadcasting — to read the speech. The
following morning readers picked up their newspapers
to find what Hughes had said. They found it — if they
looked hard enough. At least, those of them found it
whose interest was able to survive what they saw on the
first page. In blazing headlines four columns wide ap-

[12] The words are Hughes's, years later.
[13] "Released for Publication," Oscar King Davis.

peared, not the name of Hughes but that of Roosevelt.

The headlines epitomized a message Roosevelt had sent to Congress at five o'clock the evening before (after afternoon newspapers had gone to press), the most pro-

THE MORE HE BOOSTS, THE MORE IT HURTS

From the Philadelphia "Record."

vocatively sensational utterance of his career; headlines beginning with two words that had become familiar — current humor said the newspapers used to keep these words standing in type —

ROOSEVELT FLAYS . . .[14]

— headlines which shouted:

HOTTEST MESSAGE EVER SENT TO CONGRESS[15]

[14] Chicago *Tribune*.   [15] Chicago *Tribune*.

ULTRA-RADICAL MESSAGE[16]
MESSAGE DAZES[17]
ROOSEVELT'S ONSLAUGHT[18]
"BIG MEN" ROASTED[19]

— headlines followed by the text of the most violent message Roosevelt had ever given out. The epithets, the flaming phrases that blazed from it, were so sensational that an editor of the New York *World* was moved to print them in a double-column box:

Web of corruption.	The strong, cunning men.
Apologists for corrupt wealth.	Law-defying wealth.
Hypocritical baseness.	Vindictive and terrible radicalism.
Criminals of great wealth.	Mammon of unrighteousness.
Powerful wrongdoers.	
Peculiarly flagrant iniquity.	With envenomed bitterness.
To shackle cunning.	Notorious railroad combinations.
Laying up a day of wrath.	
Flagrant dishonesty.	Bitter and unscrupulous craft.
Rottenness.	
Unhealthy seeming prosperity.	Very wealthy criminals.
	Corruption of organized politics.
Greed, trickery and cunning.	Corruption of high finance.
Representatives of predatory wealth.	With frantic vehemence.
	Evil eminence of infamy.
Wealth accumulated by iniquity.	The death knell of the Republic.
Puppets who move as the string is pulled.	Purchased politicians.
	Domineer in swollen pride.
Corrupt men of wealth.	Wealthy malefactors.

The speech made a blazing sensation. Though Roosevelt stopped just short of naming the "wealthy malefactors" whom he meant to designate by his thundering epithets, a newspaper correspondent close to him (J.

[16] Cincinnati *Enquirer*.   [17] New York *Times*.   [18] New York *World*.
[19] Chicago *Tribune*.

Callan O'Laughlin, of the Chicago *Tribune*) supplied
the identifications by printing the names of "some of the
men the President had in mind when he wrote the
message": "John D. Rockefeller, Standard Oil mag-

From *"Puck,"* December, 1907.

"How the diabolo can I keep this going till nomination day?"

nate; Edward H. Harriman, railroad financier," and nine
others. One enemy and critic of Roosevelt found himself sufficiently identified in Roosevelt's speech as an
"apologist for successful dishonesty . . . who in writ-
ings and speeches in the colleges serve these their masters
of great wealth to the cost of the plain people." Chancellor James R. Day[20] of Syracuse University stepped
forward in a newspaper interview to say that "not a
nickel or dime was ever offered to me by any person,
company, or corporation, for a sentence or a paragraph"
in any of Day's criticisms of Roosevelt. The scholarly

[20] Chancellor Day, whenever Roosevelt attacked the Standard Oil Company,
or the conservatives generally, had a permanent self-imposed rôle of coming
forward with a reply, somewhat in the spirit of "Fireman, save my child."

Chancellor, out of the resources of literary and pathological judgment his academic position provided him, solemnly asserted that Roosevelt's message was, as to some parts, "the ravings of a disordered mind," and as to others, the expression of an "adroit and cunning . . . shrewd but reckless demagogue." "These are strange times," said the Chancellor, "when American citizens are to be assailed under cover of a message to Congress for exercising their inalienable right of the discussion of the policies and acts of the Administration. If this liberty is taken from us what is left of the democracy of which we boast?" Finally, the Chancellor exclaimed, little knowing how his words would sound twenty years later, "What better are we than Russia!"

The explosive thunders of Roosevelt's message to Congress left little space in the newspapers and only an obscure position for the speech of Hughes — the Chicago *Tribune's* typographical presentation began with two words that constituted a relative rating for its impact — "Hughes also . . ." —

HUGHES ALSO HITS
RICH EVIL–DOERS
Outlines Platform on Which He
Will Make Fight to Become
Chief Executive

Hughes' careful statements about public policy, intended to be, as the Cincinnati *Enquirer* put it and as everybody understood, his "formal declaration of his entrance into the race for the Republican nomination," were not only dwarfed in space and relegated to inconspicuous positions, but were given the effect of pallid feebleness by Roosevelt's savage epithets. Hughes' temperate, sane, well-thought-out discourse could no more compete for public attention with Roosevelt's effulgence than a crystal spring with a volcanic eruption. Hughes' calm advocacy of a commission to revise the tariff, and an employers' liability law, his scholarly delineation of the field of Federal power compared with State — all that was reduced to a kind of feeble ignus fatuousness by the flaming provocativeness of Roosevelt's torrid denunciations. Against the reverberating thunders of Roosevelt's address, Hughes' scholarly exposition became an unheard whisper. "That," said Oscar K. Davis,[21] "wound up the Hughes candidacy."

Persons who knew or inferred that Roosevelt must have prepared so important an address several days in advance, and who made further inference from Roosevelt's expert understanding of the mechanics of publicity, charged Roosevelt with having timed the sending of his message to Congress, three hours in advance of Hughes' speech, with the deliberate purpose of blanketing the latter — "Timed to Dwarf Hughes," said the New York *Times* headline. Roosevelt, when friends imputed this adroitness to him,[22] just grinned.

v

Taft as Roosevelt's Shadow

With Hughes out of the way, Roosevelt dedicated himself to persuading the country to accept Taft. Resourcefully, persistently, Roosevelt assured the country that Taft was the equivalent[23] of himself, and tried to make his assurance good by attempting to make Taft

21 "Released for Publication."

22 Whether Roosevelt consciously timed his message to drown Hughes' speech, there is no proof: When I humorously implied that he had, he merely remarked, cryptically, "If Hughes is going to play the game, he must learn the tricks."

23 In one quarter, characteristically credulous, Wall Street, Roosevelt's picture of Taft as the duplicate of himself was for a moment believed. When Wall Street, thus believing, muttered that Taft was "unsafe" and began to look about

be Roosevelt. His closest friend, Henry Cabot Lodge, told him he could not do it: "You can do and say things which neither Taft nor any other man can do or say, because you are yourself and not another; you cannot put Taft into your place with the American people."

Roosevelt continued the attempt. He inducted Taft into the rudiments of the game. After Taft had arranged to make his opening speech in Boston he happened to be with Roosevelt in the bedroom of the latter's daughter Alice, who was recovering from an appendicitis operation. Roosevelt asked Taft what he was going to discuss. Taft said he had prepared a speech about the Philippines. Roosevelt laughed — so uproariously that his daughter, infected by the mirth, joined with such violence as to break one of the cat-gut stitches of her appendicitis wound.[24] Taft, under Roosevelt's shrewd tutelage, abandoned his speech about the Philippines, and Boston heard a discourse on a subject nearer home, the currency problem.

Throughout the campaign Roosevelt gave intimate advice, told Taft just how to make a political speech, how to become a popular campaigner. "Stay in hotels," he advised Taft, instead of the private homes whose hospitality Taft loved, "and give everybody a fair shot at you." When Taft continued his daily golf playing,

for a conservative candidate, Roosevelt, putting "reverse English" on the game he was playing, inspired stories in the newspapers favored in Wall Street to the effect that he was thinking of remaining President himself — "If they won't take Taft, they'll have to take me." Wall Street, terrified, concluded to take the lesser evil. Roosevelt never at any time had any such intention, but his political resourcefulness included a guile in which he took a Falstaffian relish.

The writer of this history was close to Roosevelt at the time, has in recent years read most of Roosevelt's letters as well as the literature about Roosevelt, and is familiar with researches made by other authors and students. I have not found, no one in my acquaintance has found, and in my judgment there does not exist, any evidence that Roosevelt during his term of office ever gave a thought to acting contrary to the voluntary pledge he had given at the time of his election in 1904, not to succeed himself.

[24] Furnishing authentication, the first in history no doubt, for the old Saxon superlative of merriment: "laughed so hard he bust a gut."

drawing to that then relatively new game in America the attention that focusses on a Presidential candidate, Roosevelt sent word to him to take his exercise in some form more familiar to the plebeian. "It is true," Roosevelt explained to the messenger,[25] for repetition to Taft, "I myself play tennis, but that game is a little more familiar; besides you never saw a photograph of me playing tennis. I'm careful about that; photographs on horseback, yes; tennis, no. And golf is fatal."

Busily Roosevelt took a hand at every point in the nation-wide field, taking many of the tricks himself, advising as to the cards that were being played outside his hand. When Taft's brothers and campaign manager determined to try for the delegates from New York State, where Charles E. Hughes was still nominally the State's candidate and favorite son, Roosevelt advised them to "let Hughes alone in New York; you will need him and his friends in the election."[26]

Minutely, Roosevelt instructed Taft in the art of effective political speechmaking. "Don't talk on delicate subjects," he wrote. "Stop citing court decisions, for the moment you begin to cite decisions people at once think it is impossible for them to understand, and they cease trying to comprehend, and promptly begin to nod." "[You] must," he instructed Taft, "treat a political audience as one coming not to see an etching but a poster." "[You] must have streaks of blue, yellow, and red to catch the eye and eliminate all fine lines and soft colors." Taft humbly took the lesson in. "I think,"

25 The messenger was Mark Sullivan. Some of these instructions by Roosevelt to Taft were given before the nomination, some after.

26 It turned out to be so. In the ensuing campaign, a single speech by Hughes in Ohio was almost enough, alone, to crumple up Bryan's campaign. One who was near Bryan as he read Hughes' speech in a Pullman diner the following morning saw the Commoner's face fall, and observed that throughout the remainder of the campaign Bryan did not press again that part of his platform which Hughes had riddled.

said Roosevelt later, "Taft thought I was a barbarian and a mountebank at first. But . . . he is at last catching the attention of the crowd."[27]

The crowd, nevertheless, saw Taft as what, during the campaign, he was, a not very expertly synthesized Roosevelt, at best the approved heir apparent to Roosevelt rather than a birthright duplicate of the blood. A type of joke became common:

"That's a splendid phonograph, old man. It reproduces the sound of Roosevelt's voice better than I ever thought possible. What make?"

"We call it the Taft."

"The great current question about Taft," said *Life*, is "whether he has got a boiler of his own or is permanently belted onto a line of shafting which owes its revolutions to steam furnished by another statesman. . . . The big Secretary is one of the finest pieces of human machinery there is in sight, and works to the admiration of almost all observers, but the intimacy of his connection with the Roosevelt boiler operates undoubtedly to the prejudice of his independent aspirations." However, *Life* added, "If Taft is a shadow, he is the biggest, most substantial and most wholesome shadow that ever a President cast."

VI

In the failure of the crowd to get much more than amiably tolerant about Taft, in their rfeusal to be stirred deeply about either Taft as Taft or Taft as pseudo-Roosevelt, it came about that the principal work of Roosevelt, in nominating Taft, was to prevent the nomination from being thrust on himself.

When some members of Roosevelt's cabinet, taking a

27 "The Letters of Archie Butt."

gamble, seemed to be permitting their subordinates to work up Roosevelt sentiment, Roosevelt wrote an identical note to the secretaries of the Treasury and of the Interior and the Postmaster General — "This must not be."[28] When Senator Jonathan Bourne of Oregon invented a phrase, "second elective term," to describe a thing differing, in Roosevelt's case, from a third term, Roosevelt frowned on the etymological subtlety. When Roosevelt heard that two delegates from West Virginia were going to vote for him, he wrote to a friend in that State: "I most strenuously object to any friend of mine going for me on any ballot." When he heard that his old Rough Rider friend, Cecil A. Lyon of Texas, was going to bring a Roosevelt delegation to the convention, he summoned Lyon to the White House and, softening his firmness with humor, said, in effect: "Let your delegation be for Taft, Cassius, or never more be officer of mine"; and Lyon, sadly returning to Texas, said: "It's all off, boys, the big chief won't let us vote for him and we've got to vote for Taft."

VII

When the nominating convention met in Chicago, in June, 1908, Roosevelt sent the most expert telegrapher on the White House staff to stand immediately back of Chairman Lodge to flash a message to Roosevelt, and to receive, in case there should be a stampede[29] towards

28 "Theodore Roosevelt and His Time," Joseph Bucklin Bishop.

29 The stampede toward Roosevelt came, when Lodge, in his keynote speech, said: "The result is that the President is the best abused and the most popular man in the United States to-day." The demand for Roosevelt was so insistent that when the balloting was on the uproar was so great as to prevent any one hearing the roll call. Lodge, following, at Roosevelt's request, steam-roller methods, merely beckoned the head of each delegation to the platform and recorded the vote. Not until Massachusetts was reached on the alphabetical list did the Roosevelt adherents quiet down and admit their hope could not be.

Roosevelt, the imperative declination, which Roosevelt in the White House was prepared to send.

In another quarter of Washington, across the street from the White House, in Taft's office in the War Department, the convention proceedings were followed in a different mood. Taft had as guests some intimate friends and members of his family. Taft himself, confident and serene, by nature free from suspicion or other form of unhappy apprehension, sat among friends in the middle of the room; at his desk, occupying his official chair, was Mrs. Taft. When Taft's name was placed in nomination and the cheering began, Mrs. Taft remarked, "I only want it to last more than forty-five minutes" — the day before a demonstration at the mention of Roosevelt's name had lasted that long. Taft said, chidingly, "Oh, my dear! my dear!" When a bulletin was handed Mrs. Taft saying that a large portrait of Roosevelt on the platform had caused a new outburst of cheering, she sat "white as marble and motionless. Mr. Taft tapped with his fingers on the arm of his chair. . . . No one said a word or looked at his neighbor."[30] After several painful minutes came a bulletin saying that Massachusetts had cast 25 votes for Taft. That, to those who understood, was the signal that Roosevelt's plan to nominate Taft was being carried out successfully, for Massachusetts was the state of Senator Lodge, and Senator Lodge was at once the chairman of the convention and the known spokesman and agent of Roosevelt's wishes. "Mrs. Taft's face . . . more than regained its normal color; she was the personification of a proud and happy wife."

The next day, Roosevelt wrote a letter to a friend, Sir George Otto Trevelyan:

[30] Joseph Bucklin Bishop, "Presidential Nominations and Elections."

Well, the convention is over and Taft is nominated. . . . It has been a curious contest, for I have had to fight tooth and nail against being renominated myself. I could not have prevented it at all unless I had thrown myself heart and soul into the business and had shown to the country that Taft stood for exactly the same principles and policies that I did, and that I believed with all my heart and soul that under him we should progress steadily along the road [my] administration has travelled. He and I view public questions exactly alike. In fact, I think it has been very rare that two public men have ever been so much at one in all the essentials of their beliefs and practices.

And then, in the fine pleasure that comes of a worthy task carried to completion, Roosevelt added a sentence, struck off in the sheer exuberance of his content, which was destined later to bedevil him, destined to be momentous in the presidential campaign of four years later. "Always excepting Washington and Lincoln," Roosevelt wrote, "I believe that Taft as President will rank with any other man who has ever been in the White House."

13

TAFT IS ELECTED PRESIDENT

In Which Process, Again, Roosevelt Plays the Leading
Rôle, Being at Once Shrewd Counsellor in Strategy, Able
Tutor in Technique, Trainer and Stimulator in Belligerency.

Now, to electing Taft, Roosevelt renewed his dedica-
tion. He collaborated with Taft in composing the latter's acceptance speech — in which Taft said, as his most
effective appeal to the American electorate: "Mr. Roosevelt led the way to practical reform. My chief function
shall be to complete and perfect . . .

Painstakingly, and also joyously, Roosevelt took the
rôle of trainer: "Let the audience see you smile always,
because I feel that your nature shines out so transparently
when you do smile — you big, generous, high-minded
fellow. . . . Hit them hard, old man!"[1] When Taft's
hitting was not hard enough for his mentor's taste,
Roosevelt stepped out of the trainer's corner himself to
deliver the needed punch. When William R. Hearst
(figuring in the campaign as an independent third candidate as well as journalistic brewer of miscellaneous commotion) exploded a scandal damaging to the Republican campaign in Taft's own and critical state, Ohio, by
exposing payments of money to important Republican
Senator Foraker,[2] Roosevelt showed Taft precisely how
to meet the situation — and himself conducted on Taft's
behalf a dual manœuvre of defense and offense, first publicly disavowing Foraker, and then shrewdly writing
an open letter to Bryan, the Democratic Presidential

---

[1] Roosevelt to Taft, September 11, 1908.
[2] Foraker was able to show the payments were not for anything he did in the
United States Senate.

candidate, pointing out that a second recipient of Standard Oil money mentioned on Hearst's list was one of the
two chief officials managing Bryan's campaign.   "In this

President Taft.

Foraker affair," Roosevelt wrote,[3] "I made up my mind
that I would hit from the shoulder, inasmuch as Taft
did not."

When Taft as the Presidential nominee was an important figure at commencement ceremonies of his University, Yale, Roosevelt, conscious of the political unwis-

[3] To Lawrence Abbott.

dom of propinquity of a Presidential nominee with big business, wished "that Yale had not chosen this particular time . . . to confer a degree on J. Pierpont Morgan."[4] When a man in Ohio wrote a letter calling attention to stories about Taft being a Unitarian and therefore an "infidel" — writing, so the unctuous pseudo-friend said, "for the sole purpose of giving Mr. Taft an opportunity to let the world know what his religious belief is" — it was Roosevelt who replied with an energetic denunciation of bigotry: "In my cabinet at the present moment there sit side by side Catholic and Protestant, Christian and Jew . . ."[5]

If it was sympathy and encouragement the candidate needed, the versatile trainer could supply that, too: "Poor old boy," he wrote to Taft, "of course you are not enjoying the campaign; I wish you had some of my bad temper."[6] In Roosevelt's friendly epithets there was, perhaps, just a hint of impatience with his pupil, of dawning disappointment. And, on the other side, if Taft himself was too amiable to resent such intimate urging, others close to Taft may have hoped for the time when Taft would be free of such personal tutoring.

Throughout the campaign Roosevelt "watched over Taft like a hen over her chickens, always on the alert and never missing a trick,"[7] far and away the most expert tactician, "the greatest force in the party. . . . Without his personality there would be an awful slump."[8] At all times Roosevelt's manner was the barometer of Taft's fortunes. "Whenever Roosevelt looks worried," his sympathetic aide, Archie Butt, feels "anxious for Taft."

[4] Letter to Benjamin Ide Wheeler, president of the University of California.
[5] The letter was made public November 4, 1908.
[6] Roosevelt to Taft, July 15, 1908.
[7] "Presidents I Have Known," Charles Willis Thompson.
[8] "Letters of Archie Butt."

But if Roosevelt "is in a rollicking humor," Butt knows all is well with Taft. "We have them beaten to a frazzle" Roosevelt would say when things were going right.[8a]

When on election day Taft got 321 electoral votes to Bryan's 162, and 7,678,908 popular votes to Bryan's 6,409,104, Roosevelt was "simply radiant."[8a] It was, with one exception, the largest electoral vote and popular plurality ever received by any Presidential candidate. With a discriminating prudence relatively rare in statistics it stopped just short of equalling Roosevelt's own victory four years before[9] — making Roosevelt's happiness complete, perfect.

	1904			1908	
Roosevelt	7,624,489		Taft	7,678,908
Parker	5,082,754		Bryan	6,409,104
Roosevelt's plurality	2,541,735		Taft's plurality	1,269,804
Electoral vote, 336 to 140.			Electoral vote, 321 to 162.

II

Once more Roosevelt composed a letter to his friend Trevelyan. Expansively, dropping his modesty as he took up his pen, Roosevelt wrote:

Taft will carry on the work substantially as I have. His policies, principles, purposes and ideals are the same as mine, and he is a strong, forceful, efficient man, absolutely upright, absolutely disinterested and fearless. . . . I have the profound satisfaction of knowing that he will do all in his power to further every one of the great causes for which I have fought and that he will persevere in every one of the great governmental policies in which I most firmly believe.

In short, Taft will be me!

[8a] "Letters of Archie Butt."

[9] Actually, Taft's popular vote, though not his plurality, was greater than Roosevelt's:

III

Taft, elected, also wrote a letter. It was to Roosevelt:

I have just reached Hot Springs. The first letter I wish to write is to you, because you have always been the chief agent in working out the present status of affairs, and my selection and election are chiefly your work. You and my brother Charley made that possible which in all probability would not have occurred otherwise. I don't wish to be falsely modest in this. I know, as you have said to me when we have talked the matter over, that neither you nor he could probably have done the same thing with any other candidate, under the circumstances as they were, but that doesn't affect the fact as I have stated it, or my reason for feeling the deep gratitude which I do to you both for what has happened and the successful efforts which you have made costing time and energy and subjecting you to severe criticism, and, in some cases, the loss of personal friendships that you might have avoided.[10]

Here was fullness of gratitude on the part of Taft, fullness of satisfaction on the part of Roosevelt — pleasure to Roosevelt at once with his success in bringing about the boon he had conferred on Taft and with Taft's gratitude for the boon. Here was deep thankfulness on the part of the receiver, beaming happiness on the part of the giver — an apotheosis of the ideal relation between beneficiary and benefactor.

It was the last time this could be.

[10] This letter disproves one of the most persistent of recent American legends. In many books, scores of newspaper publications, and thousands of conversations by those who claimed to know "the inside" of what happened, the cause of the break between Taft and Roosevelt is alleged to have been a letter written by Taft to Roosevelt, in which Taft, according to the story, says, "thanks to my brother Charles and you, I shall be President," or, as put by Arthur Wallace Dunn ("From Harrison to Harding") : "Next to my brother [Charles] I owe more to you than to any one man for my election."

All the versions are alike in the essential characteristic alleged to be inflammatory, Taft's mentioning his brother before Roosevelt. All allege that to have been the excitant of Roosevelt's resentment — Dunn quotes Roosevelt as saying: "He puts money above brains."

Roosevelt made no such remark. Taft wrote no such letter. The letter Taft did write is as above and names Roosevelt as the primary beneficiary of his gratitude. It is true that rift began at the precise moment that letter was written — but the letter, as such, had nothing to do with it. For an account of the real causes, see pages 316 et seq.

14

THE BEGINNING OF RIFT

Which Constituted, for Roosevelt and Taft, the Breaking of
the Silver Bowl. And, for the Country, Made Much History.

AT precisely the instant when the election returns
showed Roosevelt had made Taft President and when
Taft had voiced his gratitude to Roosevelt, at that moment, without either realizing it, the relation into which
the two had fitted as the mortise to the groove, came to
an end and would never be renewed. The silver bowl was
broken, the time of the friendship of Roosevelt and Taft
was one with "the years that the locust hath eaten." The
subsequent incidents are pertinent not to the friendship
but to the rupture. The details were immaterial, for consciousness of the rift was bound to come to each, if not
by one way then by another. As incidents of the relations
between two men they followed the same pattern, and
were of no more consequence than the relations between
any other two men; it merely happened that because
these two were, one a President and the other a President-to-be, the incidents had consequences for history.

II

When two persons, having been friends, become the
opposite, the events composing the rift are the material
of drama. To fix the precise moment when friendship
became less than it had been, to identify the individual
grain of sand which when in the upper half of the hour-
glass basked in the warmth of affection at full-tide, but
which as soon as it had passed into the lower half felt

the chill of beginning coolness; to explore for the traits in each of the men that made cleavage possible and to identify the circumstances and influences that made it inevitable — that is the fascinating task at which poets and novelists toil.

When the two men involved are, one a President of the United States and the other a President-to-be, when one is the leading statesman of the world and the other is the first one's choice to succeed him as President, when the whole relationship between the two determines the Presidency of the United States for twelve years, determines a new tangent for the nation's destiny and affects the fortunes of the world in countless ways — in such a case the transition from friendship to enmity is the very essence of history.

Neither for historian nor dramatist is the task easy. His equipment must include, commonly, an insight giving him greater understanding of other men's souls than they have themselves, for it is rare that any one is able to recall, after a misunderstanding has passed into the stage of avowed separation, just what was the circumstance and when the moment, that one of two friends did a thing which caused disappointment in the other, and equally rare for the other to be able to recall the first faint sense of rebuff that was the beginning of cleavage. In all transitions from friendship to the opposite, whether portentous with men highly placed or trivial among the humble, the recollections of the parties to the quarrel are far from the best evidence. A judge, or a historian, who, seeking to apportion what is loosely called "blame" for a rift — as well speak of "blame" for a change of the seasons — would be unwise if he should accept the judgments of the participants themselves.

The common way is to tell the story in terms of melodrama, to say that on such or such a date, or for such and such a reason, the two quarrelled. Rarely does it happen so. The beginnings of enmity, like the beginnings of the friendship that preceded it, are composed of faint and subtle overtones of the souls of the men involved. The beginnings of such situations are as evanescent, as difficult to identify, as the moment when summer makes its first faint sigh of surrender to fall. The historian seeking to detach and record all the elements that entered into the termination of a friendship must know much besides the principals to the situation; he must know the surrounding circumstances, and the influences outside the men themselves, some one of which, at some fatal moment, pulled stronger than the tie of affection could hold. He must know, among other things, the men's friends and their kin and their wives.

In the case of Theodore Roosevelt and William H. Taft there was a circumstance that gave to their rupture a resistless inevitability as austere as a Greek tragedy, a circumstance making for disruption so powerfully that only incredible self-restraint and humility, especially on the part of Roosevelt, could have averted it — and Roosevelt did not have incredible self-restraint and humility.

There is a French proverb which says that in every meeting of lips one is the kisser, the other the kissed. In every relation of human beings, one is giver and the other receiver. These qualities, these attitudes toward life, toward others, are essential in each human being. They are permanent and in nature go on to the end. Because the personalities of each, their respective attitudes toward life are permanent, the one a temperamental bestower, the other a temperamental receiver, it commonly follows, in the lack of intrusion by some circumstance from outside, that the friendship is enduring.

In the case of Roosevelt and Taft, however, events flew in the face of nature. Events decreed that Roosevelt, having been the giver, should, on leaving the Presidency, cease to be the giver, and that Taft, having received all that Roosevelt had, the Presidency itself, was thereafter in a rôle opposite to that for which nature had designed him; while Roosevelt also, being no longer able to be giver, was likewise in a position warped out of that for which nature had designed him. The election returns on November 4, 1908, violently reversed the relation of the two to each other. Taft was now to be President; if there was to be giving now it would be with Taft in the rôle of giver, Roosevelt in the rôle of receiver — and it was not in Roosevelt's nature to be a gracious receiver. Roosevelt as President could be and loved to be a magnificent giver to Taft the Governor-General of the Philippines and Taft the Secretary of War. Taft by temperament and attitude of mind could be and was a comfortable receiver of place, and equally an able bearer of the responsibility that place involved, a dutiful payer of the loyalty that the gift to him called for. In the final phase, Roosevelt gave to Taft the very thing that had made his giving possible, the Presidency itself. Once Taft stepped into that office the rôles of the two men were violently reversed; if there was to be giving now, it must be from Taft to Roosevelt. The thing was impossible in nature.

III

The first time Roosevelt had occasion to be asker, Taft to be giver, arose casually in a conversation, ordinary when it took place but destined to be portentous. It was in the transition period, when the rôles of the two overlapped — when Roosevelt was still President, but on the way to becoming ex-, and Taft not yet President but on the way to be.

Taft, as soon as he had been nominated for the Presidency, felt he should hand Roosevelt his resignation as Secretary of War. Roosevelt, having in mind no interest of his own, but mainly Taft's and the Republican party's, told Taft that he would like to appoint as the new Secretary a Southern Democrat (Roosevelt knew well the value of such a gesture during a Presidential campaign); that he had in mind Luke Wright of Tennessee; that it would be difficult to get Wright or any other good man for so short an unexpired term, but that if he [Roosevelt] could assure Wright that Taft would continue him in Taft's administration, this might be an inducement.

It was the first occasion when, as between the two men, Roosevelt was the asker, even of a favor meant almost wholly for Taft's benefit and the party's and the country's, and little or not at all for Roosevelt's own benefit. Roosevelt shrank from the unaccustomed rôle.

"Remember," Roosevelt said, "I am not asking this as a favor to me. I am trying to get a good man. I would prefer a man whom you will continue, but if you do not care to commit yourself I will go ahead and do the best I can without involving you at all."

Taft replied that he "would be more than pleased to continue Wright."

"Then," said Roosevelt, "I can tell Wright, when I offer him the place, that I am speaking for you as well as for myself?"

"You can."

Taft went further, brought up the matter of the Cabinet as a whole. In the elation of his success in getting the Presidential nomination, in the warmth of his gratitude to Roosevelt, in the radiant benevolence that was his fundamental nature, and at a time when his family counsellors were not about him, Taft made a portentous statement to Roosevelt — whether it was only a statement, or a promise — later became material:

"I wish," said Taft, "you would tell the boys I have been working with [the Cabinet] that I want to continue all of them. They are all fine fellows, and they have been mighty good to me. I want them all to stay just as they are."

A contemporary drawing by Homer Davenport in the New York "American."

"Dance!"

"Why don't you tell them so yourself?" Roosevelt asked.

"No, I don't want to do that. I don't want to make any promises. I want to be in a position to say that I have no promises out. I wish, though, that you would tell them just how I feel and let them know that I want the Cabinet to stand just as it is."

"That cannot be," Roosevelt replied, "and should not be. [Roosevelt mentioned three members of his Cabinet who had personal reasons for not wishing to go on.] Straus, Meyer, Garfield, and Wilson, however, would,

I think, be glad to stay on, and if you really want me to talk with them about it, I will gladly tell them of your intentions."

"Yes, I wish you would,"[1] replied Taft.

As a result of that conversation, Roosevelt assumed he had Taft's voluntary statement that he would retain five members of Roosevelt's Cabinet. As to one, Wright, Roosevelt felt that Taft's assurance was more than a mere statement of intention; it was a specific promise, a promise asked for in this one case by Roosevelt, a promise which, indeed, constituted a contract because it involved in a sense a consideration given.

Roosevelt, so feeling, passed Taft's assurance on to Wright and the other Cabinet members. The Cabinet members, with that assurance, assumed they would be kept. For some six months, from the time of Taft's

[1] This conversation between Taft and Roosevelt is fundamental in the turn their relations subsequently took. No record of it was made at the time. The version quoted here is Roosevelt's recollection set down by him formally eight years after the conversation took place. A version given by Taft two years after the conversation does not materially differ from Roosevelt's.

After the breach between Roosevelt and Taft had come to have historic importance, in February, 1916, Roosevelt was for twelve days on a steamer with a friend, Henry L. Stoddard. Stoddard suggested to Roosevelt that there ought to be somewhere a formal record of the facts about the break between Roosevelt and Taft. Roosevelt said, "If you care now to take down a statement of facts, I will be glad to make one." Stoddard took down the statement, labelled it, "Statement made to me and revised by Theodore Roosevelt on steamship *Matura* returning from Trinidad," and after Roosevelt's death published it. It is from this statement that the quotations above are taken.

A similar statement was made on another occasion by Roosevelt in his own hand-writing. A friend of his, Lawrence F. Abbott, had written for a newspaper an account in which he stated: "It was his [Taft's] desire and intention to retain those Cabinet colleagues of Mr. Roosevelt who had contributed so much to the re-creation of the Republican party." This sentence Abbott showed to Roosevelt, and Roosevelt wrote on the margin: "He told me so, and authorized me to tell the Cabinet, specifically, Garfield, Straus and Luke Wright."

Those are Roosevelt's versions. Taft's does not materially differ. Taft, October 19, 1910, said to Archie Butt, and Butt that evening wrote down: "One day, just after I was nominated, I told Roosevelt that, should I be elected, I did not see how I could do anything else but retain all the old members of the Cabinet who had been associated with me. I thought nothing more about it, but I learned later that Roosevelt had practically told every member of his Cabinet that he was going to be retained should I be elected. . . . I am now placed in the attitude of breaking a promise to each of these men."

nomination when he made his statement to Roosevelt, until two months after his election, Roosevelt, his Cabinet, and everybody in his circle assumed that Taft would retain Roosevelt's Cabinet (except the three who wished to retire). One member renewed the lease on his Washington house. Others refrained from making the personal plans they would have made had they not been assured they would be kept.

IV

The first tentacle of disturbing doubt to reach Roosevelt came some weeks after Taft's election, in the form of a report from Roosevelt's secretary, William Loeb, Jr. Loeb told Roosevelt that Taft had come to see Loeb and had stated to Loeb that he had concluded not to retain Secretary Garfield. Loeb had assumed from Taft's manner that Taft meant him to repeat this information to Roosevelt. Roosevelt's mouth fell. His eyes took on the inward-looking, squinting expression that accompanied bepuzzlement, and the inward concentration that sought the answer. "I simply cannot believe it unless he tells me so himself," he said to Loeb.[2] Roosevelt was sure Taft had told him that he intended to retain Roosevelt's Cabinet,[3] and had asked, or authorized, Roosevelt to tell the men in question that they would be kept — and Roosevelt had so told them. Roosevelt was dismayed, felt a little sheepish as he came face to face in

[2] From a letter to the author from William Loeb, Jr., September 14, 1932.

[3] Not all Roosevelt's Cabinet was involved. At least three meant to retire for personal reasons. There were five who figured in this controversy, who were willing to stay on with Taft, whom apparently Taft had said to Roosevelt that he meant to keep, and who in turn had been told by Roosevelt that Taft meant to keep them. They were: James R. Garfield, Secretary of the Interior; Oscar Straus, Secretary of Commerce and Labor; James Wilson, Secretary of Agriculture; George von Lengerke Meyer, Postmaster-General; and Luke Wright, Secretary of War. Taft kept two, Meyer and Wilson.

his daily life with the men whom he had told they would be kept by Taft, and who now knew they would not.

Roosevelt's emotions were mixed. The instinct of loyalty, that was strong in him, led him to seek excuses for Taft. Pride in his own judgment in having made Taft President led him the same way. He had thought, at the time Taft said he would keep the Cabinet, that it was unwise for Taft to say that, and impolitic for him to keep all, and to this thought Roosevelt now went back. Bravely he tried to keep his attitude toward Taft the same; his letters continued to begin "Dear Will" and to end "Give my love to Mrs. Taft." Writing to Taft about the Cabinet not being kept, there was no faintest reproach, only "I think it would be well for you to write them all at once that you do not intend to reappoint them; they will be making their plans, and less than two months remain, and I do not think they ought to be left in doubt." When persons not very close to Roosevelt tried to draw him out, he justified Taft. "No," he said, "Taft is going about this thing just as I would do; I cannot find any fault in Taft's attitude toward me."[4]

There were others, however, to whom Roosevelt could not dissimulate. He had dearly wished Garfield to be kept in the Cabinet, for upon Garfield depended continuance of Roosevelt's policy of conservation; he had been pleased when Taft said he would keep Garfield, and he had taken pleasure in telling Garfield he would be kept. Now he was obliged to say to Garfield, "Jim, something has come over Will, he is changed, he is not the same man." With another Cabinet member, his embarrassment was even more acute. Luke Wright had accepted the post of Secretary of War upon Roosevelt's

[4] "Letters of Archie Butt."

assurance, given Roosevelt by Taft, that Taft would retain Wright; in short, Roosevelt had given Wright a promise, based in turn on a promise from Taft — and the promise was not to be kept. "I am distressed, Gen-

James R. Garfield.

eral," he said to Wright, "that you will not continue to be Secretary of War. Unfortunately," he added, with a touch of bitterness that was beginning to descend upon him, "you have been too close to me, I fear."[5] And Archie Butt, overhearing this first expression of Roosevelt's feeling, wrote in his diary: Roosevelt "feels very deeply the fact that Mr. Taft seems determined to sever all the ties which have bound them together in the past. Roosevelt was the only one who did not foresee this, and I think he will be bitterly disappointed when he sees many of his policies reversed. He was so cocksure that Mr. Taft would continue all his policies, and I fear that

[5] "Letters of Archie Butt."

a general reversal will be nearer the line he will follow."[6]

Taft, ineptly unaware of what was taking place, wrote[7] to Roosevelt: "People have attempted to represent that you and I were in some way at odds during this last two or three months; whereas you and I know that there has not been the slightest difference between us. . . . With love and affection, my dear Theodore."

V

That letter of Taft's was utterly sincere. The breach was not so much in his mind as in the nature of the situation, the forced reversal of the rôles of giver and receiver, and in the mental attitudes of those about Taft. It was natural for Taft's wife and his elder half-brother (and quasi-father) Charles P. Taft, to have been irked by the newspaper quips about Roosevelt making Taft President, the cartoons that pictured Roosevelt as the hen, Taft as the egg he hatched. It was natural for them to wish to feel that Taft was President on his own merits, and, wishing that, should wish to see distance between Taft and Roosevelt, should do things likely to bring distance about. At the time Taft was in the midst of picking his Cabinet, he was visited by Archie Butt:

The door was open and I heard the heartiest laugh imaginable from Mr. Taft. As I entered, Mrs. Taft was not looking quite as cheerful as Taft. He did not stop laughing, and Mrs. Taft said: "Well, I don't see anything to laugh at; now we must get to business while Captain Butt is here." Taft grabbed me by the hand and when he could control himself said:

[6] Sapiently, Butt added: "It will be a dangerous thing for Taft to do, for it will relieve Mr. Roosevelt of all responsibility of breaking the bonds and afford him every excuse to make the race in another four years if there is any demand for him from the people."

[7] February 25, 1909.

"Nothing to laugh at? I think it is the funniest thing I ever heard. I confess it would not be anything for him to laugh at if he knew for one minute how near he was to the Cabinet and how far away he is at this minute." Then turning to me he said: "I was cabinet-making early this morning and I had thought that I had settled one place at least, and just as you

President Taft and family.

were announced I had told my wife. She simply wiped him off the face of the earth. The personal side of politics has always been funny to me. But nothing has been quite as funny as to have a man's career wrecked by a jealous wife." "Not jealous at all," said Mrs. Taft, "but I could not believe you to be serious when you mentioned that man's name. He is perfectly awful and his family are even worse. I won't even talk about it."[8]

[8] Archie Butt. On a later occasion, Butt recited another instance of Mrs. Taft's forthright energy, her husband's good-natured inertness. Butt having made some suggestions and Taft having approved them, Mrs. Taft exclaimed,

As it was with Taft's wife, so it was with the elder half-brother, Charles P. Taft, who had partly made Taft's whole public career possible by his largesse, who had supplied the largest quantity of funds for the campaign, who had supplied also affection and encouragement and loyalty, had supplied, indeed, within his limits, advice and guidance — it was quite according to human nature that Charles P. Taft should wish to feel that he had had a major part in his brother's elevation. Months later, William H., in the White House, spoke of it. Smilingly, he said, "What troubles Charlie is, he is afraid Roosevelt will get the credit of making me President, and not himself. . . . I am always amused at Charlie's determined position that Roosevelt had nothing to do with my nomination and election, and he grudgingly admits that he was for me at all, whereas to deny the determining factor he [Roosevelt] became in my nomination would be, not only the basest ingratitude, but to ignore the facts."[9] Turning to the jealous brother, Taft continued playfully: "Old fellow, I will not goad you into any discussion of this subject again, for we have had some heated talks on it before, haven't we? And I will agree not to minimize the part you played in making me President if you will agree not to minimize the part Roosevelt played. Possibly I had nothing to do with it at all and just you two did together, but . . ."

VI

Correspondingly, it was natural that friends of Roosevelt, some of them dependent for their place in the world

---

"Will, you approve everything—everything Mr. Norton brings you, everything Captain Butt brings to you, and everything everybody brings to you."

Taft, smiling, replied: "Well, my dear, if I approve everything, you disapprove everything, so we even up."

[9] "Letters of Archie Butt."

upon the presence of their patron in the Presidency, should "act as if the Tafts had committed some breach of friendship by becoming occupants of the White House. . . . To hear them talk one would think that Mr. Roosevelt was being driven from the White House by Mr. Taft";[10] and that others, seeing the new sun rising should try to win warmth from it by drawing away from the old. "It is really comical," wrote Butt, "to see the petty intrigues."[11] Among those who thus brought distance between Taft and Roosevelt was Henry Cabot Lodge. Returning from a trip to Augusta, Georgia, where Taft was awaiting inauguration day, Lodge reported that "he had been in Augusta two whole days before he was allowed to see Mr. Taft alone for a minute, that he was kept constantly under the watchful eye of either Mrs. Taft or his brother."[12]

Some of the estrangement came from members of Roosevelt's family. His eldest daughter, Alice, then about twenty-four, had much of her father's vitality and genius without his outlets for using it fruitfully; and, as a step-daughter to Mrs. Roosevelt, was freer from restraint than was best for so ebullient a spirit. Once, a friend had said to Roosevelt, "Why don't you look after Alice more?" and Roosevelt had replied, "Listen, I can be President of the United States — or I can attend to Alice."[13]

Alice, among her errant energies and versatile talents, was an impish antic, given to acid remarks of the sort that a later generation called "wise-cracks,"[14] and to conspicuous public pranks, not always untouched with malice. She would, with a sweep of her hand, brush

---

[10] "Letters of Archie Butt."   [11] "Letters of Archie Butt."
[12] "Letters of Archie Butt."
[13] Owen Wister, "Story of Forty Years' Friendship."
[14] It was she, then wife of Speaker Nicholas Longworth, who in the 1920's was credited with saying of Calvin Coolidge, "He looks as if he had been weaned on a pickle."

back her hair from her forehead, twist her features into
what she deemed to be a clownish resemblance to Mrs.
Taft, and thus present to Washington drawing-rooms,
and even on the streets, a caricature of the woman who
was about to be mistress of the White House. Such incidents, in the atmosphere of Washington, were quick to
reach the ears of the person meant to be lampooned.

There were other incidents, so inevitable in the circumstances, so completely innocent on the part of those
who participated, so touched with the essence of un-
escapable tragedy, as to be poignant. Not even the most
gracious of persons could be free from embittering influences arising out of the change. Mrs. Roosevelt, gen-
tlest, serenest of women, wisest of wives, Penelope and
Sophia combined, utterly incapable of either meanness
or folly, her wisdom and humor permitting her "a little
laugh" at others' weaknesses but her spirit incapable of
doing a petty thing or thinking a spiteful one — even
Mrs. Roosevelt was affected by the inevitable circumstances. "She hates gossip," wrote Archie Butt, "and
will not permit any one to tell her any, the fairest-
minded woman I ever met." She was scrupulous about
facilitating whatever changes her successor might want
in the White House. But when she heard from Butt
that some frock-coated white ushers, men of some importance in their own personalities, were to be displaced
by Mrs. Taft with colored servants in livery, she was dismayed. " 'All of them?' Mrs. Roosevelt asked, her voice
quivering. 'Oh, it will hurt them so,' and her voice
broke and she stopped, raised her veil and for a few minutes could not speak. 'If you knew how those men
had served us, and how kind and thoughtful they have
been. . . .' " Later, recovering herself, Mrs. Roosevelt felt she had "been a little unjust possibly towards

Mrs. Taft . . . and wishes to show the friendliness she really feels for every one."[15]

VII

The estrangement, so far, was wholly concealed behind the façade of good manners which all the participants presented to the public, and remained so for nearly three years — not until 1911 did Roosevelt say publicly a word in criticism of Taft. Up to about the time of his leaving the White House, he felt no more than that his friend had done a thing that grieved him. About this point, however, in the transition from friendship to the opposite, it was human nature that Roosevelt should revise the whole of his view of his one-time friend. Partly through disillusionment that cleared his eyes, partly in justification of the new attitude toward Taft that was germinating in him, Roosevelt broadened his distance from his former friend. To what were merely the materials for a private personal disappointment, he added materials that elevated the episode into the substance of history.

The author of this book called to say good-bye to Roosevelt on the afternoon of the day preceding his departure from the White House, March 3, 1909. As I left, Roosevelt came with me to the door. Something was said about this being the last time we should meet in the White House, and something about the times we had been together there, the battles Roosevelt had fought against the standpatters. As we looked through the glass doors toward the lowering winter sky over LaFayette Park, I asked him, "How do you really think Taft will make out?" "He's all right," Roosevelt said, "he means

[15] "Letters of Archie Butt."

well and he'll do his best. But he's weak. They'll get
around him. They'll" — he came close to me, putting
his shoulder in front of my shoulder and pressing gently
with an effect of holding me back — "they'll lean
against him."

President Taft and Governor Hughes on the reviewing stand on the afternoon of
Taft's inauguration, March 4, 1909.

15

MARCH 4, 1909

A Ceremony in Which Old America Touched Elbows with New. Uniforms That Dated Back to the Continental Army Mingling with the Olive-drab That Had Been Dictated by the War with Spain. Old Units of Military Force That Preserved an Unbroken Chain of Tradition Back to the Annual "Training Day" of Colonial Times. The Last "Grand Inaugural Ball." The Ceremony at the Capitol. Enter Taft; Exit Roosevelt — though It Remained to Be Discovered that in Nature It Was Impossible for Theodore Roosevelt to Achieve "Exit" from the High Places of Activity in American Life. Taft Says "Good-bye" to Roosevelt.

In the parade that William H. Taft reviewed on the afternoon of his inauguration, March 4, 1909, America's past marched elbow-to-elbow with its present, and some vedettes of its future. It was a microcosm of the period during which Taft was to spend his years of office, the old America still pretty potent, thrusting itself rather pathetically forward as if asking for consideration on grounds of sentiment; the new America, a trifle brusque in the surge of its youthful strength, striding confidently on.

The military units of the parade were mainly of the new; they wore the olive-drab uniform, then still novel, that had been introduced during the war with Spain, when desirability of concealment against modern long-range rifles had dictated obsolescence for the gay blues and reds and yellows and gold braid of tradition. There were troops from the "Cuban Army of Pacification"; from the "Philippine Constabulary"; and thirty-three hundred sailors from the fleet at Hampton Roads, bronzed

333

from their just-finished cruise around the world (first ever taken by any American battle-fleet, our announcement that we had taken the place in the sun to which our victory over Spain entitled us). As the sailors passed, crowds along the sidewalks sang "Home Again from a Foreign Shore." Marching with the precision of youth's pride in its calling were cadets from West Point and midshipmen from Annapolis, alert with a new stimulation, inspirited with the belief that since America was now a world power, with colonies and dependencies, the career of arms would be elevated to greater dignity and importance — ambitious young fellows looking forward to be Lord Cromers, Lord Kitcheners, Lord Clives. Popular as always with the crowds were the strutting, tough-sinewed Marines, the sight of them recalling their "Marine Hymn":

> From the Halls of Montezuma
> To the shores of Tripoli,
> We fight our country's battles
> On the land and on the sea.
> First to fight for right and freedom
> And to keep our honor clean,
> We are proud to claim the title
> Of United States Marine. . . .

Interspersed with the new, giving to the sober olive-drab a touch of color and quaintness, like grandfather in a stock at a family reunion, were military units, and civilian as well, that recalled America's past, their very names evoking the flavor of old times:

The Worcester (Mass.) Continentals, organized April 10, 1776, three months before the Declaration of Independence; wearing, in the Taft parade, uniforms of buff and blue identical with the one George Washington had worn in the Revolutionary War, their appearance vividly suggesting the "Spirit of 1776," and recalling the early American "training day," when citizens practiced

From a photograph © by Enrique Muller.

The American battle-fleet returning from its cruise around the world.

From a photograph by Brown Bros.

West Point cadets in the inaugural parade, March 4, 1909.

manœuvres on the village "green" designed to equip them for protection against Indian raids.

The Richmond (Va.) Blues, organized in the year George Washington became President, having now kept for nearly a century and a quarter a uniform of dark blue with white breast and silver trimmings and leather helmets a foot and a half high adorned with white swan feathers.

Military units that bore the names of early commanders, or other distinctive designations (an individualism already largely overcome and destined by the time of the World War to succumb completely to the utility of designation by numbers alone): the "Cleaves Rifles." The "Portland Light Infantry" from Maine. The "Drake Zouaves" of Elizabeth, N. J. The "Gray Invincibles" of Philadelphia.

The "German Fusiliers" of Charleston, S. C., which had seen its first duty at the battle of Fort Moultrie in the Revolutionary War.

The Fifth United States Infantry, which proudly identified itself on the programme with its martial record, including the War of 1812, the Mexican War, the Black Hawk and Seminole Wars.

A company of Hussars from Georgia, their State flag eliciting from a few elderly men on the sidewalk as lively a repetition of the "rebel yell" as cracked voices could accomplish.

A company of the National Guard of Louisiana, the names of their officers — Labarre, Cergnois, Dermontluzin — recalling our purchase of our trans-Mississipi territory from Napoleon and the exile of the Acadians.

Troop A of the Ohio National Guard, from Cleveland — since Ohio was rather in the business of supplying tenants for the White House they were called the "personal escort of the President." The Troop had al-

ready escorted President William McKinley eight and
twelve years before.

The Temperance Pioneer Corps of South Bethlehem
(Pa.), symbol of the long period of militancy against
alcohol destined eleven years later to be successful —
and destined a few years after that to be looked upon as
having been too successful.

Among the civilian paraders were similar echoes of
America's past:

A company of full-blooded Creek Indians, Chief Eu-
fala Harpo commanding.

A "Pickaninny Band" — the word once universal for
a negro child was beginning to be obsolete, on its way to
join "Sambo" and "Dinah."

The "Young Men's Blaine Republican Club" of Cincinnati, survivor of a time when torch-light parades had
been a universal medium for expressing political emotion
in presidential campaigns.

The "Conkling Unconditionals" of Utica, N. Y., recalling the same tradition and recalling also in its name[1]
a doughty political leader already nearly forgotten by
the time of Taft, and by the years in which this history
is written not even a memory.

II

That night there was a "Grand Inaugural Ball,"[2] anticipated as a "swirl of society," at which, so the Washington *Star* assured a jealous democracy, "the every-day
American citizen will be permitted by the unwritten law
of American ethics to touch elbows with aristocratic
diplomats in the full panoply of their court costumes

---

[1] Roscoe Conkling, Representative and Senator from New York State 1859–
1881. A picturesque, combative, fiery figure in public life from before the Civil
War until his resignation from the Senate because of a quarrel over patronage
with President Garfield.
[2] The last ever held.

representing monarchies across the seas . . . and all for the modest price of $5.00."

The "every-day American citizen," we can feel sure, got his money's worth of thrill. He might have got even

DANCING

TEN O'CLOCK P. M. TO ONE O'CLOCK A. M.

1	WALTZ—"MARSOVIA"	BLAKE-BELCHER	13	WALTZ—"MERRY WIDOW"	LEHAR
2	TWO-STEP—"STAUNCH AND TRUE"	TEIKE	14	WALTZ—"MANILA"	FERAZE
3	WALTZ—"IN BALMY NIGHTS"	ZIERHER	15	TWO-STEP—"RAINBOW"	WENRICH
4	WALTZ—"WALTZ DREAM"	STRAUSS	16	WALTZ—"ARTIST'S LIFE"	STRAUSS
5	TWO-STEP—"UNDER ONE FLAG"	VON BLON	17	WALTZ—"BAD'NER MAD' IN"	KOMZAK
6	WALTZ—"THE BACHELORS"	SANTELMANN	18	PROMENADE— "LINCOLN CENTENNIAL"	SANFORD
7	TWO-STEP—"OLD FAITHFUL"	HOLTZMAN	19	WALTZ—"BLUE DANUBE"	STRAUSS
8	PROMENADE—"IN OLD BERLIN"	STARKE	20	TWO-STEP—"THE FAIREST OF THE FAIR"	SOUSA
9	WALTZ—"RED MILL"	HERBERT	21	WALTZ—"GOLDEN SUNSET"	HALL
10	TWO-STEP—"THE FORD"	ZICKEL	22	TWO-STEP—"ON THE AVENUE"	PIERSON
11	WALTZ—"VIENNA BEAUTIES"	ZIERHER	23	WALTZ—"GENEE"	LEVI
12	TWO-STEP— "THE MAN OF THE HOUR"	ARONSON	24	WALTZ—"LOLA"	FRIEDEMAN

"STAR SPANGLED BANNER"

Dance programme of last inaugural ball, March 4, 1909.

more — or less, according as he had imagination or lacked it — had he been able to see in the shadows behind the "aristocratic diplomats" some omen of what was about to happen to them and to the gorgeous courts of which they were a part, the "monarchies across the sea" from which they brought a disdain, not always successfully concealed, for what they considered our crude democracy. One within Taft's administration, and several during that of his successor, were destined to experience disillusion about the permanence of the ancient dynasties they represented, and to have a disquieting awakening from their estimate of the American democracy:

Count Johann Heinrich von Bernstorff, who was to live to see the dethronement and exile of the Imperial Highness whom he served, and to have himself a hand in the events which caused America to take part in barring Germany from the "place in the sun" she fatally coveted.

The Chinese Minister, still wearing the queue, the gorgeous Mandarin coat, the buttons, that were part of the regalia of the regime of the "old Empress" and of the state costumes of the Manchu dynasty — his successors in Washington a few years later doomed to look a little ridiculous in dress suits as representatives of a republic.

The Turk, his fez to be banned in 1927 by the edict of his own government, now intent on becoming modern by fiat, and his successors to walk Washington's streets in the undistinguished anonymity of a black derby hat.

The Russian, Baron Rosen, next but one to the last ambassador to represent the Czars at Washington, whose empire was doomed in a few short years to pass through bloody revolution and to embark upon the most colossal social experiment in human annals.

Ambassador James Bryce — his nation, Great Britain, soon to have an experience which would depose her from the proud pre-eminence she had had for more than a century.

Changes ahead might have been envisaged also in the personages of some who were not present in 1909 because they did not yet exist. For decades one of the standing jests of Washington was to speak of "the Irish Ambassador," companion to the joke about the "admiral of the Swiss Navy." Usually some agreeable or distinguished man of Irish birth in the Senate or House was made the beneficiary of the title by common consent; for a long while it was Bourke Cockran. By the time of Taft's successor, Woodrow Wilson, or a little later, and mainly through events in which Wilson had a large hand, it was decreed there should be present at the formal functions of Washington diplomacy, not only an Irish Minister but a Latvian Minister, and a Czecho-Slovakian, a Yugo-Slavian, a Finnish, a South African, a Lithuanian, a Polish, and a Canadian.

III

The ceremony in which Taft took over the Presidency from Roosevelt, by reason of snow could not take place in the open, in the presence of the multitude on the Capitol portico, and was held, for the second time in history, within the Senate.[3] The oath of office was administered by the Chief Justice of the United States Supreme Court, Melville Weston Fuller, who had been born in Maine in the year 1833, in which Andrew Jackson was inaugurated President the second time, and who still wore the flowing hair of the early days of the republic — he was the last public man in Washington who did so out of habit and retained custom (there were some later ones who did it as a pose).

IV

The two parties to the ceremony, Taft the incoming, Roosevelt the outgoing, had passed the morning and the evening of the day before in the ways that custom dic-

[3] Which had just ended its session in a filibuster conducted by Southern Democratic Senator Hernando de Soto Money of Mississippi against including, in a re-enactment of the penal code, a post-Civil War statute hateful to the South, pressed by some Northern Republicans, providing federal protection at the polls for negro voters. In 1909, it was still possible to make political capital out of "waving the bloody shirt."

tated for their rôles, as modified by their respective temperaments. Both were in high spirits, Taft because of

President-elect Taft arriving at the Capitol steps for the inaugural ceremony,
March 4, 1909.

the inevitable stimulation of the circumstances, Roosevelt because he was Roosevelt — it had been said of Roosevelt that whatever the event, he would be the chief figure present, at a wedding the bride, at a funeral the corpse, except that as corpse he would be unable to refrain from rising to preach the funeral sermon. Now, in the ending hours of his Presidency, he was more Roosevelt than ever. It was the most strenuous day he ever had in the White House, and in proportion as the day was strenuous did Roosevelt rise to it. As his last official act, he sent to Congress a message, his four hundred and twenty-first,[4] which the newspaper headlines, to the delight of the country, epitomized as:

HIS LAST WHACK AT CONGRESS
ROOSEVELT SENDS STINGING REBUKE FOR FINALE[5]

Congress had, as its own last fling at Roosevelt, incorporated in the routine sundry civil appropriation bill, a quite uncalled-for provision that "no part of the money herein appropriated" should be expended upon certain activities of Roosevelt which had irritated Congress, particularly Roosevelt's alleged use of the Secret Service to spy upon members of Congress deemed by him to be undesirable, and certain independent commissions Roosevelt had set up. Roosevelt, with only a few hours of his Presidency left, could not in any event expend money upon the forbidden purposes. Equally, of course, he could not help signing the bill, since the routine of the government depended on it. But he added an extraordinary message of defiance. "This action [of Congress]," he said, "is a benefit only to the criminal classes." As for the attempted limitation upon his commissions, "the purpose of the attempt is clearly an invasion of executive prerogative and unconstitutional and void; it is for the people of the country to decide whether or not they believe in the work done by these commissions [conservation and country life]."

That sort of message to Congress would be, to most Presidents, a matter of long hours of deliberation, ac-

[4] Roosevelt sent to Congress 421 messages and forty vetoes, more than any other President.

[5] *Washington Star,* March 4, 1909.

companied by exhausting consumption of emotion and
nervous energy. To Roosevelt it was merely a spark
struck off in the midst of his closing half-day. The scene
in his office was a repetition of the electric vitality of
hundreds of similar days before, for ever unforgettable
to any who participated in them, except that in this closing hour Roosevelt's tempo was accelerated, his vitality
at higher pitch. He dashed to the door to shake hands
with an arriving friend come to say good-by, he dashed
back to his desk to sign a bill from Congress or a letter
or a photograph, the while keeping up such flow of rail-
lery as deprived parting of all lugubriousness. He shook
hands, two hands at a time, with passing groups of callers brought by Congressmen. He button-holed one man
for a moment's confidential chat, shouted a bluff greeting across the room to another, drew a third into an al-
cove for a whispered consultation. Never was he more
characteristically Roosevelt.

V

Taft, his natural heartiness enlarged by the circumstances, played golf the afternoon of March 3, and on
the way home chuckled about the dismay of a Secret
Service man whose motorcycle failed him. In the evening he listened, at a smoker of fellow Yale alumni, to
"Boola-Boola," and

> Brek-ek ek-ek, ko ex, ko ex,
> Brek-ek ek-ek, ko ex, ko ex,
> Whoa-up, whoa-up,
> Hullabaloo, Ya-a-a-le,
> Ta-a-ft, Ta-a-ft, Ta-a-ft!

— the effulgence of the moment leading Taft to assure
his fellow graduates that "I will do my best; I feel it in
my bones that I will make good."

During the forenoon of March 4, he shook hands with four thousand people, including the inevitable "original Taft man," a type who commonly turns up to call on every new President and usually suggests that his powers of divination should be rewarded with an office; and a picked list of the "most gallant and handsome citizens in the country" — highfalutin designation for the men who had been selected to be floor committee for the Inaugural Ball; and a delegation who brought "a pair of mohair trousers made from the shearing of a Texas goat," which Taft promised to wear, as an inducement to Texas to change its views about the tariff and the Republican Party.[6] When the weather turned unseasonably stormy, doing violence to some of the plans for the inaugural ceremony, Taft merely chuckled, "I always knew it would be a cold day when I became President of the United States."

VI

About 11:45, Taft and Roosevelt took their last ride together, from the White House to the Capitol, for the ceremony of Taft's taking the oath. Roosevelt, still President, rode on the right; Taft, lacking fifty minutes of being the superior in rank, rode at the left. At the Capitol, while the two were together in the President's room, waiting to go on the Senate floor for the public ceremony, it was observed by a keen-eyed reporter of the Washington *Star*,[7] that "while they were cordial they did not spend very much time together; for nearly ten minutes they sat by each other's side without saying a word."

In the Senate, after completion of the ceremony of inauguration, Roosevelt started to leave. Passing the

[6] An inducement destined to be vain, for it was twenty years before Texas voted for a Republican President, and then for reasons remote from the tariff.
[7] March 4, 1909.

rostrum he came upon Taft, who was descending. Roosevelt ran up the steps and grasped Taft by the shoulders, possibly a closing flare-up of Roosevelt's long-time

From a photograph © by Harris & Ewing.

Roosevelt and Taft on the south portico of the White House just before leaving for the inaugural ceremony at the Capitol.

affection for Taft. Taft grasped Roosevelt in the same way. They stood a moment locked in a Gallic embrace, then broke apart, Roosevelt saying something in a low voice that caused Taft to smile. Then Roosevelt left the room. "There was a hush over the Chamber as he left, and one could almost hear the unexpressed thought of that great assemblage, 'He has gone.' "[8]

By old established custom the two men should have ridden once more together, from the Capitol to the White House, this time with Taft on the right. Roose-

From a drawing by E. W. Kemble in "Harper's Weekly," March 6, 1909.

"Good-by, Bill, I've had a perfectly corking time."

velt, whether or not because he, as Leslie M. Shaw acidly put it, "could not ride on the left," broke the usage. With Mrs. Roosevelt he went from the Capitol to the railroad station. A crowd there shouted, "What's the matter with Teddy, he's all right." A band, waiting to take its place in the parade to come later, noticing Roosevelt, picked up its instruments and played "Auld Lang Syne." Roosevelt, with Mrs. Roosevelt, entered the train, made his way to a stateroom, closed the public

8 "Theodore Roosevelt," Charles G. Washburn.

out, and went back to his home at Oyster Bay and private life.

Taft rode to the White House to begin his administration. With him, in the place assigned by tradition to
Roosevelt but abdicated by him, rode Mrs. Taft. "No
President's wife had ever done it before. . . . Of course
there was objection. Some of the Inaugural Committee expressed their disapproval, but I had my way and
in spite of protests took my place at my husband's
side. For me that ride was the proudest and happiest
event. . . ."[9]

[9] "Recollections," Mrs. William Howard Taft.

Drawn by H. B. Martin.

A cartoon which pleased and amused President Taft during the honeymoon
period of his administration.

16

TAFT'S FOUR YEARS: THE "INSURGENTS"

In the argot of politicians and Washington correspondents, there is at the beginning of every administration a "honeymoon period," during which White House and Capitol and partisan press, abjuring politics, radiate an altogether artificial and impermanent sweetness and trust and tolerance toward each other, and especially, on the part of the latter two, toward the new President. In Taft's case, the sentimental interlude was exceptionally sugary. "Never," said the New York *Sun*, "did any man come into the Presidency before with such universal good will." The *Literary Digest*, which during a long American generation made a metier of cutting from the press balanced comment pro and con, about current events, was made almost peevish by the one-sidedness it now found: "So unrelieved was the honeyed amiability of the newspaper comment which greeted the new administration that it seemed as if the . . . press had for the moment forgotten its function of criticism; we have searched the editorial pages of Democratic papers almost in vain for any fault-finding with President Taft." "All is quiet along the Potomac," quoted Edward G. Lowry; "the political mood of the national capital is as serene and soothing as that of the man who sits down alone in the dusk of the day to breathe softly into a flute the strains of 'The Maiden's Prayer.'"

II

A survey that probed beneath the surface would have revealed, however, that there had formed within the Republican party an angry cleavage, an insurgency by a minority West against a majority East.

This insurgency, diverse in its origins, had one root in a feeling on the part of the West that the protective tariff, instituted to foster Eastern "infant industries," had over-fed those industries until they were now fat and overbearing giants; another in the resentment of the West, composed mainly of individual businesses, chiefly farming, against the highly organized business East and its great corporations which drew much of their sustenance from the West but paid most of their profits to the East; another in the irritation of the granger West against the mainly Eastern-owned railroads, which had gone on from the seventies to the passage of the Railroad Rate Act in 1906;[1] another in the memories of the long controversy over currency,[2] between mainly debtor West and mainly creditor East, which had lasted from soon after the Civil War until 1896; another in the feeling that the remaining free lands, in the West, especially the mineral and oil-bearing ones, were being accumulated in the private possession of Eastern-owned railroads and other corporations — this one of the grievances, expressed in a movement called "conservation of natural resources," had many adherents in East as well as West.

All these roots drew sap from a deep undercurrent of American tradition, a spirit of resistance against authority, opposition against organized power, suspicion against vested interests. This truculent independence, now expressing itself acutely in insurgency against the Republican party, was a dominant trait of the American people, as old as America itself. Politically and socially

[1] See "Our Times," Vol. III, Ch. 7.   [2] See "Our Times," Vol. I, Ch. 9.

it *was* America. It had inspired the first settlement of the continent, had caused our separation from the mother country, had dictated the spirit and forms of the new government and institutions we set up. Our earliest settlers, as well as most of our immigrants, had been picked persons, selected by the law of their own natures on the basis of resentment against authority. In Europe in the seventeenth, eighteenth and nineteenth centuries, the individual who found himself most irked by a stratified society, who most resented organized power, whether of the church or of the system of land-tenure, or of caste of inherited place — any whose instinct urged him toward independence, moved to America. In each succeeding generation, this process of natural selection on the basis of instinct for independence repeated itself. In each generation, the most restless "went West," the first wave to central New York, western Pennsylvania, Kentucky and Tennessee; the next to Indiana, Illinois and Wisconsin; the next to Iowa, Kansas, Nebraska, and Missouri; the next to the Rocky Mountains and the Pacific Coast. By the time of Taft's administration or earlier, the people of the West were the result of three or four successive sievings of those most independent in spirit. Also a new condition had arrived; the free land was exhausted. No longer was there any "out West" to absorb those whose nature it was to resist authority, organization, to be made restless by the ruts of settled ways. Deprived of the chance of escape from what irked them, they turned to fight it.

The condition expressed itself in a division of the Republican party, in the country and in Congress, into mainly Eastern "Standpatters" (apt word[3] for conserva-

---

[3] "Standpatters" as a designation of the organized majority of the Republican party arose from an off-hand statement of Mark Hanna, then National Chairman, who in 1899 said all the Republicans needed to win the ensuing election was to "stand pat."

tive contentment with what is) and mainly Western "Progressives," translated by newspaper and popular zest for a fighting word, into "Insurgents."[4]

III

Which group the new President should stand with would be in the popular mind a test of Taft's fidelity to Roosevelt and Roosevelt's policies. Partly a misleading test, for Roosevelt had not really "stood with" the Insurgents; rather, he had used this group as one element of the power which he forged from many sources. Nor had Roosevelt ever completely flouted or directly and permanently opposed the conservative East — them, too, Roosevelt had used as one of the materials out of which he fused his power. But the legislation Roosevelt had brought about was largely in the Insurgent direction, his attitude toward public questions was mainly that of the West, the mainspring of his popularity came from that section. Now the West would instinctively view Taft in the light of whether he stood with them and their representatives in Congress, whether in his official attitudes as well as his informal intimacies he would seem to associate most with the Insurgents in Congress, or with the orthodox Standpatters who held the official places of power and were a large majority of the party.

To Taft it would be a difficult test, for Taft lacked Roosevelt's vigor which kept both factions subordinate to his own leadership, lacked Roosevelt's diversity of temperament which used to encourage Standpatters and Insurgents alternately, as each group lent itself to Roosevelt's larger purpose of the moment. Taft lacked Roose-

---

[4] The terms "Progressives" and "Insurgents" were used interchangeably. During the early period of the existence of the group, "Insurgents" was the preferred word. For that reason I have used "Insurgents" in this volume. After about the time of the organization of the Progressive party in 1912, the designation "Progressives" became more common.

velt's geniality coupled with dominating vitality, which could alternately flout Standpatter or conservative — and then immediately and cheerfully lift the victim to his feet and carry him along in Roosevelt's forward surge. This variousness of temperament, this fecundity of talent for dominance, Taft lacked. Particularly did Taft lack the primitive energy which enabled Roosevelt always to ride the wave, lead the procession. Taft with his more phlegmatic temperament, his more legalistic mind, would be prevailingly and conspicuously on one side or the other. In Taft's case the outcome of the test would make him seem all black or all white.

The static quality in Taft, his inertia, would bring it about that the label which he should finally bear would be less chosen by himself than fixed upon him by whichever side had the greater energy in surrounding him, pressing upon him, leaning against him.

IV

The Insurgent wing of the Republican party within the Senate was a group with fluctuating edges, amounting to from 10 to 14 Senators coming from Wisconsin, Indiana, Iowa, Minnesota, Kansas, Nebraska, North and South Dakota, and, so far as Borah then new in the Senate voted with them, Idaho. Calling themselves Republicans, at all times careful to keep that label (because in their States the Republican was the dominant party and almost the only one), they more often voted against than for the measures put forward by the Republican majority that controlled the Senate. They were, at the time Taft took office, hardly numerous enough or compact enough, to be called a wing of the party. It was of the essence of their natures that they lent themselves only with difficulty to organization or leadership. They were of a type that stands off from the herd, whether the herd be large or small. Their agreement in voting upon any issue was a coincidence rather than the fruit of organization. The same quality that made them insurgents against the majority made them unsympathetic to co-

President Taft and his Cabinet.

operation with each other. All had large egos; of the sum of the egos[5] of all 96 Senators, the 10 Insurgents had more than half. Their exile from the places of power was, publicly, their chief cause of complaint; inwardly, the exile was of their own choosing and most of them felt their martyrdom as a luxury which pleased their egos. They had an instinct for the dramatic, were agreeably conscious of the conspicuousness of being in-

[5] This emphasis upon the egos of the Insurgents may mislead. The word is used here mainly in the sense of a hard, inflexible personality, unwillingness or inability of a man to merge his personality into a group, a driving quality of intense preoccupation with one's own opinion and desires. Some of the Insurgents, especially LaFollette and Beveridge, had egotism in the ordinary sense. Others, like Clapp of Minnesota, were men of rather easy-going personality. Dolliver was utterly without the egotism that his ability would have abundantly justified.

surgents. They had a high average of ability to make their causes and their grievances vocal, overt, heard. The most prominent and forceful among them was La-Follette, but he could hardly be called their leader, for he exacted too dictatorial a subservience to his individual views ever to be a leader among equals having the same title to power and the same unbending quality as himself. None among them had the combination of forcefulness with urbanity and willingness to compromise and co-operate that was essential to leadership and organization in a group so diverse. Up to the time Taft took office their status as a group was ineffective; they were but little more than individual sharp-shooters who annoyed, rather than seriously threatened, the Republican majority and its leader, Senator Nelson W. Aldrich of Rhode Island.

v

Aldrich

It was against Aldrich and his leadership that the Insurgents cried out; against him they hurled their crowd-rousing epithets, "boss," "dictator," "despot," "tyrant"; him they denounced to the country as the all-powerful personification of the forces and influences they fought. "All powerful" was not too serious an exaggeration. One of the Insurgents, Beveridge of Indiana, though given to superlatives, did not exceed literalness when he said that Aldrich exercised greater power than any other individual in any legislative body in the world.

Much of Aldrich's power was an attribute of his position. The rules of the Senate went on the assumption that the party having the majority, now the Republicans, should control; the rules and practices of the Republican organization conferred much authority on the leader.

He controlled appointments to committees; by that power he could at once place on committees only Senators likely to carry out his will, and at the same time receive

Drawn by Herbert Johnson for the Philadelphia "North American."

The famous tariff cartoon. Roosevelt glares, the big stick gathers cobwebs, while Taft pleads and Aldrich says, "Aw, hang the consumer!"

willing subservience from those whom he favored. By his power to promote some measures and suppress others, he could command gratitude from the beneficiaries of legislation, especially of the tariff. Since the gratitude often took the form of campaign contributions, Aldrich could extend to a loyal Senator, or withhold from a recalcitrant one, funds important for State campaigns. As things then were, the leader of the Republican party in the Senate was spokesman of most of the country's commercial interests, the symbol of all conservative sentiment.

That part of Aldrich's power accrued to him as an attribute of the office he held; much more of his authority flowed to him from his personality. In any body of men in any place, Aldrich would have been likely to come to leadership. He had the outward aspect of it, six feet of body that was neither heavy nor slender; an eye so luminous, penetrating, full-orbed and brilliant that the painter of his portrait confessed inability to transfer it to canvas; in his features a combination of force and firmness which carried to lesser men instantly and invincibly the effect of dominance. As he moved about the Senate floor, his sense of confidence in his power was as evident yet as unostentatious as his head upon his shoulders. For the crowd outside the Senate, for the masses of the people, his contempt, his sense of their folly and their ignorance, was so much a part of his nature that he never showed it or thought about it. The impression of power made by his outer being was fully carried out by the directness and exactness of his mind. His flexibility of temperament gave him ease and skill in the exercise of his authority; to the submissive and the loyal, a charm and helpfulness that conveyed stimulation and elicited fervent admiration; to the too-independent, or the ignorant or foolish, a coldness that chilled, a ruthlessness that often passed arrogance and sometimes became cruelty. Much of his power lay in his ability to judge men; one of the Insurgents, for example, Bristow of Kansas, he recognized instantly as a man of narrow and obstinate independence — Aldrich "passed him by as he would a servant in his house or an attache of the Senate."[6]

Aldrich's ability to judge men served him well. Once he made a mistake, and the consequences made history.

[6] Claude G. Bowers, "Beveridge and the Progressive Era."

VI

Dolliver

There was in the Senate, and among the regulars of the Republican party, a man whose traits were quite incomparable with those of Aldrich, but the sum of whose qualities made him equally outstanding — indeed, considering that Jonathan Dolliver held no office of leadership and therefore depended upon himself for his eminence, it would be fair to say that Dolliver rather than Aldrich was the greatest Senator of his time. The phrase that Beveridge later uttered at Dolliver's grave, "Beyond any possible doubt the greatest orator in the contemporaneous English-speaking world," at once understates Dolliver's bigness and misleads about the qualities that contributed to it. With Dolliver, oratory was as easy-going, as offhand, an expression of his rich personality as ordinary conversation. He did not seek occasions for speechmaking, rather he avoided them; he had not the aggressiveness of an orator, nor even of one who consciously regards himself as a public man. He was utterly without pose; to a physical figure and a personality so patently big, pose was unnecessary — the most effective pose Dolliver could adopt was merely to be Dolliver. Part of his immense charm lay in his preference, as a rule, to be a spectator upon life, a spectator who ever regarded mankind as interesting, amusing, and on the whole likeable; and who brought to his observation of life rich resources of reading and reflection. By one figure of speech, Dolliver was a mountain of a man —his bulk, as well as his personality, justified that; by another figure he was a deep, quiet lake, restful to the spirits of those fortunate to come in contact with him; it was in the rôle of companion that he lived longest in the affections of those who remembered him.

In his political convictions, Dolliver was, moderately, of the newer Western type. He had progressive leanings, was slightly disposed to "get off the reservation" but was by no means an outright Insurgent. A phlegmatic good nature that went with his bulk, a personal philosophy which taught him that things didn't matter much, and an intellectual tolerance that arose from his wide reading as well as his contacts with men, led him to have distaste for the harsh hates, the unceasing suspicion, the shrill stridency, of most of the Insurgents. He was as often against as identified with the positions, usually extreme, taken by the Insurgents. Indeed he was, during his early years in the Senate, one of Aldrich's lieutenants, occasionally entrusted with duties of diplomacy and conciliation for which Dolliver's amiability and largeness of personality strikingly equipped him.

Once LaFollette, who understood the latent immensity of Dolliver's persuasive and hortatory powers, undertook to make of him a more complete convert to the Insurgent cause, by reciting to him a shrill catalogue of the Standpatters' crimes, closing with an intimate personal appeal designed at once to reproach Dolliver and allure him. "Your place, Jonathan," LaFollette said,[7] "is at the head of a movement here in the Senate and in the country for the public interest." Dolliver's brief and amiable reply was, "Bob, your liver's out of order; cheer up."

A few days later, just after Taft became President, Aldrich had occasion to make shifts in his committees. The death of an Iowa Senator of the older conservative type, William B. Allison, one of the "big six" who with Aldrich dominated the Senate, made a vacancy on the Senate's most important committee, Finance. Allison's

---

[7] LaFollette's Autobiography.

colleague was Dolliver, and Dolliver felt he was entitled, by precedent, on geographical grounds, and by his personal status, to the vacancy.

President Taft and Senator LaFollette on the way to the Farmers' National Convention at Madison, Wis.

Aldrich withheld it; in re-organizing the committee, he gave two places to men serving their first terms, Smoot of Utah and Flint of California, and lifted Cullom off the Appropriations Committee to put him on Finance. The passing over of Dolliver for three men who

Dolliver could justly feel were not his equals, amounted to a flagrant flout.[8]

The incident was observed by the shrewd LaFollette who presently contrived occasion to approach Dolliver with a beckoning look in his eye. Dolliver responded, in words that spread over a conference of hours in La-Follette's room, words which LaFollette summed up (with perhaps a melodramatic heightening of literalness):[9]

> From this time on [Dolliver said] I am going to be independent. I am going to serve my conscience. I have been lecturing, I have saved my dollars and put them into a farm up there in Iowa. I am going to judgment in the next twenty years, and I am going so I can look my Maker in the face. I do not have to stay in public life. I can take my books, my wife, and my children, and if I am dismissed from the Senate for following my conviction I will go out to my farm and stay there until the call comes.

Dolliver brought to the Insurgents not only the largest personality among them, but a quality of amiable bigness and urbanity which at once enabled them to achieve unity among themselves and to make converts. Dolliver was persuasive. LaFollette and the other Insurgents could say things that pleased themselves and pleased those who already felt as they did; no one among them until Dolliver had the gift of saying the same thing in a manner that would please also the public and the rank

---

[8] In this same re-organization of committees, Aldrich made a second mistake. Borah of Idaho had just come to the Senate. Aldrich, making enough investigation to learn that Borah had been the leading lawyer in his State and as such had represented great corporations, judged Borah to be "safe." In that impression he put Borah on the Committee on Judiciary. Before the Committee was a proposal — strongly opposed by Aldrich and other conservatives — for a constitutional amendment for election of Senators by direct vote of the people. Borah provided the deciding vote which approved the proposal, reported it out of committee to the Senate, and sent it on its way to fulfilment. On the same committee and in the same way Borah was influential in bringing about the constitutional amendment inaugurating the income tax.

[9] LaFollette's Autobiography.

and file of Congress, and thereby make their causes popular.

This conversion of Dolliver from Saul to Paul was, to Aldrich, most untimely, for the Congress then organizing had been called into special session for the writing of a tariff, in which Aldrich and the New England interests he represented had much at stake.

Jonathan Dolliver.

17

TAFT'S FOUR YEARS: THE TARIFF REVISION

THE last revision of the tariff, the Dingley bill of 1897, had been upward, by the Republicans. Almost at the moment it was written increased gold supply from a newly found source in Alaska, from other new mines in Australia, and from the new cyanide process of treating ore, had caused slowly rising prices of goods. Rising prices had given rise to complaint about the "high cost of living." High cost of living had given rise to demand for downward revision of the tariff. Roosevelt, impulsively, had toyed with the idea. Once, in a preliminary draft of a message to Congress, sent to the newspapers for future publication, he had incorporated a vague suggestion that at some future time he would send another message recommending that the tariff should be revised[1] — but had deleted it by telegraph upon urgent warning from hard-boiled Standpatter Speaker Cannon, whose cunning instinct told him there was political dynamite in tariff revision. "No matter how great an improvement the new tariff may be," said Cannon, "it almost always results in the party in power losing the election."[2] "Anyhow," said Cannon on another occasion, "whence comes this so-called demand for tariff tinkering? Aren't all our fellows happy?"[3]

More enlightened Republican leaders, such as Elihu Root, felt throughout Roosevelt's administration that the party could not go before the voters in the Presidential election of 1908 without undertaking to reduce the tariff.

[1] "From Harrison to Harding," Arthur W. Dunn, Vol. II.
[2] "Uncle Joe Cannon," L. White Busbey.
[3] From the Washington *Post,* November 17, 1905.

II

Taft, from the time he first thought of himself as a Presidential possibility, had recommended reduction, beginning in September, 1906, with a speech at Bath, Maine, destined later to be minutely examined for its exact meaning, in which, "speaking my individual opinion and for no one else," he expressed the view that "since the passage of the Dingley bill there has been a change in business conditions, making it wise and just to revise the schedules of the existing tariff." On several occasions Taft had repeated his suggestion. The national convention that nominated him in 1908 had endorsed revision in its platform; the Republican majority of the Ways and Means Committee in Congress, so soon as the election of 1908 determined the Republicans would be in power, had held hearings. Taft, immediately after being inaugurated, called a special session of the new Congress to revise the tariff, to convene eleven days after his inauguration, on March 15, 1909. A bill was written in the House and sent to the Senate.

The early, general controversy broke out over whether the revision was downward. Newspapers[4] prevailingly

[4] Speaker Cannon, Standpatter and friend of high duties, always insisted in private conversations, and in some guarded public utterances, that the newspapers, because of their wish for free Canadian pulp and print-paper, had created the sentiment which demanded tariff revision, and then, because their commodity had not been put on the free list, created the impression that the bill was an upward revision. On one occasion Cannon made the public statement, without mentioning names, that he had been the victim of an attempted rape of his scruples: "Another publisher, childlike in his frankness, comes direct to the Speaker's room in person with the proposition to throw the whole newspaper press of the country over to support any ambition [meaning the Presidency] the Speaker may have, if he will secure just one desired piece of legislation, and the threat that he will turn this terrible engine of publicity against the Speaker if he refuses."

For Cannon's charge there was some foundation. It is a fact that the newspapers wanted free pulp and news-print. A few, but not many, owners and business managers of important newspapers would not hesitate to make the offers and threats of which Cannon complained. Arthur Wallace Dunn, very much on the inside of the situation, wrote, "The demand for free pulp and print-paper had more to do with forcing a promise of tariff revision than anything else."

said it was not. The New York *Evening Post* emitted a thundering threat: "A voice like the sound of many waters is rising from the country to show where the consumers are, and what is their state of mind."

Over this issue, whether revision downward had been pledged by the Republicans, and whether the bill fulfilled the pledges, arose the first break between Standpatters and Insurgents. The Standpatters, callous to President Taft whose fortunes they were destroying, asserted, with incredible impudence, that no one had promised that this tariff revision should be downward.

"Where," asked Aldrich, "did we ever make the statement that we would revise the tariff downward?"[5] "Nobody," said Standpatter Lodge, "ever pledged me to revision downward, any more than to revision upward."[6] "This talk of being under obligations to revise the tariff downward," said Standpat Senator William B. Heyburn of Idaho, "comes from somewhere, I do not know from where, from some political, I was going to say swamp, like a miasma. It was a concession, a sop, thrown by those lacking in confidence to the voters whose support they thought they had to have. There is nothing in the platform of the Republican party which requires us, as suggested by the Senator from Iowa [Dolliver] to make any concession, because some one may have promised a revision downward."[7] The constant cry of revision downward," said Standpat Senator Hale of Maine, "was never put into the Republican platform."[8]

Search of the Republican platform revealed that the cynical plea was true, that it contained only delphic words, a use of the virtuous adverb "unequivocally" in

[5] *Congressional Record*, April 22, 1909, p. 1499.
[6] *Congressional Record*, May 8, 1909, p. 1911.
[7] *Congressional Record*, June 8, 1911, p. 2950.
[8] *Congressional Record*, May 9, p. 2275.

a way ingeniously contrived as to achieve equivocality: "The Republican party declares unequivocally," the text of the platform said, "for a revision of the tariff. . . .

Hastily the Insurgents and their journalistic allies turned back to the speeches of the President who had run on the platform. Equivocality was not in Taft's nature. Plainly he had promised revision downward. He had said (in his acceptance speech at Cincinnati September 2, 1908) "a revision which shall reduce excessive rates." He had said (at Milwaukee September 24) "The necessity for maintaining the tariff at the former rate has ceased; the tariff . . . should be reduced." He had said (in his inaugural speech March 4, 1909) that the change in conditions since the passage of the Dingley Act "will permit the reduction of rates in certain schedules and will require the advancement of few if any." He had said (at Milwaukee, September 24, 1908): "I do not hesitate to say, with all the emphasis of which I am capable, that if the party is given the mandate of power in November, it will perform its promises in good faith."

The Insurgents, buttressed by these quotations, proclaiming that they were the true friends of Taft, the authentic spokesmen of Republican policy, began a spectacular fight for reduction. From these Insurgent Senators bearing the label Republican came a more thorough attack on the high tariff than Democrats had ever made. Laboriously, the Insurgents toiled through the long, hot Washington summer. Systematically they divided the schedules among them, to Dolliver, cotton; to LaFollette, wool; Bristow, sugar; Cummins, metals. Every night, after the close of the day's Senate session — which toward the end lasted until 11 at night — each Insurgent Senator devoted laborious midnight hours to mastering the technicalities of the schedule assigned him. "Every

Insurgent," Beveridge wrote to a friend, "seriously impaired his eyesight during that session."[9] Many nights they met together (the host on each occasion supplying a case of beer for the un-Insurgently genial Mose Clapp of Minnesota) to lay out the plan of battle for the coming day.

For this sort of fighting Aldrich and the Standpatters were unprepared; they had written the schedules on figures supplied to them by the respective industries; the fact that the statistician of one industry was carried on the pay-roll of the Senate committee which wrote the bill became an explosive scandal in the debate. Aldrich, with his associates, unequipped to meet the detailed figures of the Insurgents, was reduced to a futility galling to him and ridiculous to the country. The Standpatters, Insurgent Dolliver said, are "now engaged, with hired help and outside experts, in an endeavor to have their own bill explained to them."

Dolliver it was — Dolliver made apostate and insurgent by Aldrich's arrogant slight, Dolliver with his pungent humor and apt figures of speech — Dolliver it was who constituted perhaps the principal weapon of the Insurgents. When Standpat Senator Francis E. Warren of Wyoming defended a tariff on raw wool, Dolliver called public attention to the Senator's immense holdings of sheep and pasturage in a phrase which, bringing smiles to millions of lips, did more to damn the tariff than tons of statistics. Warren was, said Dolliver, "the greatest shepherd since Abraham." The wool schedule as a whole — as Schedule K it became famous, or, more accurately, infamous, to the country — was, Dolliver said, "offspring of the wedding of the shepherds and the weavers." "The past year," he continued, "witnessed two events of unusual interest, the discovery of the North Pole by Doctor

[9] Claude G. Bowers, "Beveridge and the Progressive Era."

Cook, and the revision of the tariff downward by the Senator from Rhode Island, each in its way a unique hoax and both promptly presented to the favorable notice of the people by the highest official congratulations."

To all of which and everything else Aldrich's reply, much too incoherent to qualify as repartee, was to charge Dolliver with "assault on the very citadel of protection. . . . The Republican party stands for protection no matter where it strikes." Often Aldrich's only response was not to respond, to walk from the Senate floor, red-faced, for the first time in his life successfully defied.

III

That Taft should take account of a situation which involved not only his political fortunes and those of the Republican party but his personal honor, seemed axiomatic. Privately and publicly, by friends in his closet and foes in the press, he was urged that he had "his own reputation to guard as well as his party to lead, that it was his duty to speak out and let the country know what he thinks of the Aldrich dishonesties." "It is not necessary," admonished the New York *Evening Post*, "for the President to wait till a bill comes before him to sign or veto; by letter or by speech he can make his position clear."

Taft made no speech, took no public step. The "sentinels on the editorial watch-towers," said the *Literary Digest*, discern "two leaders of the Republican party — one [Aldrich] forcing a high-tariff measure through the Senate with consummate skill; the other [Taft] sitting silently in the White House, waiting."

Privately Taft followed a course fatal to any man in his position — vacillation. To Insurgents who called on him he gave encouragement — "Saw Taft, he is with us," Beveridge wrote[10] to his wife. To Standpatters who called on him he gave the impression that he would sign whatever bill was passed. Taft's course, seen as a pattern after the event, shows that his hope and intention — so far as he had anything as definite as an intention — was to have the Insurgents bring about as low a tariff as they could,[11] and then, if it was not low enough, to make his own fight when the bill was "in conference" —the stage at which the bill as written by the House and the differing bill as written by the Senate go before a committee of representatives from the two chambers for compromise and final agreement.

That plan, on the part of Taft, reflected unique ineptness, reflected indeed incredible ignorance of parliamentary procedure — and parliamentary procedure was what the Standpatters knew best. When the conference period came Taft attempted to act, attempted vigorously — but encountered a parliamentary "practice as old as the government itself, so old that it amounted to law, that where the House proposed one rate in the tariff bill and the Senate proposed another, the conferees could not go below the lower rate nor above the higher rate. In betwixt the House rate and Senate rate they could do as they pleased."[12]

IV

Whether the bill was materially higher or materially lower is not easy to say. A change in the tariff which is made by an opposition party, which goes frankly and as

10 June 12, 1909. Quoted in "Beveridge and the Progressive Era," Claude G. Bowers.

11 Taft took two steps pleasing to the Insurgents. On June 16, 1909, he sent the Senate a message recommending an amendment to the tariff bill laying a 2 per cent tax on incomes of corporations, and a proposal for an amendment to the Constitution authorizing an income tax.

12 Champ Clark, "Quarter-Century of American Politics," Vol. II.

a whole in a reversed direction, can be recognized; but a modification made by the same party and keeping the old direction can be made to appear one thing or the other. The calculation whether the net change in the sum of several thousand items, many intricately related to each other, filling some three hundred pages of fine print, is upward or downward, embodies such movable factors of specific and ad valorem duties, of percentages based on past imports and estimated future imports, that it becomes a case in which the figures can be, and now were, made to prove either result.

The statement of Aldrich and Lodge that there had been reductions on 379 articles and increases on only 33 could easily mislead; equally misleading could be Insurgent LaFollette's retort that the increases affected ten million dollars of imports, the decreases only forty-five thousand. The official estimate of the author of the bill in the House, Sereno Payne,[13] was that the "equivalent ad valorem of the preceding Dingley law was 42.58 per cent and of the new law 41.61 per cent," a reduction of .97 per cent. The official estimate of the Democratic leader in the House, Champ Clark, was that the new bill raised the tariff 1.70 per cent. Perhaps as good evidence as any was the informal judgment of a high-tariff advocate and beneficiary, Representative Asher C. Hinds of Maine: "Massachusetts never went away from Congress carrying more in her craw than she has got in that tariff bill."[14]

Whatever might be the truth, the press said the revision was upward, and the country believed the press. Summaries of roll-calls on the tariff were constructed[15] in which Senators were pictured to the public as good or evil, depending upon the number of times they had voted

13 *Congressional Record*, p. 4914, July 30.
14 "From Harrison to Harding," Arthur W. Dunn.
15 In *Collier's Weekly*, then militant against the Standpatters.

with Aldrich or against him. Perfect good was the Senator who voted *against* Aldrich on every roll-call, 106 times — LaFollette was the only one, followed by Bristow of Kansas with a score of 101. Absolute evil was the Senator who voted *with* Aldrich 129 times — Smoot of Utah was the only one, followed by Kean of New Jersey with a score of 125.

One list was set up as infamy, defined as the Senators "who have voted with Mr. Aldrich on every one of the schedules." Another list was set up as virtue, composed of the 10 Senators who consistently voted against Aldrich. They were Albert J. Beveridge of Indiana, Joseph L. Bristow of Kansas, Norris Brown of Nebraska, Elmer J. Burkett of Nebraska, Moses E. Clapp of Minnesota, Coe I. Crawford of South Dakota, Knute Nelson of Minnesota, Albert B. Cummings of Iowa, Jonathan P. Dolliver of Iowa, Robert M. LaFollette of Wisconsin. A map showed as virtuous white the states from which these Senators came: Kansas, Nebraska, South Dakota, Iowa, Minnesota, Wisconsin, Indiana. The rest of the United States was unregenerate black.

In that state of public opinion the bill went to Taft. It was to be the most important decision of his Presidency, the most determining on his own political fortunes. Already, under the necessity of making his own decisions, in the rôle now of standing on his own feet, no longer a subordinate leaning on Roosevelt, Taft had become irritable, rather frequently lost his good nature and had a manner of snarling in the presence of newspaper men. When Insurgent Medill McCormick called on Taft to warn him that unless he vetoed the tariff bill the West would bolt, would saddle him with a Democratic Congress, and would defeat him for re-election, Taft pounded the table, swore angrily,"[16] and otherwise

[16] Charles Willis Thompson, "Presidents I Have Known."

emitted the angry defiance of a man who knows he is in the wrong but feels he cannot help it.

Taft, on August 5, 1909, signed the bill. The act fixed upon him the judgment that Dolliver had passed, the most damaging sentence ever uttered by any of Taft's critics, a sentence whose aptness did more than anything else to crystallize the public impression about Taft. "President Taft," said Dolliver, "is an amiable man, completely surrounded by men who know exactly what they want."

v

Taft signed the bill, and took himself off to his belated summer vacation. Into his golf-playing, after some six weeks, intruded Standpat Republican leaders, the very ones who had betrayed him, reporting insurgency aflame in the West and pleading that Taft put out the fire. Specifically they asked that he do something to help Standpat Congressman James A. Tawney, who was threatened with political extinction in his Minnesota district. Taft, reluctantly dropping his golf, took train to Winona, where, September 17, 1909, he explained that he "did not promise that everything should go downward," admitted that the wool schedule "is too high and ought to be reduced," and, with amazing naïveté proclaimed, "This is the best tariff bill that the Republican party has ever passed, and therefore the best that has been passed at all."

"Shades of Theodore Roosevelt!" exclaimed the Des Moines (Iowa) *News*, "may ghosts of the animals he has killed in Africa ever haunt him for having foisted on the country this man Taft." "Those Western Republicans," said the defiant St. Paul *Pioneer-Press*, "have made up their minds that they are not going to be ruled by New England and for New England."

All of which, and the infinitely much more there was, was put in picturesque words by a journalist of that day[17] — "a reverberating roar; the Rocky Mountains stood on their heads, the Great Lakes turned inside out, and the Sierra danced like the hills of Scripture."

Taft, when he heard the reverberating roar, made about the only further mistake possible; explained that he had dictated the speech to a stenographer "on the cars between two stations, and I glanced through it only enough to straighten out the grammar."

Instantly erupted a campaign, journalistic and political, to supplant the Republican House with a Democratic-Insurgent one. It succeeded.[18] Taft, during the last two years of his term, would have a House controlled by the opposition party, certain formula for grief.

Aldrich, letting it be understood he was weary of life in the Senate, announced some months later that he would retire at the end of his term, March 4, 1911.

[17] Charles Willis Thompson, "Presidents I Have Known."
[18] In this election, in November, 1910, was elected the first Socialist ever sent to Congress, Victor L. Berger of Milwaukee.

18

TAFT'S FOUR YEARS: THE FIGHT ON THE RULES

As Aldrich was to the Senate, so was Joseph G. Cannon to the House. And as the Insurgents arose in the Senate, so did a similar group arise[1] in the House, coming from roughly the same States, Wisconsin, Iowa, Nebraska, Minnesota, Kansas and the Dakotas, in all about thirty out of a total Republican House membership of 219. They, like their fellows in the Senate, were exiles from the places of power. They were strongly individualistic in character, they chafed under the conditions that held them down, and they were of a temperament indisposed to chafe in silence. One, the best-known, Victor Murdock of Kansas, by the color of his hair contributed a dominating red to the polychromatic picture of the group, enabling the newspapers to characterize them, with adequate accuracy, as "fiery." Another among them, studious, self-contained, gentle but with intense convictions, destined to leave Congress inconspicuously and to die in quiet obscurity, was destined also to have, years later, a dramatic vicarious return to public notice. In the year 1927, when a youth with strongly individualistic traits of character startled the world by making the first airplane flight from New York to Paris, the name of the lone eagle, flaming sensationally across the skies, recalled to a few his father of the same name, who as an Insurgent in Congress a dozen years earlier had written a book about the crimes of bankers, Charles A. Lindbergh.

The grievance of the Insurgents in the House was

[1] So far as there was material difference, the Insurgent movement arose earlier in the House.

against the Speaker, and the autocratic authority which the rules enabled him to exercise; against "Czarism," epithet of odium interchangeable with "Cannonism."

II

Cannon

Cannon was an old man. He had emigrated with his family from North Carolina to Illinois at a time when the journey, by covered wagon, consumed four months, and he could remember when a box of matches was a modern luxury costing "a shilling." Coming to Congress in 1873, at the age of 36, he had been a rustic, a "hay-seed," a plain man from the plain people — and he had preserved the reputation through fifty[2] years in Congress, during which he had become the most sophisticated man in American public life, the most familiar with every subterranean channel of politics, the most cunning in its devious ways, the most artful in the tricks of the craft, the most adroit in picking his secretive path through the intricate field where politics overlaps upon business. He told bucolic stories, dwelt lovingly on old times in rural Illinois when an independent American citizen "could stand in his doorway, bite his morning "chaw" of tobacco and spit eighteen feet without trespassing on his neighbor," pointed his arguments with tales about frontier "hard-shell" Baptist preachers, was called "Uncle Joe." His voice, diction and manner, and the substance of the tales he told, had at once, in extraordinary intermingling, the quality of the mourning-bench exhorter and the bar-room Boccaccio. In one and the same story or adage he would combine the religiosity of the pulpit with the profanity and Rabelaisian raciness of the horse-sheds behind the meeting-house. Once, to a man who proposed com-

[2] Less two years he was out.

bat against Roosevelt, Cannon gave advice in backwoods Anglo-Saxon terms which, elevated to Latin derivatives, may be translated as, "Never engage in a uriniferous competition with a mephitic master of aromatic warfare."

From a photograph by Underwood & Underwood.

Speaker Joseph Gurney Cannon.

His pose of untutored countryman, of a quaint character, a primitive personality, a vulgarian, he preserved no more for any personal advantage to himself than as a deliberate contribution to his function of keeping the United States a going concern. Behind the mask of simplicity operated one of the most complex and subtle minds that ever practiced statecraft. He knew that the public, as a mass, thinks and acts in large part through symbols and that for him the pose of commonness, of Lincolnian simplicity, was useful to keep the faith which the public must have in the occupants of high place. The secret of his personality might have been gathered, by the discerning, from his eyes. In his mainly Quaker ancestry was a dash of French Huguenot, and within that facial circle of whiskered Quaker artlessness were two of the most knowing eyes in the modern world, Talleyrand eyes that saw everything, revealed nothing, eyes which, William Hard said, "might have been forged at Pittsburgh out of actual steel." As a detail of his technique of inscrutability he smoked, or rather held in his mouth, a cigar — card-players and traders know that time may be gained to consider a move or compose an answer, and the emotions betrayable by mobile lips may be concealed, by rolling a cigar in the mouth. Cannon's "restless teeth bit off large untidy sections from the near end of a maltreated cigar, until his wet lips from one side of his long mouth to the other were strewn with sodden, shredded tobacco leaves, and the neglected, fitful smoulder at the cigar's far end seemed to be in greater danger from flood than from fire."[3] Physically he was slim, sinewy, erect, elastic, "compounded of equal parts of granite and whipcord"; one hunderd and forty pounds of flexible, controlled, directed personal force. He would turn up at three or four dinners in the course of an evening, utter a quip or tell a homely story at each, and at midnight sit down to a poker game. His poker playing, like nearly everything else he did, was part of his technique for the exercise of his official function — it enabled him to measure the men with whom he had to deal, the material out of which he must forge government. He would play

[3] William Hard.

until dawn, and then at eleven pound the Speaker's gavel with the force and firmness of an incomparable master of men. To see him, lithe, poised, confident and immovable, exerting his will upon 391 men, more than half of whom yearned to defy him, was to elicit utter admiration,[4] willing or unwilling, for a man who is perfect in the function for which fate designed him. His standpatter quality, his resistance to any and all innovation whatever, was, again, in part his native temperament, in part a detail of his job of keeping the United States a going concern. He considered that of all proposals for change fifty per cent are harmful, the rest useless. Ten chances out of ten, the new would be no improvement on the old. It was said of him that "if he had attended the caucus on creation he would have been loyal to chaos." He stood by what is. Once the new was forced upon him, it took on the sanctity of "is," and he became loyally Standpatter on that.

III

Cannon really had as much power as the thunderous slogans of the Insurgents attributed to him. Much of it was personal, lay within the boundaries of his sinewy brain; more of it was embodied in the rules of the House — and to preserving those rules as they were Cannon devoted all his force. That was the one ideal left to him after close to forty years of illusion giving way to reality and cynicism, a reverence for the heritage that had come down to him with his office, a determination to pass it on undiminished. His other ideal was a religiously held conviction that two-party government as practiced in America was the best — not merely the best, the only

[4] The author of this history wrote, at the time, probably more harsh words about Cannon and the influences he represented, than any other person who ever held an insurgent pen.

good — way of running a country, and that two-party
government was best preserved and promoted by compact
organization, stern party discipline, centralized responsibility and authority. Under the rules of the House as
they then were, Cannon as Speaker appointed a majority
(all the Republican members) of the Committee on
Rules, and the Committee on Rules interpreted and administered the eight thick volumes of rules and precedents which to the average member were baffling Greek;
if any member of the House outside the Speaker's satel-
lites on the Committee should attempt to introduce in the
House an amendment to the rules, Cannon had absolute
power of recognition — more accurately of non-recogni-
tion — he could "ignore the presence of the recalcitrant
member as completely as if he did not exist."[5] Cannon
appointed all Republican members of all committees; he
had, that meant, personal and arbitrary power to give or
withhold everything in the form of power or ambition
that Members prized. The recipients of his shrewdly
distributed favors were, in consequence, a unit in sup-
porting Cannon for re-election to the Speakership each
two years. For the same reason they were willing to
withhold in committee — "chloroform," "put to sleep"
were the phrases used to describe the operation — such
proposed bills as Cannon disapproved, reporting for action by Congress only such proposals as Cannon deemed
desirable to pass.

If a Member, after being favored with a committee
appointment by Cannon, acted upon any legislation in a
manner disapproved by him, the reckless one found himself, at the beginning of the succeeding session, no longer
on the committee. In the course of this harsh exercise
of discipline, Cannon removed Insurgent Henry Allen
Cooper of Wisconsin from the Committee on Insular Af-

---

[5] George Rothwell Brown, "The Leadership of Congress."

fairs, and Charles N. Fowler of New Jersey from the Committee on Banking and Currency, and demoted Victor Murdock of Kansas from fifth place to tenth on the Committee on Post Offices and Post Roads.[6]

Cannon in short had arbitrary power to determine what legislation should be enacted and what should not; he really was the dictator that his opponents shrilly called him.

IV

All this, inevitably, was a shock to a new Member who came to Washington fully believing he had been elected to an open forum, fully believing he would have equal privileges with every other Member, fully believing he could at any time rise in his seat, address the chair, propose a measure, make a speech in advocacy of it and bring it to a roll-call. [Four-fifths of them, ultimately, adapted themselves to what they found, conformed to the system, became acolytes of the hierarchy, and grew to what measure of power they were able to achieve by impressing their talents, including their docility, upon Cannon. The more impatient, the more recalcitrant, the more stiffnecked or the more independent of spirit became Insurgents.

The Insurgents felt deeply and charged loudly that Cannon used his power to promote the interests of business, to check the wishes of "the people." There was little in that. That Cannon was a realist goes without saying. He knew that at all times politics is merely the name for the process by which whatever force or group

---

[6] Cannon was able to say, in defense, that the members he demoted had "failed to enter and abide by a Republican caucus and this being a government through parties, for that, as well as for other sufficient reasons, the Speaker of the House, responsible to the House and to the country, made the appointments with respect to these gentlemen as he conceived it to be his duty in accordance with the trust reposed in him."—*Congressional Record,* 61 Cong., 2d Sess., p. 3321.

is at any time dominant in society achieves its will in government. That is axiomatic. He knew that in the United States the dominant interest — dominant with the willing consent and complete satisfaction of the country — was business, materialism. It is doubtful if Cannon ever made a bargain for his personal advantage, or improperly deferred to any interest for a corrupt consideration. Deals he made, tricks he devised and carried out, but they were for the advantage of the one ideal he recognized, party government as he conceived it, and the supremacy of the Republican party. The one consideration that determined his course, the one limitation that dictated his concessions, was a shrewd estimate of the mind of the House and of the country, an estimate of what he could "get by with," of what he could not safely deny and keep himself and his party in power. The historical test, the adequate answer, is that under Cannon and under the rules so bitterly complained of, the House enacted the Pure Food Bill and the Railroad Rate Bill. Cannon had immense power, but his power was dependent on his party remaining in office. He was careful to use his power to make at least as many concessions to popular feeling as would insure the Republicans keeping their hold in Congress, as many to the sentiment of the House as would enable him to keep his job.

V

It was part of Cannon's shrewd talent, his bigness, that as a rule he saw the need of yielding before others did, made the concession before rebellion arose. By March, 1910, however, nearly a year after the overturn of Aldrich by the Insurgents in the Senate, there was in the air a spirit of rebellion for rebellion's sake, an insurgency aimed not toward passing any particular legislation, but toward sheer revolution which should throw off the shackles from individual members, a movement to liberalize the rules fundamentally. One among the Insurgents, George W. Norris of Nebraska — he had been a county judge and had a first-class mind — began by patiently mastering the intricacies of the rules and precedents until he knew them as well as Cannon himself. He could find no hole in the iron ring of rules within which Cannon was intrenched. Nevertheless, with a streak of patience that was part of his combative equipment, Norris wrote out a resolution providing the most drastic liberalization of the rules that had been proposed for half a century. This he carried in his pocket until its folds were worn ragged. On March 16, 1910, Cannon and his associates controlling the House pushed his autocracy to a farther point than ever before, attempting to do away with "Calendar Wednesday," a day on which Members had slightly more than their usual prerogative. The attempt shocked some of the less hard-boiled of Cannon's own followers. On a roll-call, the Speaker lost — and that was the first breach in Cannon's power. Into the breach rushed the ready Norris. Rising with his dog-eared resolution in his hand, he moved to have the Committe on Rules elected by the House instead of appointed by Cannon. It was March 17, 1910. The newspapers, heralding the battle in headlines which left nothing larger for the Great War, saw a special significance in the fight coming on St. Patrick's day. There were twenty-nine hours of continuous debate. Norris won, the combination of Insurgent Republicans and Democrats casting 191 votes against 156 — "the most severe defeat administered to a Speaker since the establishment of the government."[7]

In the tumult that followed, Cannon stepped to the

[7] "The Leadership of Congress," George R. Brown.

front with a gallant gameness that made him as loser no less the hero of the day than the winner. He would, he said, entertain a motion to declare his office vacant, in effect an offer to abdicate. His opponents had counted on nothing like that. The move startled them, disrupted their ranks. To change the rules, the system, was one thing. To depose Cannon personally would be too formidable, the prestige of the man made the idea seem shocking. The resolution to declare the chair vacant was lost by 192 to 155. Cannon remained Speaker, but stripped of his power.

VI

The fight on the rules should have had no direct effect on Taft. But the cleavage between Insurgents and Standpatters had existed for a year; Taft had been obliged to give his countenance to one side or the other. He lacked Roosevelt's ability to embrace neither, dominate both. Taft had given his approval to Cannon, not that he liked Cannon personally or approved the rules — but in a division between some 30 Insurgents against some 189 regulars, there had been but one way for the President, as head of his party, to go — he could not possibly side with a rump. Taft had no kinship with Cannon — "simply hates him," wrote Archie Butt. Yet partly in the interest of party solidarity, partly out of amiability and inertia, Taft allowed himself to be "photographed with his arms about Cannon's neck," and appeared to endorse him whenever they spoke together. Now Cannon's sinking carried Taft downward with him. Now Taft's prestige was further diminished, the prestige of the Insurgents elevated. It was one more ring in the downward spiral of Taft's fortunes.

19

TAFT'S FOUR YEARS: THE BALLINGER CASE

From the time the first Puritan set foot on New England soil, the American idea of what to do about land was to get the Indians off, and settle it. The settlement invariably took the form of private, individual ownership. In all the territory from the Atlantic Coast to the Missouri River, in which the first two hundred and fifty years of the white occupation of America took place, not one tract of land was reserved for public ownership and common use. (Excepting an acre here and there for a "common" or "green" in a New England village, or for a public school or a church or a state capitol.) Wherever there was unoccupied land, a settler could squat on it, and by occupying it twenty-one years acquire title. In all that stretch of continent there was no equivalent of what later came to be known in the extreme West as a "national park" or a "forest reserve." No one thought of such a thing. The purpose for which land existed was individual ownership. When the federal government came into possession of new areas, such as the territory west of the Mississippi, the accepted way to treat it was to lay it out in tracts of 160 acres, and get each tract as promptly as possible into possession of an individual owner. The price was deliberately made nominal; the government regulations for acquiring title were simple, and were interpreted in the spirit of facilitating settlement. As late as 1901, when McKinley's death put Roosevelt in the White House, it was the "firmly fixed" habit of the General Land Office, Roosevelt wrote,[1] "of deciding,

[1] In his "Autobiography."

whenever possible, in favor of private interests . . . and technical compliance with the letter of the law was all that was required."

Nowhere was this point of view so strong as on the successive fringes where settlement was taking place. Once a settler had "taken up" his quarter-section of government land, his hope was that others would promptly take up the neighboring sections, so as, among other reasons, to bring increase of value to his own land. In the town-sites that sprang up along each successive frontier, the most earnest hope of each little banker, merchant and professional man was to see the vacant land nearby taken up as soon as possible. For those already there, each new settler meant growth, business, increase of value of the land they themselves owned, taxes to support schools and local government, voters to send the ambitious into public office. Quick settlement conformed to the American emphasis on growth, bigness. As late as the 1890's a visitor to any Western state or territory was conscious of a spirit of urging by the community to take possession of unoccupied land, to "homestead." If he had enough money to pay the small government fee for filing, it was difficult for him to escape the importunities of the town "boosters." If he could not conveniently stay long enough to meet the government requirements of a few months' occupancy in person, eager neighbors would help him meet the technicalities, or cheerfully connive in evading them. To get the free land into private ownership was the universal wish. If the new settler came in the form of a corporation, so much the better — the corporation taking up land would presumably build a railroad, or conduct lumbering operations, or mine coal, or erect a mill or water-power plant. It was satisfying to the community — the waterpower owner would bring industry, and additional settlers as labor. Corporations acquired water-power sites on Western rivers as informally as early settlers in the East had acquired grist-mill sites on tiny streams.

II

About 1900 came reversal of this point of view. It came through realization that the nation's supply of free land was nearing an end, and that considerable quantities of it in immense tracts had passed into the possession of corporations which through use of "dummy" entrants — a short-cut hitherto good-naturedly condoned — had acquired forests, mineral lands, water-power sites. Often these corporations oppressed the small individual homesteaders; always of course their ownership limited the opportunity of the individual to acquire free land.

Almost overnight, the evasion of red tape technicalities which yesterday had been a virtue became to-day a crime. It was one of those shifts of common point of view which prove, among other things, that what are called "moral standards" vary with time as well as with place; and that in some cases morality is closely associated with economics. The change that came in the West in the 1890's found a considerable number of persons mid-way of perfecting their titles to public land; many were harassed by the government, and not a few went to jail.

III

Pinchot

With a fervor almost passionate, idealists dedicated themselves to saving for the people and for posterity such tracts of land as had not yet passed into private ownership. Chief among these was Gifford Pinchot, young descendant of old New York merchant families, whose dominant inner passion was to flee from the ease that inherited wealth invited him to; almost he seemed to have a terror of the temptation to self-indulgence, seemed always to be fighting it as if it were his most dangerous and malevolent enemy. In a spirit partly of hardening his flesh, partly of crucifying his spirit, he slept on the floor with a wooden pillow, and each morning for his bath had his valet throw buckets of icy water over his sinewy body. With his discipline of the body went a mystic spirituality; "for years he wore a black band on his sleeve, understood to be for a loss so long passed that none of his friends could recall it." He was tall, lean; in his large, vision-lit eyes modified by austere lips was a suggestion of his Huguenot ancestry. In his face, which in his youth was one of "marked and particular beauty," "enthusiasm and asceticism seemed to mingle about equally . . . It would serve as a model for Leonidas bidding welcome to his destiny. There is a suggestion of zeal in excess of restraint, the possibility of following some idea too far. Neither History nor Letters qualify this countenance, nor the temper of a judge. The eyes do not look as if they read books, but as if they gazed upon a Cause."[2] Pinchot was of those whose eyes, as they pass through the world, instinctively look about for a hero, and for martyrdom in the hero's service. "Gifford," said Roosevelt, who understood Pinchot perfectly, "truly has an affection for

[2] The quotation is from the gallery of portraits of the "familiars" of the White House during Theodore Roosevelt's administration, which Owen Wister wrote in his "Story of a Forty Years Friendship" (with Roosevelt). Pinchot, after Roosevelt left the White House, and especially after Roosevelt died, became, in his running for Governor of Pennsylvania and other public activities, bitter, strident. Lacking the leadership, and the restraint, which Roosevelt had supplied to him, and lacking the quality to be a great leader himself, the impression he made lost some of its early charm, took on a harsh, intolerant pugnacity. In his early career he seemed to love many men, the mass; in his later, he seemed to hate a few picked enemies. Owen Wister, writing of him in 1930, regretfully admitted the change. Gently Wister said: "[His early] service to the nation cannot be wholly obliterated by his subsequent career. . . . As I cannot speak well of it, I will not speak of it at all."

me; it is almost fetish worship, and I have figured it out that Pinchot truly believes that in case of certain conditions I am perfectly capable of killing either himself or me; if conditions were such that only one could live he

THEN.   NOW.

Gifford Pinchot.

knows that I should possibly kill him as the weaker of the two, and he, therefore, worships this in me."[3] As Pinchot sought heroes to worship, so did he seek demons to fight. He found them, in the persons of those who opposed Roosevelt, the Standpatters. One of these, Senator Boies Penrose of Pennsylvania, last of the political barons, last of the old-time state-wide political bosses — though as Harvard graduate he knew perfectly the French pronunciation of Pinchot's name — habitually spoke it in a way that enabled him to compress into it his scorn for two of the minutest, least consequential objects in the physical world, "Pin-shot."

[3] "Letters of Archie Butt."

IV

Pinchot, graduating at Yale in 1889, spent three years in Germany and Switzerland, studying there an art, forestry, then unheard of in an America still lavishly rich in wood, though highly developed in old European countries whose supplies needed to be carefully preserved and administered for the common good. Returning to America, Pinchot began, in the privately owned mountain lands of one of the Vanderbilts at Biltmore, North Carolina, the first systematic forest work in America. By 1896, he was leading spirit in an organization for altruistic propaganda, the National Forest Commission, and a little later head of a tiny "Bureau of Forestry" (later the "Forest Service") in the United States Department of Agriculture, of which the annual budget, at the time Roosevelt became President, was only forty thousand dollars.

To Pinchot and his cause,[4] as to many other men ardent for new ideas, the accidental Presidency of Roosevelt was a gift from the gods. Promptly Roosevelt had Pinchot as a member of his intimate "tennis cabinet," and was preaching to Congress in his first annual message, December 3, 1901, that "the forest and water problems are perhaps the most vital internal problems of the United States." "The whole future of the nation is directly at stake."[5]

By 1902, two new words, connoting a new phase of American national affairs, were becoming familiar to an America destined to be made conscious of many new terms for rapidly changing conditions. "Reclamation" meant the fostering of waste land, especially the bring-

4 Pinchot did not originate the idea of forest reserves. The first, or at least an early, conception came from the naturalist, John Muir, at a time in the 1880's, when John W. Noble had charge of the public lands as Secretary of the Interior in the administration of Grover Cleveland.

5 Speech at Memphis, October 4, 1907.

ing of water by irrigation to arid desert land; by June 17, 1902, Roosevelt with others had urged through Congress a "Reclamation Act"[6] under which in subsequent years some 160 millions of government money was expended in irrigation. A broader term for the new idea was "Conservation" (of natural resources), which, appearing in Nelson's Encyclopedia for 1911 (in a definition written by one of Pinchot's associates, P. P. Wells), meant "foresight and restraint in the exploitation of the physical sources of wealth as necessary for the perpetuity of civilization and the welfare of present and future generations." The word had a social implication leaning toward the philosophy known vaguely as "Socialism," a dogma that the "unearned increment" of the natural resources should be retained for the public. Conservation, Wells said, "was only a means to an end and the end was economic justice."

Associated with "Conservation" were words like "vision," in a literature which rebuked our past wastefulness, warned of impending extinction, and called excitedly for restraint. Pinchot predicted that persons then alive would eat on concrete or metal tables, due to the exhaustion of forests; that at the existing rate of increase of use "our supplies of anthracite coal will last fifty years and bituminous a little over a hundred." Unless we practice conservation, Pinchot said, "those who come after us will have to pay the price of misery, degradation and failure for the progress and prosperity of our day." Even hard-boiled old James J. Hill, president of the Great Northern Railroad, implacable individualist and arch-developer of the Northwest, infected (against his

[6] Twenty to thirty years later, after agriculture as an industry had fallen upon hard times, there was some questioning of the policy of reclaiming new land to add to a farm area which already produced more than could be sold at satisfactory prices. The history of reclamation included no small quantity of money lost, by the government and by individuals; of wasted effort, foiled hopes, broken lives.

inclinations and interests) by Pinchot and Roosevelt, foresaw[7] "in the year 1950 an iron-less age; iron will have retreated almost to the company of precious metals. . . . The peril [as to both iron and coal] is not one of remote geologic time, but of this generation."

V

To Roosevelt, infected by Pinchot's zeal, stimulated by an approval of crusades that was characteristic of the time, Conservation became a holy cause; perhaps his leadership in it would be the thing that every President, if he has any imagination, thinks about, the thing marking off his administration in history. With high gusto he fought the private interests who were offended by the new policy, the timber, mining and water-power corporations whom he designated "land-grabbers." When they, acting through Senator Fulton of Oregon, undertook to put a statutory curb on Roosevelt's zeal, the subsequent developments constituted one of the most spirited and characteristic episodes of Roosevelt's Presidency.

Roosevelt's leverage for practical conservation, his fundamental power to preserve the forests, rested on his authority to withdraw by executive order from entry, and to set aside as forest reserves, any part of the public domain which could reasonably be described as forest — Pinchot's young men were constantly ranging the mountains to find land sufficiently wooded to justify Roosevelt in withdrawing it. Fulton manœuvred through the Senate, as a "rider" to the Agricultural Appropriation bill, a provision that the President could no longer do this,[8] that future withdrawals must be made, not by executive order, but by act of Congress.

[7] At the Minnesota State Fair, St. Paul, September, 1906.

[8] In six Northwestern States—Oregon, Washington, Wyoming, Idaho, Colorado, Montana.

Roosevelt knew he must sign the appropriation bill as a whole to keep the Department of Agriculture functioning. While the bill was still in the Senate, Roosevelt and Pinchot conferred. To Pinchot and his subordinates Roosevelt said, in effect, as it was repeated later with possibly some admiring exaggeration: "Bring me maps showing every piece of public domain in those six States that contains a bush." Pinchot's subordinates and his office drafting force worked day and night. Roosevelt with their maps before him signed executive orders withdrawing sixteen millon acres. Then he signed the bill which forbade him to do what he had just done. Grinningly, he wrote years later in his Autobiography: "The opponents of the Forest Service turned handsprings in their wrath."

VI

This aggressiveness of Roosevelt in behalf of Conservation, his assumption, as a broad rule of practice, that the President can and should do anything in the public interest (as conceived by him) that the Constitution did not expressly forbid, gave rise to the atmosphere of angry controversy in which Conservation was when Roosevelt was succeeded by Taft. Roosevelt's official spear-head in the fight had been James R. Garfield, who as Secretary of the Interior had authority over the public domain. (While Pinchot was the principal inspiration and most earnest zealot, he was, officially, only a subordinate in the Department of Agriculture.) For this reason Roosevelt wished Taft to keep Garfield in the cabinet. Taft did not. From that, the rest followed.

Taft appointed Richard Achilles Ballinger of Seattle, Washington. Taft may readily have thought that Ballinger was an adequate appointment, for Ballinger had been, up to a few months before, a subordinate in Garfield's department, head of the General Land Office, and as such had seemed to be in sympathy with Garfield, Roosevelt and Conservation. Taft was loyal to Conservation, and would not consciously have appointed a Secretary of the Interior who would reverse the policy.

To Pinchot and the ardent young zealots who had gravitated round him, the dropping of Garfield was complete justification for acute distrust; in their state of mind hardly any successor whom Taft might appoint could fail to be under suspicion. Pinchot was now without the governor that Roosevelt had been to his impulses. With Roosevelt out of touch in Africa, Pinchot became what Roosevelt described him,[9] one "who would expend his great energy in fighting the men who seemed to him not to be going far enough forward."

Ballinger (and Taft) had been in office less than six months when Pinchot put his suspicion into action. To a young subordinate in Ballinger's department, Louis R. Glavis, Pinchot gave a letter of introduction to Taft. Glavis, calling[10] on Taft, charged that his superior, Ballinger, was improperly expediting transfer of a hundred thousand acres of government coal land in Alaska to a group of capitalists (composed mainly of the Guggenheim family) on claims which, Glavis charged, were in part invalid. Taft sent the charges to Ballinger. Ballinger delivered to Taft a defense and explanation — with buttressing documents it contained upward of half a million words.

Taft addressed[11] to Ballinger a "ponderous, sweeping letter of exculpation and endorsement intended to be a permanent seal of sanctity, to refute all present charges

9 Letter to Henry Cabot Lodge.   10 August 17, 1909.
11 September 13, 1909.

against Ballinger and make future ones impossible."[12] Taft told Ballinger that he had "examined the whole record most carefully" and that he had "reached a very definite conclusion." Taft's conclusion was that "the case attempted to be made by Mr. Glavis [is] without any substantial evidence to sustain his attack [and] embraces only shreds of suspicions" — this phrase, catching the public fancy, became conspicuous in the subsequent commotion. Taft authorized Ballinger "to dismiss L. R. Glavis from the service of the government for filing a disingenuous statement unjustly impeaching the integrity of his superior officers."

To the support of Glavis quickly came Pinchot. His support took the form in part of having some of his subordinates furnish to the newspapers information from the government files tending to support the charges Glavis had made, tending to reflect on Ballinger and, by this time, inferentially, on Taft. When this activity became known, Pinchot wrote a public letter to Senator Dolliver saying that his subordinates "broke no law and at worst were guilty only of the violation of official propriety."

Pinchot's action was, of course, flagrant insubordination. Taft dismissed him from office, saying:

Your letter was in effect an improper appeal to Congress and the public to excuse in advance the guilt of your subordinates before I could act, and against my decision in the Glavis case before the whole evidence . . . could be considered. I should be glad to regard what has happened only as a personal reflection, so that I could pass it over and take no official cognizance of it. But other and higher considerations must govern me. When the people of the United States elected me as President they placed me in an office of the highest dignity and charged me with the duty of maintaining that dignity and proper respect for the office on the part of my subordinates. Moreover, if I were to pass over this matter in

[12] This description of Taft's letter is from a bitterly hostile source, *Collier's Weekly*. It was written, in 1910, by Mark Sullivan.

silence it would be most demoralizing to the discipline of the executive branch of the Government. By your own conduct you have destroyed your usefulness as a helpful subordinate of the Government, and it therefore now becomes my duty to direct the Secretary of Agriculture to remove you from your office as Forester.

Now to the support of both Pinchot and Glavis came *Collier's Weekly*, many newspapers, practically all the cult of Conservation zealots, as well as miscellaneous altruists. "Glavis" became one of those names which achieve a febrile, ephemeral fame in the headlines for a few months. *Collier's* printed Glavis' charges under a headline asking "Are the Guggenheims in charge of the Interior Department?" illustrated by a giant corporate hand reaching out to seize the nation's heritage. Such journalistic exclamations were sufficient excitant to a public which never grasped, to the end of the case or since, the meaning of "clear-listing," "lieu lands," "filing" or the other technical intricacies that made up the substance of the charges and the evidence. The Conservation zealots demanded that Ballinger be investigated by a committee of Congress. When the committee met, *Collier's* paid a fee of $25,000 to an able Boston lawyer and reformer, Louis D. Brandeis,[13] to represent Glavis and in general the forces hostile to Taft. Brandeis asked for and the committee demanded from Taft, all "reports, statements, papers or documents upon which he acted in reaching his conclusions."

Among the papers sent the committee by Taft, in response to their demand, was a document of about 50,000 words signed by Taft's Attorney-General, George W. Wickersham, a "report and summary" of the case, purporting to be one of the documents upon which Taft had based his decision to dismiss Glavis and support Bal-

---

[13] Later Associate Justice of the Supreme Court of the United States by appointment from President Woodrow Wilson.

linger. The document was dated September 11, 1910. Brandeis showed — chiefly through testimony volunteered by Wickersham's private secretary — that Wickersham had written the document not on September 11 but some three months later, after Congress had called on Taft for the papers upon which he had based his exculpation of Ballinger. Taft explained that the ante-dating of the report had had as its object merely to stress the date when the Attorney-General had rendered an oral report.

Within the committee, a majority, Republican, reported that Ballinger was "a competent and honorable gentleman, honestly and faithfully performing the duties of his high office with an eye single to the public interest," that the charges against Ballinger "appear to have had their origin in a strong feeling of animosity created by a supposed difference in policy respecting Conservation." The minority, Democratic and Insurgent Republican, reported otherwise. About everybody agreed that Ballinger was, to put it very mildly, in that state, insecure for a holder of public office, in which his "usefulness was impaired."

Ballinger, six months after the report of the committee, resigned.[14] To his retirement he took a letter from Taft, which may have reflected Taft at his best as a human being, if not happy as a President:

I do not hesitate to say that you have been the object of one of the most unscrupulous conspiracies for the defamation of character that history can show. I have deemed it my duty not only to the Government, but to society in general, to fight out this battle to the end, confident that in the end your fellow citizens would see that the impressions of you as a man and as the administrator of a high public office were false and were the result of a malicious and unprincipled plan for the use of

14 March 7, 1911.

the press to misrepresent you and your actions, and to torture every circumstance, however free from detrimental significance, into proof of corrupt motive.

Upon which the New York Evening *Post* observed:

Mr. Taft consents to Mr. Ballinger's departure in a blaze of indignant relief.

VII

Pinchot took ship for the White Nile to pour out his tale to Roosevelt. Roosevelt by this time knew that Taft was not expert in administering the government of the United States. He knew too that Taft was failing in adequate support of Roosevelt's policies. But Roosevelt also knew Pinchot, knew the touch of fanaticism in him, his disposition to court martyrdom. And Roosevelt knew the rules of conducting an executive office. Remembering his own experiences with Congress, he knew the utter impossibility of having in the executive branch of the government a subordinate who would conspire with men in Congress to embarrass the President. "I am not yet sure," Roosevelt wrote,[15] "whether Taft . . . could have followed any course save the one he did."

Roosevelt's following, however, knowing little and caring less about the question of administrative discipline involved, thought only in terms of Conservation, and as Pinchot as a disciple of Roosevelt. Conservation, they felt, had been betrayed by Taft, Pinchot humiliated. The Ballinger case was yet another ring in the downward spiral of Taft's fortunes.

[15] To Lodge, April, 1910.

20

TAFT'S FOUR YEARS: HIGH HOPES WRECKED

THE most ambitious constructive step taken by Taft during his administration was the initiation of reciprocity treaties. Reciprocity, in the stage to which in 1910 it had evolved after a century of cursory trial, meant agreement between two nations permitting exchange of commodities either free of tariff duties or at rates less than those in force against other countries. During Roosevelt's administration a reciprocity treaty between Cuba and the United States, giving each country a preferred position in the markets of the other, had turned out to be mutually satisfactory.

Taft, for his venture, chose Canada. A form of reciprocity between Canada and the United States had been in force half a century before, and after it had ended Canada had made numerous overtures for a new treaty. To Ottawa, in the Fall of 1910, Taft sent two commissioners to negotiate with the Dominion government. A treaty was drawn, and, on January 7, 1911, signed by the negotiators. In substance, the treaty was an approach to free trade between Canada and the United States. It called for placing on the free list more than one hundred articles and for reducing the tariff on more than four hundred others.[1]

Since the treaty had to do with the tariff, which is a form of taxation, and since taxation is a matter over which the Lower House[2] of Congress has prerogative, Taft was obliged, perforce, to submit his measure to the

[1] "Contemporary American History," Charles A. Beard.
[2] Ordinary treaties are subject to ratification by the Senate only.

double jeopardy of approval by both House and Senate. He sent it to Congress January 26, 1911.

In the House, now Democratic, the pact met with no formidable opposition and was passed, by the aid of Democratic votes, in February.

The Senate, despite all Taft's cajolery, refused to do anything. "In the last days of the Session there was in the Senate the novel and anomalous spectacle of the most important Administration measure utterly ignored and without a friend to champion it."[3] Thus, without action, the Session ended.

Taft, with an aggressive energy unusual in him, less than half an hour after the old Session ended issued a call for a special one, to meet April 5, 1911. On convening, the House again passed the bill (265 to 89), April 21, 1911. In the Senate formidable opposition arose. Taft had counted confidently on the Insurgent Republicans, believing reciprocity precisely the sort of Utopian legislation that would appeal to their proclaimed highmindedness, and was consequently astonished and pained to discover that the Insurgents were unsympathetic, almost to a man opposed. They justified their resistance on the ground that the treaty would discriminate against the farmers of the West by encouraging imports of foodstuffs from Canada, while at the same time benefitting Eastern manufacturers by creating larger markets for them in Canada. Farm papers encouraged their readers to write to Washington condemning the treaty. Agents of farm organizations protested against it. To a group of delegates from the National Grange, calling to warn Taft, he said petulantly that he would insist on reciprocity even if it should cost his party the farmer vote.

To bring public pressure to bear on the recalcitrant and

3 Harold J. Howland, *The Outlook,* March 18, 1911.

slow moving Senate, Taft energetically made speeches, one in New York and another in Chicago which the admiring New York *Times* considered the "equal of the best efforts of Gladstone." In his speeches Taft fought back at the enemies of reciprocity, with charges that the opposition was inspired by a "contemptible union" of the lumber and print-paper interests with "those who claim vociferously to represent the whole farming industry of the United States."

On June 8, belatedly, the Finance Committee of the Senate reported the bill out, ominously without recommendation. Thereafter, on and off for three weeks, reciprocity was a football over which a hybrid alliance of Democrats and Standpat Republicans contended against a no less anomalous union of Regular and Insurgent Republicans. The disruption of party lines made the Senate chaotic, kaleidoscopic. Finally, the Senate passed the treaty June 21, 1911, by a vote of 53 to 27. Of the votes against it, only three came from the Democrats and twelve each from the Republicans and Insurgents. Jubilantly Taft thanked the Democrats, acknowledged "the credit that belongs to [them] . . . for their consistent support of the measure in an earnest and sincere desire to secure its passage."[4]

Likewise jubilantly, Taft made another acknowledgment, which did not turn out so innocuously. For no other reason, probably, than to pay a debt and to give expression to his kindly amiability, he put the treaty in jeopardy, furnished its opponents with the one weapon capable of destroying it. To the publisher of a string of sensational newspapers, William Randolph Hearst, Taft gave a statement expressing his "high appreciation of the energetic work of the seven Hearst papers and of your

[4] June 22, 1911.

staff for their earnest and useful effort to spread the gospel of reciprocity."

Hearst had been during some months advocating reciprocity with Canada — but Hearst for some years had been advocating annexation of Canada. At a time when the United States apparently had imperial ambitions, had recently acquired the Philippines and Porto Rico, annexation was to the Canadians a national bugaboo. Fear that reciprocity might be the first step toward absorption was the reason reciprocity had been opposed by some Canadians and many Englishmen, some particularly influential, among them Sir Gilbert Parker, and Rudyard Kipling who wrote that he could not understand "how 9,000,000 people can enter into such arrangements as are proposed with 90,000,000 strangers on an open frontier of 4,000 miles and at the same time preserve their national integrity. . . . It is her own soul that Canada risks to-day. Once that soul is pawned for any consideration Canada must inevitably conform to the commercial, legal, financial, social, and ethical standards which will be imposed upon her by the sheer admitted weight of the United States."

Now, opponents of reciprocity in Canada exploited the apparent identity between Taft who favored reciprocity, and Hearst who favored annexation. Taft's words to Hearst became a tocsin in Canada; a hundred Paul Reveres spread them from Halifax to Vancouver. At the elections, reciprocity was overwhelmingly defeated. To everybody's surprise, the Canadian agricultural provinces voted as strongly against it as did the manufacturing East, proving that fear of eventual annexation had been more powerful than hope of economic advantage.

"Gloom prevails in official Washington," unfeelingly wrote Hearst's Washington correspondent. "The defeat of President Taft's pet measure is acknowledged on all sides to be a serious setback to the President's aspirations for a second term." Taft said: "For me it is a great disappointment. I had hoped that it would be put through, to prove the correctness of my judgment that it would be a good thing for both countries. It takes two to make a bargain, and if Canada declines we can still go on doing business at the old stand."

If Taft regarded the failure of reciprocity as a "great disappointment," the country as a whole looked upon it as an irritating repulse by Canada to a friendly gesture from us, and upon Taft's course as a whole as inexcusably blundering. Taft had called Congress into special session to sit through the long hot summer to pass the treaty. He had assured Congress and the American people that Canada wanted it. To get the bill passed he had practically wrecked the organization of his own party in the Senate. And the final result of these manœuvrings, labors, and sacrifices had been that the hand which the American people had stretched in commercial fellowship across the border had been rudely rejected — through Taft, the nation had laid itself open to rebuff.

II

Peace Treaties

In Taft's progress from disaster to disaster there seemed an inevitability like that of a natural law. "President Taft," said the *Ohio State Journal*, "hardly gets fairly settled down to golf and the other duties of his high office when something else happens."

Taft, on entering the Presidency, carried with him a wish long dear to his heart to lead his country to do something effective for the cause of world peace. To the forwarding of this ambition he devoted the most moving part of his speech accepting the Republican nomination. After his election, as a first step, he opened negotiations with France and Great Britain looking to the extension of the already existing arbitration treaties between the United States and those nations to include all controversies "justiciable" in character, even though they might involve questions of "vital interest and national honor" — "all questions determinable by the principles of law and equity" were to be submitted to the Hague Tribunal. The negotiations prospered. In August of 1911 treaties embodying Taft's extensions were signed, to the hymned plaudits of peace-lovers everywhere.

When the treaties went to the Senate they met with the atrabilious welcome which the Senate reserves for Presidential excursions into foreign relations. The Senate, after drastically amending them, ratified the treaties on March 7, 1912. They had been so changed, however, that Taft considered that all the merit had been amended out of them and so, regretfully and a little sullenly, he declined to sign them. The disappointment, to the genuinely altruistic and world-minded Taft, was personal, poignant. The more representative portion of the press sympathized with him, condemned the Senate. "Ratification," said the New York *Evening Post*, "would have given prestige to a Republican President who is a candidate for re-election and Mr. Taft's political and personal opponents struck hands to prevent it." The Chicago *Record-Herald* said that "partisanship, peanut politics, opposition to the President, the desire to withhold from him something that might give him strength and prestige, were factors in the deplorable and humiliating outcome."

III

Taft's Four Years: The Better Part

In spite of wreck after wreck of major matters, Taft's administration as a whole justified the verdict of Doctor

Arnold B. Hall, professor of political science in the University of Wisconsin, a strong supporter of LaFollette in State matters, that Taft had "made more real and lasting progress than any two Presidents since the Civil War"; [5] and the judgment of John Bassett Moore about the many reform measures which Taft helped to carry through Congress — "never has the attention of the people been more vigorously directed to matters connected with the development of good government on a democratic basis." [6]

Taft, as a result of vacancies occurring during his administration, practically made over the Supreme Court, named six out of its nine Justices — as he signed the commission of Edward D. White to be Chief Justice, he sighed, "To think I am giving this commission for the office that I wanted myself!" [7]

Taft appointed fully 60 per cent of the occupants of the inferior Federal courts — incidentally causing Taft's sensitive standard of ethics to make it impossible for him to become a practicing lawyer after he left the White House.

Taft proposed [8] in a special message, and Congress passed, a constitutional amendment enpowering Congress to levy a general income tax which, after ratification by the necessary number of States, became effective [9] before the end of Taft's administration.

Taft recommended and Congress created a Customs Court of five judges to hear appeals in customs cases; and a tariff commission to render opinions on questions having to do with the tariff.

[5] *Current History*, April, 1912.   [6] "Short History of the United States."
[7] Taft reflected that if Chief Justice White should achieve to the normal longevity of Supreme Court justices, he would be in the post until long past the time when Taft himself might still be considered eligible. As it turned out, White died in 1921 and President Harding appointed Taft as White's successor — Taft becoming the only man who was ever both President and Chief Justice.
[8] On June 6, 1910.   [9] February 25, 1913.

Taft recommended and Congress created a Court of Commerce to which appeals could be taken from decisions of the Interstate Commerce Commission — the Court, after a brief, hectic, and unhappy existence, including a scandal and impeachment of one of the judges, was abolished in 1913.

Taft recommended and Congress established a postal savings system, in which deposits could be made up to $500, at 2 per cent interest.

In Taft's administration was created[10] the parcels post, which, as instituted January 1, 1913, would carry eleven pounds or less of fourth-class matter at a rate of five cents for the first pound and one cent for each additional pound.

Taft recommended and Congress set up a fact-finding body called the "Economy and Efficiency Commission," out of which later evolved the national budget.

Taft, by executive order, placed 8,000 assistant postmasters under the Civil Service — a long step toward removal of postmasters from the field of patronage and politics.

In Taft's administration Congress passed a constitutional amendment providing for direct election of United States Senators.

Taft recommended and Congress enacted a 2 per cent tax on the net income of corporations — the tax during the war and after went much higher and became one of the principal sources of federal revenue.

Taft recommended (June 16, 1909), Congress passed (the Senate by unanimous vote on July 5; the House on July 12) and the States ratified, a constitutional amendment permitting the federal government to levy and collect an income tax — the first change that had been made in the Constitution in forty-three years.

[10] Signed by the President August 24, 1912.

IV

Taft's Four Years: A Good Policy That Had an Unhappy Result

The Democrats, having won the Lower House of Congress in the November, 1910, election, having come into power with the calling of a special session the following year, 1911; being now in the traditionally advantageous political position of having a majority in one Chamber of the Government without responsibility for the government as a whole, proceeded to make the traditional use of the advantage, with a view to making political capital[11] for the Presidential election the following year, in which Taft would go before the country for a second term. Ingeniously they bedevilled Taft. Three times they introduced "pop-gun" tariff bills, measures aimed at schedules odious to the public, such as "K," the woollen schedule, designed to reiterate in the public eye emphasis upon the iniquities of the Payne-Aldrich bill; tortuously they prolonged the investigation of Taft's Secretary of the Interior Ballinger to advertise to the country that Taft was faithless to Conservation and subservient to the great corporate interests engaged in grabbing the nation's mineral and forest resources.

In their campaign to prove Taft a reactionary the Democrats charged him with friendliness to the trusts; and to prove it created a committee to investigate the United States Steel Corporation, which had been organized, had its growth and its whole history in the Republican administrations of McKinley and Roosevelt, and which had never been brought into court — which, indeed, the Democrats charged, had been the beneficiary of favor from the Republican administration.

[11] Strictly according to the morals of party warfare.

Taft, at this stage of his rapidly falling fortunes, did a thing of the sort that men in desperation sometimes do when they find the strength of the tide running against them too strong for their mental footing. Not Taft so much as his advisers, for it was not in Taft's nature to do a desperate thing; left to himself he would have let the tide against him go on to whatever fate it might bring him. But some of his advisers suggested that the tide adverse to Taft might be reversed, the Progressives placated, and the Democrats disarmed, by a policy of thoroughgoing prosecution of the trusts. The advice coincided with Taft's fundamental conviction that the law, being on the statute books, should be enforced. In this spirit were started a number of anti-trust suits which, in the aggregate of all that were prosecuted in Taft's administration, exceeded by far the number prosecuted in Roosevelt's, or any other — made the Taft administration the outstanding one in American history for prosecution of trusts.

Within three years, Mr. Taft had twenty-two bills in equity and forty-five indictments under the Sherman law to his credit. During Harrison's administration there had been four bills in equity and three indictments; during Cleveland's administration, four bills in equity, two indictments, two informations for contempt; during McKinley's administration, three bills in equity. Roosevelt had to his credit, eighteen bills in equity, twenty-five indictments, and one forfeiture proceeding.[12]

As a spectacular high spot in Taft's prosecution of the trusts, his Attorney-General, George W. Wickersham,[13] on October 26, 1911, filed a suit for dissolution of the United States Steel Corporation, citing, as one cause for its being a monopoly, its purchase of the

---

[12] "Contemporary American History," Charles A. Beard.

[13] A member of Taft's Cabinet, Knox, said subsequently that the suit had never been discussed in the Cabinet. "Henry Clay Frick, the Man," George Harvey.

Tennessee Coal and Iron Company four years before, and alleging that the act of purchasing had included securing approval from Roosevelt, and that Roosevelt's approval had been procured by deceit.

That suit against the Steel Corporation, with its reflection upon Roosevelt, while it might have seemed the solution of one of Taft's present troubles, was the beginning of a future and a more serious one[14] — was, indeed, the most disastrous act of Taft's political career, led to the most calamitous episode in the history of the Republican party.

[14] For the effect of Taft's Steel Trust suit on Roosevelt's emotions, and the subsequent developments, see Chapter 24.

21

TAFT'S FOUR YEARS

By the time Taft had been a year in the White House, the fat man jokes about him, which when he was Secretary of War had been genial and kindly, began to take on a caustic tang — the 1907 jest about Taft being "the politest man I know because he gave up his seat in a street-car to three women," now supplanted by the 1910 one about a fat woman trying to get off a street-car: because she was stout, she was obliged to go down the steps backward, but at each stop the conductor and the friendly passengers, seeing her facing forward, assumed she was getting on the car, and by giving her a helpful push facilitated her progress in the direction she did not want to go, so that she was carried past four stops before she could make it clear that it was off, not on, that she wanted to go.

The very things Taft had done to please the crowd, his patting Demos on the head, which had evoked plaudits at the time he did it, was now criticized. He had sat in the bleachers at a baseball game at Pittsburgh, declining to take a box, and had been praised by the press of the country — "he refuses to be exclusive," he is "one of the people."[1] He had made tours of the country and journeys from Washington so numerous as to cause him to conclude that "the major part of the work of a President is to increase the gate receipts of fairs."[1] Now, in the changed mood of the country, those excursions and his diversions were turned against him. Too much of his time was "occupied in pleasure seeking, attending baseball games in a number of different cities, frequent

[1] "Letters of Archie Butt."

408

attendance at theatres, playing golf and riding around Washington and other places in automobiles."[2]

Even the comment that was meant to be fair, or generous, carried a hint of disappointment, a trace of jeering, a suggestion that his physical bulk overtopped his intellectual.

> Thou art the cosmic bulge, the overspill;
> Thou art America, Brobdignagian Bill,

wrote London *Punch*. The same chord was thrummed by a rhyming polemist in the New York *Sun:* "A solid man, both fore and aft, is he who's known as Mr. Taft. He sits high in the halls of State, a man of most unquestioned weight. He has the manners of a Judge, and hence is rather hard to budge; and as the man, so the official, moves slowly on through paths judicial. . . ." The jibe, as if with an after-thought of justice, ended by conceding the fundamental goodness that every one recognized in Taft: "If he could have eternity to make things as they ought to be, when time hath reached its end afar we'd all dwell in Utopia."

Inevitably, much of the criticism, whether caustic anger or merely gentle jibing or sad disappointment, took the form of comparison with Roosevelt, as in:

> Dear Teddy, I need you; come home to me quick,
> I am worried and weary and worn.
> And as hope long deferred only makes the heart sick,
> I am sadly in need of your potent "Big Stick";
> So, Teddy, please haste your return. . . .[3]

Taft recognized the change in the public mood, and, though brave about it, was distressed. His family and intimate friends "felt as unhappy at the way things were going as Taft himself; I feel so sorry for him I could almost cry," wrote the faithful Butt.[4]

[2] Quoted from a Republican criticism of Taft's action about the tariff.
[3] By Timothy Hay, originally printed in the San Francisco *Bulletin,* widely copied.
[4] "Letters of Archie Butt."

II

It was a pity, and it was unfair. Taft was not a bad President, he was a good one. He had absolute integrity, was "honest, simply honest, transparently honest." Considerably less than Roosevelt would Taft relax the highest standards of public service to name a friend to office or pay a debt to a politician. Indeed, Taft leaned backward. "The trouble with Taft," said Cannon, in a moment of irritation about patronage sought and refused, "is that if he were Pope he would think it necessary to appoint a few Protestant cardinals." Taft was highminded, just-minded; clean-minded, clear-minded; no lawyer or judge of his time could excel the sure-mindedness with which he thumbed through great stacks of legal papers, his mind absorbing their contents, his judgment finding the gist. He was clear-minded and discriminating about men, too, and could on occasion exercise a unique power of characterization — one of the Insurgent senators he described as "so narrow he can see through a key-hole with both eyes at once without squinting." His appointments to the bench and to executive positions were above the average. Taft had much less capacity for self-delusion than Roosevelt. If a man was of dubious character Taft's instinct knew it and his rigid rectitude did not condone it. If a man was evil, Taft knew it; if one had done wrong, either in the general sense or to Taft, Taft remembered it. "He does not say much, he does not show his dislike, or rather he does not waste his dislike when there is no need for it, and those whom he dislikes never suspect it until the crucial moment."[5]

Far less than most Presidents would Taft practice hy-

[5] "Letters of Archie Butt."

pocrisy, even the relatively harmless political variety, or compromise with it. Anything devious was abominable to him. In all the 330 pounds of him, not a pound nor an ounce nor a gram was deceit. Furtiveness he despised. At his desk, if a politician leaned to whisper to him, Taft's end of the conversation would rise until the window-panes rattled. Courage he had, too, at all times the quiet kind, and, when roused, the energetic kind. Never did he yield to any organized militant minority — his scorn for that was a chief cause of his downfall.

"No President in recent years," one of his most powerful critics was forced to concede, "has won for himself more widespread personal admiration for kindliness, for candor and for integrity."[6] And when this critic sought justification for his condemnation he found it, mainly, in the vague charge that Taft was too Constitution-minded, that he "is primarily an interpreter of laws rather than an administrator of laws." In other words, that Taft should have been a judge rather than a President. The charge, of course, was true.

III

Easy-going Taft was, and that was part of his own contribution to his tragedy. Left to himself the easy-going quality of him would have carried him to the career where easy-going would not have been a detriment, the Supreme Court. But it was part of his fate — at first good-fortune, later less so — to have a wife with a quality of managing energy, one more ambitious for her husband than he for himself, one having initiative in starting things which it was not easy for her husband's inertia to finish. She had kept him off the Court and in the course that led to the Presidency. Then, soon

[6] Lyman Abbott in *The Outlook,* at a time, in 1912, when *The Outlook* was dedicated to defeating Taft for re-election.

after the election, and even before Taft took office, she found that "My own problems [as mistress of the White House] became to me paramount and I began to give them my almost undivided attention and to neglect the political affairs which had for many years interested me so intensely."[7] After she had been in the White House only a few months, illness pulled her down. She became almost room-bound. Taft was deprived of her energy throughout the time he needed it most.

IV

Taft knew the public attitude toward him had changed, knew that major events in his administration had gone against him. "I have not played in much luck during this administration," he said to Archie Butt.[8] Earlier he had said, self-consolingly, looking toward hope rather than on reality, "Archie, do you realize that my administration is not half over and that a lot can happen in that time?"

In that Taft revealed a part of so much of the blame as rested on him. If there should be a turn for the better for him, it would have to "happen" — Taft would not bring it about, would not see to it that it should happen. If it came, it would be through "luck" or not at all. Taft was static, his power that of inertia, not of momentum. It was not in him to start things and keep pushing on them. In the conditions that arose around him and determined his fate, it was the politicians who, with vigilant alertness, knew the kind of man they had to deal with, and supplied the initiative, acted betimes; Taft's rôle was that of belatedly trying to catch up with situations after it was too late.

Taft knew his failing, spoke of it with complacency, and also with a humor that softened the fault. One of

7 "Recollections," Mrs. William H. Taft.   8 January 15, 1912.

his favorite stories was about a colored boy fishing in the Potomac; when Taft asked what he was fishing for the boy replied, "Just to be a-fishin'." "Roosevelt," Taft said to Butt, "could always keep ahead of his work, but I cannot do it and I know it is a grievous fault. It is too late to remedy it. The country must take me as it found me. Wasn't it your mother who had a servant girl who said it was no use for her to try to hurry, that she was a 'Sunday chile' and no 'Sunday chile' could hurry? I don't think I am a Sunday child, but I ought to have been."

v

All Taft's personal failings were immaterial, whether those of inertia before ill-fortune asssailed him, or those of irritability later. His tragedy was merely that he was a placid man in a restless time, had a judicial temperament when the country was in a partisan mood, was a static man in a dynamic age. Under other conditions, or in many a four years of the country's history, Taft's elephantine bulk, his good-nature, his easy-going pace, might have commended him to the country, made him a hero at the time and subsequently a legend of gargantua, made him an ideal President. During any period of national quiescence Taft might have been uniquely in tune with the universe. His heartiness, genuineness and sincerity might have been a tonic to similar qualities in the country. But the people had recently drunk deep of the very different qualities of another personality; having been stimulated by the heady wine of strenuousness they could not be content with the tepid nectar of Taft's milder qualities.

Taft's chief failing was that he differed from Roosevelt, his chief misfortune that he followed Roosevelt in the Presidency. The country had been tuned to the tempo of Roosevelt, and inevitably therefore could only be out of step with the tempo of Taft. To accent the maladjustment, Roosevelt had told the country that Taft was like himself. Taft could not live up to that picture; and to fail to live up to expectations created in others is a sure cause of failure. Taft might be an excellent President in a score of ways; all would do him no good if he was not excellent in the precise way the country had been led to expect. Pathetically, with earnest good-will, Taft had hoped, had tried, to be what Roosevelt had said he would be. "I do nothing," he had written to Roosevelt as the latter took ship for Africa, "without considering what you would do in the same circumstances, and without having in a sense a mental talk with you over the pros and cons of the situation."

Taft had written that, in all sincerity, during his first month in the White House. He had meant to live up to it. He did not foresee that the rôle of trying to be Roosevelt involved a pose which his forthright simplicity would not permit him to continue. For Taft, any pose was distasteful to his character, impossible to his nature. He had to be himself. And Taft as himself, placid, easygoing, slow to decide, was a far cry from the strenuous, quick-acting Roosevelt whom the country, with some important exceptions, had come to regard as the model of what a President ought to be.

22

THRU!

Roosevelt in Retirement — if That Word Could Describe
any State of Being in Which Roosevelt Could Ever Find
Himself. His Journey to Africa, and His Good Hunting There,
"of Fowls According to Their Kind, and of Beasts in Their
Kind, and of Everything That Creepeth on the Earth Ac-
cording to Its Kind." His "Bully Row" at Rome, and the
Commotion He Caused at Cairo, and His Visits to Royalty,
Including the Enjoyable Experiences He Had at What He
Called the "Wake" of a King. His Lectures before Euro-
pean Universities, and before Monarchs — and to Them.
Concluding with a Letter Which He Received from Taft.

MEANWHILE Roosevelt:

On the afternoon of March 4, 1909, he left Washington and the Presidency, attended by a whirlwind of
comment of which the almost universal characteristic
was partisanship, for or against. About Roosevelt while
he lived there was hardly such a thing as a balanced judgment. From the day he first became a public character,
all America was divided between those who felt the devil
had artfully omitted to provide him with horns, and
those who justified the saying of a magazine writer, "I
still insist that Roosevelt would be applauded for stoning
his grandma." Of the encomiums that attended his departure from the Presidency, one of the most exalted
came from Taft, who "verily believe[d]" that "the historian[1] twenty-five years hence . . . will accord to
Roosevelt a place with Washington and Lincoln." Most

[1] The "historian twenty-five years hence" is an arbiter often appealed to. The
present one, writing twenty-three years after Taft spoke, regrets his inability,
as a small fraction of the aggregate of all historians, to make Taft's prediction
good; and doubts if two more years (to make Taft's twenty-five) will bring
the judgment that Roosevelt has an equal "place with Washington and Lincoln."

of the encomiums were in the reverent mood of an American versifier and humorist,[2] who, becoming anonymous

From the "Literary Digest," 1909.

All America chuckled over Davenport's cartoon picturing the panic among the denizens of Africa's jungles caused by the news that Roosevelt was coming.

for the purpose of being serious, expressed the characteristic sentiment of millions of average Americans in:

I'm glad I've lived when he was President —

2 Wallace Irwin.

The dispraise of Roosevelt was invariably acid, epi-
thetic. If it were possible to arrive at an adverse judgment of Roosevelt by a logical statement of disapproved
actions, no one attempted it; the detractors were too
angry for anything but etymological brickbats. A "per-
petual self-seeker," said the Worcester *Telegram*, "a
foxy twister of the facts," a "daringly pernicious and
noisy politician." "If you wish my opinion of Theodore
Roosevelt," said a distinguished author-diplomat of the
day,[3] "it is that he might make a passable king, a very
fair newspaper man, an admirable circus impresario; but
as President he is as monstrous as would be Mrs. Mary
Baker Eddy in a Salome dance." Some achieved their
dispraise of Roosevelt by praise of Taft. "There will
now be a reign of reason in the White House" — by
such comparisons they made the contribution that out-
siders often make to the materials, already abundant in
this case, for rift between friends. Such detractors as retained enough calm to put their malice into the forms of
wit, wove infinite gibes. Of this, the exquisite essence,
the perfect summation, was compressed by the New York
Sun — Roosevelt's ancient, consistent, and able enemy
— into an editorial which may reasonably be described in
superlatives, at once the briefest and the most forceful,
the most pungent, and the most pointed ever printed. Expressing itself in the manner of an explosive breath of
relief after prolonged and almost unendurable strain, and
taking adroit advantage of the least successful of Roosevelt's adventures into extra-official omnipotence, his attempt to bring about "simplified spelling,"[4] *The Sun*, on
the morning of March 4, 1909, in the editorial space in
which other papers published page-length summaries

[3] Poultney Bigelow.

[4] For an account of Roosevelt's adventure into improvement of orthography,
see "Our Times," Vol. III. For an account of part of *The Sun's* long battle
against Roosevelt, see "Our Times," Vol. III.

of Roosevelt's administration or ponderous comments about the ending of it, *The Sun* printed one word:

"Thru!"

ruaea in CKENZIE ion and ertaking PIERCE, s Secre- he plans ?, which 't office, hose he Var. ;imental ?ractical ?KENZIE	BEVERIDGE'S term expires in 1911. Mr. FAIRBANKS will then be 59. He is accustomed to public life and likes it. Obviously there are interesting possibilities in the immediate future of Hoosier politics. _____ Thru! _____ The liquor question in Vermont never seems to be settled to the satisfaction of either the wets or the drys. One year Rutland votes for license, and the next year it swings the other way. Burlington also oscillates between the saloon and the	Trees makes be rals $3.30 a Inter compou Retur white p most pi $160; wt at the The acc the cor a net pi cent. co NEW

An excerpt from the editorial page of *The Sun*, March 4, 1909.

II

In the period of private life into which Roosevelt now entered, the first since his early 20's, he was observed with as much affection by the part of the public who loved him, as much acerbity by those who did not, as when he had been in the goldfish bowl that the Presidency is. In truth, the phase into which Roosevelt now entered was not "private life." Wherever he might be, whatever rôle he might be filling, there was that about him which caused eyes to turn to him. "He was his own limelight and could not help it: a creature charged with such voltage as his became the central presence at once, whether he stepped on a platform or entered a room."[5]

The magnetism he generated was able to reach back across the ocean from Africa. His going as a mighty hunter, as the lion killer, added to him the glamour that the average man has always seen in dangerous adventure, the deference the tribe has always paid to "Bah Ram,

[5] The quotation is from "Roosevelt, the Story of His Friendship," by Owen Wister.

the great hunter." His taking with him his twenty-
year-old son Kermit made him kin to every father who
ever tramped the edges of the autumn woods to induct

From a photograph by Kermit Roosevelt.

Bwana Makuba and group of Nandi warriors.

his boy into rabbit shooting, and even more to the city
father who vainly dreamed of repeating that scene of his
own youth.

With eager and benevolent interest America, almost
as if it shared what he was doing, observed his preparations: The three rifles, including the double elephant

one; the nine pairs of glasses; the canned goods and the tooth-brushes and the soap; the gold-mounted rabbit's foot that John L. Sullivan gave him; the two hundred

From a photograph by Kermit Roosevelt.

Colonel Roosevelt examining the carcass of a lioness.

rockets, in case he should — terrifying thought to many, bearable to some — get lost; the books he took for reading, bound in pig-skin and packed in an aluminum case to resist the mandibles of African ants — their titles, published and widely discussed, became the "Pigskin Library."

The affection for him, as he sailed out of New York[6]

6 March 23, 1909.

was so easy to be observed, so strongly felt, as to be almost a thing one could touch — an affection not at all diminished by the jokes about "may every lion do his

From a photograph by Kermit Roosevelt.

A water buffalo, one of the most dangerous of African big game, killed by Roosevelt.

duty!" a glamour heightened by the strange new words that America became familiar with, "safari,"[7] "sais," "mimosa"; the alluring names of the places he went and from which despatches came to American newspapers, Mombasa, Nairobi, Uganda, Gondokuro — to America

[7] African word for a hunting trip. Roosevelt dated his letters home "on safari."

it was like receiving daily bulletins of the travels of Marco Polo. "The people," Lodge wrote him, "follow the account of your African wanderings as if it were a new Robinson Crusoe." The title the natives gave to Roosevelt, "Bwana Makuba"[8] — it became to the America of that day almost as familiar a phrase as "the big chief." And the extraordinary names of many of the animals he slew: he, with Kermit, killed a total of 512 (Roosevelt 296, Kermit 216), including: 17 lions, 11 elephants, 2 rhinoceroses (9 square-mouthed, 11 hook-lipped), 8 hippopotamuses, 9 giraffes, 47 gazelles, 29 zebras, 9 hyenas, together with miscellaneous numbers of animals whose names contributed an extraordinary, if ephemeral addition to American faunal information — the bongo, the kudu, the dikdik, the wildebeest and the

[8] Great Master.

From a cartoon by Harding in the "Brooklyn Eagle," 1910.

Back in the old place.

hartbeest, the giant eland and the common eland, the impala, the wart-hog, the aardwolf, the klipspringer, the great bustard and the lesser bustard, the bushbuck, the waterbuck, and the reedbuck — they were not the

Roosevelt at Naples, Italy.

imaginary fauna of Alice in Wonderland; they were real animals and Roosevelt slew them; many, stuffed, were to be seen in the National Museum at Washington in 1932.

III

He emerged at Khartum, where, so he wrote to Lodge[9] with some naïveté, "Everybody turned to me precisely as if I were in my own country; they were hoping and praying for leadership." Such a prayer Roosevelt was not the man to deny, he responded as casually as if he were making a train-platform speech at Decatur, Ill., and with repercussions as explosive as ever attended anything he said

[9] "Correspondence of Theodore Roosevelt and Henry Cabot Lodge," Vol. II.

in America. In an atmosphere tense with dissension between ruling English and fanatically anti-English Egyptians, Roosevelt, with as much confidence as if he were a Clive on the one hand or a Pharaoh on the other, told the English they must continue to rule Egypt, the Egyptians that they must be loyal to the English.

Before the thunders from that episode ceased echoing over a startled world, Roosevelt proceeded to Rome, where, by one and the same act, he publicly rebuked, on the one hand, a Papal Secretary of State[10] whom he described[11] subsequently as a "furiously bigoted reactionary . . . a sixteenth-century Spanish ecclesiastic," and on the other an American Methodist clergyman whom he described as "a crude, vulgar, tactless creature, cursed with the thirst of self-advertisement."

Roosevelt, as he approached Rome, sent, through the American Ambassador, a message asking the Pope to grant him an audience. The Papal Secretary of State sent back word that the Pope would be "delighted," but hoped that Roosevelt would not while in Rome call upon the headquarters of some American Methodist missionaries, one of whom had called the Pope the "whore of Babylon." Roosevelt had not intended to call on the Methodists — he detested the action of the one who had been vulgarly offensive to the Catholic Church. But refraining of his own will was one thing, refraining because of a stipulation imposed by the Vatican was another. Roosevelt sent word to the Pope that "It would be a real pleasure to me to be presented to the Holy Father, for whom I entertain a high respect both personally and as the head of a great church" — but "I must decline to submit to any conditions which limit my freedom of conduct; I trust on April 5th he [the Pope] will

[10] Merry del Val.   [11] In a letter to George Otto Trevelyan.

find it convenient to receive me." The Vatican replied that "His Holiness will be much pleased to grant an audience to Mr. Roosevelt, for whom he entertains great esteem, both personally and as President of the United States; His Holiness quite recognizes Mr. Roosevelt's en-

Roosevelt at lunch, Naples.

tire right to freedom of conduct; on the other hand, in view of the circumstances, for which neither His Holiness nor Mr. Roosevelt is responsible, an audience could not occur except on the understanding expressed in the former message."

Roosevelt was not presented. As to the Methodists, when one of them issued a new attack upon the Vatican, Roosevelt cancelled an engagement to meet them. Roosevelt, remembering the lesson of American politics, that in a controversy the first party to get his story into the newspapers acquires a long lead, made the whole incident public. As he left Rome, the gentle priests at the Vatican must have felt a little as they did when Attila the Hun turned his back on the Holy City. As for Roosevelt, his emotion, as expressed in a letter to Lodge, was that he had "had an elegant row."

IV

He visited the King of Italy,[12] whom he found reading James Bryce's "American Commonwealth," and who

From a cartoon by Minor in the St. Louis "Post-Dispatch," 1910.

Seeing Roosevelt.

explained to Roosevelt that he was training his son to be equipped, if necessary, to be the first President of the Italian Republic — Roosevelt used to say, after he returned to America, that Victor Emmanuel was "a good fellow, in American politics he could have carried his ward." And the King[13] and Queen[14] of Norway, whose situation appeared to Roosevelt "much as if Vermont

12 Victor Emmanuel.　　　13 Haakon.　　　14 Maude.

should off-hand try the experiment of having a king" — "they were dears," he added. And the Crown Prince of Sweden, whom Roosevelt found "a thoroughly good fellow, very serious and honest." And the King[15] and Queen

Roosevelt and the Kaiser at the German army manœuvres. The "Colonel" was the only private citizen ever allowed to review the troops of Germany.

of Belgium — the Belgian Queen, with the King of Italy, were the only royalties with whom Roosevelt found he could talk books. And the Queen of Holland[16] and her consort. And the Crown Prince of Denmark. And the Emperor of Austria,[17] who, with sixty years of reigning behind him, and with a prescience destined to be poignantly fulfilled, said he "was the last representative of the old system," whereas Roosevelt "embodied the new movement, the movement of the present and future." — Roosevelt's conversation with Franz Joseph

[15] Albert.   [16] Wilhelmina.   [17] Franz Joseph.

was carried on in French, which, Roosevelt said, "I speak with daring fluency."

And the Emperor of Germany — destined also to be the last of his line — who, as a distinguished treat, permitted Roosevelt to participate with him in five hours of a ceremony which gave the Kaiser the opportunity to say: "Roosevelt, mein freund, I ask you to remember that you are the only private citizen who ever reviewed the troops of Germany." The Kaiser had photographs made of the scene, upon the backs of which he wrote, in his own hand, inscriptions designed to convey a Hohenzollern humor: "The Colonel of the Rough Riders lecturing the Chief of the German Army," and "Kaiser and Rough Rider review German Army — old peace bore Carnegie go way back and sit down."[18] "When we shake hands we shake the world." Roosevelt had the photographs mounted with glass on both sides, so as to reveal both photograph and the Kaiserliche inscription — to show them to visitors at Sagamore Hill was one of the pleasures of Roosevelt's closing years.

All of which contact with royalty equipped Roosevelt to say later, when in the Progressive campaign critics accused him of wishing to be king of the United States, "I know kings and they don't. A king is a kind of cross between a vice-president and a leader of the Four Hundred."[19] A less epigrammatic and therefore more accurate expression of Roosevelt's serious feeling about the royalty he met was that "I thoroughly liked and respected almost all the various kings and queens. . . . They struck me as serious persons, devoted to their people and anxious to justify their own positions by the way they did their duty. The average among them was not very high as regards intellect and force. I cannot imag-

[18] This inscription is given from memory.
[19] "Impressions of Theodore Roosevelt," Lawrence F. Abbott.

ine a more appallingly dreary life for a man of ambition and power."[20]

V

He delivered an address at the University of Christiania, and received the degree of Doctor of Philosophy

From a photograph by H. C. Ellis, Paris.

The ex-President Roosevelt talking with General Gallieni.

— the only one ever granted by the University. And before the Nobel Prize Committee at Christiania. And at the Brussels Exposition. And at the University of Cambridge, which conferred on him the degree of LL.D.

He made an address at the Sorbonne, in English — the "Gaulois" approved the introduction of American spellbinding arts to an audience of French scholars. "M. Roosevelt's oratorical style is clear, his utterance prodigiously audible, he speaks slowly, hammers home each word; he knows how to master an audience, he communicates his own heat to it, he arouses it or he amuses it, and he knows how to be, by turns, grave and humorous,

[20] "Theodore Roosevelt and His Time," Joseph Bucklin Bishop, Vol. II.

authoritative and persuasive; he has at times glorious flights or exquisite mannerisms."

He spoke at the University of Berlin, where he was given the degree of Doctor of Philosophy, and where the

From a photograph by Brown Brothers.
Roosevelt at Oxford University.

Kaiser honored him with the All Highest presence — Roosevelt "fixed his eyes directly on the Kaiser, showing all his magnificent teeth at once."[21] A German naval officer, later to be widely known outside his own country, named Von Tirpitz, paying Roosevelt the most exalted compliment he could think of, said he had often heard that Roosevelt and the Kaiser were alike, and he was

21 "Impressions of Theodore Roosevelt," Lawrence F. Abbott.

now able to assure Roosevelt that the resemblance did indeed exist. Roosevelt's Berlin lecture was on "The World Movement." It made no mention of the pending high mortality among dynasties, nor of other world movements destined shortly to collide with each other along the Hindenburg line.

He delivered the Romanes lecture (on "Biological Analogies in History") at Oxford University, where Doctor Henry Goudy introduced him as: "A noted sportsman and lover of natural history; he has recently, after his arduous labors as Head of the State, been seeking relaxation in distant Africa, where his onslaughts on the wild beasts of the desert have been not less fierce nor less successful than over the many-headed hydra of corruption in his own land." Lord Curzon recited a facetiously commendatory couplet of his own composition:

Before whose coming comets took to flight
And all the Nile's seven mouths turned pale in fright.

The Chancellor of the University, injecting a parenthetical prediction into his complimentary designation, saluted him as: "Most strenuous of men, most distinguished of citizens to-day playing a part on the stage of the world, you who have twice administered with purity the first Magistracy of the Great Republic (and may perhaps administer it a third time), peer of the most august Kings, queller of men, destroyer of monsters wherever found, yet the most human of mankind, deeming nothing indifferent to you, not even the blackest of the black; I, by my authority and that of the whole University, admit you to the Degree of Doctor of Civil Law, *honoris causa.*"[22]

He was made a Freeman of the City of London, in gratitude for which, in a speech at the Guild Hall, he

[22] "Theodore Roosevelt," Charles G. Washburn.

gave the British admonition about how to run the Empire: "Either you have the right to be in Egypt or you have not. . . . If you feel you have not, then by all means get out; if, as I hope, you feel that your duty to civilized mankind and your fealty to your own great traditions alike bid you to stay, then make the fact and the name agree, and show that you are ready to meet in very deed the responsibility which is yours" — a Rooseveltian frankness which the horror-struck London *Standard* deemed "a social crime not far from a sacrilege." It gave rise to serious debate in Parliament, caused the London *Star* to suggest mildly that "Mr. Roosevelt should learn that he is not exempt from the customs of civilized nations"; gave aptness to a cartoon in *Punch* picturing the marble lions in Trafalgar Square, symbols of England's power, guarded by a placard saying, "These lions are not to be shot"; and conferred a perhaps Delphic quality on some words Rudyard Kipling wrote about Roosevelt in a letter to an American,[23] "Take care of him, he is scarce and valuable."

VI

While Roosevelt was in Europe, King Edward VII died, and President Taft asked the ex-President to serve as special Ambassador of the United States to the funeral. The experience provided Roosevelt with two stories which entertained his friends until he died.[24] The tales had the comedy inherent in juxtaposition of an American citizen with kings; in the exalted posturings of royalty at a moment when royalty is exceptionally and very solemnly royal, as seen through the eyes of a plain, humor-

[23] Brander Matthews.
[24] The version of these stories given here is as Roosevelt told them at a lunch at my home soon after he returned from Europe. It agrees with a version written immediately after King Edward's funeral by Roosevelt in a letter to David Gray, which was made public after prudently waiting until most of the kings and other personages mentioned had died.

ous, and rough-and-ready man to whom one king looks much like another, and all look not greatly different from anybody else. As Roosevelt, on his return to America, told the stories to friends, and observed the relish of those who heard them, his own pleasure in the telling grew; he came to put gusto into them. Among his friends, it came to be a saying that Roosevelt could readily make a living on the vaudeville stage relating his adventures at what he called King Edward's "wake." It was in his rôle of teller of these tales that the memory of Roosevelt lingered most vividly with some who knew him best and loved him most.

A special train made up at Vienna to carry mourners from southeastern Europe to the funeral at Windsor included the private cars of Archduke Ferdinand of Austria (the same who was later assassinated at Sarajevo) and the Czar of Bulgaria, the latter called by Roosevelt, in terms of American baseball, "one of those 'bush league' Czars from the Balkans." Before the train could start, a delicate question of relative rank had to be settled, involving the order of the two private cars on the train. The essential question, whether an archduke and heir to the throne of a major empire, Austria, should precede or follow the incumbent czar of a minor country, was intensified by the fact that the Czar was a comparative newcomer in the fraternity, having attained his czarship in part by a process which, as the more securely seated dynasties looked upon it, would have been described in American slang as "crashing the gate." In truth, the tyro's czarship was self-assumed and very recent; it was less than two years before (October 5, 1908) that he had declared his country independent, and himself a czar. These dynastic reasons for disdain for the parvenu czar were intensified by certain qualities of the

tyro's personality. The interloper was, measured not only
as czar but as man, deficient in those qualities of personal majesty which established members of the fraternity have a right to expect in a candidate for full standing; the Czar, even to Roosevelt's easy-going American
standards, seemed lacking in impressiveness — Roosevelt
called him a "twittering wagtail." In the controversy
over precedence on the funeral train, the mutual distaste
of the respective principals was emphasized by the even
greater mutual hostility of their respective retinues, expressing itself in a quantity of angry vociferation, belligerent gesturing, which, to an American point of view,
was, as a prelude to a funeral, either unseemly or comic
or both.

After some hours of argument, which seriously delayed the start of the train, the dispute was won by the
Archduke, whose reward in prestige was that his car
should be next the engine, hence closest to the cinders
and noise, the order being, first the Archduke's car, second the Czar's, and third a dining-car.

By the time the train could get under way, since angry
pride and heated argument are exhausting experiences,
hunger added itself to the other emotions. The Archduke sent a functionary from his suite to ask a functionary of corresponding rank in the other's suite to ask the
Czar if the Archduke could pass through the Czar's car
on a trip which the Archduke earnestly craved to take to
the dining-car. The request led, with the Czar and his
retainers, to a discussion of the international questions
involved and the precedents bearing upon them. The
conclusion was that since the Czar's car was, construc-
tively, Bulgarian territory, it would be inexpedient to
give the Austrian Archduke a visé to pass through it until the matter could be referred to legal and diplomatic
advisers of the Czar's government, who, unhappily, were

some hundreds of miles away at their posts in the Bulgarian capital. The consequence of the decision was that the Archduke, by this time very hungry indeed, was obliged to wait until the train came to one of its scheduled stops, when he, followed by his stiffly uniformed suite, strode austerely around the Czar's car, ate his belated dinner, and then waited again until the next stop of the train should give him opportunity to get back to his own car without crossing titular Bulgarian territory.

Probably the inconvenience the Archduke endured weighed little in his mind compared with his successful defense of the prerogatives appertaining to the ancient dynasty of Austria; and undoubtedly his satisfaction was disturbed by no premonition of the assassin's bullet that was destined shortly to make these prerogatives of little worth to him, or of the ensuing war that was to end the dynasty itself.

The night preceding the funeral, the new British king, George V, gave a dinner to the special ambassadors and other official mourners, some seventy in all, including most of the czars, emperors, kings, and lesser royalties of Europe and Asia. The event, to Roosevelt's American standards, seemed a little festive, considering the occasion that had brought the guests together. To another American present, Henry White, the affair resolved itself into one central lion, the ex-President of the United States, with another central figure, the German Kaiser, making himself a kind of master of ceremonies, in a scene which consisted of the Kaiser leading one king after another up to Roosevelt, introducing his royal friend, and saying to Roosevelt, "Now tell him that story about Ben Daniels."[25]

[25] Which of the Ben Daniels stories Roosevelt had told the Kaiser is not recorded. There were several, any one of which would have struck the kings as reflecting an extraordinary state of life in the United States. Ben Daniels

One among the guests did not share the spirit of humor or gayety. Pichon,[26] Special Ambassador from France, was as serious as the most meticulous sense of obituary propriety could call for, though for a reason special to himself. Pichon was, indeed, glowering. He with Roosevelt were the representatives of republics, and were therefore the two wearing plain black clothes, in a gathering which contained such a quantity of gold and purple as could only be assembled at a first-rank royal funeral or coronation. Pichon's and Roosevelt's conspicuous inconspicuousness of dress was self-imposed and therefore not to be complained of. Pichon had observed, however, that those having charge of the rites seemed disposed, to an uncalled-for degree, to put upon him and Roosevelt the same estimate of lowly rank that their own choice of raiment implied. Pichon had noticed that the two coachmen sent to bring himself and Roosevelt to the Castle had worn plain black livery, while the coachmen sent for other guests had worn red. Upon Pichon's mind dawned the suspicion that in the public funeral procession the following day, he and Roosevelt might be assigned places which would have the effect of demeanment upon them, and of not-to-be-borne humiliation to the republics they represented. With the purpose of bringing about an emergency Franco-American alliance in the interest of the relative dignity of republics compared to monarchies, Pichon sought out Roosevelt. Roosevelt was instantly aware of the Frenchman's excitement — Pichon's hair, Roosevelt said, telling the

---

was one of Roosevelt's Rough Riders. He had been marshal of Dodge City, Kans., in the days when that town was probably the toughest abode of civilized man to be found on the American continent. In the course of the exercise of Daniels' rather lurid functions as peace-officer he had lost half an ear — "bitten off" he explained offhandedly to Roosevelt.

26 Stephan Jean-Marie Pichon, journalist-politician-diplomat, in 1910 Minister of Foreign Affairs in Briand's Cabinet. After the Great War he served as one of France's representatives at the Paris Peace Conference.

The funeral procession of King Edward VII. Roosevelt is on the right of picture in a dress suit.

story afterward, "stood out like a head of lettuce." The
effecting of so improvised an entente was impeded by
Pichon's inability to speak English, while Roosevelt's
French was more daring than fluent. Roosevelt, grasp-
ing Pichon's concern as much from his excitement as
from his words, was moved to assuagement, saying he
felt sure everything would be all right, but that, in any
event, "we must not make a row at a funeral" — Roosevelt could not recall whether the French phrase for
funeral is "cortège funerale" or "pompe funebre."

The next day Roosevelt and Pichon were assigned to
the same carriage. Roosevelt was careful to put Pichon
on the right, taking for himself the left. Roosevelt's
achievement of a properly funereal spirit was made difficult by the necessity of repeatedly patting Pichon's knee,
as the latter, sticking his head in and out the window,
saw representatives of countries he deemed inferior to
France, especially tiny Portugal, escorted to carriages
ahead of that to which Roosevelt and Pichon had been
assigned. When Pichon exclaimed "Ce Chinois!" and excitedly pointed to a gorgeously robed mandarin being led
to the carriage just ahead, Roosevelt repeated very solemnly his admonition that whatever happens the primary obligation upon a participant in a funeral procession is not to make a row. The climax of Pichon's per-
turbment came when the master of ceremonies brought
to the same carriage in which Pichon and Roosevelt sat
the representative of the Shah of Persia. Pichon's black
look and scornful "Ce Perse!" put upon Roosevelt the
double anxiety of making the palpably scared Persian
feel at ease and at the same time placating the Frenchman, which he partially accomplished by having the Persian sit on the small seat with his back to the head of the
procession. "Ce Perse," Roosevelt observed, telling the
story later, was a "deprecatory, inoffensive Levantine of

Parisian education, about as unaggressive as a rabbit in a cage with two boa constrictors."

By the time the seventh Edward had been securely interred in Westminster Abbey, Roosevelt, what with the strain caused by the excitable suspicions of his republican colleague, and his disillusionment with the light-weighted triviality of most of the scions of monarchy present, entertained no zest ever again to participate in the ceremonials of a royal funeral. "I felt," he said, "if I met another king I should bite him."

In that democratic mood Roosevelt set out to return to the America from which he had been absent fifteen months.

VII

At Southampton, as Roosevelt took ship,[27] he found letters from America making up a total of two thousand invitations to make speeches so soon as he should get home, and a not smaller number of urgent solicitations that he resume his leadership in American politics.

One further letter he found. It was from Taft, and it read:

It is now a year and three months since I assumed office and I have had a hard time. I do not know that I have had harder luck than other Presidents, but I do know that thus far I have succeeded far less than have others. I have been conscientiously trying to carry out your policies but my method of doing so has not worked smoothly.

[27] June 10, 1910.

23

ROOSEVELT'S RETURN

A Chapter in Which Roosevelt Passes from Zenith to Nadir. Against His Better Judgment, He Enters Politics; against His Essential Nature, He Tries to Walk in the Middle of the Road — and Suffers the Fate in Which That Course Usually Ends. Temporarily in Eclipse, He Feels Very Sad.

From Herbert Johnson's Scrapbook.

The "common people" awaiting "Teddy's" return.

ROOSEVELT returned to America on June 16, 1910, to a lavishness of ceremonial reception, an ecstasy of popular applause, which caused one of his biographers[1] to feel that that day was the "zenith of Roosevelt's fame";

[1] Charles G. Washburn.

which led Roosevelt himself to say, "It is a kind of hysteria," but to add: "They will soon be throwing rotten eggs at me. . . . I am like Peary at the North Pole, there is no way for me to travel except South"; a reception made salty, rather than minimized, by a prayer on behalf of those who did not like him:

Help us to bear the man; help us to listen with patience and forgiveness; help us to thank our lucky stars for this last year's vacation; for rested nerves; for freedom from sudden shocks; for mothers'[2] long immunity; for cumulated strength to bear the future.[3]

— a reception which as respects national politics, and Taft in the White House, expressed itself in a metrical appeal by *Life:*

Teddy, come home and blow your horn,
The sheep's in the meadow, the cow's in the corn.
The boy you left to 'tend the sheep
Is under the haystack fast asleep.

Whether or not Roosevelt would "blow his horn" was the common question. The condition — Taft "under the haystack fast asleep" — appealed to the country as one which invited Roosevelt, almost called for him. Every chance word he said, every expression that flickered over his countenance, was spied upon by the microscopes of the press for evidence of political ambition. In the brief address which he could not avoid making in response to his welcome back to New York, he had said he was "ready and eager" to "help solve problems." "Ready and eager?" the suspicious press had said. Did this mean willingness to be President again?

II

Roosevelt at this point could, subject to the law of his nature, make his own fate, and whatever fate he should

2 The allusion was to Roosevelt's preaching to mothers to bear large families.
3 *Life,* May 26, 1910.

make for himself would determine the fates of many another — would, indeed, lay out a tangent for his country's history.

Conceivably he might have retired to Oyster Bay, permanently, might have practiced painstakingly the scrupulous self-restraint from active politics that ex-President Cleveland had followed before him, and Calvin Coolidge[4] after him. For the moment, that was his mood. "One thing I want now is privacy," he said as he landed; "I want to close up like a native oyster."[5] In a spirit that in part was absolutely sincere — yet in part a subconscious seeking of sanctuary from an at-the-moment unpleasing alternative — he looked forward to quiet days at Sagamore Hill. "Mrs. Roosevelt and I have . . . our own home, with our books and pictures and bronzes and big wood fire and horses to ride and the knowledge that our children are doing well."[6] He genuinely loved his home and all that it meant. "Edith and I are enjoying every hour," he wrote once to Lodge, "the walks through the woods, the red sunsets across the Sound, the brilliant moon, the great log fires indoors."

The nostalgia Roosevelt at all times had for Sagamore Hill was made stronger now by distaste for the alternative of participating in public affairs under the handicap put upon him by his relation to Taft. To the swarms of newspaper men who sought to interview him — always with the motive, or the effect, of dragging him into politics — he had nothing to say; and he asked them, almost with irritated abruptness, to stay away from Oyster Bay. The two thousand invitations to make speeches that had piled up on him while he was in Europe, and were accumulating at the rate of more than twenty a day, which ordinarily would have pleased and stimulated

4 Up to the year this is written, 1932.   5 New York *Times,* June 19, 1910,
6 "Theodore Roosevelt and His Time," Joseph Bucklin Bishop, Vol. II.

him, gave him now only irritation — he was almost bitter at their "kindly fatuity." Of his callers he complained, "I have almost no protection against the pressure." He wished he had remained away from America longer, until after the congressional elections that would be held in

Sagamore Hill.

the Fall. "Ugh!" he had written to Lodge, "I do dread . . . having to plunge into this cauldron of politics."[7]

III

That was, for Roosevelt, an extraordinary mood. Normally, prospect of activity was the breath of life to him. But now, when he contemplated participation in public affairs, his mind was obliged to go stumbling about in a maze which balked him whatever way he

[7] May 5, 1910. The several quotations in this chapter from Lodge and from Roosevelt's letters to Lodge, are taken from the two volumes of "Selections from the Correspondence of Theodore Roosevelt and Henry Cabot Lodge."

turned, inhibited all his normal impulses, seared his usual spontaneity, turned his spirit sour. Some motives drew him toward activity, others toward silence, both encountered frustration. Every zest of his normal taste turned to ashes in his mouth.

The heart of the maze, the thing that raised one kind of wall or another against him whatever way he turned, was his relation to Taft in the White House. He had put Taft in the Presidency, therefore was responsible for him — that called for support of Taft. But he could not support Taft because Taft had departed from his policies. On the other hand, to criticise Taft would be to apologize for his own act in making Taft President. Not even did silence offer him solution of his perplexity, for silence would be interpreted by some as condonation of Taft, by others as criticism. To be silent about Taft's mistakes was to be disloyal to those policies of his which Taft had departed from, and those friends of his, such as Pinchot and Garfield, whom Taft had flouted or put away from him.

Even if silence could have made Roosevelt comfortable, which it could not, he was unable to be wholly mute, for he had engaged himself (more than a year and a half previous, before leaving the White House) to act as contributing editor of *The Outlook*. He knew the public would expect him to write about public affairs — neither the public nor his publishers would be satisfied by critiques on Irish sagas — and to write about public affairs without mentioning the President of the United States was impossible.

His problem was made complex, and also imminent, by the approach of the Congressional elections, in November. He knew the Republican party managers would expect him, and have a right to expect him, to pay his obligation to the party that had given him two terms in the White House, by helping in the campaign to elect a Republican Congress. But to campaign for a Republican Congress was to approve the one already in existence — and he could not well approve of that without approving of the President under whom it had sat, Taft. If he should campaign for a Republican Congress, his sincerity would be indicted; he knew he could only help any cause by saying to the people what he sincerely believed — and he did not sincerely believe the Republican party had been behaving well. Ugh! The thing was a mess.

Lodge, artful in intention if not in effect, tried to tell him how he could at once campaign yet not campaign. Lodge would "not ask you to stump for the Republican party"; but only "to give such support to it as will show you regard it as the best instrument. . . . All I want you to say is that you want the Republican party to win." Craftily Lodge tempted Roosevelt with an appeal to what Lodge knew to be a weak point in Roosevelt's armor, consideration for his place in history: "I do not want you to be left in a position where any one could say, or any historian in the future, that in the dark hour you stood aside and allowed the party which you had led, and which . . . had followed you loyally, to go to defeat without a word of sympathy or help." Lodge saw "the extreme difficulty of framing a course which will meet these two points, but I think it can be done," though, Lodge admitted, it "will require time and thought and very careful consideration." But Roosevelt, clear-sighted and honest-minded, knew "I cannot without stultifying myself. . . ."

Silence would not serve him, for silence was impossible to achieve. Politicians from both factions asked to come to see him and he could not well refuse. As the visitors returned to New York, reporters pounced upon them; and the visitors, partly to achieve advantage for their respective sides, partly to elevate their importance as individuals, repeated what Roosevelt had said, or what they wished he had said, or their interpretation of what he had said — all with the effect of embarrassing Roosevelt, pulling him this way and that in the factional fight, making public confusion about his position and intentions. Callers from the Taft side were "wild that I should come out in a flaming general endorsement of the Taft administration," and intimated that he would. Visitors from the Insurgent side created the impression that he would denounce Taft. When Beveridge of Indiana, calling on Roosevelt on July 8, said his talk with Roosevelt had been "satisfactory," the country put upon that word the inference that went with Beveridge's position as an ardent Insurgent. "Roosevelt's jaw has a new angle of determination," said Insurgent Senator Bristow of Kansas, after calling on July 2. "I want to tell you," said Senator LaFollette, who visited him on June 25, "that Colonel Roosevelt is in fighting trim."

Roosevelt was not "in fighting trim" at all, for the reason that there was nothing he could fight. In neither one direction nor the other could he strike out freely.

IV

In that mood of frustration he turned with boyish pleasure to attend a reunion[8] of his Harvard class at Cambridge. There, of all places, in that academic calm, literally while he walked beneath the elms, and within thirteen days after his return from Europe, he got himself embroiled in politics — and not in major politics,

[8] June 29, 1910. It was Roosevelt's 30th reunion.

not in the nation-wide fight of Insurgent against Stand-patter, but in a parochial eddy in New York State. With Roosevelt in the academic procession was Gov-

Governor Charles E. Hughes of New York in the Yard at Harvard on June 29, 1910. Walking with Mr. Hughes is William M. Chadbourne, and behind him, to the right, is the author of this volume, Mark Sullivan. It was on this day, at Cambridge, that Mr. Hughes persuaded Theodore Roosevelt, then recently returned from Africa and Europe, to take an active part in New York State politics.

ernor Charles E. Hughes of New York, present to receive an honorary degree. The two, walking together in the procession, were observed to be talking so earnestly as to slow up the march. A half hour later Roosevelt, making an address to the alumni, said he "had intended to keep absolutely clear from any kind of public or polit-

ical question . . . [but] our Governor has a very persuasive way with him." That evening Roosevelt gave
out a public statement taking Hughes' side in a fight
for a direct primary bill which Hughes was trying to
force through the unwilling New York Legislature.

By that impulsive act Roosevelt was back in politics,
and not in the best way — it does not exalt an ex-President's prestige to become involved in a local state fight.
The squabble in New York was no part of the controversy in the nation between Insurgents and Standpatters,
no part of the Western uprising against Taft. Neither
did the New York fight have any particular relation to
the rift, still latent, between Taft and Roosevelt — in
the New York fight many friends of Taft were on the
side of Roosevelt. Taft publicly and specifically disavowed having any interest in it. It was strictly a local
incident.

In the New York fight Hughes lost, and, of course,
Roosevelt with him. Now Roosevelt was made to feel
a sense of rebuke. He must be vindicated. That drew
him further in. His friends and those who wanted to
make use of his prestige persuaded him to let his name
be proposed for chairman of the Republican State convention. Ruefully, without heart in it, Roosevelt con-
sented. The State committee rejected him — insult-
ingly declined to give a trivial honor to the most distinguished man in their party, the only living ex-President.
Now Roosevelt's partisans said he must make a fight for
it, put his name before the delegates. He entered the
fight — and wrote[9] to Lodge, quoting the classic reluctance of the Black Douglas, "We have come to the
ring, and now we must hop." He won, by a close vote,
568 to 443 — unappetizing triumph to a man who had

9 September 12, 1910.

fed upon nation-wide victories — and wrote to Lodge: "It is not the kind of fight into which an ex-President should be required to go. . . . Twenty years ago I should not have minded it. It would have been entirely suitable for my age and my standing. This whole political business now is bitterly distasteful to me."

V

Deeply involved in New York — and hating himself for it — he was now approached by the national Republican leaders with the solicitation he had feared, that he make a Western trip in the interest of the Congressional campaign. He would go, he said — his instinctive understanding of the danger contending against his zest for action — only on the condition that his trip should be made under the auspices, not of the Republican committee, but of *The Outlook;* and only provided it should be publicly announced that he would "represent myself entirely, nobody else."[10] He started off, and wrote to Lodge: "I look forward with dread to . . . the effort to combine a straightforward enunciation of my own beliefs with freedom from anything looking like criticism of the [Taft] administration."

In that spirit of looking two ways, he made the speeches. Necessarily they were equivocal; more accurately, he tried to balance one speech looking one way with another looking the other way.

Trying to be helpful in "securing a fairly united party support for the Republicans," he approved the new tariff as being, though imperfect, "better than the last, and considerably better than the one before the last."[11] In the same spirit of approving, so far as he could, the Standpatters, he "praised Taft for every action of his as

10 New York *Times,* August 20, 1910.
11 *Outlook* editorial, September 17, 1910.

to which I could conscientiously praise him; where I could not praise him, or disapproved of what he had done, I kept silent."[12] Then, trying to balance his praise of Taft and the Standpatter tariff by a degree of progressiveness which would even the account in the minds of the Insurgents (and in his own), he went so far toward radicalism as to reach in a speech at Ossawatomie, Kans., a position described by the New York *Evening Post* as "not only the most extreme utterance that he himself ever made previously, but [that of] the most radical man in public life in our time."[13] By that, in turn, he alienated the Standpatters, of course, and also many moderate conservatives who hitherto had thought well of him.

The sum of it was that by campaigning for the whole of a party, in only half of which he believed, he had offended not only both halves but his independent personal following as well. Most of all he offended his own soul. To a friend[14] he wrote his judgment of the double-edged effect of his speeches in the West: "The lunatic Insurgents . . . were not contented with anything short

[12] "Theodore Roosevelt and His Times," Joseph Bucklin Bishop.

[13] Two of Roosevelt's speeches on this Western trip were of historic importance, in the development of those ideas of Roosevelt which subsequently became the platform of the Progressive party, and were otherwise familiar under the generic designation, "the New Nationalism." At Ossawatomie, Kans., on August 31, 1910, his words went far towards Socialism, which actually Roosevelt despised. The "New Nationalism," he said, "implies far more governmental interference with social and economic conditions than we have yet had. . . . Every man holds his property subject to the general right of the community to regulate its use to whatever degree the public welfare may require." His assertion that he stood "not merely for fair play under the present rules of the game, but for having those rules changed so as to work for the more substantial equality of opportunity and reward," conveyed to conservatives an ominous condonation of departure from the Constitution.

In his speech before the Colorado Legislature, August 27, 1910, he went farther than he ever had before in advocating a check on the power of the courts to declare legislative acts void.

These two speeches are important to any student of the rise of the Progressive party and the ideas it embodied.

[14] Joseph Bucklin Bishop, November 21, 1910.

of denunciation of Taft; the reactionaries literally went insane in their opposition" (to his extreme progressive utterances about the courts). To Root he wrote of the effect on his own spirit, "I have never had a more unpleasant summer."

He was unhappy because the course he had followed ran counter to his nature, because he felt the course would turn out to be ineffective in saving the Republicans at the coming congressional elections, and because of the more distant prospect that if the Republicans lost the congressional elections in 1910 they would lose the Presidential election in 1912.

He had failed for the party, he felt, and he had failed for himself. He had paid out his personal prestige as endorser for the party, and the party would get nothing in return. The personal loss, he could see, was serious. In a course that attempted to go down the middle of the road he had offended both Insurgents and Standpatters. It was not that his middle-ground course had been weak. He had not tried to placate both sides. He had attempted to repeat what, while he possessed the authority of the Presidency, he had often been able to do, treat both sides imperiously, clout them and force them into line. Now he had paid out the authority that he had held over from the Presidency but he had got nothing for the party, and as for himself was very poor indeed.

"If only he had kept silent!" wrote, years later, his most intimate friend, Owen Wister.[15] "But," Wister added, "the duck had taken to the water, and it had car-

---

[15] In "My Forty Years Friendship With Theodore Roosevelt." To speak of Wister as Roosevelt's most intimate friend is justified by explaining that Wister was that one of Roosevelt's friends who had the deepest and most accurate insight into Roosevelt's nature. Wister knew more of the subtleties of Roosevelt's soul than any other man, far more than Roosevelt himself. To read Wister's chronicle of their friendship is to hear the most delicate overtones of Roosevelt's voice.

ried him from the original pond down into a raging river." He only needed to be silent — and to be silent he only needed to be cautious, selfish.

VI

The elections (November 8, 1910) bore out Roosevelt's gloomy judgment, and then some. It was a Republican debacle. The Democrats won control of the Lower House of Congress by a majority of 66, 228 to 162; carried the governorships of 26 States out of the 48; carried Taft's own State, Ohio; carried New York; carried New Jersey — and by that elevated into the Governorship and into public life a Democrat who was recognized to be the greatest future menace to the Republicans since Grover Cleveland, a university president (of Princeton) named Woodrow Wilson.

The debacle was not only Republican. It was personal to Roosevelt himself. In the West, insurgent States in which he had campaigned had gone Democratic; in the East, conservative New York in which he had campaigned had done the same. The defeated Republican candidate for Governor in New York, Henry L. Stimson, was Roosevelt's particular friend and protégé: "Our Harry."

This New York outcome was interpreted as a direct rebuke to Roosevelt. The Democratic New York *World* which during the campaign had repeatedly said that a "vote for Stimson for Governor in 1910 was a vote for Roosevelt for President in 1912," now said that Roosevelt was extinguished — by 1912 he would be a half-forgotten myth. Cartoons elected him to the "Down and Out Club," picturing him there in the friendly fraternity of common disaster with the Lorimers and the

Tawneys whom Roosevelt had consigned there during years when he had been the one-man and self-appointed committee on admissions to the club. Newspapers which a year before, when he was in Africa, had wished him "back from Elba," now revised their slogans, consigned him "back to St. Helena."

Publicly, Roosevelt's only comment on the debacle of the election took the traditionally trite form of affirmation of continued gameness in the face of defeat: "The fight for progressive popular government has merely begun," he wrote, somewhat beside the point, in *The Outlook*, November 19, 1910, "and will certainly go on to a triumphant conclusion in spite of initial checks and in spite of the personal success or failure of individual leaders."

Privately, Roosevelt had no such certainty about the ultimate "triumphant conclusion" of his cause. About the "personal failure," the permanent extinction of the principal "individual leader," he was certain. To friends he spoke with resignation of his conclusion that his influence in public life was ended. He was very downcast. "I have been almost ashamed," he wrote to a friend,[16] of his emotions since the election.

On the Sunday after the election, the writer of this history visited him at Sagamore Hill. As I started to leave, he said, "Don't go. The time will come when only a few friends like you will come out to see me here." After a while, as I started again to leave, he suggested that I should not take the train from Oyster Bay but that the two of us should walk four miles across the Long Island fields to another station on the main line, at Syosset. At the station, as we parted, he made me a present of the cane he had carried, as if he wished to make some

[16] "Theodore Roosevelt and His Times," Joseph Bucklin Bishop, Vol. II.

kind of enduring seal of what he regarded as probably a diminishing number of his future friends. As I looked out the window of the car and Roosevelt waved a final good-by and turned back toward Sagamore Hill, I felt sorry for the thoughts I knew would accompany him through the four miles of winter dusk.

24

ROOSEVELT AND TAFT: OPEN BREAK

Roosevelt in Eclipse from One Cause, Taft from Another.
The Two Meet Casually Three Times, but the Old-time
Warmth Is Gone. Publicly Neither Says Anything Adverse
to the Other, Privately Each Has the Sense of Separation.
Taft's Attorney-General Takes a Step Which, Probably
Unwittingly on Part of Taft, Causes Roosevelt to Erupt.

ROOSEVELT was in eclipse, definitely, notoriously. For
almost exactly a year, from the disastrous election of November 8, 1910, until November 17, 1911, his personality was in the shadows — his magnificent energies,
that had once had a continent for their arena and the
world for their sounding board, now dissipating themselves feebly in the shallows of scummy backwaters.
The stream of visitors to *The Outlook* tapered off. Such
as came were more and more the type of professional
secretaries of uplift organizations, or extremists whom
Roosevelt in his heart shrank from — later he kicked
them from him with an epithet, "lunatic fringe."   In
March, 1911, he started on a six-weeks' trip to the South
and West, on which, significantly, no car of newspaper
correspondents followed. At Atlanta he delivered an address to negroes about industrial education. At Austin,
Texas, he spoke on the campus of the University. At
Berkeley, California, he uttered the unfortunate words,
"I took the Canal"; and a part of the press and public,
which likes to have either a hero to worship or a victim

to harry — and is sometimes willing to turn the first into the second — interpreted the phrase as an admission that he had "taken" Panama in an odious sense. Public disesteem for him increased. The prediction he had made at the time of his zenith, that he, like Peary, had no way to travel except South, seemed fulfilled.

He felt that he was himself to blame. That was his sorrow's crown of sorrows. He had put Taft in the White House and Taft had not pleased the country — had, from Roosevelt's standpoint, failed. From that, the rest had flowed: debacle to Taft himself, debacle to Roosevelt, debacle to the Republican party.

Looking forward, Roosevelt could see no way out. He accepted the party rule that Taft, as a President serving his first term, should be renominated. He accepted the law of political tides that defeat of the party in power at the mid-elections of a Presidential term, as had now happened in 1910, forecasts complete defeat and ejection from the Presidency in the succeeding Presidential election. Roosevelt hated that, not only on personal and party grounds but for broader reasons. He was really a strong Republican partisan, believed the country could not truly prosper or be well managed by the Democrats.

With these public reasons for gloom and self-reproach went a private, inner one, one which, to such a nature as Roosevelt's, weighed much. He saw a man in the White House functioning badly in a job which Roosevelt knew he himself could do well. The common phrase, "Roosevelt could not stand seeing Taft occupying his bed," was inexact. What Roosevelt saw was Taft on the bridge of the ship which Roosevelt had captained better, and could captain better now.

II

Three times during this period Roosevelt and Taft met. Once, Roosevelt, being in the neighborhood of Taft's summer home,[1] sent word to Taft that he would call. Significantly, Roosevelt brought another with him. Butt and a Secret Service man told by Taft to watch for Roosevelt's coming "felt a quiver of excitement when we saw a big motor-car turn into the roadway leading to the house and recognized a minute later the ex-President and Senator Lodge." Taft, coming out on the porch just in time to meet Roosevelt as he stepped from the machine, held out both hands, exclaiming: "Ah, Theodore, it is good to see you." Roosevelt said: "How are you, Mr. President, this is simply bully."

"See here now," said Taft, "drop the 'Mr. President'."

"Not at all," said Roosevelt, "you must be Mr. President and I am Theodore."

A little self-consciously, the two, together with Lodge and Butt and Taft's secretary, moved to seats on the porch. "Both were a little strained," wrote Butt, "and I looked at Taft for some sign but his face was a blank when he caught my eye." In the lack of any hint from Taft, Butt whispered to Lodge, "Do you think they want to be left alone?" Lodge replied that he had asked Roosevelt that very question and Roosevelt had said he preferred Lodge should "remain during the visit, that he wanted it to be like any other social call and not to be left alone with the President." The talk was impersonal, about politics in New York State, Roosevelt's experiences in Europe, the Kaiser, Germany. As Roosevelt left, Taft said, wistfully: "This has taken me back

[1] Beverly, Massachusetts, June 30, 1910.

to some of those dear old afternoons when I was Will
and you were Mr. President."[2]

Once a New York politician brought the two together
for help he thought he might get from conjunction.
Roosevelt crossed Long Island Sound in a motor-boat to
meet Taft passing through New Haven. As the two
rode together Taft "wreathed his face with a purely
physical smile and laughed aloud, but it was all
strained."[3] Some one in Taft's retinue, attempting to
serve him more well than wisely, inspired a newspaper
account which implied that Roosevelt had sought the
meeting to ask Taft for help in New York State. Roosevelt, offended, issued a denial. Taft, reading Roosevelt's
statement, "looked alarmed and then began to laugh, but
it was rather forced and full of concern as when one
whistles in a graveyard. . . . The two men are farther
apart than ever."

The two met once more, at the fiftieth anniversary of
the priesthood of Cardinal Gibbons.[4] Roosevelt, arriving first, "was waiting for Taft in the gymnasium adjoining the armory, where there were several hundred
persons." As Taft entered, Roosevelt came forward,
grasped his hand, called him "Mr. President," and "expressed his great pleasure at seeing him. Taft called him
"Theodore," and they both stood for a few minutes talking. . . . They played the game beautifully through the
programme. The eyes of the thousands in the hall were
riveted on the faces of the President and ex-President,
eager to catch any sign which might be construed into
friendship or hostility. Once, when they whispered together and got to laughing, it so pleased the people that
they all broke into cheering and applause."

[2] The quotations given here from Taft and Roosevelt are from the "Letters
of Archie Butt: Taft and Roosevelt."
[3] Butt, September 20, 1910.   [4] Baltimore, June 6, 1911.

III

Throughout all this period Roosevelt had uttered no public word of dispraise for Taft. From the time he left Taft in the White House, March 4, 1909, for two years and eight months, Roosevelt, publicly, made no allusion to Taft that Taft could resent.

Privately, Roosevelt's evolution of thought about Taft took first the form of disillusionment, a disillusionment made possible by distance from Taft's side. "For a year after Taft took office," he wrote to Lodge,[5] "for a year and a quarter after he had been elected, I would not let myself think ill of anything he did. I finally had to . . . admit to myself that deep down underneath I had all along known he was wrong on points to which I had tried to deceive myself by loudly proclaiming to myself that he was right." Once Roosevelt had taken himself out of an emotional attitude toward Taft, once he became clear-eyed about his former friend, once he put his reason, unclouded by affection, to analyzing Taft's nature, he came to the same conclusion as most of the discriminating public. Taft as a subordinate, Taft when geared to the generator that Roosevelt was, had been one thing; Taft, standing on his own feet, was another. "The qualities shown by a thoroughly able and trustworthy lieutenant are totally different," Roosevelt wrote to Lodge,[6] "from those needed by the leader." "It took eighteen months," Roosevelt wrote years later, "to convince me that he was a first-class lieutenant but no leader." To a question asked him by a friend,[7] "How did it happen, Mr. Roosevelt, that feeling as you do about Mr. Taft, you were so much in favor of him for the Presidency?" Roosevelt replied, "I'll tell you, I

5 On May 5, 1910. 6 April 11, 1910.
7 Mrs. Robert Grant, wife of a Boston jurist and author.

never realized at the time how much of myself I had put into Taft."

All this was private, to friends. For the first thirty months of Taft's administration Roosevelt said no public word in dispraise of Taft.[8]

Nor had Taft said, publicly, anything to give offense to Roosevelt. Privately, he had spoken often, sometimes sadly, sometimes reproachfully, in the earlier days of their separation affectionately, with a sense of loneliness over Roosevelt's absence from his side. "When I hear some one say 'Mr. President,'" Taft said in an intimate moment to his aide, "I look around expecting to see Roosevelt." When circumstances began to make Taft feel that rift was opening, he was reproachful, not yet toward Roosevelt but toward Roosevelt's friends. "I am not criticising Roosevelt," he exclaimed,[9] "but I get rather tired hearing from his friends that I am not carrying out his policies and when I ask for one instance they cannot name one." Later, by the time Taft was obliged to feel that he must be, from Roosevelt's point of view, an unsatisfactory President, he hoped Roosevelt would not come to visit him "because I cannot argue my case with him or before him." Later yet he was gently reproachful toward Roosevelt. "Archie," he said to his aide, "I am very greatly distressed [about Roosevelt]; he sees no one but my enemies, and if by chance he sees any supporters of the Administration he does not talk intimately with them. . . . I confess it wounds me

8 There was one slight, immaterial exception: Roosevelt, among his contributions to *The Outlook,* had printed a mild, quite unprovocative criticism of the arbitration treaties Taft was negotiating with Great Britain and France. Roosevelt's strongest sentence was, "The United States ought never specifically to bind itself to arbitrate questions respecting its honor, independence, and integrity."

9 To Archie Butt, December 19, 1909. All the expressions by Taft about Roosevelt here quoted are from Butt's letters in "Taft and Roosevelt."

very deeply. I hardly think [Roosevelt] is playing it exactly square with me." On another occasion: "If I only knew what [Roosevelt] wanted I would do it. But he has held himself so aloof that I am absolutely in the dark. I am deeply wounded and he gives me no chance to explain my attitude or to learn his. . . . You know how I have tried to do everything in my power to show my gratitude for what he did for me. Do you know where I could have done differently from what I have done? . . . I could not ask his advice on all questions. I could not subordinate my administration to him and retain my self-respect, but it is hard, very hard, Archie, to see a devoted friendship going to pieces."

In time Taft began to let his repining about Roosevelt be heard not merely by his intimate aide, but by visitors at his table. As he became less discreet he became less restrained, began to express resentment. "If you were to remove Roosevelt's skull," Taft said, "you would find written in his brain '1912.'" Constantly "mutual friends" — ironic phrase sometimes! — were repeating to Roosevelt what Taft had said, to Taft what Roosevelt had said. While Roosevelt had been President and Taft Secretary of War, Taft would never allow any one to asperse Roosevelt in his presence. By September 1910, however, the growing rift between the two had become so wide that Butt could jot down in his notebook: "[Taft] listens to everything that can be said against Mr. Roosevelt and from the most irritatingly insignificant quarters . . . by every person who wants to curry favor by abusing Mr. Roosevelt."

All remained, however, private, within the circle of personal gossip-carriers, schemers, intriguers.

Newspapers, through the nature of their function, because amity is not drama and quarrel is, kept the atmosphere constantly favorable to rift by assuming or im-

plying, or asserting, in innuendo, quip and direct aver-
ment, that Roosevelt wanted to be President again and
would like to take the nomination from Taft in 1912.
When Roosevelt took a hand in the New York State
fight in 1910, he was "laying the basis for getting the
New York delegation in the 1912 nominating convention." When Roosevelt went on his Western speaking
trip the same year, he was "after the Western delegates"
for the 1912 nomination.

Never, however, from the time Roosevelt left Taft
in the White House, March 4, 1909, until November,
1911, could any newspaper cite anything said by Taft
derogatory to Roosevelt or by Roosevelt derogatory to
Taft. All recrimination between them was private,
within the circle of their friends and acquaintances.

IV

Then, on the morning of October 27, 1911, Roosevelt read in the newspapers an item that, to millions of
Americans had only casual interest, an announcement
that Taft, through his Attorney-General,[10] had the day
before begun a dissolution suit against the United States
Steel Corporation, charging, among other counts, that
the Steel Corporation was a monopoly, that it had
achieved its monopoly in part by purchasing the Tennessee Coal and Iron Company four years before, and
that in acquiring the Tennessee Company the Steel Corporation had misled Theodore Roosevelt, who had been
President at the time.

To Roosevelt, the announcement was infuriating.

Hundreds of friends of Roosevelt and of Taft have

[10] George W. Wickersham. The suit was handled by a special assistant, J. M.
Dickinson.

made surmises about the cause of the split between them, scores of historians have searched to find it, thousands of newspaper articles have assigned one cause or another, millions of the curious have wondered. The Steel Corporation suit was it. To be sure, there was, as in all such cases, no one cause; it was a growth. But so far as one incident contributed more than another, so far as one episode detonated the antagonism into flame, so far as there was any "*the* cause," the Steel Corporation suit was the climax, without which the antagonism might have remained beneath the surface, and events might have taken a different course.

In October, 1907, the country had been in a panic. Thousands of shares of the Tennessee Coal and Iron Company had been pledged with important banks in New York. The panic had driven the price of the stock down to a point where it was not equal to the amounts of the loans for which the stock was pledged. If the stock should be thrown on the market, the banks would fail, the panic pass into a worse phase.

In this situation, J. P. Morgan — acting, by common consent, through virtue of his personality and power, as commander-in-chief of the financial community — had sent for Judge Elbert Gary and Henry C. Frick, the two men who, next to Morgan himself, were the dominant figures in the United States Steel Corporation. To them, after a Saturday and Sunday of practically continuous conference, Morgan suggested — more probably, since Morgan was Morgan, he told them — that they, as heads of the United States Steel Corporation, must buy the Tennessee Coal and Iron, that they must buy it before the Stock Exchange opened Monday morning, that they must pay a price roughly twice what the shares were then selling at, a price high enough to protect the

loans in the endangered banks and that they must pay
for it in Steel Corporation bonds, which, a sound security selling close to par (84), could be substituted in
the banks for stock of Tennessee Coal and Iron.

Gary was willing, but told Morgan that it would be
desirable to get the consent of the government at Washington, because otherwise the purchase might be construed as an illegal act in restraint of trade, a violation of
the Anti-Trust Act, and the government might enjoin
the purchase, in which case the panic would be made
worse rather than cured.

Promptly a telephone message to Secretary Loeb in the
White House made an engagement for Gary and Frick to
see President Roosevelt the next morning; promptly another telephone message assembled a special train of locomotive and Pullman; speedily Gary and Frick made the
midnight dash to Washington; eagerly, before Roosevelt had had breakfast, they appeared at the White
House; anxiously they explained what they wanted to
Roosevelt and Elihu Root[11] (whom Roosevelt had with
him in the absence of Attorney-General Bonaparte).

Gary and Frick told Roosevelt that "as a mere business transaction they did not care to purchase"[12] the Tennessee Coal and Iron; that "under ordinary circumstances they would not consider purchasing"; that "little
benefit will come to the Steel Corporation from the purchase"; that they were "aware that the purchase will be
used as a handle for attack upon them on the ground
that they are striving to secure a monopoly." But, they
told Roosevelt, they "feel it is immensely to their interest as to the interest of every responsible business

---

11 Root at this time was Secretary of State.

12 This version of what Gary and Frick said to Roosevelt and Roosevelt to
them is from a letter written by Roosevelt to Bonaparte at the close of the
interview and while Gary and Frick were still present; this version agrees substantially with another written by Gary.

man to try to prevent a panic, and general industrial smash-up."

Roosevelt "answered that while of course I could not advise them to take the action proposed, I felt it no public duty of mine to interpose any objections."

After the crisis was averted and the country righted, cynics, pooh-poohing, invented the theory that purchase of Tennessee Coal and Iron had not been necessary at all. By a series of ingenious ex post facto hypotheses, they proved the panic would have ended anyhow. Cynically they charged that the Steel Corporation had used the occasion to acquire a valuable property at an exceptionally low price.

Necessarily inherent in these attacks were charges against Roosevelt: One, making Roosevelt out an innocent, said that Gary and Frick had deceived him. The other, making Roosevelt out a conspirator, said that he had consciously connived in the scheme in payment for past favors or expected ones in the shape of political campaign contributions, or because of his friendship with a Steel Corporation director, George W. Perkins. These charges the Democrats and every other enemy or critic of Roosevelt took up. Over and over they exploited them. So soon as the Democrats had control of the House of Representatives they investigated the Steel Corporation and put Roosevelt on the stand.

Of all the charges ever made against Roosevelt, this one enraged him most. Whenever, wherever, and by whomever it was made, he went to extreme pains to denounce it. He denounced it on the stump, he denounced it before a Congressional investigating committee, he denounced it in magazine articles, he took pains to denounce it in his autobiography. His sincerity and indignation led him to such frequency and emphasis of denial as to cause his friends to smile. Defense of himself from this charge became a principal detail of his concern about his place in history. Repudiation of the charge was almost an obsession with him.

Now, four years after the event, here was the Taft administration which Roosevelt had put in power as-

From a cartoon by Ketten in the New York "World."

Listening. A cartoon based on the artist's suspicion that T. R. may have had a hand in managing some of the events that led to the demand for him as President.

serting to be true, with the authority of a legal document, what Roosevelt had frequently, publicly and indignantly asserted to be untrue; here was the Taft administration declaring that Roosevelt had been deceived, and necessarily implying that if he had not been deceived then he must have consciously connived — "making me out either a fool or a knave," Roosevelt snorted.

V

The Steel Corporation suit had been filed on October 26.[13] The first number of *The Outlook*, stately gaited weekly, in which Roosevelt could speak was the one dated November 16. Angrily Roosevelt repudiated the aspersions upon him. The Administration's allegation that "I was misled . . . is not correct. The representatives of the Steel Corporation told me the truth. . . . I was not misled. . . . The representatives of the Steel Corporation did not deceive me. . . . Any statement that I was misled . . . is itself not in accordance with the truth. . . . I reaffirm everything."

In addition to his repudiation of the attack on his honor or his intelligence, he vigorously criticised the principle upon which the suit was based. Big business organizations, he said, should be prosecuted only when they have committed crimes; size alone is not a crime. With italicized emphasis he made himself clear — "nothing . . . is gained by breaking up a huge industrial organization *which has not offended otherwise than by its size*"; such organizations, guiltless of wrong-doing, should be handled by regulation, not prosecu-

---

[13] The suit, an American equivalent in real life of Dickens' Jarndyce vs. Jarndyce, was filed October 26, 1911, and hung in the courts throughout the Great War and for more than a year afterward. A decision of the District Court favorable to the Corporation was handed down June 3, 1913. Appeal was filed October 28, 1915. Argument before the Supreme Court took place March 7-14, 1917, and re-argument October 7-10, 1919. On March 1, 1920, almost ten years after the Department of Justice had instituted its suit; nine years after the open break the suit had caused between Taft and Roosevelt; eight years after Taft's defeat in the elections of 1912 which the campaign against the trusts had been designed to prevent; six years after the death of the Progressive Party which had come into being and lived through a short but lusty existence largely because of the suit; a year and more after the close of the World War during which men's minds had been focussed on far different preoccupations than the no-man's-land between monopoly and not-monopoly, and public thought on the economics of big business had vastly changed; a year after Roosevelt, long since purged of his bitterness toward Taft, had died—on March 1, 1920, the Court, by a 4 to 3 decision, absolved the Corporation.

tion; to do as Taft was doing now about the Steel Trust was an attempt to treat the problem by "destructive litigation" instead of "constructive legislation,"[14] "not progressiveness but an unintelligent . . . toryism." With caution, to make certain no one should charge his present outburst with being inspired by approval of trusts, he called the roll of the antitrust suits he had brought. Invidiously he added that when he was President antitrust suits were instituted "only where we felt so sure of our facts that we could be fairly certain there was likelihood of success."

[14] Roosevelt's distinction between trusts charged with specific crimes and those that were trusts only because they were big, and his advocacy of an administrative government body to deal with the latter class, became a fundamental tenet in the programme of the Progressive party. It is described on page 539.

25

ROOSEVELT: HIS HAT IN THE RING

Rooseveltians, Their Hearts Awakening to New Hope, Supplicate Their Idol to Take Command of the Progressive Movement, Foundering under LaFollette, and Join Battle with the Standpatters for Control of the Republican Party. The Faithful Begin an Anabasis to Sagamore Hill.

ROOSEVELT's angry public reply to the charges affecting himself in the Taft administration's suit against the Steel Corporation, his public criticism of the governmental policy on which the suit was brought, his private expressions of anger against Taft — repeated in a word-of-mouth transmission that quickly reached about every important person in the country — combined to awake everybody who had wished — hitherto with resignation to disappointment — that Roosevelt might contend against Taft for the Presidential nomination. Something electric passed among Roosevelt zealots everywhere, telling their hopeful instincts that Napoleon might now leave Elba, that "his boat was on the sea, his foot was on the shore." There was no radio then, but among the Roosevelt followers the ether of fraternity was enough. From one to another the tidings were relayed as if from beacons on the hills. Eyes that for three years had been dulled by prosaic days lighted up to watch for the fiery torch, alert ears listened for the tocsin.

Quickly, like strewn iron filings mobilizing to the pull of a revitalized magnet, there converged from every section of the country an anabasis to Oyster Bay. By ones and twos and threes they came: Rough Riders — Frank Knox of Michigan, who dared to tell Roosevelt he would be "yellow" if he did not lead the fight his old followers were aching for; tall Colonel Lyon of Texas, all of whose politics was compressed into one dictum, military in its terse directness, "Whatever Teddy says, goes." Old ranch companions of the Colonel — Seth Bullock of South Dakota. Serene idealists — Jane Addams of Chicago. Impetuous reformers — Gifford Pinchot of Pennsylvania, Everett Colby of New Jersey, Judge Ben Lindsey of Colorado. Leaders of big business who liked Roosevelt's proposal for dealing with trusts — George W. Perkins. Newspaper owners — Alexander Moore of Pittsburgh, Henry L. Stoddard of the New York *Evening Mail;* William R. Nelson of the Kansas City *Star*, whose political creed was "I am for Roosevelt first, last and all the time, I am for him right or wrong,"[1] compressed by another, William Allen White of the Emporia (Kan.) *Gazette*, into "Roosevelt or bust." Newspaper editors — E. A. Van Valkenberg of the Philadelphia *North American*, Henry Allen of the Wichita (Kan.) *Beacon*, Chester H. Rowell of the Fresno (Calif.) *Republican*. Authors — Hamlin Garland and Will Irwin. Cartoonists — John T. McCutcheon and Homer Davenport. Former members of Roosevelt's Cabinet — fine-spirited James R. Garfield of Cleveland, gentle Oscar S. Straus of New York. Belligerent crusaders—Francis J. Heney and Hiram W. Johnson of California. A few Republican bosses of the old-time type who through some mysterious alchemy had been infected by Roosevelt's spirit or for other reasons had concluded to stand with him — hard-bitten Bill Flinn of Pittsburgh. New York periodical publishers — Frank A. Munsey, Robert J. Collier. New York and Washington journalists — Gilson Gardner, Henry Beach Needham. Insurgent Republican Senators and Members

---

[1] "Released for Publication," O. K. Davis.

of the House — Albert J. Beveridge of Indiana, Joseph
M. Dixon of Montana. Republican governors who had
taken the progressive turn — scholarly Herbert Hadley
of Missouri, red-haired Walter R. Stubbs of Kansas,
quiet Robert P. Bass of New Hampshire, Chase S.
Osborn of Michigan. Regular Republican leaders who,
because they believed Taft could not win or for other
reasons, wished Roosevelt to get the nomination — J.
Hampton Moore. College professors — Albert Bush-
nell Hart of Harvard.

The types of them, their temperaments, their interests, were as various as the country itself. Their common denominator was that they were "Rooseveltians,"[2]
men who had found life joyous when Roosevelt was in
the White House, drab when he was out of it. If Roosevelt was at Oyster Bay, they came to him there:

> On Sagamore's lawn stood reporters with tabs
> And hosts of Progressives drove up in their cabs.
> And now and anon galloped out of the west
> Some envoy. . . .

Days when Roosevelt was in New York, they came
to him in *The Outlook* office; the buzz of their eager

[2] The burden of the political convictions of most of those who urged Roosevelt
to run could be compressed into three words, "We want Teddy." It was by
their affection for him, the stimulus they got from him, that most of them were
inspired. In the conferences in Roosevelt's study at Oyster Bay, or in his *Outlook*
office, there was some high talk about "progressivism" and the like. What most
of the visitors wanted was that Roosevelt should be in the White House again.
Some real discussion there was about expediency and time, whether Roosevelt
would do better to let Taft have the nomination and take his licking, and postpone his own running until 1916. A material factor was that the people wanted
Roosevelt in 1912, and there could be no certainty they would continue to want
him until 1916. On this point, a diary kept by one of *The Outlook* editors,
Harold Howland, describes a conference of Roosevelt, Everett Colby, W. Fel-
lowes Morgan and Mark Sullivan, held January 20, 1912. "All agree time . . .
is here." Sullivan contributed practical wisdom learned in a youth spent on
the farm, "The time to set a hen is when the hen wants to set." Roosevelt,
taking the adage in, elevated it to "The time to use a man is when the people
want to use him." The barnyard advice, as it turned out, was not wise; Roosevelt's running for the Republican nomination in 1912 was a major political mistake. Still, was it?

voices drove away the ordinarily semi-religious hush, the very elevators in the building seemed to move with a quicker tempo. At midday a troop of thrilled admirers trotted after Roosevelt across Gramercy Park to lunch at the National Arts Club. Eagerly they looked into Roosevelt's eyes for a sign, watched his words for encouragement. With whatever they got they returned to their homes, to be met at distant railroad stations by lesser orders of Rooseveltians, corporals and privates in the ranks, who looked into their eyes for the same sign they had sought in Roosevelt's.

Roosevelt did not, at first, tell them he would run. For some ten weeks after his November 16 blast at Taft his attitude was one which the New York *American* compressed into a compact question, "T.R.: R U or R U not?" "Almost overnight," said *Current Literature* in January, 1912, "has this Roosevelt obsession risen and spread until it has become the dominant feature in the political discussions of the country."

II

One among the Insurgent Republican Senators did not come to Oyster Bay. LaFollette had hoped to be the beneficiary of the discontent with Taft, had organized the "National Progressive Republican League"; had, naïvely, invited Roosevelt to join it — "The name of a former President would give strength to the organization," the unhumorous LaFollette wrote in his autobiography. Not sufficiently rebuffed by Roosevelt's declination to join, LaFollette, for the purpose of making the way absolutely clear for himself, demanded that Roosevelt formally declare he would not become a candidate for the Republican nomination. Roosevelt ignored him.

To the LaFollette standard — so long as there was lit-

tle or no expectation that Roosevelt would run —
flocked many of the Insurgents, mainly the more mor-
dant ones, together with a sprinkling of others, not Insurgents in a real sense, who attached themselves to La-
Follette not because of fealty to him or his programme,
but for motives of hatred against Taft and a wish to do
him damage, or because they hoped that by nursing the
revolt along the time might come when Roosevelt could
no longer refuse to accept the leadership of it. They
were a strange ill-assorted band, so riven and criss-
crossed with jealousies, suspicions, and ambitions as to
be constantly on the verge of explosive disintegration.
LaFollette was no leader for them. They could be dominated, held together, and made to work for a common
purpose only by an inspiring generalship of the highest
order, such as LaFollette was hardly capable of providing.

When the flare-up over the Steel Corporation suit occurred, the first overt rift in the friendship between Taft
and Roosevelt, Roosevelt's friends among the group
about LaFollette took heart. Roosevelt, having tossed a
pebble at Taft, might, as things got warmer, throw
weightier missiles. Now it seemed not altogether impossible that Roosevelt should make a fight for the nomination. The Rooseveltians in LaFollette's camp impor-
tuned Roosevelt to take over the movement. At the same
time their real feelings for LaFollette began to manifest themselves; where formerly had been a patient deference was now a growing indifference. Discipline vanished. To LaFollette's sensitive ego they seemed worse
than traitors, and he fell into a mood of chronic complaint. To this his disciples responded with flouts. In
the midst of an abusive harangue against Roosevelt,
Pinchot cut him short: "What can you do? You must
know he has this thing in his own hands and can do what

he likes." From then on LaFollette, as a serious contender for the Presidency in 1912, was through. The final debacle came some weeks later. LaFollette, tired by a long speech-making tour of the West, worried over the illness of one of his children, went to Philadelphia to speak at a newspaper publishers' dinner, an audience before whom it was acutely desirable for any seeker of a Presidential nomination to make the best possible impression. The impression LaFollette made was described by Owen Wister:[3]

Manuscript in hand, LaFollette began. He was going to tell, he said, the true story of money in the United States; by whom it was actually earned, into whose hands it had invariably gone, by what means it had been stolen from those to whom it rightfully belonged. He prefaced this with an attack on journalism and journalists. As he was the guest of journalists, this was an unusual beginning. Presently everybody at our table had begun to look at each other. Next, I saw the faces at neighboring tables staring in the same surprise. We were soon listening to not even a pretense of accurate financial history, but a harangue of distorted denunciation, aimed apparently at us all. The speaker's voice grew acid, raucous, his statements ceased to be even caricatures of reality. . . . People began to leave. He shook his fist at them, saying: "There go some of the fellows I'm hitting. They don't want to hear about themselves." The chairman called him to order, telling him personal abuse would not be permitted. He continued his speech, and a new astonishment came over us; whole passages were being repeated. At first one was not sure, then it was obvious. The repetitions made havoc with his coherence, all consecutive meaning departed. It was noticed by those sitting close to the speaker's table that LaFollette was not laying the finished pages of his address down but shuffling them about. At half-past eleven the hall was empty. He had been speaking since ten and continued until half-past twelve, then sank forward on the table.

Immediately there was a scurrying to flee the sinking LaFollette ship. Gifford Pinchot telegraphed a St.

[3] In "Roosevelt, the Story of a Friendship." Some sentences in this quotation are paraphrased.

Paul meeting: "In my judgment LaFollette's condition is so serious that further candidacy is impossible." George L. Record of New Jersey announced in a public meeting that the LaFollette movement had collapsed and Roosevelt was now the Progressive candidate. In Chicago, the whole Progressive movement, under the lead of Medill McCormick, shifted to Roosevelt almost overnight. Even LaFollette's manager issued a manifesto urging LaFollette's friends to work to have delegates elected not for LaFollette but "for the thoroughgoing and definite principles which he has advocated." The spectacle inspired pity even in the conservative New York *Tribune:* "The haste with which most of the insurgent leaders are seeking to clamp the lid down on Senator LaFollette's candidacy must excite the compassion of those who believe that there should be at least some moderate standard of honor among politicians. . . . He is being hustled ruthlessly inside the hearse, although he still insists that he is strong enough to occupy a seat alongside the driver."

LaFollette went, if not all the way to the hearse, certainly to the limbo of Presidential impossibilities, and spent much of the rest of his life brooding to himself, and declaring to sympathetic listeners that he might have been President but for a plot of Roosevelt and Roosevelt's friends.

III

Among those soliciting Roosevelt to make the race against Taft were seven Republican governors.[4] From passages in letters they wrote him, from ideas supplied by

[4] They were: Walter R. Stubbs of Kansas, Chase S. Osborn of Michigan, Herbert S. Hadley of Missouri, Chester H. Aldrich of Nebraska, Robert P. Bass of New Hampshire, W. E. Glasscock of West Virginia, and J. M. Carey of Wyoming.

others around him, and with some passages contributed
by himself, Roosevelt composed a form of round-robin
letter addressed to himself asking him to make the race.

From a photograph by Brown Brothers.

A characteristic gesture of Roosevelt during the 1912 campaign of the
Progressive ("Bull Moose") party.

This he turned over to Frank Knox who, January 22,
1912, started out over the country getting the signatures; some he got at a Progressive conference at Chicago attended by several of the governors.

Roosevelt, with this call in hand, not yet made public, went to a convention at Columbus, Ohio, engaged
in drawing up a new state constitution. There, on February 22, he delivered an address, meant to be a state-

ment of his personal platform, called by him a "Charter of Democracy" — translated by the Democratic New York *World* into "Charter of Demagogy." One phrase in the address, "recall of judicial decisions," misinterpreted to mean a popular vote on all decisions of all courts, so shocked conservatives as to cause the rest of the address to fail to get much notice — "recall of judicial decisions"[5] was almost as damaging to Roosevelt as "rum, Romanism and rebellion" to James G. Blaine. Actually, Roosevelt's "Charter of Democracy" speech had been shown in advance to and approved by several of his most conservative friends, millionaire Frank A. Munsey, millionaire E. C. Converse, and conservative Republican leader William L. Ward.

On his way home from Columbus, Roosevelt, in response to a question asked him in the railroad station at Cleveland, gave the country another of his unforgettable phrases, "My hat is in the ring," adding "the fight is on and I am stripped to the buff." The public, ignoring the terminology of mediæval combat, but pleased with the modern, gave the former phrase universal currency.

Two days later, at New York, Roosevelt made his challenge formal, giving out the letter signed by the seven governors and his own reply: "I will accept the nomination for President if it is tendered to me, and I will adhere to this decision until the convention has expressed its preference."[6]

---

[5] For a statement of what Roosevelt meant by "recall of judicial decisions," see Chapter 30.
[6] New York *Times*, February 26, 1912.

26

FRIENDSHIP IN RUINS

Epithets Encounter Epithets. Charge and Countercharge
Bring to an End Roosevelt's Twenty Years' Friendship with
Taft. "This Wrenches My Soul!" The Startling Spectacle of a President and an ex-President, Once Close Intimates, Now Calumniating Each Other, while Listeners
Cheer and Howl Approval. History Is Set to a New Tangent.

To Taft, knowledge of Roosevelt's purpose, now definite
after long suspense, came in a note handed to him at the
White House from the Associated Press, just before dinner on the evening of February 25, 1912. For weeks, under the strain of his official duties, his consciousness of his
ebbing popularity and his anxiety about Roosevelt,
Taft's health had been bad — "his flesh looks like wax,
his lips are thin, he is getting unhealthy bags under his
eyes."[1] He read the news in silence, and passed the note
to the others. Silently all filed in to dinner and sat
down. Mrs. Taft was the first to speak. Femininely she
said: "I told you so and you would not believe me."
Taft, with tired impatience, retorted, "I know you did,
my dear, and I think you are perfectly happy now, you
would have preferred him to come out against me rather
than be wrong yourself."[2]

Taft's mood was not, as yet, anger. Though his
friends and some of the public saw Roosevelt's announcement clearly as an attempt to — so the New York
World put it — "bulldoze Taft out of the Presidency,"
Taft's mind turned back to the older, happier days. A
mutual friend of Taft and Roosevelt, Henry White,

---

[1] "Letters of Archie Butt."　　　[2] "Letters of Archie Butt."

moved to a gentleman's attempt to preserve decorum in what seemed to him a terrible situation, talked with Taft about the clash, and about the future of it. Taft assured White, and White wrote[3] to Roosevelt, in a letter

From a cartoon by K. K. Knecht in Evansville "Courier."

Roosevelt giving Taft the nomination in 1908—and demanding it back in 1912.

now pathetic, that "he [Taft] said that nothing would induce him to say — or to allow any one whom he could control to say — anything against you personally; and that he never can forget the old and happy relation of intimacy. . . . [He] said that he could not help hop-

3 March 3, 1912.

ing that when all this turmoil of politics had passed, you and he would get together again and be as of old."

That was Taft's intention, that his state of mind. So far as Taft became a contributor to the public exchange of angry epithets in which he and Roosevelt were soon to engage, the most sensational ever indulged in by any two Americans similarly placed, it was the consequence of accident.

Unfortunately, already, Taft, without intending to, had given Roosevelt and Roosevelt's friends opportunity to say later (in phrases of such a defense as is made by one himself ashamed) that Taft started it. Taft, in a speech[4] on February 12, 1912, had discussed the Progressive movement and its leaders. "Such extremists," Taft had said, "would hurry us into a condition which would find no parallel except in the French Revolution. . . . Such extremists are not Progressives, they are politically emotionalists or neurotics."

The word neurotic was explosively unfortunate. Taft meant it as a generic expression. So far as he had any one of the prominent Progressives in mind, it was not Roosevelt but another.[5] Roosevelt, however, and Roosevelt's friends, now seeking excuse for their own belligerency, chose to regard the word as directed at Roosevelt. Their justification lay in the fact that to call Roosevelt "crazy"[6] had become a detail of political war-

[4] At the Lincoln Day dinner of the New York Republican Club.

[5] A man active in the Progressive movement, whom Taft particularly detested and who had been under the care of neurologists.

[6] There had just come to America from Vienna a new pseudo-science called Freudism (see Chapter 9). Acolytes of it were applying it to public characters, whose position left them open to any interpretation the psychoanalysts, amateur or professional, chose to put upon their conduct. A distinguished psychiatrist, Doctor Morton Prince, said in an article published about this time, that Roosevelt would "go down in history as one of the most illustrious psychological examples of the distortion of conscious mental processes through the force of subconscious wishes"—meaning that Roosevelt's leadership of the Progressive movement was inspired wholly by a subconscious desire to be President again. Another alienist, Doctor Allen McLane Hamilton, wrote a per-

fare which many of his opponents indulged in, and which he did not much mind, until it came from Taft. In the angry public resentment of Roosevelt and Roosevelt's friends against Taft's unfortunately chosen word and utterly unintended application; and in the whole bitterness that arose, Taft was driven into a mood expressed by his other unfortunate phrase: "Even a rat will fight when he is driven into a corner."[7] In that mood Taft, on April 25, went to Boston and delivered the most remarkable speech ever delivered by a President about an ex-President.

II

For two hours Taft stood before his audience denouncing with all the vigor of language he possessed "one whom in the past I have greatly admired and loved." Following an unusually vehement outburst he paused a moment, his great kindly face quivering with emotion, and exclaimed: "This wrenches my soul!" He had been driven to his present course, he explained, by "the unjust, unfounded charges against me . . . that Mr. Roosevelt is now making to the public." Roosevelt had, he declared, attempted to discredit him by "adroit appeals to discontent and class hatred"; had "garbled" his language, "misrepresented" his actions. All this, and more to the extent of ten newspaper columns, Taft charged, with perspiration streaming down his face, in the presence of ten thousand people who sang "We'll hang Teddy's hat to a sour apple tree," under the sponsorship of a presiding officer[8] who declared that "Theo-

fectly serious article in the New York *Times* in which he gravely considered the question of Roosevelt's sanity.

[7] This was subsequent.

[8] Governor John L. Bates of Massachusetts.

dore Roosevelt is following the footsteps of Julius Cæsar and Napoleon Bonaparte, and unless we stop him it will be but a question of time when he usurps a dictatorship of the American people" — the setting and manner of the scene accenting the substance of the indictment to a degree which caused the New York *Times* to say, and nearly everybody to feel, that "these damning charges, made by a President of the United States against an ex-President," constitute "one of the most deplorable occasions in the history of our politics."

III

Twenty-four hours later, and only forty miles away, at Worcester,[9] Mass., Roosevelt struck back. He had read, in the morning newspapers, the full text of the castigation of him the night before by his one-time friend, and, in a temper defiant alike of the restraining voice of decorum and the placatory counsels of friends, he replied with what stands as the most extraordinary speech ever made in the United States by an ex-President about a President. He had before him an audience of his own partisans, familiar with Taft's speech the night before, and tense with a belligerency that accelerated Roosevelt's own. With fists clenched, head thrust

---

[9] The meeting at Worcester was pre-arranged, one of the dates in a campaign Roosevelt was making for the Massachusetts delegates to the Republican National Convention of 1912. To offset this campagn Taft had gone to Boston and made his speech the night before. Roosevelt thereupon threw away the prepared speech he had planned for Worcester, and devoted himself to replying to Taft.

Of the two speeches that composed this exchange, Taft's was the more orderly. Taft had written it out carefully, in the form of eleven numbered points, each supported by quotations from documents. Taft's speech was printed verbatim in the Boston newspapers. Roosevelt's reply was extemporaneous. The newspapers, so far as the author of this history is able to find, printed only detached passages, and it is from the fragmentary report in the Boston *Post* that the detached sentences here reproduced are taken.

forward from his stocky body, his voice at times hoarsely
shrill with emotion loosed from all restraint, his features
straining with the anger that blazed within him, he
used anathemas about Taft not only sensational as coming from an ex-President, or being hurled at a Presi-

PUNCH, OR THE LONDON CHARIVARI.—June 26, 1912.

PLATFORM AMENITIES.

President Taft (*conductor of the White House Express*). "YOU CAN'T GO ON THIS TRAIN."
Colonel Roosevelt. "WELL, IF I CAN'T, YOU SHAN'T!"

[*After Charles Keene.*]

From a cartoon by G. R. H. in "Punch," June 26, 1912.

dent, but "such as seldom have been heard on a public
platform in this State."[10] "President Taft," Roosevelt
said, "has not only been disloyal to our past friendship,
but he has been disloyal to every canon of decency and
fair play. . . . The assaults made upon me by his campaign managers have been foul to the verge of in-

[10] Boston *Post,* April 27, 1912.

decency." Implying that Taft had called him a "neurotic," Roosevelt retorted: "Mr. Taft had better preserve his self-respect by not pretending that it gives him great pain to attack me. No one uses such epithets in pain. President Taft served under me for over seven years without finding fault with me. He only discovered I was dangerous when I discovered that he was useless to the American people. I wanted from President Taft a square deal for the people of the United States. If he had given the people a square deal he could have counted on my enthusiastic support. I do not believe he has given the people a square deal. I believe that he has yielded to the bosses and to the great privileged interests. Every boss in the country is with Mr. Taft and to deny it is ludicrously false." Referring to one of Taft's acts, Roosevelt said:

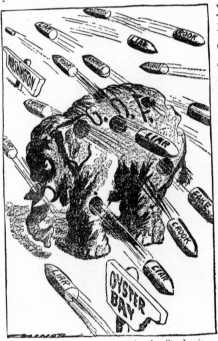

From a cartoon by Minor in the St. Louis "Dispatch."

Plight of the Republican elephant felled by missiles fom both sides in 1912. "I can't stand much more of this!"

"This is the crookedest kind of a crooked deal; it's an attempt to dodge the consequences of his mis-statement by the most deliberate misrepresentation."

Roosevelt's anger carried him to words and actions sensational in the extreme. He denounced as "an unpardonable sin" Taft's reading the night before of an old letter from Roosevelt — and then Roosevelt himself drew from his pocket an old letter that Taft had written to him, and read:

I can never forget that the power I now exercise was voluntarily transferred from you to me, and that I am under obligation to you to see that your judgment in selecting me as your successor and bringing about the succession shall be vindicated according to the standards which you and I in conversation have always formulated.

Excoriating Taft's ingratitude, Roosevelt said: "Mr. Taft is President only because I kept my promise in spite of infinite pressure to break it. It is a bad trait to bite the hand that feeds you.[11]

All this, and more to the extent of two hours, Roosevelt said, to an audience that cheered: "Hit him again, Teddy! Hit him between the eyes! Soak him! Put him over the ropes!" — the scene and the background causing the Boston *Post* to sum up with sad resignation: "Roosevelt, with his roaring epithets, his prize-fight vocabulary, his complete abandonment to rage; Taft, with his ill-adapted attempts to fight back in kind. . . ."

It was appalling, terrible; yet also Titanic, justifying

[11] Roosevelt's reading of this old letter from Taft damaged both writer and reader. *Life,* appalled, wrote:

"What was it that Mr. Roosevelt's since-bitten hand fed to Mr. Taft? It was us, our country, the headship of our Government. WE were that dog-biscuit, for which Mr. Taft was so grateful, and which Mr. Roosevelt conferred with such magnanimous fidelity. WE were that morsel; we, the people, whom Mr. Roosevelt is now so solicitous to have rule! Come, Brethren; how do you feel about it? What kind of sustenance is it that you wish to receive from this hand that fed you to the grateful Taft? "To our mind this little note of Mr. Taft to Mr. Roosevelt is one of the most appalling documents in American political history. But, at the same time, it is pathetic, because Mr. Taft evidently had no conception how bad it was, nor Mr. Roosevelt, either. To be sure, it was a note that Mr. Roosevelt's instincts would have guarded him from writing, but he does not seem to have been much shocked to have it written to him. If he had been adequately shocked, he would never have let it get out. He would have put dust on his head and gone out into the backyard and burned it."

the setting of Homeric epic in which a writer of newspaper verse[12] recited:

T. R. TO W. H. T.

Or ever the knightly fight was on,
The skirmish of smear and smudge,
I was a king in Washington
And you were a circuit judge.[13]

I saw, I took, I made you great,
Friendly I called you "Will."
And back in Nineteen Hundred and Eight,
Out in Chicago, Ill.
I made the convention nominate,
And now — the terrible chill.

For many a sun has set and shone
On the path we used to trudge
When I was a king in Washington
And you were a circuit judge.

I passed the lie and you passed it back;
You said I was all untruth;
I said that honesty was your lack;
You said I'd nor reck nor ruth;
You called me a megalomaniac —
I called you a Serpent's Tooth. . . .

12 Franklin P. Adams in the New York *World.*
13 Poetic license. Mr. Taft's days as a circuit judge long antedated Mr.
Roosevelt's accession to the Presidency.

27

OPEN FEUD

Brother Is Set Against Brother, Friend Against Friend.
New Groups and Enemies Assail Roosevelt. In Thirteen
State Primaries the Country Shows It Prefers Roosevelt to
Taft — but the Control of the Republican Party Is in the
Hands of the Old Guard. Roosevelt Fights On.

ROOSEVELT's fight against Taft, the cleavage in the
Republican party it precipitated, divided brother from
brother, father from son, friend from friend. More
than the Civil War — because that was sectional — the
Roosevelt-Taft feud drove its rending force into the
hearts of communities, churches, clubs, families. Of
the friendships sundered, the most exalted, next to that
between the principals themselves, was between Roosevelt and Lodge, Lodge who had been Roosevelt's intimate
more than thirty years, who had talked with him at least
once a day whenever both were in Washington, and written him when they were separated at least once a week on
the average, letters which on Lodge's side began "Dear
Theodore" and on Roosevelt's "Dear Cabot"; letters
ending, "Give my love to Nannie [Lodge]" or "to
Edith [Roosevelt]." Now was parting. Publicly, in the
austere spirit of New England, Lodge announced, within
forty-eight hours after Roosevelt's Columbus speech: "I
am opposed to the constitutional changes advocated by
Colonel Roosevelt." Privately he wrote to Roosevelt:
"I have had my share of mishaps in politics but I never
thought that any situation could arise which would have
made me so miserably unhappy. . . . There is very
little of the Roman in me toward those I love best."

Gaily Roosevelt replied:[1] "I don't know whether to be most touched by your letter or most inclined to laugh over it. My dear fellow, you could not do anything that would make me lose my warm personal affection for you. . . . Now don't you ever think of this matter again. Tell Nannie how delighted I was to see John and Mary. . . . Ever affectionately, Theodore Roosevelt."

II

Roosevelt, by his present fight, had added wholly new groups to the host that had criticized him while Presi-

From a drawing by McCutcheon in the "Bull Moose," Aug. 24, 1912. By courtesy of Roosevelt House.

Types of the old-time bosses who would rather see the Republican party destroyed than let Roosevelt have the 1912 nomination. *On the reader's left:* Boies Penrose of Pennsylvania; *in the middle:* William Barnes, Jr., of New York; *on the right:* Murray Crane of Massachusetts.

dent. To the stodgy conservatives, who during his Presidency had hated him merely because he held a club over big business, were added a group of old-time sentimental Republicans, whose personal memories ran far back toward the Civil War, to whom the Republican party was really something a little sacred, and who now saw the ark of the covenant soiled by an attack upon a Republican President and an attempt to deprive him of the renomination to which by custom he was entitled; and another group, shocked to the bone at the notion of the recall of judicial decisions; and another group to whom

[1] March 1, 1912.

the rule against a third term was a sanctified thing, and who now saw, as they viewed it, Roosevelt trying to violate that rule by attempting a third term, as they considered, for himself; and yet another group whose distaste for Roosevelt arose out of what they regarded as his lack of loyalty to his friend Taft, coupled with the lack of sportsmanship inherent in his fighting a President whom he himself had placed in office; and yet another group who were repelled by Roosevelt's violence; and by still another one whose attitude toward the show was one of cynical amusement. From all these, with their various reasons for opposing Roosevelt, through their several media of editorial, cartoon, or speech, came upon Roosevelt's head a tornado of assault, a rain of epithet, a biting sleet of satire.

The assaults on Roosevelt took in many cases the direction of two assumptions: one, that Roosevelt was crazy — crazy was the word, no euphemism like "unbalanced"; the other, that he aimed at a life tenure in the Presidency and, thereafter, hereditary succession. "Does any sane person believe," asked the Philadelphia *Evening Telegraph*, "that if Theodore Roosevelt is nominated and elected in November, he will ever quit the Presidency alive? . . . An election in 1912 will be equivalent to an election for life and hereditary succession." Colonel Henry Watterson's Louisville *Courier-Journal* managed to compress both caustic assumptions, insanity and ambition for life tenure, into a double-barbed sentence: "Unless he breaks down under the strain and is taken to a lunatic asylum . . . there can be in his name and person but one issue, life tenure in the executive office."

There erupted, of course, accusations of inconsistency, violation of a pledge — the charge was put with characteristic succinctness and force in an editorial which the New York *Sun* printed on March 6, 1912, and kept repeating with iterative emphasis throughout the campaign:

THE DEADLIEST OF ALL PARALLELS

President Roosevelt's Decision on November 8, 1904:
"Under no circumstances will I be a candidate for or accept another nomination."

Ex-President Roosevelt's Decision on February 25, 1912:
"I will accept the nomination for President if it is tendered to me."

To this, necessarily foreseen by Roosevelt, he replied:

My position on the third term is perfectly simple. I said I would not accept a nomination for a third term under any circumstances, meaning of course a third consecutive term. . . . The precedent which forbids a third term has reference solely to a third consecutive term. A President of the United States can, if he knows how to use the machinery at his disposal, renominate himself even though the majority of the party is against him. But after he has been out of office for a term he has lost control of that machinery. He is in the position absolutely of any private citizen.

All of which was put by the sedate *Outlook* into a homely parable: "When a man says at breakfast in the morning 'No, thank you, I will not take any more coffee,' it does not mean that he will not take any more coffee to-morrow morning, or next week, or next month, or next year."

Above the thunders about the third term tradition, the solemn warnings of threatened dictatorship, played the American sense of humor — expressed in the Brooklyn *Eagle's* "No place feels like home after you have once lived in the White House," and the *Ohio State Journal's* "There is a fairly well-grounded impression that Colonel Roosevelt also favors the recall of former Presidents," and the *Wall Street Journal's* "Those most enthusiastic over the recall of judicial decisions are prevented by prison rules from working for the Colonel," and *Life's* "The popular demand for Colonel Roosevelt is steadily increasing; but however great the demand

WHERE WILL HE LAND ?

From the Denver "Post." By courtesy of Roosevelt House.

A cartoonist's conception of Roosevelt's attempt to get over the anti-third term hurdle in 1912.

may become, it can never be as great as the supply." Even *Life*, however, found it not easy to be funny. Its deeper emotion was expressed in a passage: "The cold chills race up and down our spine. . . . The Roosevelt Presidency was one of the most interesting national moving picture films that was ever unrolled before us. We haven't a single regret for the time and money we spent upon it. But to have to sit through it again!"

III

Roosevelt in his formal announcement of his candidacy had said, in a shrewd combination of high principle with the best advantage for himself:

One of the chief principles for which I have stood is the genuine rule of the people. I hope that the people may be given the chance, through direct primaries, to express their preference as to who shall be the nominee.

There had been under way, as an incident of the Insurgent uprising — as, indeed, perhaps the main detail of their programme — a movement for "Presidential primaries,"[2] to be substituted for conventions as the mechanism for selecting (and instructing) delegates to national conventions. The movement up to now had had no marked success — about as much, let us say, as would reflect the momentum of the early Insurgent leader, LaFollette, as a candidate for the Republican Presidential nomination.

With Roosevelt's announcement of his candidacy, the comparatively few who had been tepidly interested in direct primaries as a cause were now joined by the very many who were ardently interested in Roosevelt as a hero, who desired him to have the Republican nomination, who knew that the conventions would be controlled by Standpatters and office-holders, and who saw in the presidential primary Roosevelt's only chance.

Immediately "Presidential primaries," from a sluggishly moving cause, became a torrential crusade. "GET THE DIRECT PRIMARY FOR YOUR STATE,"

[2] At this time, three terms were in use: "Presidential primary," "Presidential preference" or "preference primary" and "direct primary." By 1932, the generic term "direct primary," covering all, had become universal.

cried a fierce young eagle of the press of that day, Mark Sullivan,[3] ardent for Roosevelt. Vividly he explained what the new device was: "The Presidential primary means that you can go to the polls (if you are a Republican) and say whether you want Taft or Roosevelt. If you don't do the choosing the bosses will." With emphasis of reiteration he amplified: "The Republican nominee will be Roosevelt or Taft; the choice between these two will be made in one of two ways, either by bosses in back rooms or by the people at primary elections. Which is the more desirable?" "Do you," he asked of "every Republican voter," paying his reader the compliment of italicized type:

Do *you* have an opinion as to whether Taft or Roosevelt ought to be the nominee? Do you believe you ought to have a right to express your opinion at the pools? With presidential primaries you will have the chance; without them, the choice between Taft and Roosevelt will be made by the bosses.

Evangelically he supplied his readers with arguments to heckle the politicians:

Ask the Republican politicians this question: If the plain voter is capable of choosing between Taft and Wilson, assuming they should be the candidates, why isn't he also capable of choosing between Taft and Roosevelt?

Urgently he stirred his readers to act:

Get the Presidential primary for your State. Don't let the politicians tell you it is too late. The politicians in Michigan refused it a long time but they called a special seession of the legislature last Monday to pass the law. The Presidential primary can be got for every State if the people demand it vigorously enough. Don't let the politicians dodge this issue. GET THE DIRECT PRIMARY FOR YOUR STATE.

Under such hectic urging, in a spirit almost of national emergency, Presidential primary laws were

[3] In *Collier's Weekly,* February 17, 1912, and again and again and again in subsequent issues.

adopted by special or regular sessions of the legislatures in Massachusetts, Pennsylvania, Illinois, Maryland, Ohio, and South Dakota.[4] In Illinois, when the Governor demurred to calling a special session of the Legislature to enact a primary law, the Chicago *Tribune*, ardent for Roosevelt and ardent for the direct primary as a means of helping Roosevelt, forced the Governor's hand by obtaining signatures from more than a majority of the Legislature.

Roosevelt won and got the delegates in practically every State in which the direct primary method was used. He carried Illinois by 139,436; he carried New Jersey by 17,213; he carried Pennsylvania by 105,899; he carried California by 69,218; he carried Nebraska by 16,769 more than Taft and LaFollette together; he carried Taft's own State, Ohio, by 47,447. In thirteen States that had primaries, there were 388 delegates — Roosevelt got 281, Taft 71, LaFollette 36.

From that showing the inference was indisputable: the people, the rank and file of Republican voters, wanted Roosevelt.

But if Roosevelt got substantially all the delegates from the Presidential primary States, he got relatively few from the States in which the old convention system prevailed. And of these there were rather too many.

The outcome was clouded by the fact that in several States the election of the delegates (either by convention or primary) was not conclusive; contesting delegations were sent to the convention, in some cases by Roosevelt partisans, in some others by Taft's. The number of contests was 252 out of a total of 1,078 delegates in the convention. The settlement of these contests would

---

[4] They had previously been adopted in Oregon, in 1910, and in Wisconsin, New Jersey, Nebraska, California, and North Dakota, all in 1911.

determine whether Roosevelt or Taft would have a majority in the convention.

The contests would be tried and decided, in the first instance, by the Republican National Committee. In that fact lay Roosevelt's weakness. The National Committee in 1912 (and in every Presidential year) is made up four years before — the method is fixed by long custom. At the national convention four years before, in 1908, the delegates from each State had selected the State's member of the National Committee, and the forty-eight thus selected remained in power until the succeeding convention in 1912. It was these forty-eight who would now try the contests. They reflected a convention four years before which had nominated Taft; they held over from a time when there were no Presidential primaries; they belonged prevailingly to the old, standpat wing of the party; they were, as a body, loyal to Taft.

To try the contests (in the first instance) the National Committee met in Chicago twelve days before the convention itself. The only chance Roosevelt would have to influence their decision must be by focussing publicity upon them. To do this, Roosevelt retired to Oyster Bay, whence twice a day went out to the country a barrage of protest, appeal and miscellaneous excitants to public emotion.

28

EVE OF BATTLE

Roosevelt at Sagamore Hill Fights a Battle of Headlines.
Going to Chicago, He Injects a Tinge of Evangelism into the
Battle, Leading His Host in a Determined and Resourceful
Effort to Wrest Control of the Party from the Conservatives.

WITH the primaries over and the State conventions all
held, with the processes of producing delegations (and
contesting delegations) completed, Roosevelt remained
at Oyster Bay, but decidedly not in retirement. Through
countless messages to lieutenants over the long distance
telephone (then still somewhat a novelty) to Chicago,
and through a private telegraph wire with one end in the
attic at Sagamore Hill and the other in the bedroom of
his manager at Chicago, Senator Joseph M. Dixon of
Montana; through verbal messages carried by friends
who raced from Oyster Bay to take the Twentieth Century Limited westward; through inspiration poured into
the eager ears of subordinates who on their way to Chicago stopped at Oyster Bay for contact with the master,
Roosevelt directed the preliminary moves at Chicago.

With equal energy and adeptness he executed the
other of the two functions that were important at this
time, the fighting of that part of the battle of which
the field was the public mind. Through the avenues of
publicity eagerly opened to him and through other
mechanisms that his resourcefulness laid hold upon, the
cheered his followers, subtly insinuated discord among
his opponents, pleaded with the "in betweens." With
charge and reply to charge (though not often the latter),
now with satire, now with furious denunciation; with
solemnity, with gaiety, and always with vitality, Roose-

velt kept the public eye upon the Chicago battlefield, the public mind upon the issues, the public emotions at mounting fever heat.

To the reporters who twice each day trudged the mile of hill from their headquarters at Oyster Bay to Roosevelt's front porch, he exclaimed, on May 31, "Fake, pure fake," as his comment on a rumor that he would go

Roosevelt with his secretary on the lawn at Sagamore Hill where he received Progressive pilgrims asking him to run for President again.

to Chicago. "I may alter my plans," he added, with a second thought of throwing a menace in the general direction of his opponents, "if circumstances demand, of course I'll go." On June 1, he demanded that the contests over rival delegations at Chicago be open to the press, and complained that the Republican National Committee, in its distribution of seats, was denying a fair share to his supporters, indicating, he said, "a deliberate purpose to use ten thousand tickets to stuff the gallery with shouters who would try to overawe the convention." June 2 being a Sunday, Roosevelt, following family custom and deferring to the old American feeling about how the Sabbath should be observed, remained in seclusion, silent.

June 3, when the National Committee, which had charge of convention details and was partial to Taft, revealed an intention of making Elihu Root permanent chairman of the coming convention, Roosevelt took a notice which had to be carefully phrased. Of Root, who had been Roosevelt's Secretary of State and Secretary of War; of Root, whom he had described as the "ablest statesman on either side of the Atlantic Ocean in my time" and of whom he had said: "I would rather see [him] in the White House than any other man now possible, I would walk on my hands and knees from the White House to the Capitol to see Root made President";[1] of Root who during Roosevelt's Presidency had been flint to his steel, Damon to his Pythias, safety-valve to his multitubular boiler — of Root, now in the camp opposed to him, Roosevelt had to say something condemnatory, something castigatory of his present activities. Roosevelt must, in a word, picture Root as a horrible example of a good man gone wrong. "In the past," began Roosevelt's curious indictment, "Mr. Root has rendered distinguished services as Secretary of State and Secretary of War." "But in this contest," began the philippic part of Roosevelt's comment, "Mr. Root stands as the representative of reaction. He is put forward by the bosses and the representatives of special privilege. He has ranged himself against the men who stand for progressive principles within the Republican party; that is, against the men who stand for making the Republican party what it was in the days of Abraham Lincoln" — the sum of which turgidity

[1] "Released for Publication," Oscar K. Davis.

merely amounted to Roosevelt saying "Root is against ME:"

On June 4, when the Ohio Republican convention gave the eight "at large" delegates to Taft, although in the direct primary Roosevelt had carried the State by 47,000, he cried, "political brigandage," "frank and cynical defiance of the emphatic action of the people" — adding to a reporter who asked him, as he handed out his statement, whether he had "hit hard," "This is no time for excited utterances. I prefer to underestimate and understate facts and conditions and make as conservative a statement as possible." "That's bully," he said on June 5, grinning jovially as he told of receiving a telegram from South Dakota. "Why," he chuckled, "my vote there was larger than that of Taft and LaFollette put together. They are running very close." "Stuff and nonsense of the most tawdry description," he said on the same day, of a report that Wall Street interests offended by Taft's anti-trust suit had raised a fifteen million dollar fund for Roosevelt. June 6, he received at Oyster Bay a hard-boiled Pittsburgher, William Flinn, who had temporarily ousted Penrose as boss of Pennsylvania. "I am sending Flinn to Chicago," said Roosevelt to the newspaper men, creating the impression that if at Chicago strong-arm tactics were to be resorted to, champions would not be lacking on the Roosevelt side. June 7, spending the day at his *Outlook* office in New York, Roosevelt received in the corridor outside his office and therefore peculiarly publicly, Director Samuel McCune Lindsay, Director of the New York School of Philanthropy, John A. Kingsbury, of the New York Association for Improving the Condition of the Poor, and Secretary Homer Folks, of the Charities Aid Society; whom he permitted to state, for the newspapers: "We called on Colonel Roosevelt to submit planks for the national Republican platform, to give definite form to the conception of social and industrial justice, which Colonel Roosevelt has made the dominant issue in his campaign" — Roosevelt knew well the persuasive publicity value of the concatenation of altruistic affiliations and implications.

In reply to a question by a newspaper man picturing a parallel between the 1912 Republican convention and the one of 1880, Roosevelt said: "If they act honestly, there will be no occasion for any one to bolt." June 8, receiving from Chicago news of a decision adverse to him, he said that "again and again we have sent to the penitentiary election officials for deeds not one whit worse than what was done by the National Committee at Chicago yesterday." June 9, another Sabbath, contributed no emanation from Oyster Bay. June 10, asked if it was true a special train was waiting to take him to Chicago, he snapped, "Nonsense!" June 11, Roosevelt, in his rôle of Contributing Editor of the *Outlook*, erstwhile decorous and polite journal of opinion, denounced the seating of certain of Taft's delegates at Chicago as "a fraud as vulgar, as brazen, and as cynically open as any ever committed by the Tweed régime in New York forty years ago." In this editorial he brought into use a new and not entirely pat adjective of combat: "The contest for the Republican nomination has now narrowed down to a naked issue of right and wrong; for the issue is simply whether or not we shall permit a system of naked fraud, of naked theft from the people, to triumph" — causing Roosevelt's sly enemy, the New York *Sun*, to mimic him: "So much for the naked issue, now for the naked truth . . ." June 11, he denounced an action of the Republican National Committee at Chicago as "dangerously near being treason," and continued: "To whom does the Republican party belong? I hold that it belongs to the plain people. Mr. Taft, through his lieutenants, acts on the belief that the party belongs to the bosses." Roosevelt defined the issue as being "simply whether the people ⁂have the right to nominate whomever they wish for the highest office in their gift, or whether by deliberate theft and fraud certain machine leaders, acting in the interest of special privilege, are to be permitted to deprive the people of this right." June 12, Roosevelt denounced the acts of Taft's men at Chicago: "There is no form of rascality which the Taft men had not resorted to."[2]

The whole of the Colonel's objurgations, denunciations, accusations, calumniations, and miscellaneous fulminations causing the indispensable "Mr. Dooley" to remark:

I had no idee it was so bad. I wint to bed last night thinkin' th' counthry was safe, so I put out th' cat, locked th' dure, counted th' cash, said me prayers, wound th' clock, an' pulled into th' siding f'r th' night. Whin I got up I had a feelin' that somethin' was burnin', th' same as I had th' mornin' iv th' big fire. But I cudden't find annything wrong till I opened up th' pa-apers an', much to me relief, found that it was not me pants but th' republic that was on fire. Yes, sir; th' republic is doomed to desthruction again.

II

For response or counter-attack to Roosevelt's barrage of denunciations from Oyster Bay, Taft in the White House was impotent by temperament, handicapped by his office or his sense of the dignity of it. The news

---

[2] All of which was impishly paraphrased by Roosevelt's enemy, the New York *Sun:* "The bestial nature of the indecent hordes of pirates, second story men, porch climbers, gun men and short card dealers who oppose me is now perfectly manifest. . . . This strikes at the very foundation-stone of pure democracy, for it misrepresents me. It has been known ever since pure democracy became respectable through my adherence to it. This despicable effort to confuse and obscure the public mind I denounce as a machination of the special interests in their loathsome campaign for the submergence of innocence, childhood, motherhood, womanhood, and Abraham Lincoln."

coming out of the White House dealt practically wholly with Taft's official duties — at the moment rather oner-ous. Almost the only news emanating from Taft that had to do even faintly with the fight was a despatch say-

From a cartoon by Glackens in "Puck." By courtesy of Roosevelt House.

Sad effect on the Republican elephant of Roosevelt and Taft pulling in different directions.

ing that Taft had chosen, to make his nominating speech, an Ohio Republican, a "fluent speaker with a strong voice" — his name was Warren G. Harding. On June 14 he was quoted as saying: "All the information I get is that I will be nominated on the first ballot."

If Taft himself was inept and otherwise barred from the sort of repartee that Roosevelt's barrage called for, Taft's lieutenants, while willing, were hardly a match

for the Colonel. When the Roosevelt forces charged the
National Committee with refusing to give Roosevelt's
friends an adequate supply of tickets for the convention gallery, the Committee chairman, Harry S. New,[1]

From a photograph by Brown Brothers.

Taft on the stump during the 1912 campaign.

retorted that the Roosevelt manager was a "pettifogging
falsifier," — anemic verbal shadow of the Colonel's
robustious "shorter and uglier word." When a Roosevelt man telegraphed the National Committee's sergeant
at arms, William F. Stone, asking for tickets, Stone
wired back, "Not a damned ticket to any Roosevelt

[3] Later Postmaster General in President Harding's Cabinet.

man." The retort, while forceful, somehow lacked the public appeal of the Roosevelt method. On June 9, the Taft managers decided to "draw a contrast between themselves and the Roosevelt headquarters," and in that purpose "not to answer the Colonel's charges," to "give the Roosevelt forces a monopoly of the publicity" — an abnegation of which the virtue lay in recognition of inferiority, somewhat like the rabbit, in a contest with the porcupine, preferring weapons other than quills.

If Taft was unwilling, and his managers unskilled, in the arts of vocal barrage, their deficiency was abundantly supplied by volunteers from the sidelines. The most effective missiles came from the New York *Sun*, in the form of satire. On June 13, *The Sun*, in a pseudo concern for Roosevelt's place in history, advised him to quit. He had already had honors enough, *The Sun* said, listing them:

> For a man whose feet have already surmounted almost every pinnacle of human ambition; who has been statesman, ruler, philosopher, warrior, reformer, preacher, historian, faunal naturalist, autobiographer, sage, idol, instructor of the other nations of the earth and swayer of the minds of millions of his own fellow countrymen by sheer personal force; who has figured not only as the maker of peace between two of the greatest of world powers engaged in one of the most tremendous conflicts in military annals, but has himself taken the sword against a formidable European antagonist and charged on horseback up San Juan hill in a picture by Frederic Remington, and, if we are not mistaken, in another picture by Vasili Verestchagin; who has not only held for two terms the most exalted office in the world but has also won uncounted minor triumphs with pen, mouth, elephant rifle, boxing gloves and epigrams — for such a man . . . not much is left to be desired.

For which reasons *The Sun* slyly urged that Roosevelt abandon his present ambition, and particularly that he should not go to Chicago in person.

III

At Oyster Bay June 14, Roosevelt arose early, breakfasted early. In a flurry of instructions to servants and good-byes to neighbors who had come to wish him luck, he climbed into the tonneau of an open car and, with Mrs. Roosevelt, started for New York, forty miles away. It was noticed by the little group who saw him off that the Colonel's afflatus suggested more militancy, more snap and crackle, than usual, due, in part, to the new hat he was wearing, a hat among hats, big, tan, with a deep crown and a wide brim, having a sombrero effect; the hat of a soldier, of a Rough Rider.

Just before noon Roosevelt reached his office in *The Outlook*. In the corridor outside his door were jammed hundreds of people, through whom Roosevelt shouldered a way, smiling, responding to greetings. As he reached his door, a newspaper man asked a question. Roosevelt turned around, waited for silence: "When am I going to Chicago? I do not know yet. I may return to Oyster Bay this afternoon. But sometimes things move quickly these days." Grinning, he pushed open the door, backed through, and closed it.

In the corridor the hum of excitement went on. Inside, Roosevelt talked over the telephone with his aides in Chicago. The Convention was only two days away.

Presently Roosevelt came out, handed around copies of a statement — he was going to Chicago. Reporters rushed to telephones. In the afternoon Roosevelt started.

At Chicago, police had made preparations to control the crowd at the railroad station. The plan, from the moment Roosevelt appeared, evaporated. The sight of the Colonel, teeth agleam, romantic headgear, burly arms waving greetings, was catalytic. A mob, shouting, laughing, cheering, shoving, engulfed the police and took Roosevelt to its bosom. The drive to the hotel was through lines of sensation-mad people, "who greeted him as they might have greeted a successful Roman general returning from the wars." They followed him into his hotel, jammed the lobby, almost crushed the breath from his body. Finally he escaped to an elevator and thence to his headquarters, and ten minutes later emerged onto a balcony and gave a short talk: "It is a naked fight against theft, and the thieves will not win."[4] The crowds in Michigan Avenue and Grant Park roared back, "Soak 'em, Teddy! Give it to 'em!"

To a reporter who asked him a commonplace question about his health and spirits, Roosevelt achieved — in this case without planning it — one of the most potent for effect of all the striking phrases that sparkled along the path of his career. "I'm feeling," he said, using a quite artless simile that came to his mind from his hunting experiences, "like a bull moose" — bringing it about that BULL MOOSE should stalk in heavy black letters across the front pages of 10,000 newspapers (conveying, one wonders, what mystic significance, to a nation in which not one of a hundred had ever seen an antlered animal, or could know how a bull moose feels under any set of circumstances). Crudely drawn pictures of the animal appeared in immense posters on the walls of hotels and as placards at the head of improvised parades, the biological details giving some pain, doubtless, to the curator of the Field Museum on

4 The somewhat overwhelmed correspondent for the New York *Times*, reporting the speech, quoted a few blistering fragments, such as: "The thieves, robbers and high-binders [who] steal the people's liberties"—and then, in fear apparently that he might be suspected of gilding the lily, added: "The quoted words are his as used in his public utterances here to-day, and each time that the Colonel uses them he gathers new frenzy."

Michigan Avenue, but the spirit adequately grasped by Roosevelt's exalted followers. Manufacturers of campaign buttons telegraphed frantically to their factories, where harried artists made unaccustomed demands on local libraries for a picture of "alces Americanus." The name, "Bull Moose," the idea, the spirit, was taken into the national consciousness, became an established thing, a symbol universally understood. Roosevelt's political following was the "Bull Moose Party," a partisan of him was a "Bull-mooser."[5]

IV

The spirit into which Roosevelt at Oyster Bay had whipped the scene and which rose to surround him as he arrived on the field in person, was not what might have been expected from the angry epithets which Roosevelt had been using to stimulate his followers. It was a fighting spirit, of course — it could hardly have avoided that, but the kind of fighting spirit that is described as martial, and the precise shade of martial which verges into religious. Due to the presence of women in large numbers in Roosevelt's ranks, entering into politics for the first time and taking it with exalted seriousness; due to the implications, vague but always elevated, of the phrase Roosevelt had made a slogan, "social justice"; and due perhaps to a certain solemnity, a fatefulness in the fact that the Republican party, then still remembered as having fought the Civil War and saved the Union, was now in its own grapple of life and death — due to these and whatever causes, the emotion Roosevelt inspired expressed itself in what had already begun to be sung and what became the practically official

[5] The phrase "Bull Moose" had its great burgeoning less at the Chicago Republican Convention, June, 1912, than during subsequent weeks, and especially at the August convention in which the Progressive party was born.

and universally used battle songs of Roosevelt's party,

> Onward Christian soldiers
> Marching as to war . . .

and the "Battle-Hymn of the Republic":

Mine eyes have seen the glory of the coming of the Lord,
He is trampling out the vintage where the grapes of wrath are
  stored.
Glory, glory hallelujah!
Glory, glory hallelujah!
Glory, glory hallelujah,
His truth is marching on.

Even the arguments, the most violent of them, were expressed in symbols of religion, Biblical quotations. The Chicago *Tribune*, earnest Roosevelt organ, as an appeal to the National Committee for justice to the Roosevelt delegations, printed in large type across the entire page, and on all the pages of its issue of June 18:

THE EIGHTH COMMANDMENT: THOU SHALT NOT STEAL

Solemnly, with utter seriousness, almost reverently, *The Tribune* said of the convention hall that "the coliseum is the temple at Gaza and Samson is between the pillars."

In that spirit, on the night preceding the opening of the convention, Monday, June 17, Roosevelt made perhaps the most moving speech of his career. The Auditorium would hold 5,000 — four times that many struggled to enter. Roosevelt began on a high note: "Disaster is ahead of us if we trust to the leadership of men whose souls are seared and whose eyes are blinded, men of cold heart and narrow mind, who believe we can find safety in dull timidity and dull inaction." As for his own fortunes, he offered himself in the spirit of utter sacrifice: "What happens to me is not of the slightest consequence. I am to be used, as in a doubtful battle any man is used, to his hurt or not, so long as he is useful, and

is then cast aside or left to die. I wish you to feel this
and I shall need no sympathy when you are through with
me, for this fight is far too great to permit us to concern
ourselves about any one man's welfare." In his peroration he achieved a climax which in emotional intensity
equalled Bryan's "crown of thorns, cross of gold," which
was comparable to the most elevated oratory in the language — and which made a very old word newly familiar to an America that was beginning to lose acquaintance with its Bible:

We fight in honorable fashion for the good of mankind; fearless of the future, unheeding of our individual fates, with un-
flinching hearts and undimmed eyes; we stand at Armageddon,
and we battle for the Lord.

Something about the word "Armageddon," an implication at once mystic and martial, made it overnight part
of the language of the street. Embattled righteousness
was the meaning commonly ascribed to it; its pronunciation varied with individual preference. Scores of songs
and poems were inspired by it:

We stand at Armageddon, and we battle for the Lord,
And all we ask to stead us is a blessing on each sword;
And tribes and factions mingle in one great fighting clan,
Who issue forth to battle behind a fighting man.

Not all that "Armageddon" inspired was reverent,
not all took either the word or its discoverer seriously.
The New York *Sun* found in it material for jeering wit.

In spite of some hesitancies of pronunciation the brethren
got a holy joy out of "Armageddon." There is a mystic wonderful charm to it; it is like "Abracadabra" or "parallelo-
pipedon," a word of might with magic in the vowels and the
bowels of it. Seth Bullock believes it to be a township in
Oklahoma. The Hon. Angelo Perkins is positive that it is
Welsh. Medill McCormick holds that it was an early skirmish
in the Revolution. . . .

Of all the satires and ironies that arose out of the religious flavor which Roosevelt's 1912 crusade took on,

the most penetrating came from one unknown to the present historian, or, I suspect, to any other. His performance was of a sort that does not get itself into the official records, nor even into the newspapers. His name is

From a photograph courtesy of Roosevelt House.

A characteristic pose of Roosevelt campaigning in 1912.

forgotten, if indeed it was ever known. Only the thing he did is recalled. But I can visualize him. A homely philosopher he must have been, one, I imagine, with some small income, sufficient to save his cerebration from being dissipated in the pursuit of livelihood, one having a bent for reading and able to indulge it, having a bent also for observation of mankind and above all one with capacity to reflect fruitfully upon what he read and observed. A sense of humor he must have had, yet I suspect the thing he did was not so much in the spirit of humor as of adequacy — it seemed called for and he did it.

I can visualize him strolling down the quieter side of Michigan Avenue, the Park side. I can imagine him pausing to observe the Colonel going by, and the crowds that followed. He noticed the rapt quality of them, the visionary gleam in their eyes, the frenzy in some. Seeing it he recalled from his reading the age-long disposition of men to set up heroes, to expect Messiahs. Seeing and reflecting, it occurred to him that the scene called for a comment on mankind and his incredible ways. Being a laconic person, his comment took the form of action. Waiting until the crowd had hurried by, he crossed the street, sought a small printer, had a brief order filled, and employed some small boys, with the result that throughout Chicago's streets were scattered thousands of dodgers reading:

At Three o'Clock
Thursday Afternoon

THEODORE ROOSEVELT

Will Walk

on the

WATERS OF
LAKE MICHIGAN[6]

---

[6] In this bit of narrative the only authentic detail is that the dodger was circulated. How it came about is imagined, wholly. The authorship, far from what is here surmised, may have come from some perfectly serious follower of the Colonel—there were among them ones who, in the fervor of that occasion, were equal to it. Another possibility, even more obvious, is that the impishness may have been committed by some Standpatter Republican.

Mr. James P. Hornaday remembers the incident, but is uncertain whether it happened at the Republican convention in June or the Progressive one in August.

29

THE BATTLE

Roosevelt Forces Contend, Parliamentarily and Almost Physically, Against Taft Forces in the Coliseum at Chicago. A Battle in Which Polemic Arguments Came to be Subordinated to Vocal Brickbats. The "Steam Roller." Epithets, Threats, and Alarums. A Young Woman Who Suddenly, and Pleasurably, Became Conspicuous. End of the Fight — and End of the Tragedy of Roosevelt and Taft.

"Am I goin' to th' convintion?" said Mr. Dooley. "What a question to ask a spoortin' charakter! If a fellow was to come to ye an' say: 'Here's a free ticket f'r a combynation iv th' Chicago fire, Saint Batholomew's massacree, the battle iv th' Boyne, th' life iv Jesse James, an' th' night iv th' big wind,' wud ye take it or wud ye not? . . . Iv coorse I'm goin'! I haven't missed a riot in this neighborhood in forty years, an' onless I'm deceived be th' venal Republican press this man will rejoice th' heart, as Hogan says. I'll get a seat somewhere that I can see th' sthruggle f'r human rights goin' on but fur enough away so I won't be splashed. If anny wan comes up to me an' begins 'Fellow Republican,' I'll cry out: 'Take ye're hand off y're gun. Ye have nawthin' agin me. I'm a Dimmycrat.'"—"Mr. Dooley," by Finley Peter Dunne, Chicago *Tribune*, June 16, 1912.

THE official[1] for the formality of opening the convention was Victor Rosewater, whose gentleness of voice, paleness of face, and slightness of figure, were apt for the status he had in private life, editor of the Omaha (Neb.) *Bee*, and would have been appropriate for a musician or a Hebraic poet — might, indeed, have marked him for almost any possible rôle before that of presenting his frail breast to a political tornado. Rosewater, his shortness of stature emphasized by the length of the gavel he now grasped, and the height of the reading desk behind which he stood, his thinness of voice almost grotesquely in contrast with the hoarse passions raging

[1] By virtue of his post of Chairman of the Republican National Committee.

in the hall, his manner that of a man whose certainty that bombs will strike near him is accentuated by anxious uncertainty whether they will fall to right or to left, to front or to rear, or, as happened, on all sides at once — Rosewater had quiet for just two perfunctory acts. Without interruption from the floor he was allowed to introduce the clergyman[2] — whose invocation ventured only so far into the faint umbra of the matters on hand as to ask God to "direct all our actions by Thy holy inspiration" — and then retreated to the safe neutrality of repeating the Lord's Prayer. Upon the heels of the "Amen," Rosewater, who had a manner of nervous hurry, directed the Secretary[3] to read the routine call for the convention; and hardly had the closing syllable dropped from the Secretary's lips when the first thunder of the storm broke out.

The National Committee had made up, as usual, the "temporary roll" of delegates and had placed upon it the 72 Taft delegates whom the Committee a few days before had adjudged winners of the contests. This roll, the Roosevelt forces now challenged, denouncing the 72 as "not honestly elected" and moving that in place of them there be substituted the "seventy-two [Roosevelt] delegates who have been elected by the honest votes of the Republican voters" — that, in short, as it was expressed again and again by the Roosevelt spokesmen, with no attempt at delicacy, "the roll be purged of fraud." To this motion the Taft forces interposed a parliamentary objection, on the ground that "no business of any character is in order until after the Convention shall have been properly organized."

[2] Reverend James F. Callaghan, of St. Malachy's Roman Catholic Church, Chicago.
[3] Of the National Committee, William Hayward, then of Nebraska City, Nebraska, later of New York City.

Rosewater, facing the necessity of deciding whether or not the Roosevelt motion was in order, rather timorously[4] disavowed personal responsibility for the decision he was about to make, saying that he had apprehended the question would come up, that therefore he had had it "under advisement for several days," that he had "had advice upon it from many distinguished gentlemen more learned in parliamentary law than myself," that he was "greatly indebted to these gentlemen" for "elucidating the question" for him, and that he would have the clerk "read a statement" containing the arguments, precedents, and conclusions with which his advisers had provided him. The statement of course, reached the conclusion that the motion of the Roosevelt leaders was "out of order," that the 72 contested Taft delegates should remain on the temporary roll. With that decision announced, Rosewater, with the eager manner of hurrying toward an end to his disquieting responsibilities, went on with his one remaining function, the election of a Permanent Chairman[5] to preside over the coming and certain-to-be-stormy session.

II

With that, the convention passed into its tensest phase, for it was known to every delegate, to every spectator in the galleries — not "every spectator," rather "every partisan," for there was no spectator who was not a partisan

[4] Finley Peter Dunne in *The American Magazine* said about Rosewater's decision: "He made the decision, there is no doubt about that. It is in the official record written down by the official reporters—the night before. But no one heard him make it. The actual physical disposition of the decision is unknown. The impression of those who sat in front of the chairman and watched the play of his throat muscles, was that he swallowed it.

[5] The permanent presiding officer of the convention was called, for technical parliamentary reasons, and appears in the record as "temporary chairman" until the closing day, when he became "permanent chairman." Throughout this narrative I have, for clearness' sake, referred to the occupant of the chair as the "permanent chairman."

— and to every citizen waiting tensely before newspaper bulletin boards in every corner of the country, that the election of the permanent chairman would be the first test, that whichever side mustered a majority in that test would, if its ranks held and its determination endured, have the same majority (substantially) for the nomination of the Presidential candidate. Whichever side won the permanent chairmanship would win the presidential nomination.

The Roosevelt candidate for permanent chairman was Francis E. McGovern, put in nomination by a Wisconsin delegate[6] as "the brilliant, the able, the impartial, and the fearless Governor of my commonwealth."

McGovern did not really live up to all those adjectives. He was chosen by the Roosevelt forces as their candidate for permanent chairman partly with the shrewd notion that they thereby could muster the maximum number of votes against the Taft candidate. All the Roosevelt delegates would (and did) vote for McGovern as a matter of course; the Roosevelt forces hoped that the little group of 26 Wisconsin delegates, who were not for Roosevelt but for LaFollette, would, on the vote for chairman, be led by state pride to support McGovern. But the Roosevelt leaders did not know, as the country did later, LaFollette's limitless intransigence. LaFollette, speaking through one of his delegates (Walter L. Houser), coldly informed the convention that McGovern was not his candidate, that McGovern did "not represent the interests of LaFollette."[7]

The candidate of the Taft forces for permanent chair-

[6] Henry F. Cochems.

[7] Ultimately, in the roll-call for permanent chairman, twelve Wisconsin delegates voted with the Roosevelt forces for McGovern, fourteen threw their votes

man was Elihu Root.[8] To put his name before the convention, they relied upon the speech-making talent and other versatile abilities of a New York delegate, Job E. Hedges, who was the one man in the Taft forces equipped with, or able to retain in this moment, any qualities of poise and humor. With irony, with serenity; with the capacity, as occasion arose, for what a later generation would have called "a snappy come-back," this proposer of Root won an opening trick in the forensic game by quoting a panegyric about Root which had been uttered by Roosevelt himself a few short years before — "Elihu Root is the ablest man that has appeared in the public life of any country in any position in my time." When, upon this quotation being read, cheers broke out more for Roosevelt than for Root, Hedges urbanely assured the Roosevelt rooters that "you need not hesitate to cheer Roosevelt in my presence; I cheered him seven years. . . . Elihu Root was good enough for Roosevelt and he is good enough for me."

III

There followed, on both sides, a welter of seconding speeches which, heard and seen as a whole, including the cross-fire among the delegates and the frequent remarks from the galleries, had the effect of a lake of fiery lava on the surface of which erupted detonating bombs of anger and malediction, humor and irony.

A good many of the seconders of McGovern forgot

to two obscure LaFollette lieutenants, and one did not vote. This refusal of fourteen LaFollette delegates to unite with the Roosevelt forces for McGovern for chairman did not materially affect the outcome, for McGovern had only 501 votes to Root's 558.

In the subsequent balloting for Presidential nominee, Wisconsin's 26 delegates voted all for LaFollette, to the end. This was the course of the Wisconsin delegates, or so much of them as LaFollette from time to time controlled, in every subsequent Republican National Convention until LaFollette died.

8 Strictly, Root was "put in nomination" by the National Committee; Hedges' was a seconding speech.

McGovern and talked about Roosevelt — or, in another spirit, about Root. Francis J. Heney of California, in a long speech seconding McGovern (on the rare occasions when he thought of it) reviewed the history "of the conduct of the national committee" in a vocabulary and a spirit with which Heney had become familiar through his practice as prosecutor in the criminal courts. Scornfully he designated a Taft leader with a term from the argot of the underworld, "Big Steve of Colorado." Shockingly pointing his finger at the victim of his acid words, he said, of this Taft leader, that he "differs from Abe Ruef[9] of California only in the fact that Abe Ruef was in the penitentiary last week while Big Steve was helping to make this temporary roll" — leading to a demonstration which the official stenographer embalmed for history, rather mildly, as "disorder and confusion in the hall." To permit the seventy-two disputed Taft delegates to vote on the question of chairman when they "have no legal, moral, or ethical right to be in this convention," was, Heney said, simply "the proposition that a corrupt judge shall sit in his own case." "You may as well hear me out," he continued, "because you are going to hear me if it takes all summer."

A delegate from West Virginia, William Seymour Edwards, rising to second McGovern, began in the manner of Rome and Shakespeare: "Gentlemen and fellow-delegates: Give me your ears" — but quickly, upon hearing unpropitious sounds from the gallery, changed his tempo to something more consistent with the present occasion, saying, in the next sentence, "Boys, give me a chance."

When a Kentucky Senator, W. O. Bradley, undertook to second Root with a tribute of the conventional sort,

---

[9] Notorious boodler, mayor of San Francisco, whom Heney had prosecuted.

a Roosevelt delegate,[10] recalling a not universally admired episode in Bradley's senatorial career, called out,
with effective irrelevancy, "You voted for Lorimer."[11]

Senator Bradley of Kentucky in the speech in which his peroration, extempo-
rized to meet the occasion, was "Liar! liar! liar!"

This interpolation into the proceedings of a happening
rather far removed from the matter of electing a chairman of the convention, was greeted with manifest satisfaction and approval by the Roosevelt delegates, who

[10] Meyer Lisner of California.

[11] William Lorimer, Senator from Illinois, expelled from the Senate on the
ground that several members of the Illinois legislature had been paid to vote
for him.

with good heart and ample lung-power united in a chant,
"Lorimer! Lorimer! Lorimer!" Bradley, exasperatedly
resigning himself to the change of theme forced upon
him by the Roosevelt partisans, singled out a conspicuous
Roosevelt delegate from California, and addressed him
in a shout of such volume as to be heard above the

Calling the roll at the 1912 Republican National Convention under conditions
which demanded strong lungs and the largest megaphone available.

tumult: "Yes, I voted for Lorimer and when I did I
voted for a man ten thousand times better than you. . . .
I want to say that the time will never come when the
great State of Kentucky will be so low and degraded as
to accept moral advice from Francis J. Heney."

Bradley, his creative spirit pleased at having invented
so apt a retort, swung back into his panegyric of Root,
and as he approached his conclusion found himself in a
mood sufficiently charitable to say, "I want to thank

you gentlemen for your decorous and courteous attention." To which the Roosevelt delegates, in ungracious
repudiation of the virtues Bradley had attributed to
them, repeated their chorus, "Lorimer! Lorimer!
Lorimer!" Whereupon Bradley, with a quick change of
tempo into both the mood and the melody, the lilt of the
precise moment, retorted "Liar! Liar! Liar!"

IV

Finally, the oratory of seconding the nominees for
permanent chairman exhausted itself, the calling of the
roll began. At each point where the name of a contested
Taft delegate was called, shrill protest arose from the
Roosevelt leaders, expressed in forms that did not always
take the trouble to adhere strictly to the ceremonious
locutions of parliamentary procedure. When the Secretary called the name of a Taft delegate from Pennsylvania, Roosevelt-leader Flinn of that State challenged
the vote. When the chair declined to entertain the protest, Flinn expressed his appeal from the decision of the
chair by a simple affirmation, "Steal! Thief! You are a
pack of thieves." When the chair seemed not disposed
to entertain this form of appeal and proceeded with the
calling of the roll, Flinn informed the chairman, the
convention, and the world that "You'll have a happy
time calling any roll here this afternoon unless you give
us justice; we are going to be heard in this convention
or you are not going to have any roll call." "Do you
want me," he added, "to come up [on the platform]
where I can talk to you?" Flinn had a reputation that
gave validity to his threat, gave substance to the innuendo which the chair saw in his words, and justified the
apprehension, plain in the chair's manner, that if Flinn

should come up on that platform his processes of persuasion might not be confined to talk.[12]

Finally, when Flinn's and all other protests had been

Elihu Root as presiding officer of the 1912 Convention, being called upon to use extra-parliamentary devices for the preservation of decorum, orders "Bill" Flinn of Pennsylvania to "resume his seat."

ignored, the roll call was completed and the chair announced that "a majority of the delegates have voted for Senator Root." As Root took the chair, the outraged Flinn made his so-to-speak minority report in a simple epithet. To the very face of Root, to the former Secretary of State of the United States, to one of the half-

[12] To forestall just such an action, the stairs leading from the floor to the platform had been removed on the opening day. The chief of the Chicago police had been asked to stand in front of Flinn and watch him throughout the convention.

dozen leading statesmen of the world, Flinn exclaimed: "Receiver of stolen goods." He was informally seconded by another Roosevelt delegate who, with an attempt at fine discrimination, reduced the charge to "Protector of stolen goods." Whereupon the listening Chicago chief of police, out of a criteria of violence including the Great Conflagration, the Haymarket riots, the Pullman strike, and the daily alarums in the stockyards district, expressed juridical condemnation, in a voice loud enough to be heard and included by the stenographer in the permanent record: "This is a plain breach of the peace."

To all this Root's cool response was to enter calmly upon the delivery of his prepared address, consisting chiefly of a laudatory review, in the usual form and spirit, of the achievements of Taft's administration. Root concluded, climactically, with a tribute to "the courts, state and federal . . . Their judges will not be punished for honest decisions; their judgments will be respected and obeyed. The keystone established by our fathers will not be shattered by Republican hands. 'For there is no liberty where the power of judging be not separate from the legislative and judicial powers.'[13] 'To what purpose are powers limited, and to what purpose is that limitation committed to writing, if these limitations may at any time be passed by those intended to be restrained?' "[14]

By which every one understood that Root was putting the emphasis of the climax of his speech not, according to the tradition of Republican convention keynote oratory, upon the wickedness of Democrats but upon that of a Republican; that Root was subtly creating an effect

13 The sentence is quoted by Root from *The Federalist*.
14 This sentence is quoted by Root from John Marshall.

upon the convention and the country by recalling, and condemning, Roosevelt's fatal phrase "the recall of judicial decisions."

V

The vote for permanent chairman had been Root 558, McGovern 501.[15] Had the 72 contested Taft dele-

Governor Hadley, of Missouri, floor-leader of the Roosevelt forces, attained much of his impressiveness by his restraint.

gates been prevented from voting, Root would have had less than a majority, Roosevelt's candidate for chairman would have been elected, Roosevelt's friends would control the convention, Roosevelt would be nominated. Unless these 72, or an appreciable proportion of them,

[15] Lander 12, Houser 1, Gronna 1, not voting 5.

could be unseated, Roosevelt's cause was lost. To the unseating of those delegates, therefore, or to successfully indicting their right to vote, the Roosevelt leaders now proceeded to devote their parliamentary battle.

Governor Hadley of Missouri, floor leader of the Roosevelt forces, had already at the opening of the convention moved that the 72 Taft delegates, against whom contests had been made, be removed, and that there be substituted the 72 Roosevelt delegates on whose behalf the contest had been made. This motion the chair had ruled out of order. Now Hadley renewed it as the opening move in a long parliamentary battle, in the course of which his motion became standardized, that "List 1," the 72 Taft delegates, be stricken off, and "List 2," the 72 Roosevelt delegates, be substituted.

When the Roosevelt forces realized that the motion in this form would be lost, they modified it, to the effect that the 72 contested Taft delegates as a group should not be permitted to vote in any matter affecting their titles as a group to their seats. Shrewdly, by iteration Hadley emphasized that a contested delegate voting upon his own title to the seat he claimed was as being defendant and juror in the same case. "It is written in the law of England," said Hadley, quoting a classic of jurisprudence, "that no man shall be a judge of his own case." The same axiom, expressed in less classic words, was on the banner which the California delegation jiggled up and down in the face of the delegates every time this question was before them: "We refuse to try title to property before the thief who stole it."

To which Root as presiding officer made a distinction between an individual voting on the title to his own individual seat, and a group voting on questions affecting the title of the whole group to their several seats. Root conceded that "no man can be permitted to vote upon the question of his own right to his seat" but held, and quoted the parliamentary manual of the House of Representatives to sustain him, that "the disqualifying interest must be such as affects the member directly, and not as one of a class." The rule does not disqualify any delegate whose name is upon the roll from voting upon the contest of any other man's right. "Otherwise," Root pointed out, "any minority could secure control of a deliberative body by grouping a sufficient number of their opponents in one motion, and by thus disqualifying them, turn the minority into a majority, without any decision upon the merits of the motion."

The Roosevelt forces lost their motion by 567 to 507. Then as the separate cases of contesting State and district delegations were brought up, Hadley each time moved that the Taft delegates be unseated, the Roosevelt delegates substituted. Each time, the Roosevelt forces lost, by 569 to 499, by 564 to 497, and votes closely similar in numbers. The nearest the Roosevelt forces came to winning any contest was in the case of two California delegates, when the Roosevelt forces had 529 to the triumphant 542 of the Taft forces.

It was clear, and had been since the vote on permanent chairman, that the Taft forces had control of the convention.

Those of the Roosevelt leaders who had had hard-boiled experience, either political or parliamentary, knew well that once the Taft forces had secured control of the convention (through the action of the National Committee in deciding in favor of Taft contesting delegates) there was no parliamentary means by which they could be unseated. "The national committee," conceded an ardent Roosevelt partisan, George Ade, "fixed things so that they couldn't be unfixed by anything short of an earthquake."

VI

But the hope of the Roosevelt forces did not depend wholly, or even, at this stage of the contest, greatly, on their delegate strength or on success in unseating contested Taft delegates. Indeed, fully half the Roosevelt hope and objective, fully half the Roosevelt method of battle, was to convince the Taft leaders and especially the officials of the National Committee and the other custodians of the destinies of the Republican party, that Taft was the weaker candidate, Roosevelt the stronger one; that Taft if nominated could not win the election, that only Roosevelt could; that in the circumstances under which the contest had developed and in the pitch to which it had now come, millions of Republicans would vote for a Democrat rather than for Taft; that, as it was put, in effect, again and again, "you can nominate Taft, but only the people can elect him, and the people won't." Hadley, in the very midst of his technical legal argument against the right of the contested Taft delegates to their seats, interjected an irrelevance, not so much in deliberate shrewdness as in naïve expression of what was in his mind:

I do not know whether a majority of this Convention agrees with me that Theodore Roosevelt ought to be our candidate for President, but there can be no difference upon the proposition that he can command the support of more people, and he can lead a larger number of American voters in a cause for which he fights, than any other man.

VII

Only to a slight extent, however, did the Roosevelt leaders make this appeal in formal argument to the Taft

forces. They did not need to. The appeal, the proof of
Roosevelt's greater popularity, and of the disapprobation
into which Taft sank deeper each day came in spontaneous demonstrations from the crowds in the gallery,
from the milling masses in Chicago outside the convention walls, from every corner of the country. It came in
the infinitely varied forms to which spontaneity gives
birth; and the whole of it composed a characteristic picture of the American spirit, expressing itself at one moment in deeply earnest devotion to something the crowd
vaguely understood to be the "Spirit of Social and Industrial Justice," the next moment in such a fecund gamut
of humor and good-natured jeering as only the American spirit produces. The crowd had taken the fancy that
the operations of the Taft political machine, in the stolid
impassiveness with which it had gone about the business
of seating Taft delegates and casting out Roosevelt ones,
had a resemblance to a steam-roller. "Steam-roller,"
therefore, the management of the convention became,
with Root in the rôle of driver. Every time he rose to
make a decision, from a thousand vocal cords, bass and
tenor, alto and soprano, came a myriad imitations, each
with its individual over-tone of irony, of a steam-roller
getting under way, "toot, toot," followed, as the week
went on, by an imitation of steam escaping from a labor-
ing engine, achieved by rubbing two pieces of sand-paper
together — by the end of the convention there could
hardly have been a square inch of sand-paper left in any
Chicago shop. Whenever Root made a decision unpleasing to the Roosevelt partisans, their comment took a vocal form which would have led a visitor from Mars to
assume that some ten thousand persons had suddenly suffered a simultaneous and universal stomach-ache. When
Chairman Rosewater announced that the photograph
of the convention was about to be taken, and that the

photographer would be pleased if the crowd would look pleasant, a delegate expressed the loud opinion that it would be the first and last time. When Rabbi Joseph Stolz prayed that "the counsel of righteousness and truth of the everlasting God prevail over the waves of passion and the tumult of voices," an audible titter through the hall indicated lack of faith in the power of prayer. From time to time rumors went about that Roosevelt in person would come to the convention, that he would address the convention, that he would march down the aisles at the head of his followers and seize the convention by force, that he would grasp a moment when the hall was empty — three o'clock in the morning was the hour commonly assigned by this rumor — and would, with his followers, take possession of the hall, the platform, the gavel, and the other symbols, forms, and insignia of the Republican party. That particular one of the rumors caused the nervous managers of the Republican party to ask for an extra detail of police — additional to the 500 already employed — to guard the hall at times when its only occupants were the rats in the basement.

Once the crowd, or the nine-tenths of it that was for Roosevelt, merged itself into a remarkable mass demonstration, in which the precipitant was a young woman in the galleries, destined to be described minutely later by the newspapers as wearing a suit of cream-colored linen, a blue straw turban hat, and a bouquet of sweet peas, and as having a "radiant and infectious smile." She had been, during the morning, merely a face in the gallery, no more noticed than any other of the thousands of women who, in the genteel restraint of that day, confined their expressions of Roosevelt emotion mainly to decorous waving of their handkerchiefs. At one point, however, Mrs. Davis, moved by some incident to an exceptional exaltation, seized a poster of Roosevelt, leaned with it far over the edge of the gallery, and waved it in time with music the band happened to be playing. The

W. J. Bryan in the press seats, a sandwich in one hand.

crowd began to turn toward her; she, stimulated by the crowd, rose to a rare height and ingenuity of emotional leadership. Holding the Roosevelt poster at arm's length in one hand, she greeted it with her handkerchief in the other. In pantomime she coaxed the Taft leaders to be fair to her hero, holding out her hands in mute appeal, and expressing in her mobile features a gamut of appropriate manifestations of feminine winsomeness. By this time, the delegates, the crowd, and the band had turned to her leadership. Roosevelt delegates from California, bearing an immense golden bear that served at once as the State's emblem and as a Teddy-bear, went to the gallery, placed themselves behind Mrs. Davis, marched her up the aisles of the main floor with the Roosevelt State delegations and placards falling in line, and thrust her on an elevation occupied by the press. Under her spell the hall passed into an orgy of Roosevelt cheering that lasted forty-two minutes, throughout which by no means the least interesting spectacle was the features and manner of Mr. Root, and of his associates on the platform, faced with a development of political conventions not provided against by any paragraph in Jefferson's manual of parliamentary procedure. William Jennings Bryan, occupying a seat with the reporters, recorded in the following day's newspapers, that "It is only fair to the Taft delegates to say that they preserved a proper decorum during the entire performance, their faces wearing an expression suited to the occasion."

VIII

From the Roosevelt point-of-view, all was vain, and had been since the first parliamentary decision against them. Parliamentarily, the Taft forces controlled. As for persuasion or intimidation, neither beautiful women in the galleries nor catcalls from the crowd, neither hint of bolt nor certainty of Roosevelt's greater popularity, could move the Standpatter forces. They would rather lose the election, even destroy the Republican party, than let Roosevelt have the nomination. It was in terms of political death that all had come to think — death for the Republican party and for the two principals, Taft and Roosevelt. "The only question now," said Chauncey M. Depew, "is which corpse[16] gets the most flowers." Roosevelt, when he realized he could not win, an-

The birth of the new party.

nounced through Henry Allen of Kansas that the Roosevelt delegates would continue to sit in the convention but not vote nor otherwise participate. When the convention ended he called an informal meeting of his followers, announced a new party, the Progressives, and

[16] Some months after the election, at the funeral of Whitelaw Reid at Grace Church, New York, Roosevelt was present together with Taft accompanied by his Cabinet. At the end of the services, Taft was uncertain whether he should, according to the custom of the Presidency at ceremonies, leave first or follow the casket. Roosevelt, observing Taft's confusion, leaned toward a friend and said, "This is the first time I ever saw a competition for precedence between corpses."

perfected the organization of it at a new convention two months later. In the election he carried six States to Taft's two, got 4,117,813 votes to Taft's 3,486,316.

But the Democratic candidate, Woodrow Wilson, carried forty States, got 6,294,293 votes, and became President.

30

MEANING OF THE PROGRESSIVE MOVEMENT

WHAT was it all about? Apart from the personal aspect, apart from the wish of Roosevelt to be in the White House again and the wish of millions of Americans to have him there, what was the meaning of the Progressive party? What the fundamental difference, in terms of governmental policy, between the old Republican party and the new Progressive one? What, aside from the emotion generated by the angry epithets, "Socialist" hurled by one side, "reactionary" by the other — what differences of principle separated the two? What was decided when the Republicans controlled the convention, and what when the Progressives had the larger popular vote? And what would have been decided had the Republicans under Taft won the Presidency, or the Progressives under Roosevelt? And what was decided when the Democrats actually won it?

Only to a comparatively slight extent did the average man think of the conflict in terms of principle at all; he saw it mainly as a duel between personalities, Roosevelt on the one side, Taft on the other. More accurately, the issue was pro-Roosevelt and anti-Roosevelt; for Taft as a personality had no great magnetism, did not attract any large personal following — Taft's rôle in the fight was largely as a symbol for those who hated Roosevelt, or the smaller number who merely deplored him. The average man, indeed, did not so much *think* about any theories of government involved as *feel* the emotions stirred up by the slogans: those of odium, "standpatism,"

"Cannonism," "Aldrichism"; or those of altruism, "social and industrial justice." The average man in the mass, the whole of the America of that day, was divided — mainly by temperament, by differing responsiveness to certain appeals — into two groups; those whose eyes became rapt in the thrill of singing "Onward, Christian Soldiers" behind the banner of Roosevelt; and those who were indifferent to Roosevelt or were moved to acute distaste by his actions and utterances.

Most of the shouting and tumult was emotion and little more. By far the greater amount of the Roosevelt and Progressive speech-making and hymn-singing proceeded from and was aimed at those areas of the cerebellum where spinal tremors originate. Those portions of Senator Beveridge's keynote speech at the Progressive National Convention that were most effective in inspiring cheers — a delirious salvo at each semicolon — would have been difficult to parse in the austere terms of political economy or social philosophy: "We stand for a nobler America; we stand for an undivided Nation; we stand for a broader liberty, a fuller justice; we stand for social brotherhood as against savage individualism; we stand for intelligent co-operation instead of a reckless competition; we stand for mutual helpfulness instead of mutual hatred; we stand for equal rights as a fact of life instead of a catch-word of politics; we stand for the rule of the people as a practical truth instead of a meaningless pretense; we stand for a representative government that represents the people; we battle for the actual rights of man."

Just what did those eloquent affirmations mean in terms of concrete legislation? And when Roosevelt electrified the nation with his "We stand at Armageddon and we battle for the Lord," just what did the average man assume would be the consequence of winning the battle or losing it — other than that in one case Roosevelt would be in the White House and the air would

From a photograph by International.

Roosevelt returning from a campaign tour during the 1912 campaign.
On his right is Mrs. Roosevelt.

sparkle, while in the other Roosevelt would be at Oyster Bay and the world would be drab?

II

One clear difference of fundamental principle there was: The Progressive party and Roosevelt stood for the universal participation of all men and women in all the mechanisms of government (with very slight exceptions, if any). That was new, and far-reaching. Between that and the representative form of government supported by the Republicans, the difference was wide and deep, and the question of national policy thus laid before the country may possibly have been, as the excited disputants on both sides heatedly declared, the most important since the Civil War.

Direct popular government, as expressed in Roosevelt's sequence of "I believe's" in his "Charter of Democracy,"[1] embraced: direct primaries for the nomination of all party candidates for all offices, including, as respects candidates for President, direct preferential primaries in which the voter should instruct delegates as to the voter's choice; direct election of United States Senators by vote of the people — as distinct from the historic method of election by State legislatures; the initiative, whereby the people by petition could initiate laws, could, in effect, command the legislature to enact laws; and the referendum, whereby the people could pass upon laws enacted by the legislature; and the recall, whereby the people could by popular vote remove from office any official, including judges,[2] regardless of the length of term for which he had been elected.

As against that, the Republicans in their platform, with a manner of declining to dignify these upstart innovations by mentioning them, stood firm for the old

[1] This was the title Roosevelt gave in his speech before the Ohio constitutional convention at Columbus. See Chapter ***.
[2] Roosevelt qualified slightly his endorsement of the recall of judges.

way: "We believe in our self-controlled representative democracy."

One other deep-reaching difference of principle there was. Roosevelt and the Progressives believed in the "recall of judicial decisions" — that was Roosevelt's phrase in his Charter of Democracy speech. It is doubtful if any political term since "nullification" had so startled the nation. In part the shock was due to popular misunderstanding. When newspapers carried the phrase in headlines, great numbers of people understood Roosevelt to mean that immediately after any judicial decision in any sort of case, criminal trial for murder or civil case of trespass, the public would have the right immediately to act as a court of appeal. As the deeply shocked New York *Sun* put it: "Roosevelt proposed to establish on the street corners a higher court of law, the Court of Crowd, with supreme jurisdiction — the craziest proposal that ever emanated either from himself or from any other statesman. . . ."

Actually, Roosevelt meant only that in cases involving judicial interpretation of the Constitution the people should have a right to pass upon the decision: "I very earnestly ask you clearly to provide means which will permit the people themselves, by popular vote, after due deliberation and discussion, but finally and without appeal, to settle what the proper construction of any constitutional point is. When a judge decides a constitutional question, when he decides what the people as a whole can or cannot do, the people should have the right to recall that decision if they think it wrong."

Roosevelt's limited, actual meaning, as expressed in the text of his Charter of Democracy speech in February, was never able to catch up with the broader, incorrect meaning inferred by the public from the early news-

paper headlines. After trying to make his meaning
clear, and succeeding only in intensifying the opprobium
of the idea, he resigned himself to the rueful conclusion

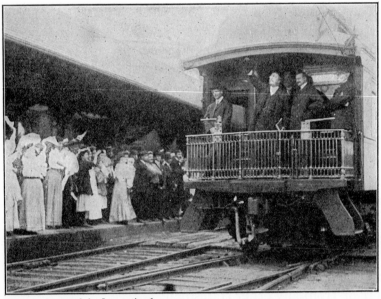

From a photograph by International.

Roosevelt making a rear-platform appearance during the 1912 campaign. This
sort of scene had been characteristic of American political campaigns for
a generation preceding 1912 and continued until 1932.

that it is a major error for a man in public life to fail to
make himself clear; by the time the Progressives were
ready to write their platform in August they were careful to state the idea with meticulous exactness — and
with avoidance of the fatal phrase:

The Progressive party demands such restriction of the power
of the courts as shall leave to the people the ultimate authority to determine fundamental questions of social welfare and
public policy. To secure this end, it pledges itself to provide:
That when an act passed under the police power of the state
is held unconstitutional under the state constitution by the
courts, the people, after an ample interval for deliberation,
shall have an opportunity to vote on the question whether

they desire the act to become law, notwithstanding such decision.

Against that the Republicans, in their platform, affirmed their unqualified support of

An untrammelled and independent judiciary. . . . The Republican party reaffirms its intention to uphold at all times the authority and integrity of the courts, both state and federal, and it will ever insist that their powers to enforce their process and to protect life, liberty, and property shall be preserved inviolate. . . . We regard the recall of judges as unnecessary and unwise.

There was yet another difference: The Republicans in their platform — though most of them hated to do it — endorsed the Sherman law making all trusts criminal, pointed with pride to having originated the law in 1889, congratulated themselves — with some polemic license — upon having "consistently and successfully" enforced it. The Progressives presented the country with a new attitude, advocating, not dissolution by prosecution but rather fostering through regulation:

We demand a strong national regulation of interstate corporations. We insist that [commercial power] shall be exercised openly, under public supervision and regulation of the most efficient sort which will preserve its good while eradicating and preventing its ill. To that end we urge the establishment of a strong federal administrative commission of high standing which shall maintain permanent active supervision over industrial corporations engaged in interstate commerce.[3]

Those three tenets of Progressive doctrine, direct participation of all voters in the processes of government, a

---

[3] An epitome of other Progressive policies included:

"We pledge ourselves to work unceasingly in state and nation for—

"Effective legislation looking to the prevention of industrial accidents, occupational diseases, overwork, involuntary unemployment, and other injurious effects incident to modern industry; the fixing of minimum safety and health standards for the various occupations, and the exercise of the public authority of state and nation, including the federal control over interstate commerce and the taxing power, to maintain such standards; the prohibition of child labor;

check by the people upon judicial interpretation of constitutions, and "constructive regulation of trusts instead of destructive litigation,"[4] would presumably have made progress had Roosevelt and the Progressives won the election of 1912. Yet it is by no means certain the public was strongly determined upon any or all; actually, during twenty years following, direct primaries made no progress but rather some recession, the recall of judicial decisions acquired no foothold whatever, and trusts in 1932 were treated the same as in 1912. And it is fairly certain that whatever change Roosevelt, had he been elected, might have made along any of these lines would have been unimportant compared to the consequences of his directing the country with respect to the Great War.

The War, lurking just ahead in the corridor of years, utterly unanticipated in 1912, gave a new tangent to everything, making it impossible to say and futile to guess what might have been the future of the Progressive movement in a normal world.

---

minimum wage standards for working women; to provide a 'living wage' in all industrial occupations; the general prohibition of night work for women, and the establishment of an eight-hour day for women and young persons; one day's rest in seven for all wage-workers; the eight-hour day in continuous twenty-four hour industries."

One observes that in neither the Progressive platform which combed the world for issues upon which to take a position, nor in the Republican platform equally wide-garnering in its inclusion of questions of public interest—in neither did there appear the word "Prohibition," destined within a few years to be the most controversial subject that bedevilled platform makers.

4 This is a paraphrase of a dictum of James R. Garfield.

1909-1913

1909

The Coming of a New Hero, Jack Binns. We Withdraw from Cuba, Again. Prohibition Captures Indiana. New Transatlantic Records, and New Achievements in Human Flight. Death of Edward H. Harriman. Cardinal Gibbons on Prohibition. The Hudson-Fulton Celebration. The "Hobble Skirt." A. Lawrence Lowell Succeeds Charles W. Eliot as President of Harvard. Books and Plays of 1909.

January 23. The steamship *Florida* rammed the steamship *Republic* amidship in a blind fog off Nan-

From a photograph by Brown Brothers.

The S. S. *Florida* making for port under her own steam after sinking the *Republic*.

tucket. Three passengers of the *Republic* and three seamen of the *Florida* were killed at the moment of impact. Thereafter, due to the discipline of the two

541

crews and to the fact that the *Republic* was equipped
with wireless and had a cool and resourceful radio operator, there was no further loss of life, no serious injuries,
no panic. The ramming opened a deep gash in the side
of the *Republic*, which let the sea into her engine-room,
but because of her airtight compartments—like wire-

From a photograph by Brown Brothers.

Jack Binns.

less, another innovation—she did not sink at once. The
bow of the *Florida* was crumpled back for thirty feet,
but she was able to keep afloat and later made her way
into port under her own steam.

The accident gave to the world a new hero in the person of Jack Binns, wireless operator of the *Republic*.
Although Binns's wireless outfit was damaged by the impact of the collision, and his current cut off by the stoppage of the *Republic's* engines following the flooding of
the engine-room, he made repairs and, connecting up a
battery for power, was within ten minutes after the acci-

dent occurred sending out the distress call of the sea. He was heard and soon ships within a radius of two hundred miles were steaming to the rescue.

Crew and passengers of the *Republic*, with the exception of Captain Sealby, were transferred to the *Florida*. Captain Sealby stayed with his ship until it sank and was then picked up with the aid of searchlights after half an hour in the water. The first of the rescue ships, the *Baltic*, reached the scene of the accident thirty-eight hours after it occurred and took aboard the passengers of both the *Republic* and the *Florida* and the crew of the former.

January 28. Major-General José Miguel Gomez was inaugurated President of Cuba. Charles E. Magoon, American provisional governor, left Havana for the United States. All American troops were retired by March 31. This, the second American military occupation of Cuba, had its beginning in the collapse of President Palma Estrada's administration in 1906.

February 22. The world cruise of sixteen American battleships under Rear Admiral Sperry ended at Hampton Roads.

March 17. Prohibition suffered a setback with the decision of the Federal Circuit Court in Richmond, Virginia, that shipments of liquor into "dry" territory on bona fide orders were legal.

March. A strong prohibition movement was sweeping over the State of Indiana. Daily, county after county, sometimes four or five in a single day, were added to the "dry" column. By the tenth of March more than fifty of the State's ninety-two counties had ousted the saloon, while only one had voted "wet."

April 28. After remaining unnoticed for nearly a century beneath the soil of an obscure Maryland farm, the body of Major Pierre Charles l'Enfant, the French engineer who remodelled the City Hall in New York and was chosen by Washington to plan the city of Washington, was removed to Arlington National Cemetery. He had had the vision to foresee America's future and had planned a city worthy of it. It is a tribute to his

The *Mauretania.*

genius that the success achieved in the development of the nation's capital have come from the faithful following of his noble plans.

May 3. The first wireless messages were sent between New York and Chicago. In March wireless telephone messages were sent by Lee DeForest from the Eiffel Tower in Paris to Marseilles, a distance of 550 miles. The experimenters in wireless telephony predicted that in the not far distant future it would be possible to telephone across the Atlantic.

May 10. The *Mauretania* broke the Atlantic record eastward, making the run from the Ambrose lightship to Daunt's Rock in four days, eighteen hours, and eleven minutes. On September 20, she ended a trip that broke this record, arriving at Queenstown in four days, thirteen hours, and forty-one minutes out from New York. On September 2, the westward record was broken, by the Cunarder *Lusitania* (later sunk by the Germans during

From a photograph by Brown Brothers.

Edward Payson Weston.

the Great War). Time: four days, eleven hours, forty-two minutes.

July 14. Edward Payson Weston completed a walk from New York to San Francisco, covering 3,895 miles in 105 days and five hours.

July 25. A bench-mark of history: Louis Bleriot, French aeronaut, crossed the English Channel in his white-winged airplane, circled twice above Dover, and settled gracefully to earth. For the first time a traveller had reached Britain who did not come by water. Bleriot's feat was the most widely proclaimed air victory until Lindbergh flew to Paris in 1927.

July 27. In an endurance-test flight at Fort Myer, Orville Wright made a new world's record for an airplane carrying a passenger, remaining in the air one hour, twelve minutes, and forty seconds.

August 7. The Lincoln penny, designed by Victor D. Brenner, was issued by the Philadelphia Mint, replacing the familiar copper coin bearing the Indian head, which had been in circulation for fifty years.

August. Two New York school boys, Walter Drew and John Munnich, accompanied by the Rev. A. A. King and J. J. Conway, made a trip around the world in forty-one days and eight hours. Nellie Bly had made the trip in sixty-seven days in 1890 and for years this stood as a remarkable achievement.

September 9. Edward Henry Harriman, railroad magnate, died. The New York *World:*

Born February 25, 1848.

His birthplace—a little frame parsonage attached to St. George's Episcopal Church at Hempstead, L. I.

His deathbed — in the heart of a palace atop a mountain of his own at Arden, Orange County, N. Y.

At the start — a penniless boy, son of a poorly paid preacher.

At the end — worth $50,000,000 to $100,000,000; a national and international figure of consequence; the peer of any man living in the game of railroad finance.

His education — two years in church schools.

At sixteen he obtained his first job, which was as office boy in a brokerage house in Wall Street.

At eighteen he was a clerk with a share in the profits of his employers.

At twenty-two he bought a seat on the Stock Exchange with $20,000. He quickly earned the reputation of being one of the most parsimonious floor traders on the Exchange.

At twenty-five he married Miss Mary Averill, of Rochester, daughter of a banker of large means.

At thirty-five he was worth $1,000,000 and made his debut as a railway man, becoming a director of the Illinois Central.

At forty he became vice-president of the Illinois Central.

At fifty he undertook the reorganization of the Union Pacific, in the face of the failure of J. P. Morgan's attempt.

At sixty he realized the ambition of his career — an ocean-to-ocean railway system under his personal control.

Much but not all of the comment evoked by Harriman's death was eulogistic. The Springfield *Republican*, while admitting Harriman's genius, declared:

There are countries where Mr. Harriman would never have been heard of, save as an unscrupulous gambler in stocks. But the American system of private ownership and operation of the highways of commerce made possible that extraordinary Harriman decade which has culminated so dramatically

Edward Henry Harriman.

in his recent return from Europe to die, with the entire financial world feverishly awaiting the bulletins from the sick man's chamber. . . . Unmoral he was, if not immoral, and the end was everything, the means nothing, to his restless and boundless ambition for achievement and aggrandizement. . . . It may be suspected that in those last years he got glimpses of the American people that told him a new era was in the dawning. It will be an era in which men of his type will shrivel and disappear, since the public interest is in the future to dominate the field of natural monopoly rather than private gain.

September 13. "Prohibitionists all over the country," Cardinal Gibbons told a confirmation class at Baltimore, "are making an effort to suppress the use of intoxicating liquors, and while I hope they will succeed, I don't think they will. Reform must come from within and not from without. You cannot legislate for virtue."

September 25. The opening day of the Hudson-Fulton Celebration in New York. The Celebration commemorated the 300th anniversary of the arrival of Hen-

The *Clermont* proceeding up the river under her own steam, greeted by salutes from the line of warships during the Hudson-Fulton Celebration.

drik Hudson and the 100th anniversary of the work of Robert Fulton. The opening naval parade was led by the replica of Hudson's *Half Moon* and a reproduction of Fulton's *Clermont*. As the *Half Moon* breasted her way down the bay under tow, she was in full view of two homely shacks on Governors Island in which were sheltered the airplanes of Wilbur Wright and Glenn H. Curtiss. Her swell washed at once the giant hull of the incoming *Lusitania*, one of the two greatest ships of commerce at that time afloat, and the iron sides of the great British and German war squadrons shouldering their way to their anchorages. The history of three centuries of development, the revolutionary influence of steam and steel on shipbuilding, were written in an instant in the contrasting vessels assembled in the harbor.

Of the deeper significance, symbolically and histori-

The *Half Moon* at the time of the marine parade on the Hudson.

cally, of the celebration, the very able editor of *World's Work*, Walter Hines Page, wrote:[1]

The rebuilding of Hudson's *Half Moon* and of Fulton's *Clermont*, and the appearance on them of persons in the dress of the period of each; the dazzling effects on land and on water of artistic designs and devices in electric light; the amazing achievements in decorative illumination by electricity; the aptness that we are showing in the representation of pageantry of historical events; the comprehensiveness of collections of all kinds, from great paintings to historical curiosities; most of all, our returning love of color and form — these things show a capacity for enjoyment and a certain merriness of temperament that have not always been characteristic of American life. We wore black clothes and lived in square, white houses and frowned on dancing and most other graceful and gleeful things; we had little music; and we thought little of form — for a long time in our national life. But we are passing that somewhat gloomy era, without loss, too, to sturdiness of character and surely with great gain to the adornment of life.

September. The "hobble skirt," strange whim of aberrant fashion, clumsy, ugly, a hindrance to its wear-

[1] *World's Work*, November, 1909.

er's locomotion, was lampooned ingeniously by Mabel E.
Brooks in *Puck:*

> Hipless, curveless, long and lanky,
>   Is the girl of nineteen nine;
> Wouldn't you be cross and cranky
>   With
>   a
>   form
>   j u s t
>   l i k e
>   t h i s
>   l i n e
>   ?
> Foolish virgins change their figures
>   At Dame Fashion's wild caprice;
> Uncomplaining, bear the rigueurs;
>   Dreaming, tho, of night's release!

A far more praiseworthy innovation in women's raiment than the hobble skirt was the growing use of bloomers by women instructors of gymnasium classes in the
vacation playgrounds of the cities. Seemingly this
healthful and common-sense custom had everything to
recommend it; nevertheless, there were many to con-
demn.   In New York City, Doctor Edward E. Bruce,
heading a committee of inspection of the Board of Education, told reporters, after a visit to the playgrounds,
that he was shocked by what he had seen.   He considered bloomers "unnecessary and unladylike, giving the
children a false notion."   Young women should wear
bloomers only in a gymnasium, he said, as it was not
proper to wear them where men were.

October 6. Abbot Lawrence Lowell was inaugurated
President of Harvard University, succeeding Doctor
Charles W. Eliot.   The New York *Sun* editorialized:

[He] fulfills the most rigid conditions which the most august
member of the corporation could require. He is of the Brah-
min caste; he is distinguished in letters; he has had experi-

Abbot Lawrence Lowell, President of Harvard University.

ence in financial affairs and administrative boards; he is an
inheritor of reasonable wealth, one of the class of Bostonians
who devote themselves to the public in general and to Harvard
in particular. He is a public speaker of force and distinction,
even if he cannot equal that admirable lucidity of style which
President Eliot has made for himself. Finally, and this may be
preached to the undergraduates in mitigation of his intelligence and his accomplishments, he was a mighty runner in
his youth.

December 5. One of the big locomotives on the Pennsylvania Railroad, in a test, made a fraction more than
ninety-nine miles an hour, the world's record for steam
locomotives. On December 6, an electric locomotive
belonging to the New York, New Haven and Hartford

Railroad, known as the Jamestown Exposition engine, travelled at the rate of ninety-two miles an hour at Clayton, N. J.

December 26. Frederic Remington died, at the age

© *1909 by Frederic Remington.*

"The Luckless Hunter," by Frederic Remington.

of forty-eight, following an operation for appendicitis. *Life* paid him this tribute:

Frederic Remington used to say: "When I die, put on my tombstone, 'He knew the horse.'"

Mr. Remington is dead — sad to say. He knew the horse, and much more — the cowboy, the red Indian, the cavalryman, the frontiersman, the red soil of some parts of the West, the look of the sage brush, the mountains, the sky.

He was full of talent and capacity. His death, so much before its natural time, is a very serious loss to art, and, in a way,

John Fox, Jr.   Richard Harding Davis.

Two writers of the period.

to history. The consolation is that he had done so much. While we still had a mid-western frontier he studied it, and now that it is pretty much gone its scenes and activities will be best realized and remembered by Remington's pictures.

December. Father John B. Tabb, Southerner, Catholic priest, poet, died. His best known poem was:

EVOLUTION

Out of the dusk a shadow,
    Then a spark;
Out of the cloud a silence,
    Then a lark;
Out of the heart a rapture,
    Then a pain;
Out of the dead, cold ashes,
    Life again.

The Books of 1909

"Peter," by F. Hopkinson Smith. . . . "The Testing of Diana Mallory," by Mrs. Humphry Ward. . . .

"The Red City," by S. Weir Mitchell. . . . Two books by George Barr McCutcheon "The Man from Brodney's" and "Truxton King." . . . "Out-of-Doors in the Holy Land," by Henry van Dyke. . . . "Septimus," by William J. Locke. . . . "The Missioner," by E. Phillips Oppenheim. . . . "The Red Mouse," by William H. Osborne. . . . "54–40 or Fight," by Emerson Hough. . . . "The Man in Lower Ten," by Mary Roberts Rinehart. . . . "Katrina," by Elinor M. Lane. . . . "The Bronze Bell," by Louis Joseph Vance. . . . "The Chippendales," by Robert Grant. . . . "The Story of Thyrza," by Alice Brown. . . . "The Goose Girl," by Harold MacGrath. . . . "The Romance of a Plain Man," by Ellen Glasgow. Of Ellen Glasgow *The North American Review* said: "There is no exaggeration in saying that what Thomas Hardy has done for the folk of the south of England, Ellen Glasgow has done for Virginia." . . . "Mr. Opp," by Alice Hegan Rice, which Annie Russell Marble said "has sustained insight and charm." . . . "The White Sister," by F. Marion Crawford. . . . "The Bride of the Mistletoe," by James Lane Allen. . . . "The White Mice," by Richard Harding Davis. . . . "The Silver Horde," by Rex Beach. . . . "A Certain Rich Man," by William Allen White. Two thousand five hundred persons out of the total population of ten thousand in Emporia, Kansas, White's home town, bought copies of this big outstanding novel, as a proof of loyalty and affection for its author. . . . "The Danger Mark," by Robert W. Chambers. . . . "The Calling of Dan Matthews," by Harold Bell Wright. . . . "Bella Donna," by Robert Hichens. . . . "Trail of the Lonesome Pine," by John Fox, Jr. *The Review of Reviews* said "Three things can be said of all Mr. Fox's novels: They are strong; they are clean, they are never dull." . . . "Lewis Rand," by

Mary Johnston, who "wrote the history of Virginia in romances."

The Theatre in 1909

"The Passing of the Third Floor Back," "supremely excellent, unconventional and wholesome," with Forbes Robertson, most distinguished member of the English-

From a photograph by Pach Brothers.

Clyde Fitch, dramatist.

speaking theatre, opened in New York October 4. Robertson's acting, said *The Theatre*, "was strangely beautiful, wondrously delicate and convincing, but the play is not a play; it is a succession of sermons." . . . John Barrymore, not yet having joined the motion pictures, was playing in the Gaiety Theatre in a comedy called "The Fortune Hunter." . . . "Texas" Guinan, who twenty years later was to achieve to a kind of international renown because of certain qualities of her diamond-like

Montgomery and Stone in the "Wizard of Oz." The chorus of this period wore stockings or tights.

personality (and also because of her greeting to patrons of the cabarets over which she presided as hostess, "Hello, Sucker!"), was reported in the theatrical journals to be winning a modest success playing one-night stands in the West in a musical comedy called "The Gay Musician." . . . A problem play, the best in its field, was "A Man's World," written by a woman, with a woman as its chief exponent. . . . From France came Mme. Yvette Guilbert, flower of the Parisian concert halls, to sing her French and English ballads at the Colonial Theatre in New York. "She appears in a Victorian gown, with short white gloves and with her auburn hair dressed in curls." Mme. Guilbert practiced at her art nine hours a day, so she said, which assiduity doubtless contributed something to her continuing mastery over audiences; so great was her skill that all laughed with her or cried with her, or did whatever she would have them do. . . . A blow to the American stage was the death of Clyde Fitch, dramatist, at Chalons-Sur-Marne, France, September 4, age 44. Fitch, most prolific of American playwrights, wrote 60 plays, and at the time of his death three new pieces from his pen, "The City," "The Manicure Girl," and "Modern Marriage," were

Lillian Russell.

in rehearsal. He early recognized the value and beauty of technique; never posed as a genius superior to his art. In an interview he said: "I wrote 'Beau Brummel' when I was twenty-three, but soon learned from Mr. Mansfield that I didn't know anything about technique." In the interval between the production of "Beau Brummel" and the "Moth and the Flame" and "Nathan Hale," which plays first established him, he passed a number of years without further recognition or reward, and these

years he devoted to the study of the drama. The critic
of *The Theatre* in just praise said that in Fitch's handling of detail "he has perhaps not been surpassed by any
writer of any time." . . . Miss Lillian Russell appeared
in "The Widow's Might," opening September 14. Miss
Russell was — well, Lillian Russell, as audiences had
known her for years; her beauty and her charm as an
actress were unchanging. . . . "The Wizard of Oz"
played on; its author, L. Frank Baum, attempting to explain why it should survive and maintain its popularity
for almost ten years, said he had written it "as a child's
book three years before it was put on as a play." . . .
1909 and thereabouts was the heyday of prosperity for
the theatre and for some playwrights. Hall Caine's
drama, "The Christian," brought him, for two seasons,
an average of $1,800 in royalties per week; for the third
season, $1,000 per week. Two companies played it the
fourth season and brought him about $800 a week. In
all, it earned for him more than $250,000. "The Music
Master" and "The Lion and the Mouse" earned over
$100,000 for their author, Charles Klein, in a year.

Edmund Breese in "The Lion and the Mouse."

1910

Mark Twain Dies. Halley's Comet Passes the Sun. The Glidden Tour. Johnson Beats Jeffries, to the Enrichment of the Vernacular. Censoring the Movies. Ladies Take to the Cigarette. Settlement of the Newfoundland Fisheries Dispute. Dynamiting of the Los Angeles *Times*. Woodrow Wilson Elected Governor of New Jersey. Mary Baker Glover Eddy Dies. Progress in Aviation. Amundsen Reaches the South Pole. Prohibition Marches On. Books and Plays.

January 1. State-wide prohibition went into effect in Tennessee.

March 2. A bill was introduced in the Senate providing for the incorporation of a "Rockefeller Foundation" to which, it was announced, John D. Rockefeller would donate more than $100,000,000, to be administered under government supervision for general humanitarian purposes. A few Senators manifested a fear that if the charter were granted, the Foundation would be a threat to the welfare of the country, and the bill was withdrawn.

April 21. Samuel Langhorne Clemens (Mark Twain) died at Redding, Conn., aged 74. President Woodrow Wilson, of Princeton, wrote a tribute of affection:

All the world knows that in Mark Twain it has lost a delightful humorist, a man able to interpret human life with a flavor all his own; but only those who had the privilege of knowing him personally can feel the loss to the full — the loss of a man of high and lovely character, a friend quick to excite and give affection; a citizen of the world, who loved every wholesome adventure of the mind or heart; an American who spoke much of the spirit of America in speaking his native thoughts.

April 25. President Taft appointed Governor Charles E. Hughes of New York to the Supreme Court to succeed Justice Brewer, deceased.

May 18. Halley's comet passed the sun, but there were no signs of the earth's passage through its tail, as had been predicted. Many lurid articles had been published in the newspapers, telling of the dire things that might happen to the earth when it passed through a million miles of the comet's tail at a speed of 2,500 miles a minute, and these had filled the ignorant and the superstitious with apprehension. With the coming of dusk people on lonely farms in the West betook themselves to their cyclone cellars, and in the industrial centres the bulk of foreign workmen stayed at home, believing that their last day on earth should be spent with their families. New York City, according to *The World*, was disappointed at the lack of fireworks:

The town had prepared itself for a new sensation. It was keyed up to a high pitch of expectancy at the prospect of being sprinkled with star-dust, and the possibility of being smothered by noxious gases or bombarded by meteorites lent a keener zest to the interest. But the show did not come off, and New York went home feeling that it had been buncoed. . . .

June 16. The Senate passed a bill, approved by President Taft four days later, enabling New Mexico and Arizona to form state constitutions and governments.

June 25. The eleven contesting cars remaining in the Glidden Tour out of the thirty that started left Chicago for Kansas City. Those still in the contest were two Premiers, two Chalmerses, two Maxwells, one Cino, one Lexington, two Molines, and one Ohio. This list is a commentary on the quickness of change in American industry; not one of the makes represented was still being manufactured in 1932.

July 4. Jack Johnson, ex-Galveston stevedore, heavyweight prize-fight champion of the world, defeated

James J. Jeffries in fifteen rounds at Reno, Nev. Jeffries' share of the "gate" was $50,400, Johnson's $70,-
600. "Tex" Rickard was the promoter. There was not
much cheering. It was not particularly brutal; there

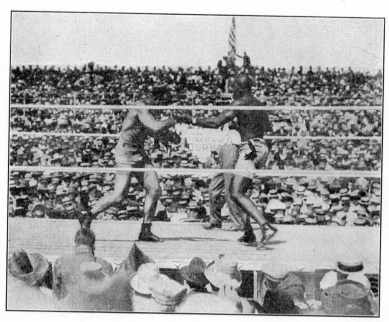

The Jeffries-Johnson fight at Reno.

was neither malice nor hate in it. Johnson comported
himself skillfully and good-naturedly and Jeffries took
his beating like a man. The crowd sympathized with
Jeffries and had no enthusiasm for the victorious negro.

Johnson's mother, "Tiny" Johnson, sat on the stage
of a colored theatre in Chicago during the fight listening
to bulletins from the ringside. When the announcement
came that her son had won, her mother's pride led her
to make an observation which had the unlooked-for result of enriching the vernacular with a slang phrase so
pithy and so expressive that in 1932, twenty-two years
after it was uttered, it was embedded in the common

speech and gave promise, because of its enduring vitality, of out-living the most weighty pronouncement of the most eminent public men of the day: "He said he'd *bring home the bacon*, and the honey boy has gone and did it."

Because of the crusade against the fight, before it was held, by church people, and of the race friction afterward — there were several small riots — conclusions were drawn as to the future of prize fighting that turned out to be completely at variance with the facts. Confidently didactic, John L. Sullivan, dean of the heavyweights, predicted: "It will probably be the last big fight in this country." To which the periodical *Life* agreed:[1] "We have outgrown prize fights; that's all there is of it. The next one — if there ever is another big one — will follow the lottery to Mexico or some other nearby country, where sentiment on this subject has not yet crystallized."

July 20. A state-wide movement to abolish the exhibition of all motion pictures of "improper tone" was started by the Christian Endeavor Societies of Missouri. It was proposed to put the ban on "spooning" scenes and on films that depicted kissing on the part of any except relatives or married persons.

July 22. The report that Mrs. Alice Longworth smoked cigarettes caused a lively discussion among the members of a well-known Pittsburgh woman's club. It was ended, rather abruptly, when a prominent Daughter of the American Revolution arose and said: "We needn't all get up our feathers simply because Mrs. Longworth smokes cigarettes. Why, a hundred years ago our great-grandmothers sat with their husbands and smoked corn-cob pipes."

August 9. Mayor Gaynor of New York was shot by a discharged Dock Department employee on the Atlantic

[1] July 21, 1910.

From a photograph by Brown Brothers.

Mayor Gaynor on his customary morning walk across Brooklyn Bridge from his home to his office in City Hall, New York.

liner on which the Mayor was about to sail for Europe.

September 7. Five judges of the International Court of Arbitration at The Hague handed down a decision in the Newfoundland Fisheries case. Since 1783, fisheries problems had come up from time to time. Because of disputes arising under the British-American treaty of 1818, Elihu Root, when Secretary of State, asked for arbitration. This decision settled the discussion: it gave to Americans the right to take on necessary water and buy bait in Newfoundland, unhampered by local laws

and restrictions, and it provided for a commission to settle disputes over fishing regulations.

October 1. Nineteen persons were killed in a fire following an explosion which wrecked the plant of the Los
Angeles *Times*. During the same day bombs were found

The Los Angeles *Times* Building after the explosion.

under the houses of General Harrison Gray Otis, owner
of the newspaper, and the secretary of the Merchants'
Association. As *The Times*, General Otis, and the Merchants' Association had for years waged a bitter fight
against the labor-unions, the charge was made that labor
was behind all three outrages. On the day following the
destruction of its building, *The Times* said:

The union has struck. The great coup consists of broken
hearts of innocent workers. That is all. The rest is as nothing.
Nothing has been accomplished except to give the world one
more example of the insane murderous folly of the rabid labor-
unions. . . . The devils in human form who murdered and
maimed the men employed in its news and mechanical depart-

ments, will not escape. Ropes are dangling for them and prison
doors are yawning for them. With all their cunning, traces of
their work are picked up every hour. There is no quarter of the
earth to which they can flee, where they will not be followed
and from which they will not be returned.

Labor leaders denied that they were responsible. They
suggested that "faulty gas mains . . . due entirely to

The McNamara brothers charged with the bombing of the Los Angeles *Times.*
Samuel Gompers is standing between them.

the unsanitary condition of *The Times* plant," had
caused the explosion. One union official even charged
that General Otis had himself blown up his own newspaper with the object of casting odium on the unions.
Organized labor itself offered a reward of $7,500 for
the arrest of the perpetrators.

November 8. Woodrow Wilson, having resigned as
President of Princeton University on October 20, 1910,
won his first election to a public office, the Governorship
of New Jersey.

November 19. Count Leo Tolstoy died peacefully at Astapova in his eighty-third year. He was taken ill on his journey to the Caucasus, where he hoped to spend his last days close to the Tolstoyan colony on the shores of the Black Sea.

December 3. Mary Baker Glover Eddy, founder of Christian Science, died aged ninety at her home in a Boston suburb. Throughout the latter part of her long life she was a lodestone for criticism.

December 14. Captain Roald Amundsen, Norwegian explorer, reached the South Pole.

December. Nineteen ten was a year of triumphs and of tragedies in aviation. A number of record-breaking flights were made, two of them in the United States. There were more than thirty fatalities throughout the world, three American aviators being on the list. On the last day of the year two of the country's most famous flyers, "Arch" Hoxsey and John B. Moisant, were killed, the former at Los Angeles and the latter at New Orleans. On August 27, J. D. A. McCurdy sent the first wireless message ever transmitted from a plane in flight and received by a land station. On June 13, Charles K. Hamilton flew from New York to Philadelphia and back, alighting at Philadelphia and at South Amboy, where a broken propeller delayed him. The total distance covered was 175 miles and the total elapsed time was eleven hours and four minutes, of which three hours and thirty-four minutes were spent in the air. On September 30, Claude Grahame-White, the English aviator, won the international trophy at Belmont Park by beating the world's aviation speed record. He travelled sixty-two miles at an average speed of sixty-one miles an hour. By his feat he earned $5,000 and won the James Gordon Bennett trophy for the Royal Aero Club of the United Kingdom. Glenn H. Curtiss flew from Albany to New York City, where he won a prize of $10,000 offered by the New York *World:*

At[2] 5 A.M., [May 29] Curtiss left his hotel, ate breakfast at a quick-lunch counter, donned a life-preserver, and getting into his airplane rose seven hundred feet above the roofs of Albany. At Poughkeepsie, seventy-five miles away, he descended to replenish his gasoline tank, landing on the front

From a photograph by H. M. Benner.

Curtiss ready for Albany to New York flight, 1910.

lawn of Farmer Gill, a friend of his. Before leaving Albany he had telegraphed Gill to have a supply of fuel ready but the telegram hadn't travelled as fast as he had and there was no gasoline. This lack was remedied by borrowing a few gallons from a motorist and again Curtiss took to the air. . . . From Poughkeepsie south the Hudson flows through the Highlands, from whose valleys and hills vicious, eccentric gusts swoop down on the river. Into this dangerous region Curtiss flew his frail craft. From right and left sudden gusts assailed him. A dozen times he escaped disaster by an eyelash. Something went wrong and he began to lose oil. Just as the oil-gauge sank to the danger point he came within sight of the Metropolitan Tower in New York. He was able to keep going long

2 Condensed from a contemporary newspaper despatch.

enough to land in Manhattan. He took off again at 11:42, blowing off the hats of onlookers and entirely upsetting one small boy, and 18 minutes later came down beside his shed on Governors Island in New York Bay.

The Books of 1910

Most popular among this year's novels, according to *The Bookman*, were "The Rosary," by Mrs. Florence

Frances Hodgson Burnett.

Booth Tarkington.

Barclay (by 1928, half a million copies had been sold); "A Modern Chronicle," by Winston Churchill; "The Wild Olive," anonymous; and "When a Man Marries," by Mary Roberts Rinehart. Better than any of these, if less popular as determined by copies sold, was Robert Hichens' lovely "Bella Donna," William De Morgan's "It Can Never Happen Again." Other "best sellers" were "Truxton King" (published in 1909), by George Barr McCutcheon; "The Silver Horde," by Rex Beach;

"Tower of Ivory," by Gertrude Atherton; "The House of Whispering Pines," by Anna Katherine Green; "Ailsa Page," by Robert W. Chambers. . . . In 1910, according to John O'Hara Cosgrave, there were eight American writers in what he called the thousand-dollar class — that is, who were in a position to ask one thousand dollars for a story of five thousand words, or thereabouts, a rate of twenty cents a word. These were Robert W. Chambers, Richard Harding Davis, Booth Tarkington, Jack London, John Fox, Jr., Owen Wister, and Frances Hodgson Burnett. . . . A distinguished fall book was Arnold Bennett's "Clayhanger," the first of a trilogy. Its length, 700 pages, was a sad handicap in a time which knew not leisurely reading. The dearth of outstanding books in this and preceding years caused *The Dial* to lament:

Literature, if not on the verge of bankruptcy, is at least threatened by an impairment of credit for which the natural remedy would be a drastic overhauling of its securities and a general retrenchment in most directions. There are no evident signs that this remedy is likely to be applied. The number of people who write flimsy novels and perpetrate bad poems and bad plays goes on steadily increasing, and the number of editors and publishers who encourage these misguided persons seems to grow at nearly the same rate. . . .
During the last half-century the world has passed through one of the golden ages of literature; but the age in which we now live is at best one of silver, if not one of lead or plated metal. The most enthusiastic spokesman of modernity would not claim for the best score of living writers anything like a parity of importance with the best score of those whose deaths we have been called upon to chronicle with such painful frequency since 1880.

The Theatre in 1910

Douglas Fairbanks, an actor renowned, in addition to many other accomplishments, for his ability to spring from the centre of a stage to a balcony or other foothold seemingly well beyond the reach of human muscles, opened, November 1, in a clever farce, "The Cub," by Thompson Buchanan. A contemporary account said that

From a photograph by Moffett in the "Theatre Magazine," 1913.

Douglas Fairbanks and his son (1913).

"the lines are witty and lose nothing when spoken by Mr. Fairbanks, who gave a performance marked by a rare sense of humor, naturalness, and sincerity." . . . In late September, Marie Dressler celebrated the 300th performance of "Tillie's Nightmare" at the Herald Square Theatre in New York; an advertisement prom-

ised "souvenirs for the ladies." . . . The musical
comedy, "The Chocolate Soldier," also passed the 300-
mark. . . . Both records were excelled by Forbes-
Robertson who on March 7 played his 500th perform-

From a photograph by Keystone View Company.

Douglas Fairbanks and his son, Douglas Fairbanks, Jr., in 1932.

ance in "The Passing of the Third Floor Back." . . .
In the spring Ben Greet and his players produced Sheri-
dan's "The Rivals." . . . A much-discussed event was
the staging of Puccini's opera, "The Girl of the Golden
West," on December 10, at the Metropolitan Opera
House; the opera was based on the drama which won

great success as a production of David Belasco. . . .
Ethel Barrymore, having become a convert to woman
suffrage, was reported to have cabled her manager,
Charles Frohman, in London, asking permission to take

From a photograph by White.

Enrico Caruso in "The Girl of the Golden West."

part in three plays Miss Beatrice Forbes-Robertson was
arranging to be given "for the cause." . . . In early
December Sam Bernard celebrated his 150th performance of "He Came From Milwaukee." . . . In "The
Fortune Hunter" John Barrymore found a comedy "perfectly suited to his agreeable personality and dramatic

scope." . . . "Your Humble Servant," by Booth Tarkington and Harry Leon Wilson, gave Otis Skinner a part well fitted to his "excellent elocution and graceful, florid style."

Forbes-Robertson and Haidee Wright in "The Passing of the Third Floor Back."

1911

Some "Firsts" in the New Art of Aviation. Mexico Flounders in Revolution. The Supreme Court Dissolves the Standard Oil Trust — and Stocks Rise. Governor Woodrow Wilson Shows Serious Concern over the "Money Trust." "Mona Lisa" Disappears from the Louvre. Kaiser Wilhelm Celebrates a Birthday. Books and Plays of 1911.

January 26. San Diego, Calif.: For the first time in the history of aviation an airplane rose from the surface of the water, sailed about and returned to the starting point, where it settled on the water as easily as a gull. The feat was achieved by Glenn H. Curtiss. Another milestone in aviation was passed March 1, when for the first time a man leaped from an aeroplane (at Jefferson Barracks, St. Louis), and descended safely to earth in a parachute. Captain Albert Berry made the spectacular leap of 1,200 feet.

January 27. To Emperor William of Germany, celebrating his fifty-second birthday, President Taft sent congratulations, expressing "the good will that this government and people bear for your country." The day was celebrated with great pomp at the embassy in Washington, Ambassador and Countess von Bernstorff receiving about 400 guests. In honor of the anniversary Admiral von Tirpitz was promoted to be Admiral of the German fleet.

March 1. Superior Judge William P. Lawlor committed Abraham Ruef, one-time "boss" of San Francisco, to the San Quentin penitentiary for a term of fourteen years for the bribing of Supervisor John J. Furey.

March 7. Twenty thousand American troops were ordered to the Mexican border of Texas. Throughout all

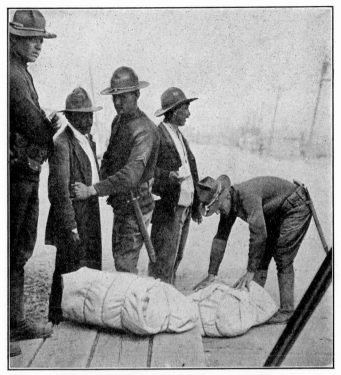

Photograph © Underwood and Underwood.
U. S. Troops on the border searching incoming Mexicans for arms.

this year conditions in Mexico continued chaotic. Fighting between Federals and irregulars occasionally took place so close to the border as to attract crowds of thrilled observers.

March 24. The Workmen's Compensation Law was declared unconstitutional by the New York Court of Appeals.

March 26. Notre Dame, Ind. The Laetare medal, annually awarded by the University of Notre Dame to a lay member of the Catholic Church in the United States who has performed a conspicuous work in literature, art, science, or philanthropy, was awarded to Miss Agnes Repplier, of Philadelphia.

May 12. Secretary of War Dickinson resigned and President Taft immediately appointed Henry L. Stimson to his place.

Standard Oil Company Dissolved

May 15. The Standard Oil Company was ordered by the U. S. Supreme Court to dissolve within six months.

Chief Justice Edward Douglas White.

The opinion, as read by Chief Justice White, declared that those trusts are unlawful only which act in "unreasonable" restraint of trade. Justice Harlan dissented strongly on this point.

In the discussion that followed the Court's decision the fate of the Standard Oil Company played a minor part compared with the new interpretation the Court had given to the Anti-Trust law.

Justice White, in explaining the manner in which he had arrived at his decision, stated that in 1890, when the

Anti-Trust law was passed, the trusts were busily changing from one form to another to evade the many laws aimed at them, so "in view of the many new forms of contracts and combinations which were being evolved from existing economic conditions, it was deemed essential by all-embracing enumerations to make sure that no form of contract or combination by which an undue restraint of interstate or foreign commerce was brought about could save such restraint from condemnation."

The strongest critic of the decision was on the Supreme Court itself, in the person of Mr. Justice Harlan.

President Taft was represented by the Washington correspondents as feeling a disappointment he very thinly concealed. Taft when on the bench had resisted this interpretation of the Act and in January, 1910, in a message to Congress had said:

It has been proposed, however, that the word "reasonable" should be made a part of the statute, and then that it should be left to the court to say what is a reasonable restraint of trade, what is a reasonable suppression of competition, what is a reasonable monopoly. I venture to think that this is to put into the hands of the Court a power impossible to exercise on any consistent principle which will insure the uniformity of decision essential to just judgment. It is to thrust on the courts a burden that they have no precedents to enable them to carry, and to give them a power approaching the arbitrary, the abuse of which might involve our whole judicial system in disaster.

Senator LaFollette said: "The Court has done just what the trusts have wanted it to do, and what Congress has refused steadfastly to do."

James M. Beck, former Assistant Attorney-General of the United States, said:

The greatest tribunal in the world, after deliberating for more than a year and writing an opinion of 20,000 words, has failed in any tangible way to interpret a law which business men must, under the peril of possible imprisonment, infallibly interpret from day to day as occasion arises. This in itself justifies a grave doubt as to the policy of a law which yields so little to judicial interpretation. If the Supreme Court, after twenty-one years, cannot tell the business men of the country what is "reasonable" and what is "unreasonable" in the combination of energy and resources, it is clearly oppressive to require laymen to do so. . . .

Among those who applauded the decision, and they were a majority, was Andrew Carnegie, who thought it marked "a crisis in judicial decisions," because "it is founded on common sense and the spirit of the law rather than on the letter of the law." The New York *Times* said: "It leaves malefactors, actual and intending, where they were, in peril of the law. It frees honest business men from their doubts, from their dread, from their want of confidence almost kin to despair. It is an emancipation proclamation issued to the industries of the United States."

On the day following the decision stocks rose strongly in the New York Exchange. On July 31, the Standard Oil Company made public its plan for dissolution, to take effect December 1.

May 28. The Tobacco Trust lost its case in the Supreme Court, whose finding was almost the same as in the case of the Standard Oil Company, save that the reorganization of the Tobacco Trust was left in the hands of the lower courts. Justice Harlan again dissented to the broad interpretation of the Sherman Anti-Trust law. Chief Justice White, who wrote the decision, asserted that the new "reasonable" interpretation actually strengthened the arm of the law, giving it efficiency in cases which, under a literal interpretation, it would be powerless to reach. He declared: "We took nothing out of this statute by the rule of reason; we gave it a vivifying potentiality."

July. Apprehension of a monopolization of the nation's credit was quickened by the formation of the National City Company by the National City Bank of New York. The new company was to have a capitalization of $10,000,000 and was so organized that it might "make investments and transact other business, which, although often very profitable, may not be within the express corporate powers of a national bank." Thus it would have the power, explained the Springfield *Republican*, to "speculate in the stock-market, and even buy and hold the stocks of national banks, which is a power expressly denied by the courts to national banks under the National Bank Act."

Governor Woodrow Wilson of New Jersey said:

The plain fact is that the control of credit is dangerously concentrated in this country. The great monopoly in this country is the money monopoly. So long as that exists, our old variety and freedom and individual energy of development are out of the question. A great industrial nation is controlled by its system of credit. Our system of credit is concentrated. The growth of the nation, therefore, and all our activities are in the hands of a few men who, even if their action be honest and intended for the public interest, are necessarily concentrated upon the great undertakings in which their own money is involved, and who necessarily, by every reason of their own limitation, chill and check and destroy genuine economic freedom. This is the greatest question of all, and to this statesmen must address themselves with an earnest determination to serve the long future and the true liberties of men.

Some time previously ex-Senator Aldrich had formed a plan for a new currency system. President Taft endorsed it before a gathering of the New York State Bankers' Association:

There is no legislation — I care not what it is — tariff, railroad, corporation, or of a general political character, that at all equals in importance the putting of our banking and currency system on the sound basis proposed in the National Monetary Commission plan.

In Congress, however, there was strong opposition to it. Representative Lindbergh attacked it and asserted:

Wall Street brought on the 1907 panic, got the people to demand currency reform, brought the Aldrich-Vreeland currency bill forward, and, if it dares, will reproduce another panic to pass the Aldrich central bank plan. We need reform, but not at the hands of Wall Street.

July 31. Upton Sinclair and nine other members of the Arden, Del., socialistic colony were convicted of vio-

From a photograph © by Edmonston

Congressman Lindbergh, of Minnesota, and his son Charles at the age of eight, to become later the famous Colonel Lindbergh.

lation of the Sunday Blue Laws and sentenced to a term in jail.

August 1. Edwin A. Abbey, one of America's greatest illustrators and a famous painter, died in London, his adopted home. His Shakespearean compositions are a monument to his draughtsmanship, and his later mural paintings give him an important place in the history of art. In 1901 he was commissioned to paint the coronation of King Edward VII of England.

August 8. The membership of the House was fixed at 435, one member for each 211,877 inhabitants.

August 22. Paris. The art world was thrown into consternation by the announcement that Leonardo da

Edwin A. Abbey.

Vinci's masterpiece, "Mona Lisa," or, as it was popularly known, "La Joconde," had mysteriously disappeared from the Louvre. A search of every nook and cranny of the museum, from roof to cellar, brought to light only the valuable frame in which the picture hung and the glass that covered it.

September 6. William Burgess swam the English Channel, a feat only once before accomplished.

September 11. Maine defeated the proposed repeal of the prohibition clause in its Constitution by about 100 votes.

October 15. Associate Justice John M. Harlan of the

From a photograph © Underwood and Underwood.

America's First Air Mail. In the fall of 1911 Postmaster-General Frank H. Hitchcock and Captain Beck flew in a Curtiss plane with a sack of mail from Nassau boulevard to Mineola, L. I.

United States Supreme Court died suddenly at his home in Washington.

The Books of 1911

"The Prodigal Judge," by Vaughan Kester. . . . "The Broad Highway," by Jeffrey Farnol. . . . "Queed," by H. S. Harrison. . . . "The Long Roll," by Mary Johnston. . . . "Miss Gibbie Gault," by K. L. Bosher. . . . "Rolf in the Woods," by Ernest Seton Thompson. . . . "The Rosary," by F. L. Barclay.

. . . "How to Live on Twenty-four Hours a Day," by
Arnold Bennett. . . . "Molly Make Believe," by
Elinor H. Coburn. . . . "Dawn O'Hara," by Edna
Ferber. . . . "The Grain of Dust," by David Graham
Phillips. . . . "The Miller of Old Church," by Ellen
Glasgow. . . . "The Winning of Barbara Worth," by
Harold Bell Wright. . . . "The Ne'er-Do-Well," by
Rex Beach. . . . "The Glory of Clementine," by W.
J. Locke. . . . "The Common Law," by Robert W.
Chambers. . . . "The Harvester," by Gene Stratton-
Porter. . . . "The Iron Woman," by Margaret Deland.

The Theatre in 1911

Most talked-of event of the year among playgoers
was the presentation of Rostand's "Chantecler" at the
Knickerbocker Theatre, New York, January 23. In the
casting both reason and precedent were flung to the
winds and the principal rôle, that of the cock, which was
nothing if not masculine, was given to a woman, Maude
Adams. Miss Adams's desire to appear in the title rôle,
said the New York *Sun* critic, was "impossible to understand. The speeches of Chantecler were a pitiful strain
on the physical powers of the actress; they left her panting for breath between every phrase. She was an alluring
specimen of masquerading womanhood, but not a whit
more masculine than the Hen Pheasant." . . . Rose
Stahl, giving a magnificent performance in "Maggie
Pepper," caused a London critic to write: "I have seen
four incomparable actresses, Duse, Bernhardt, Ellen
Terry, and Ada Rehan. With these, because of her glorious voice and her indefinable charm, I do not hesitate
to rank Rose Stahl." . . . Julian Eltinge, female im-
personator, played in "The Fascinating Widow." Many
people found him pleasing. *The Theatre*, after a tribute

of faint praise, said: "We cannot bring ourselves to laud his present effort." In the late 1920's he would probably have been booed off the stage. . . . Gilbert and Sullivan's "Pinafore" was enjoying an all-star revival, includ-

From the Locke Collection, New York Public Library.

Hazel Dawn in the "Pink Lady."

ing DeWolf Hopper, Henry E. Dixey, Louise Gunning, Marie Cahill, Alice Brady. . . . Valeska Surratt was appearing in "The Red Rose." . . . George Arliss in "Disraeli." . . . Margaret Anglin was playing in "Green Stockings," a play which the *Theatre Magazine* described as "one of the best farces seen on the metropolitan stage in recent years." . . . Julia Dean and Marie

Nordstrom in "Bought and Paid For." . . . Billie Burke in "The Runaway." . . . "Bunty Pulls the Strings," a picture of Scottish life, with Scottish actors, was a great success; "the second night saw a sold-out condition an hour before the curtain rose." . . . Fritzi Scheff was playing in "The Dutchess." . . . Frances Starr in "The Case of Becky." . . . Blanche Ring in "The Wall Street Girl." . . . David Warfield in "The Return of Peter Grimm." . . . Mary Mannering and Lewis Waller in "The Garden of Allah." . . . Hazel Dawn, Frank Lalor, and Alice Dovey in "The Pink Lady."

Ernest Thompson Seton.

1912

The Panama Canal Again Provokes Controversy. Coming
of the Self-Starter. Lord Lister Dies. China Becomes a
Republic. The *Maine* Is Buried. Sinking of the S.S. *Titanic*.
Germany Expands Its Navy. The Rosenthal Murder.
America Wins the Olympics. An Assassin Attempts to Kill
Roosevelt at Milwaukee, Wis. Books and Plays of 1912.

January 3. Rear Admiral Robley Dunglison Evans
died suddenly at Washington. He had a long and dis-

Rear Admiral Robley D. Evans.

tinguished career in the Navy, beginning before the Civil
War and ending when he commanded the American fleet
on part of its journey around the world in 1907–1908.

Panama Canal Tolls

January. The clause relating to rebating tolls to American vessels passing through the Panama Canal, in President Taft's Message to Congress, aroused the animosity of newspapers in England and on the Continent. The passage reads:

We own the Canal. It was our money that built it. We have the right to charge tolls for its use. Those tolls must be the same to every one; but when we are dealing with our own ships, the practise of many governments of subsidizing their own merchant vessels is so well established in general that a subsidy equal to the tolls, an equivalent remission of tolls, cannot be held to be a discrimination in the use of the Canal.

This proposal, the European newspapers claimed, amounted to a violation of the provisions of the Hay-Pauncefote treaty which guaranteed that "the Canal shall be free and open to the vessels of commerce and of war of all nations . . . on terms of entire equality."

The London *Outlook* ended a long diatribe with the threat:

It is obvious that, if this barefaced robbery is to be used against British vessels of commerce, the question may require the effective consideration of British vessels of war. Or will the Radical Government tolerate the tearing-up of a treaty intended to guarantee our trade and commerce against being crushed out of existence, or at least out of profitable competition — which is the same thing — by grand larceny of this description?

On May 23, the House passed the Panama Canal tolls bill, with a provision for the exemption of American coastwise vessels. The bill then went to the Senate, where an attempt was made to eliminate the exemption clause, but was defeated, 44 to 11, on August 7.

The Senate's passing of the bill was the signal for a fresh outburst of indignation abroad. A formal protest by Great Britain reached Secretary of State Knox on

December 9. Thereafter the discussion was kept up both in the newspapers and through diplomatic channels until Woodrow Wilson became President. At his behest Congress repealed the offending clause on June 15, 1914.

January 6. President Taft issued a proclamation ad-

John Grier Hibben, President of Princeton University.

mitting New Mexico to the Union as the 47th State, after fifty years as a territory.

January 7. An advertisement in the New York *Sun* marked automotive progress:

THE DISCO SELF–STARTER

THE SENSATION OF 1912

The most marked advance shown for motor cars for 1912 is the Disco Self-Starter. Safe-Sure-Simple. We can make your car self-starting and up-to-date in three hours. . . .

January 11. Doctor John Grier Hibben was elected President of Princeton to succeed Woodrow Wilson.

January 22. The first passenger train was run from Key West to the mainland over the extension of the Florida East Coast Railroad.

February 11. Lord Lister, perfecter of the antiseptic treatment in surgery, died in London, at the age of seventy. His discoveries made possible operations that were considered impossible under the old procedure, and he rendered safe many methods used only as a final resort. This he did by recognizing that nearly always the chief danger to the patient is not the operation itself but the subsequent infection by bacteria. By disinfecting wound, instruments, bandages, and everything connected with the operation, he killed the germs and obviated the unpleasant or even fatal consequences once so inevitable.

February 12. The republic of China was established by the abdication of the Emperor and the retirement of the Manchu dynasty. Yuan Shi Kai was elected President by the National Assembly February 15.

February 14. President Taft signed a proclamation admitting Arizona to the Union.

February 24. The editor of *Collier's*, then Norman Hapgood, reported: "Recently we passed an hour at a moving picture show. Between sets of pictures the audience was induced to join in singing the five most popular songs of the moment. They were these: 'Oceana Roll,' 'Mysterious Rag,' 'Alexander's Ragtime Band,' 'That Raggy Rag,' 'You Great Big Beautiful Doll.'"

"Taking it through twenty years," he said, with some sadness, "there has probably been no steady decline in musical quality, but the same cannot be said for the words."

March 16. Covered with flowers, with colors flying while the convoying ships boomed a farewell, the battleship *Maine* was sunk in the Gulf Stream off Havana beyond the international three-mile limit. After it went down millions of roses and other flowers floated to the surface, marking the spot where the ship was sunk.

In February, 1898, the *Maine* had been detached from the Atlantic Squadron and sent to Havana to pay a "friendly" visit. There it had been destroyed by an explosion February 15.

April 12. Miss Clara Barton, founder of the Red Cross Society, died at Glen Echo, Md.

Sinking of the "Titanic"

April 14, *Sunday*. At 11:40 P.M., at a point four hundred miles southeast of Cape Race, the steamship *Titanic*, travelling at full speed on her maiden journey from Liverpool to New York, struck an iceberg. Monday, at 2:27 A.M., she sank. Of the more than two thousand people on board only 705 were saved — by the *Carpathia*, which arrived about 5:30 A.M. — and 1635 were drowned. The ship's band kept playing lively airs at first, then, just before the end, the Episcopal hymn, "Autumn,"

> Hold me up, mighty waters,
> Keep my eye on things above.

Among the lost were W. T. Stead, English journalist, Francis D. Millet, American artist, Major Archibald Butt, John Jacob Astor, and Isidor Straus.

Captain Smith had been warned by wireless that icebergs lay in his path, but had not slackened speed. The ship's quartermaster, who was at the helm at the time of the collision, and was saved, gave an explanation which received universal credence:

> She was under orders from the general officers of the line to make all the speed of which she was capable. We had made 565 miles that day, and were tearing along at twenty-one knots when we struck the iceberg.

The sea was smooth — as still as water in a tumbler,
said one survivor — and there was ample time for all to
be saved. But the spaces aboard ship which might have
contained life-boats and rafts had been given over to pur-

Crowds around the bulletin boards for latest news of the *Titanic*.

poses described in a circular issued before the ship was
put in commission:

Sports decks and spacious promenades; commodious state-
rooms and apartments en suite; cabins de luxe with bath;
squash-racquet courts; Turkish and electric bath establish-
ments; salt-water swimming-pools; glass-enclosed sun parlors;
veranda and palm courts; Louis XVI restaurants; grand dining-
saloons; electric elevators.

So much care and pains had gone into the designing
and building of the *Titanic* that the public and the company actually believed she was unsinkable. As the captain of the *Carpathia* put it, "the *Titanic* was supposed

to be a life-boat herself." Not supplying the ship with enough life-boats to seat at one time all the passengers and crew was simply a gamble the company took that the occasion for a wholesale rescue could never arise.

Only a writer with the combined talents of a Dostoievski and a Mark Twain could adequately portray the scenes that were enacted while the *Titanic* lay mortally wounded. Passengers who were not asleep in their berths knew that wireless signals had been sent out and that two not very distant ships were coming at full speed. Rockets were being sent up to attract any vessels which chanced to be near. On one deck people standing around bundled in heavy overcoats were amused by the ineffectual efforts of a woman to fasten a life preserver around her pet dog. There was joking about the sartorial appearance of life-preserver-clad ladies. Nobody aboard ship — one man excepted — knew of the episode of the unanswered telephone call. At 11:38 P.M. the look-out in the crow's-nest had spied the iceberg dimly a mile away. He pressed the buzzer of the telephone connecting with the bridge. Contrary to invariable custom there was no immediate response. A minute went by and the *Titanic* pushed ahead two thousand feet. Another minute passed, the bell on the bridge jangling unheeded. The delay was disastrous. When finally the look-out delivered his message, a desperate attempt was made to swerve to one side. A head-on collision was forestalled, but as the *Titanic* swept by she scraped along a submerged ledge of the iceberg and a slit was sheared in her plates along her entire length. The iceberg was fading out of sight to the rear when a party of card players left the smoking room to find out what had caused the slight jar that had interrupted their game. They found the deck quiet and deserted and returned.

For days after the *Carpathia* reached New York with

the *Titanic's* survivors the newspapers were filled with eye-witness accounts of the tragedy. One of them:

In many instances, within the range of my vision, wives refused pointblank to leave their husbands. I saw members of the crew literally tear women from the arms of men, and throw them over the side to boats. Mrs. Isidor Straus clung to her husband and none could force her from his side. . . .

The *Titanic* leaving Liverpool for New York.

Fully two hours elapsed between the *Titanic's* striking the berg and her foundering. Not until the last five minutes did the awful realization come that the end was at hand. . . .

Deck after deck was submerged. There was no lurching, no grinding or crunching. The *Titanic* simply settled. I was far up on one of the top decks. Two minutes before the final disappearance of the ship I jumped. About me were many others, in the water. My bathrobe floated away. It was icily cold. I struck out at once. Before the last, I turned. My first glance took in the people swarming the *Titanic's* decks. Hundreds were standing there, helpless to ward off the approaching death. I saw Captain Smith on his bridge. My eyes seemingly clung to him. The deck from which I had leaped was immersed; the water had risen slowly, and was now to the floor of the bridge. Then it was at Captain Smith's waist.

I saw him no more. He died a hero. The bow of the *Titanic* was far beneath the surface. To me only her four monster funnels and the two masts were now visible. It was all over in an instant. The *Titanic's* stern rose completely out of the water. Up it went, thirty, forty, sixty feet into the air, then, with her body slanting at an angle of 45 degrees, slowly the *Titanic* slipped out of sight. There was very little suction.

Until I die, the cries of those wretched men and women who went down clinging helplessly to the *Titanic's* rail will ring in my ears. Groans, shrieks, and sounds that were almost inhuman came across the water.

I turned and swam. The water was numbing me. Only the preserver about my body saved my life. When pulled into the life-boat it was an hour later, but I knew nothing.

A Senate investigating committee under the leadership of William Alden Smith convened in New York after the *Titanic* survivors were landed. One of the witnesses examined was J. Bruce Ismay, a director of the company owning the *Titanic* and a survivor of the tragedy. There was considerable feeling against Ismay, who was charged in the newspapers with responsibility for the captain's recklessness, with having given the order to drive the ship along at a dangerous speed in iceberg-infested waters. Many newspapers regarded it as in the nature of a miscarriage of justice that he of all those on board should have been saved, when so many hundreds of passengers had been drowned. Before the committee Mr. Ismay denied having interfered in the handling of the vessel, and coolly explained how he had come to be saved:

The boat was there and a certain number of women had been loaded. The officer called out to any other women who might be on the deck to come. There were no other passengers, men or women, on the deck, so I got in. That is all there is to it.

Germany Prepares

May. An increase in Germany's naval budget, beyond anything hitherto known, aroused disquiet in Eng-

On May 4, 10,000 suffragettes marched in New York. They were lampooned in the newspapers, which, for the most part, refused to take them seriously. Those on horseback appeared at the head of the procession in Washington Square. *Above:* The procession passing Madison Square.

land. Not long before, the British First Lord of the Admiralty, in presenting his naval estimates, explained that they were "framed on the assumption that the programmes of the other naval Powers will not be increased." He declared frankly that he referred to Germany, and said the British pace would be slackened or accelerated to meet the pace of the Germans.

England was alarmed. War with Germany, ever a possibility in the minds of the English, seemed definitely nearer. Causes other than naval rivalry made it inevitable, as Archibald Hurd explained in the London *Daily Telegraph:*

Let there be no mistake — Germany aims high; the stakes for which she is competing are the greatest any nation has sought to obtain since Napoleon strode the Continent. At a colossal cost — heavy taxation on luxuries and necessities alike and heavy debt — she is pressing forward in this race in armaments, confident that she is now entering on the last lap. She has mortgaged so much in the contest that either she must achieve victory abroad or meet the storm of strife which her policy has and is still creating at home. The ruling Germans realize that this is the last lap in the race — the crucial test of endurance; either we or they must fail in the silent, bloodless war, and fail soon.

As regards the attitude of Germans toward England, Mr. Hurd stated that a steady flow of anti-British publications was pouring from the presses in Germany. Citing ten such books that had appeared in the previous month, he said:

The general tendency of these books is the same. It is that Great Britain is determined to destroy Germany; that the only way to meet the peril is to arm strongly on sea and land; that the German public must be impressed with the peril, and must call for a patriotic policy should the Government fail in its patriotic duty.

May 23. The Hamburg-American liner *Imperator*, the largest vessel afloat, was launched at Hamburg; she was 900 feet long and displaced about 52,000 tons.

May 30. Wilbur Wright, inventor, with his brother

Orville, of the first airplane that flew, died of typhoid
fever.

July 16. Herman Rosenthal, gambling-house keeper,
was shot and killed on a brilliantly lighted street in New
York City. The motive for the murder and the identity

Herman Rosenthal.

Lieutenant Charles Becker.

of the assassin were inferred by the public from the
laconic letter from District-Attorney Whitman to Police Commissioner Waldo:

First, Herman Rosenthal charged that he had been forced
into a partnership with a police lieutenant, and that other
gamblers were in a similar situation. Just as he was about to
testify on this subject and to give details and names he was
murdered publicly — dramatically. . . .

Second, The murderers of Herman Rosenthal got away
from seven policemen who were very close to the scene of the
crime, and who obtained no evidence whatever.

On July 29, Police Lieutenant Charles Becker was
indicted and arrested. To the people of New York the
question of Becker's guilt or innocence seemed of less

importance than the fact that his arrest was likely to
bring out important revelations of police corruption, its
nature, its extent, and the identity of those responsible
for it. New York was convinced that an unholy alliance
for mutual gain existed between certain members of the

District-Attorney Whitman of New York, later Governor.

police force and desperate criminals, and that there
would be neither peace nor safety until these were broken
up and made impossible for the future.

Some of the anticipated disclosures materialized. It
was shown that Becker, whose salary was $2,250, had
made bank deposits of over $65,000 since November,
1911. Later a former patrolman confessed[1] that during the preceding five years he had regularly collected
protection money from eighteen disorderly hotels, and
that in that period he had handed over $72,000 to the

[1] February 13, 1913.

"System." He said he was but one of hundreds of such "collectors." Corroboration of his story was given by the police captain named by the patrolman as the man "higher up" with whom he dealt.

Becker was convicted, October 24, of instigating Rosenthal's murder, and was sentenced to death. He was electrocuted.

July 15. A compilation of points won at the end of the Olympic games at Stockholm showed that the United States led, with 128 points; Sweden was next, with 104; and England third, with 66. World's records were broken by two Americans, J. E. Meredith of Mercersburg Academy, who ran 800 meters in 1.51 9/10, and P. McDonald, who cast the 16-pound shot 50.32 feet. "Jim" Thorp, a Sac and Fox Indian member of the American team, won the penthalon and decathlon events and was acclaimed by King Gustav of Sweden as "the most wonderful athlete in the world."

October 10. The Nobel prize for medicine was awarded to Doctor Alexis Carrell of the Rockefeller Institute, New York, for his researches and discoveries in the cultivation of tissues in vitro, the grafting of limbs and peripheral parts, and the transplantation of tissues and organs from one animal to another.

Attempted Assassination of Roosevelt

October 14. While bowing to a cheering crowd in front of a Milwaukee hotel, Theodore Roosevelt was shot in the breast by John Schrank of New York. The would-be assassin fired from a distance of only six feet, the bullet striking the bulky manuscript of the speech which Colonel Roosevelt was about to deliver, and passed through it into his breast. Roosevelt was thrown back a step or two by the force of the heavy bullet, but did not fall nor lose his presence of mind. Seeing that the crowd was about to mob the would-be assassin, he pushed to his side and protected him until the arrival of the police. Then, with the bullet still in his body and the wound unstanched, he went to a political rally and spoke for an hour and a half. What happened after the shooting was described by O. K. Davis, veteran newspaperman, who was accompanying Roosevelt on his trip:

> Cochems asked him to go at once to the hospital, and Dr. Terrill insisted upon it. The Colonel peremptorily refused. He declared that he was not hurt; that he would permit nothing to prevent his delivering his speech. When Cochems said, "Let's get to the hospital," the Colonel said:
> "You get me to that speech. It may be the last one I shall deliver, but I am going to deliver this one." . . .

After delivering his speech Colonel Roosevelt allowed himself to be taken to a hospital to have the wound dressed and afterwards took a train to Chicago, where he surrendered himself to the care of physicians.

October 30. The use of the common drinking cup was prohibited on all interstate railroad trains by a quarantine order issued by Secretary of the Treasury MacVeagh.

The Books of 1912

Fiction, with a few exceptions, was commonplace in 1912. Books in pure science were few, and history was temporarily abandoned for biography. A new science, eugenics, had caught public attention, with an accompanying crop of books. Something like a renaissance in poetry took place; Burton Stevenson, after having essayed for twelve years every kind of writing, including mystery stories, brought out the "Home Book of Verse." . . . Albert Bigelow Paine published the "authorized biography" of Mark Twain, an excellent work that de-

served the popularity it quickly won. . . . Theodore
Dreiser's "The Financier" — the story of a ruthless
magnate of industry in the America of after the Civil
War; it was not on any of the "best seller" lists. . . .

Edith Wharton.   Theodore Dreiser.

"The Squirrel Cage," by Dorothy Canfield (Fisher) —
an indictment of the struggle to live beyond one's means,
in the setting of a mid-Western city. . . . Owen Johnson's tilt against snobbery in colleges, "Stover at Yale."
"Riders of the Purple Sage," by Zane Grey — story of
Utah in 1871, when the Mormons were at the height
of their power. . . . The twenty-one best books of the
year, as listed by William Stanley Braithwaite, were:

The Autobiography of Richard Wagner.
Creative Evolution — Henri Bergson.
Jean Christophe in Paris — Romain Rolland.
The Life and Times of Cavour — William Roscoe Thayer.
The Diary of Gideon Welles.
Garibaldi and the Making of Italy — George M. Trevelyan.

Woman and Labor — Olive Schreiner.
Three Plays by Brieux.
The Life of Ruskin — E. T. Cook.
The Iron Woman — Margaret Deland.
Ethan Frome — Edith Wharton.
Love's Coming of Age — Edward Carpenter.
The Foundations of the Nineteenth Century — H. S. Chamberlain.
The Fool in Christ — Gerhart Hauptmann.
The Healer — Robert Herrick.
Hilda Lessways — Arnold Bennett.
The Painters of Japan — Arthur Morrison.
Educational Problems — G. Stanley Hall.
Lectures on Poetry — William J. Mackaill.
The Ballad of the White Horse — Gilbert K. Chesterton.
The Plays of John M. Synge.

The Theatre in 1912

In 1912 Ethel Barrymore was playing in "The Witness for the Defense"; Otis Skinner in "Kismet"; Lillian Lorraine and Eddie Foy in "Over the River"; Elsie Janis in "The Slim Princess"; James K. Hackett in "The Grain of Dust"; Louis Mann in "Elevating a Husband"; Charlotte Walker in "The Trail of the Lonesome Pine"; Billie Burke in "The Runaway"; Crystal Herne in "What a Man Thinks." "Hokey Pokey," a "potpourri in two acts," contained such celebrities as Weber and Fields, William Collier, Lillian Russell, Fay Templeton; Henry Miller and Ruth Chatterton were appearing in "The Rainbow"; Virginia Pearson in "A Fool There Was"; Gail Kane in Augustus Thomas's "When It Comes Home"; Nat C. Goodwin as Fagin in the revival of "Oliver Twist"; Grace George in "Just to Get Married." An Irish play "The Playboy of the Western World" was attended by scenes of disorder on its appearance in Boston, New York and Philadelphia. Of it the *Theatre Magazine* said: "If Mr. Synge's intent was comedy, that comedy is too subtle for

anybody of common sense or for Irishmen who attach
importance to the decent sentiments of life.   Otherwise
the play is remarkable in many ways.   But the attempt
to make comedy out of the sayings and doings of a parri-
cide fails.   The effect is offensive."

Ethel Barrymore in 1912.

1913

Impeachment of Judge Archbald. Captain Scott and Companions Perish. Continuing Turbulence in Mexico; ex-President Madero Killed "Trying to Escape." Japan at Odds with California. Vera Cruz Captured. The Trial of Governor Sulzer of New York. Books and Plays of 1913.

January 13. Judge R. W. Archbald, of the Court of Commerce, was found guilty by the Senate on five of the thirteen articles of impeachment lodged against him by the House, and disqualified from again holding office in the United States Government.

This was the first instance in fifty years, and the third in the history of the country, of a judge being removed from office as the result of impeachment proceedings.

February 3. The Income Tax amendment was adopted, being approved by the Wyoming legislature, the thirty-sixth to take favorable action.

February 10. News that Captain R. F. Scott, British explorer, and four members of his party perished on March 29, 1912, while on their return from the South Pole, was brought to New Zealand by the crew of his ship, *Terra Nova*.

February 17. Joaquin Miller, "Poet of the Sierras," died at his home near San Francisco.

February 18. President Madero of Mexico was taken prisoner, and Federal General Victoriano Huerta was proclaimed Provisional President. General Huerta immediately telegraphed to President Taft: "I have the honor to inform you that I have overthrown this Government. The forces are with me, and from now on peace and prosperity will reign." But peace proved elusive. Huerta had hardly finished celebrating his triumph when rebels attacked Federal troops in the north. Ex-President Madero and his brother Gustavo, while prisoners of Huerta, were murdered — "they had been

President Madero, of Mexico.

killed while attempting to escape," was the stereotyped explanation. Kidnapings of Americans and Europeans, and the day-by-day maraudings of roaming bands, caused President Taft to issue a proclamation directing citizens of the United States to comply strictly with the neutrality laws, and warning Americans to stay out of Mexico. This act infuriated the jingoes, who inveighed against his "surrender" of American rights.

March 4. Woodrow Wilson was inaugurated President.

March 26. Great floods in Ohio and Indiana. The number of dead in Ohio was estimated at 3,000 and in

Indiana at 200. Property loss was believed to exceed
$50,000,000. This was the famous Dayton flood.
March 31. J. Pierpont Morgan died.
April 12. Ambassador Chinda of Japan protested to

One of the flooded districts in Ohio, West State Street, Columbus.

the State Department against enactment of a proposed
anti-alien land ownership law in California. April 19 —
The President urged California to make the law less objectionable to the Japanese. April 24 — Secretary Bryan
went to California to stay the legislation. The bill passed
and was signed by Governor Johnson May 4.

April 21. A United States fleet seized custom house at
Vera Cruz, Mexico, and navy and marines occupied the
city, for the purpose of exacting an apology from President Huerta for the arrest of United States bluejackets.

May 2. President Wilson recognized the new Chinese Republic.

August 13. The New York Assembly impeached
Governor Sulzer for false statement of campaign con-

tributions and other charges. The trial began October 6 and ended October 17, with his conviction by a vote of 43 to 12.

September 4. Mayor Gaynor of New York sailed on

United States Marines in Vera Cruz.

the *Baltic* for Europe and died on board the steamer, September 10.

October 3. The President signed the Underwood Tariff bill and it became operative at midnight.

October 10. President Wilson sent the electric spark which blew up the Gamboa dike, the last obstruction to navigation from ocean to ocean through the Panama Canal.

October 18. Mrs. Emmeline Pankhurst, English suffragist leader, arrived at Ellis Island and after being detained two days was admitted.

December 23. The Federal Reserve bill became law, carrying out President Wilson's currency reform.

From a photograph by Brown Brothers.

Ty Cobb, considered by many fans the greatest baseball player of all times, as he was in 1913 at the top of his form.

Books of 1913

"The Reef," by Edith Wharton. . . . "The Inn of Tranquility," by John Galsworthy. . . . "Marriage," by H. G. Wells. . . . "Your United States," by Arnold Bennett, "in which," said *Life*, "the state of our pulse is taken by a fashionable physician with a perfect bedside manner." . . . "The Provincial American," by Meredith Nicholson. . . . "Cobb's Anatomy" and "Back Home," by Irvin S. Cobb. . . . "The Man Who Came Back," by John Fleming Wilson. . . . "The Business of Being a Woman," by Ida M. Tarbell. . . . "Auction of Today," by Milton C. Work. . . . "My

Little Sister," by Elizabeth Robins, a story of the White
Slave traffic. In commenting on this book in *Life*, J. B.
Kerfoot said: "A generation ago no one but a few particularly daring parents would have read such a book
if it had existed, and they would either have burned it
afterwards or have hidden it behind Fox's Book of Martyrs . . . whereas to-day the chances are that most of
the parents who read it will do so because . . . it has
been recommended to them by their daughters."

"New Leaf Mills," by William Dean Howells. . . .
"The Rich Mrs. Burgoyne," by Kathleen Norris. . . .
"Roast Beef Medium," by Edna Ferber. . . . "Daddy-
Long-Legs," by Jean Webster. . . . "A Personal Nar-
rative of Political Experiences," by Robert M. LaFol-
lette. . . . "V. V's Eyes," by Henry Sydnor Harrison.
. . . "A Preface to Politics," by Walter Lippmann.
. . . "The Abysmal Brute," by Jack London. . . .
"The Inside of the Cup," by Winston Churchill. . . .
"Crowds," by Gerald Stanley Lee. . . . "The Inter-
pretation of Dreams," by Sigmund Freud. . . . "The
Woman Thou Gavest Me," by Hall Caine. . . . "The
Dark Flower," by John Galsworthy. . . . "Joan
Thursday," by Louis Joseph Vance.

The Theatre in 1913

Ethel Barrymore was appearing in "Tante," by C.
Haddon Chambers. Laurette Taylor was "getting along
up into the fifth century" of the run of "Peg o' My
Heart." Jane Cowl was playing in "Within the Law";
Elsie Ferguson in "The Strange Woman." Forbes-
Robertson and his company were playing in "Othello."
A melodrama of English sporting life, "The Whip,"
was attracting the lovers of old-fashioned melodrama.
The big scene in this play was a remarkably realistic train
wreck. A comedy-opera "Firefly" was considered by

the *Theatre Magazine* to be one of the best things of the season. "There is not a coarse nor a vulgar thing in it." Pauline Frederick was playing in "Joseph and His

Mary Pickford in an early movie.

Brethren." Douglas Fairbanks was delighting thousands in the play "Hawthorne of the U. S. A." Elsie Janis was appearing with Montgomery and Stone in "The Lady of the Slipper." Grace George played in "Divorçons"; DeWolf Hopper in "The Beggar Student"; Mrs. Fiske in "The High Road"; Al Jolson and Gaby Deslys in "The Honeymoon Express"; Jane Cowl in "Within the Law"; Billie Burke in "The Land of Promise." George M. Cohan's "Seven Keys to Baldpate" was receiving the praise of the critics; "Potash and Perlmutter," a study in New York's Jewish life as connected with the cloak-and-suit trade, was providing laughter to full houses.

In 1913 moving-picture theatres were multiplying rapidly all over the country. A survey showed invest-

Billie Burke.

ment in American film theatres totalled roughly $1,000,-000,000. Moving-pictures were accompanied by illustrated songs to the accompaniment of a piano and a perfunctory travel lecture. In May, 1913, the *Theatre Magazine* stated that "the popularity of the moving picture as a form of public amusement, far from being on the wane, is increasing by feverish leaps and bounds."

Mary Pickford was known as "Little Mary" and "Queen of the Movies," and was considered by millions

IN THE "COMMERCIAL" THEATRE.   IN THE "ART" THEATRE.

Stark realities.

ONCE THEY HURRIED BY.   NOW THEY HURRY IN.

Sophistication and the drama.

From the New York "Herald Tribune" cartoons by Robert Joyce.

of "movie" fans all over the land as "the Maude Adams of the film plays." "Broncho Billy," a cowboy character, appearing on the streets of Cleveland "started a riot among the kids." The craze for "Westerns" was so great that cattlemen suffered a labor problem due to cowboys trying to get into the movies. Francis X. Bushman, one of the earliest screen idols, who "had a profile like a Greek god," was doing a two-reeler, "Tony the Fiddler," for Essanay. J. Warren Kerrigan was playing for American, independent. Alice Joyce was the leading lady of the Kalem Company. "The energy and skill she displayed when riding over the Sierra foothills and desert sands to rescue Carlyle Blackwell from so many perils meant hard work and perseverance."

INDEX

INDEX